MAR
ROO

Champion Builder Books

To Move the World: Louis G. Gregory
and the Advancement of Racial Unity in America
by Gayle Morrison

Martha Root: Lioness at the Threshold
by M. R. Garis

MARTHA ROOT
Lioness at the Threshold

by

M. R. GARIS

BAHÁ'Í PUBLISHING TRUST
WILMETTE, ILLINOIS

Bahá'í Publishing Trust, Wilmette, Illinois 60091

Copyright © 1983 by the National Spiritual Assembly
of the Bahá'ís of the United States
All rights reserved. Published 1983
Printed in the United States of America
98 97 96   5 4 3 2

Library of Congress Cataloging in Publication Data

Garis, M. R.
  Martha Root: lioness at the threshold.

  Includes bibliographical references and index.
  1. Root, Martha L.   2. Bahais—United States—
Biography.   I. Title.
BP395.R64G37   1983   297'.89'0924 [B]   83-3913
ISBN 0-87743-184-1
ISBN 0-87743-185-X (pbk.)

Design by John Solarz

To Daniel and Nancy Jordan

Contents

Part 4/
The Warp and the Weft

Page listings for photographs may be found under the appropriate headings in the index.

Preface

As with so many books, this biography of Martha Root is an outgrowth of a more modest assignment. In 1976 the Bahá'í Publishing Trust envisioned a compilation of short profiles of prominent early Bahá'í men and women. I was asked to write about Martha Root. When I started in the spring of 1977, I knew only that Martha Root had done some traveling, had told many about the Bahá'í Faith, and was considered a lovely lady.

It was not long before even limited research began to yield a vastly different picture—one of a dedicated, gargantuan spirit in a frail frame. By the time the essay was completed in June, the picture of a sweet, little lady doing some Bahá'í teaching was erased. I was astonished by the unfolding story of her global journeys; her contacts with government, educational, and cultural leaders; her writing and lecturing throughout the world, all of which required Olympian energy and endurance. It was difficult to confine Martha Root's activities and spirit to the maximum seven pages—expanded to nine to accommodate Martha's telescoped career.

When the compilation of profiles was tabled, the editors suggested that I consider doing a book on the subject. The first steps were taken in early 1980. Naively, I thought the work would be completed within eighteen months. Even with the basic knowledge of Martha's endeavors, I was unprepared for the breadth of adventures that subsequent probing revealed.

The research for the book took on an entirely different character from that done for the article, which, with one exception, relied on published sources. Letters seeking information were written to Bahá'í institutions and to individuals around the world. Newspaper notices requesting data appeared from Iceland to India, and a few priceless pearls of history resulted. Unfortunately, persons closer to Martha's age were whisked off to the next world when research was under way. However, those who were young when they met an aging and memorable Martha Root were able to add greatly to the mosaic.

As Martha's life unfolded through the mountains of archival material, personal papers, reminiscences, and Martha's published and unpublished writings, the book began to grow to twice its originally conceived size. In order to cover events and Martha's travels as they occurred at home and in a variety of countries, it became necessary to condense most incidents, eliminate many, and restrict accounts of friendships that developed through the years. It seemed infinitely more important to give the grand picture, paint the broad canvas, so that the readers would have some conception of the vastness of Martha's dedication, sacrifice, and accomplishment.

Almost any year of Martha Root's life from 1915 on would make a small volume, and most years would accommodate a full-length book. At the National Bahá'í Archives in Wilmette, Illinois, several collections with letters from, or about, Martha were not yet ready for the researcher. These, together with already available materials, will yield precious history for future studies and will serve to deepen the public's awareness of Martha's sacrifice and triumph.

In most cases dates of lectures, trips, or incidents were available or could be established, but some specific times were elusive. Nevertheless, the span between undetermined dates is not great enough to disorient the reader.

Because Martha's travels were worldwide in scope, and the reader would have difficulty locating her whereabouts if indigenous spellings of cities were used, it was decided to use spellings common in atlases and geographical dictionaries published in Western, English-speaking countries. Hence the system found in most Bahá'í publications for transliterating Persian and Arabic place names was not employed in the book.

A work of this scope is the result of a mingling of effort, of contributions from many. I am grateful to those individuals whose offerings of information were not used but rather served to round out an incomplete picture of a period or event. When knowledge of the work spread, several persons wrote to suggest possible sources of information. I am grateful to Roger

White for his numerous leads and for putting me in touch with Professor Alex Aronson in Tel Aviv; to Frances Van Deusen for leading me to Meherangiz Munsiff in London; to Dr. Pattabi Raman for pointing the path to Dr. Duane Troxel in Honolulu; to Marzieh Gail for suggesting Marion Hofman in Haifa; to Dr. Raymond Johnson, visiting from India, for bringing Monira Sohaili to me in Wilmette. I also want to thank Mildred Mottahedeh for valuable history and vibrant word pictures of Martha.

For materials used in this book I want to express my deep appreciation to: Gol Aidun, Alex Aronson, Richard St. Barbe Baker (posthumously), Anita Ioas Chapman, Joyce Dahl, Virginia Gregg, Jane Grover, Bahia Gulick, Marion Hofman, Bahiyyih Imani, Dhikru'lláh Khádem, Merwan Khosrove, Meherangiz Munsiff, Y. A. Rafaat, Monira Sohaili, Lorna Tasker, Miriam Wiener, and 'Azíz Yazdí. I am especially grateful to Martha Garman, who generously turned over to me materials she had gathered for a future work on Martha Root; of those materials, the reminiscences of Valera Allen, Edith Carpenter, Lucy Hall, and Virginia Orbison are included. I am indebted also to Mother Alexandra, the former Archduchess Anton of Austria, née Princess Ileana of Rumania, for her contribution.

For special materials that greatly enhanced the work I am beholden to Donald Kinney for use of the abundant letters given to him for safekeeping by Roy Wilhelm more than thirty years ago and to Doris McKay for lengthy, history-packed letters to me about Martha. To Bahiyyih Winckler goes a well of gratitude for cassette tapes that record years of history and amusing, poignant tales concerning Martha, and for packages of her letters sent to the Randall family.

To Dr. Duane Troxel enormous thanks is due for untold hours of research in the National Bahá'í Archives of Hawaii, the result of which was a rich and moving history of Martha's last days, only a portion of which could be used because of space limitations. The material was sorted, numbered, summarized, cataloged, and sent to me, packet by packet, along with photographs of Martha's precious mementos and other photographs of historical value. The facts about Martha's final days arrived when the research was in its infancy; they imbued Martha's earlier years, as my work progressed, with a poignancy and grandeur that was carried through to her demise.

In Cambridge Springs, Pennsylvania, I want to thank the Bedeux family, who graciously allowed me to explore and photograph the Root home on Main and Dale streets. Warm appreciation is also due to Thelma and Iris Smith for their reminiscences of Martha and her family, and to Georgia King for an informative interview. Of unusual help and warm response whenever called upon were Yetive Pulling and Edward Lederick of the Heritage Society, who provided information and photographs. I also thank Professor Lederick for making possible the use of microfilms from Edinboro State College.

Others who have rendered assistance of note in a variety of ways are: Richard Grover; Phyllis Porter Gudger; Terrill Hayes; R. Kent Jones and Stuart Kitteredge, Esperantists; Daniel MacLachlan; Dennis Ropiac; Helen Shenton; Helen and Thomas Sousa; and Frances Worthington, who provided the index.

Libraries and staff that merit citation are: the Goodell Library reference desk at the University of Massachusetts, Amherst, for precise answers to an endless number of questions; the Baron-Forness Library, Edinboro State College, Edinboro, Pennsylvania, for use of microfilms of the *Cambridge Springs Enterprise-News*; the Robert Frost Library, Amherst College, Amherst, Massachusetts, for use of microfilm equipment and other assistance; the West Pennsylvania Room, Carnegie Library, Pittsburgh, Pennsylvania, for use of microfilms and equipment, and for photographs of Pittsburgh; the Oberlin College Library and Archives, Oberlin, Ohio, where warm appreciation is due to Gertrude Jacob for lengthy research and arrangements for photographs; and the Kent State University Libraries for photographs of Queen Marie and Princess Ileana and the royal residences. For providing endless boxes of documents, photographs, and newspaper clippings my gratitude goes to Roger Dahl, Archivist, National Bahá'í Archives, Wilmette, Illinois.

I want to thank the National Spiritual Assemblies of the Bahá'ís of Austria, Germany, Hawaii, and Iceland for sending materials; the National Spiritual Assemblies of the Bahá'ís of Australia and New Zealand for photographs and other documents; the National Spiritual Assembly of the Bahá'ís of the United States for prolonged use of its archives; *Bahá'í News* for a photograph of the first Bahá'ís in Japan; and the Audio-Visual Department and Archives at the Bahá'í World Center in Haifa, Israel.

I wish also to thank The Universal House of Justice for providing an authentic translation of 'Abdu'l-Bahá's 10 January 1919 letter to Martha Root.

Special notes of gratitude are offered to Dr. Betty J. Fisher and Richard Hill, editors, for many hours of shared frustrations and rewards in bringing this work forth through countless trials and obstacles.

In this list of acknowledged support and assistance I have saved my family for the final bow of thanks, with my love: to my daughter, Leslie Garis Kopit, for hours of reading, resulting in critical and editorial assessments; to my son Brooks for endless help with footnotes, photocopying, and mailing; to my son Dalton for detailed cataloging. With a burst of clarity I realize the help given to me over years of marriage by my late husband, Roger Garis, whose example of discipline as a writer—going to the typewriter every day whether or not the muse sat on his shoulder—was invaluable. The family habit was bolstered during the thirteen years my father-in-law, Howard R. Garis, lived with us; he was at his typewriter in the study by eight in the morning every day. These deeply ingrained habits, viewed and supported by me over the years, were my mainstay in this prolonged, unabated work; I am grateful for those lessons unconsciously given and learned.

Last, I offer my largest gift of thanks for a priceless experience and education to Martha Root.

Part 1/*Beginnings*

1 Beginnings

As the nineteenth century moved into the twentieth, America was prosperous, its mood was heady, confident, strutting, and all things seemed possible. There was a vitality, an innocence, and a bravado.

The country was still close to its roots. Technology had not yet changed traditional styles of living. Houses were lit by oil or gas; the horse and carriage was the alternative to walking; bustles and high-button shoes were the fashion for ladies; a cord of wood cost two dollars; evangelists moved into cities and towns, resounding their call to salvation; the Erie Railroad waged war on tramps; new trolley lines were set up; and ocean liners plied the seas, carrying immigrants, businessmen, and pleasure-seeking passengers.

When most young women were contemplating marriage, or had achieved this station; when gardening, embroidery, and domestic arts were the primary concerns of burgeoning females, a young woman sat next to the driver of an experimental automobile moving at a rapid pace through French villages, trying to achieve a speed record. They were en route from Paris to Versailles. The year was 1902. The woman was Martha Root.

Martha was a long way from her hometown of Cambridge Springs, in the northwest corner of Pennsylvania, a long way from the numerous relatives tending the businesses and local shops and maintaining homes and farms dotting the streets and rural spaces of Cambridge Springs. Her sense of adventure moved her not only from town to city but from continent to continent. Yet she never traveled as a tourist. Every bit of information was grist for the mill—the mill being her newspaper work. She wrote of the auto races; she wrote of the *pension* where she was staying, and of fashion, roads, French chefs,

3

and gardens. Nothing was irrelevant or uninteresting. It was all part of the life that surrounded her, gave her pleasure, and fed her inquiring mind.

The life at home was left behind but not rejected. Martha passionately loved her family, her relatives, her town, and she returned to "the Springs" at every opportunity. She was virtually a one-woman public-relations unit for her town and wrote of it whenever possible. But her affection was not always returned. The townspeople and relatives were like an ocean, lifting Martha to the crest of the wave when they approved of her achievements, then thrusting her down into the hollow of the wave when her beliefs contradicted their established thinking.

Who was this girl of ordinary family, turned newspaperwoman and adventurer? Who was this woman who heard about the Bahá'í Faith, examined it, and reshaped her life to follow its teachings and to trumpet them throughout the world? What prompted her to render service so outstanding that posthumously one of the highest honors of the Bahá'í Faith was bestowed upon her when she was named a Hand of the Cause of God? What pocket of Martha's mind responded so forcibly to the teachings of Bahá'u'lláh that, with a minimum of funds and a paucity of comfort, she ventured over ice-covered mountains; faced revolutions; and risked plagues, monsoons, landslides, and earthquakes—her heart radiating with love for all of mankind? What mysterious force propelled her to remote areas of the globe with strange names, her nomadic existence only ceasing when life itself fell away?

Martha's father, Timothy T. Root, known to all as T. T., had a profound effect on her, and many of the Root-family traits were reflected in her. T. T. Root was the son of Sylvester Root, who, with his brother Daniel, had bought land in the present Cambridge Springs region of Crawford County, Pennsylvania, in 1818. They, with one other family, the Birchards, were the first to settle in the area.

Their ancestors, earlier named Roote or Rootes, had originally come from a settlement in France, on the lower Seine in Normandy, but had later moved to Cambridge, England. (In 1903 Martha took a picture of a bridge near where her forebears had lived; the word *Cambridge* was engraved on the stone where the bridge arched across a river. Martha's photograph was greatly appreciated in Cambridge Springs.) Badby, England, was the point from which three of five Root brothers emigrated. Their strong aversion to war caused them to leave England with a company of Puritans rather than fight against Charles I and the Catholics in Cromwell's parliamentary army. They sailed to America, arriving in 1640. Some of the descendants of one brother seem to have settled in the Marysville, Ohio, area, near where Martha Root was born. Another brother, Thomas Root, settled in Salem, Massachusetts, having lived first in early settlements in Connecticut and western Massachusetts. It was from his stock that Martha's paternal grandfather, Sylvester Root, was born.

Other members of the Root lineage went to the Buffalo, New York, area, where one assumed the ministry of a rich and well-established church. He later left this post to do missionary work in the roughest part of the city. At one point he was stoned and had tomatoes thrown at him by a group unsympathetic to his ideas. But he found a little street organ, organized a group of singers, and in this way penetrated the seamy side of town. He eventually opened a mission there, which became a source of help and strength to the poor and neglected.

It was the Buffalo branch of the family that produced Elihu Root (1845–1937), who became secretary of war under President McKinley, secretary of state under President Theodore Roosevelt, and winner of the Nobel Peace Prize in 1912, which acknowledged his international arbitration for peace. His family relation to Martha was first brought to the attention of the public when Martha was threatened in Japan in 1923.

The Roots were a substantial family—farmers, weavers of cloth, and tanners—and "took a prominent part in all sound movements agitated by the people in the political affairs of the communities where they dwelt." They also worked to foster "the welfare of the churches with which they united worthy citizens, substantial farmers, or skilled manufacturers. They were often Puritans disciplined in the school of severe persecution for conscience sake."[1]

Daniel Root, Martha's great uncle, was apprenticed to John Metcalf, a tanner, in Middlefield, Massachusetts. A friend,

James Birchard, who had journeyed westward, sent back word that a fine piece of timberland in western Pennsylvania was available and that Daniel and his brother Sylvester should come out and buy it. Daniel, twenty-five, and Sylvester, twenty-one, started off together in 1818. When they had gone about five hundred miles, Sylvester became ill and had to turn back; but he told Daniel to buy the land if it was worthy, and he would pay for half of it.

Daniel bought the land and returned east to marry Susannah Church on 9 September 1818. Accompanied by Susannah, Daniel went west again in November to settle. They traveled by ox team as far as Albany, New York; and when the oxen gave out, they bought a team of horses to take them through. The journey was made over primitive paths, with notched trees the only signs to guide them. Six weeks later, they arrived at their destination, about three miles southeast of the present Cambridge Springs.

Sylvester soon joined his brother and helped him clear the land, where they built a log house. Three years later, riding with a Ralph Snow, they all made the long trip back to Massachusetts for Sylvester's wedding. On 5 October 1824 he married Mercy Thomas, and in November Sylvester and his bride started westward. She was twenty, he twenty-seven.

As the snow had already covered the ground, the ox team was hitched to a pung, a sled with wooden runners, which carried the bride and groom to their land in Pennsylvania. Sometimes they would travel an entire day without seeing a house or meeting another living soul. Mercy Root had been given a small black rocking chair as a wedding present; this was placed in the wagon, packed with the wedding trousseau and household goods, for her to sit on during the trip. Her children throughout the years always referred to the rocker as "Mother's black chair."[2]

The newlyweds lived with Daniel and his wife until Sylvester's land could be cleared and his own log house built. It was soon under way, fashioned mostly of oak and chestnut, with some maple and beech.

Sylvester Root's log house was an especially large one for those days. Instead of one room with a pantry curtained off by a quilt, it had a living room, bedroom, and a partitioned-off pantry; a fireplace extended across the entire end of the house, with a chimney built of stone and mud. The roof was covered with red-oak shingles, or "shakes," two-and-one-half feet long, one-third inch thick, and six inches wide. These were held in place by poles. Mercy Root's shelves were made by boring holes into the logs, sticking in wooden pins, and laying boards across the pins. In the bedroom stood a trundle bed, four or five feet square, which could be slid under the big bed during the day.

Six children were born to Mercy and Sylvester Root in this log house—Martha, Sallie, Harmony, Beals, Justin, and Morton. A big frame house was built in 1837, and it was there, on a farm, that Timothy T. Root came into the world on 13 September 1837, followed later by a sister, Lucy. With eight children the family was complete.

Sylvester and Daniel Root, with their large families, tamed, developed, and cultivated the area. A church was started, of which Sylvester was a deacon, and a town came into being, first called Rockdale, then Venango, Cambridgeboro, and eventually Cambridge Springs.

On New Year's Day 1868 Timothy T. Root married Nancy Hart of Sherman, New York, a town about forty miles north of Cambridgeboro. She was a zestful young lady who, at age twenty-one, was ready to assume the role of wife and homemaker for which she had been trained. Both she and her husband were devout communicants of the Baptist church.

T. T. Root's interests occasionally took the family beyond Pennsylvania. There were Root relatives in the Marysville, Ohio, area (a Timothy Route and his wife, Mary, bought land there in 1847). It was there that T. T. decided to try his fortunes. He bought timberland in Wisconsin and was involved in the stave business in Ohio. During this brief residency in Richwood, Ohio, Marysville County, their third child, Martha Louise ("Mattie" on the birth certificate) was born on 10 August 1872. She had been preceded by two brothers, Clarence and Claude, born in June 1869 and May 1871.

The stay in Ohio was short, and the family returned to Cambridgeboro. There they took up residency in a spacious, Victo-

The T. T. Root farm, with stone marker in front,
was Martha Root's home on Main Street, in Cambridge Springs,
Pennsylvania, from girlhood to the beginning of her career days.

rian frame house, with numerous large windows looking out
onto rolling meadows and fields, set up with barns, and
stocked with dairy cattle and horses. The house sat at the top of
Sitler Hill, where Main Street now runs. It was here that Mattie
spent her childhood, girlhood, and young womanhood. From
here she went to grammar school and high school, then off to
college. This was home. A granite block engraved with ROOT
still stands before the house, which continues to be known as
the T. T. Root farm.

Cambridgeboro, originally part of the Rockdale area, was
one of many small, undistinguished rural towns, nestled in the
Allegheny Mountains. It was situated near the original site of
Fort Le Bœuf, built by the French in 1753. George Washington, as a young man of twenty-one, had been sent to the region
as a representative of Governor Dinwiddie of Virginia to discover the purpose of the series of forts that the French were
building, beginning with one on Presque Isle and ending with
Fort Duquesne on the Ohio River. Washington wrote a detailed
description of the activity, concluding with a count of canoes

used to convey the forces downriver in the spring: "'fifty of birch bark, one hundred and seventy of pine, besides many others which were blocked out in readiness for being made.'"[3]

John Brown, the fiery abolitionist, lived within ten miles of Cambridgeboro. The history of the town, noted and charted through the Heritage Society, is still a source of interest to the townspeople.

One of the town's residents was Dr. D. H. Gray, who discovered a spring on his property that had remedial agents in its water. Chalybeate (iron) was found in the original spring, and then other springs appeared, predominant in lithia, magnesia, and calyx-iodo. But it was the original iron spring (the Gray Spa) that created the change and first established Cambridgeboro as the home of a great water cure. Having taken a patient to Hot Springs, Arkansas, to benefit from those waters, Dr. Gray found the water on his own property to have curative powers as great as those at Hot Springs.

Martha remembered, as a child in school, this snowy-haired doctor coming to the chapel and inviting all to his spring to taste the water, where he gave a lecture on its properties. Martha described him as a "tall, slender man, with a look in his eye as if he thought too much." He pushed a rod down into the ground, and the water came bubbling up into their cups. The children nudged each other and whispered, "Daffy!"[4] They thought he was a bit odd, but they always went back to drink at the barrel spring that he had devised.

After 1884 patients began coming to the doctor, staying a week or two, apparently benefiting from the waters and publicizing the doctor's cure. Soon Dr. Gray was selling the liquid for a penny a cup; then croquet grounds were laid out nearby, and the price went up to ten cents. The town's fame grew, and during the summer there would be as many as three hundred persons waiting in line to buy the magic water, which was proclaimed to have many curative powers, was soothing to the stomach, and was said to offer a cure to the drunkard unequaled by any other.

This marvel created a constant flow of visitors to the town. The rural village was transformed into a bustling resort. Hotels were built with fine restaurants and appointments grand enough to serve the most discriminating guest. The largest and most opulent hotel in town was the Hotel Rider, thought by some to be the best appointed hotel in the United States. It was situated on the crest of a hill and accommodated six hundred guests.[5] Hotel Riverside, on Frenchman's Creek, housing three hundred, was spacious and comfortable. T. T. Root was partly responsible for its fine golf course, still a magnet for lovers of the sport. Many smaller hotels and guest houses sprang up, changing the face and climate of the town.

Cambridgeboro became Cambridge Springs in 1898; and with its hunting, nearby streams and lakes for fishing, several golf links, and fine roads for gently moving carriages, it became a resort town and a crossroads for travelers, serviced by the Erie Railroad. By the mid-1890s the summer population swelled by several thousand, and Cambridge Springs played host to these middle- and upper-class vacationers. An elderly resident, speaking of those days, remembers having to elbow her way through the crowds as she made her way to and from town.[6] In the off-season large conventions of professional groups were held at Hotel Rider. By 1903 so many private railroad cars were coming to Cambridge Springs that the Erie Railroad had to build an extra spur to hold them while sidetracked there.

In April 1904 an international chess match, which included eight of Europe's best players, was held at Hotel Rider. The importance of the event was demonstrated by a reception for the players at the White House, where the trophy was presented by President Theodore Roosevelt. During the match, F. J. Marshall made a move of historic importance that was a variation on the Queen's gambit and was called the Cambridge Springs variation. It is still used today and is referred to by that name.

The influx of a more sophisticated population obviously made an impression on a seeking, sensitive mind such as Martha Root's. This future automobile enthusiast and global traveler learned, while very young, that there were worlds outside of Cambridge Springs.

2 Growing and Learning

Despite the uncommon environment of her hometown, Mattie, as Martha was called, was raised in a typical rural family atmosphere. Her mother kept a sparkling house and was an excellent cook; she knitted, mended, sewed, and embroidered. Years later some of this needlework would find its way to places around the globe, places that Nancy Root would never see, and of which she had perhaps never heard. The family entertained a great deal and created a congenial atmosphere for their many relatives and friends.

Martha loved her mother and enjoyed her sense of fun, but the deep bond was between Martha and her father. T. T. Root was an entrepreneur. He operated a dairy farm, from which he supplied the residents with milk, and with a friend he had started a marble works. He also owned a cheese factory and a lumber business, built and sold numerous houses, and was one of the promoters of the Riverside Hotel, which, with its golf links, is still a popular resort spot.

T. T. has been described by some of the townspeople as being tight with his money and in some ways selfish; but Martha benefited from his love and generosity and had only praise and admiration for him. His frugality, if indeed it did exist, did not deny the family a fine home and simple pleasures. He was a skillful fisherman, and his successes brought him fame. He held the record for having caught the largest muskellunge, fifty-four inches long, and weighing forty-one pounds. The fish was mounted and is still a wall decoration in a lakeside building in nearby Edinboro. His picture, holding the prize catch, was hung in the Erie Interurban Station; it was also put on postcards and was one of the attractions of the region. Throughout the years the local newspaper carried notices of

T. T. ROOT
Martha's father and friend

T. T. Root's going off to Kane or Sheffield, Pennsylvania, to
fish in the streams and lakes. On one of these trips he caught
101 trout during the first day. A dedicated fisherman.

Martha described her father as being a man of few words,
not having the gift of small talk, but saying something when he
spoke. His wisdom and peace-making talents were often called
upon by townspeople to settle disputes. He would hear both
sides, then call the disputants together, use the art of consultation, and bring the adversaries to an agreement. Friendships
were restored and lawyers' fees saved.

"God gave him the big gift of humor," Martha wrote, "and
the tact to laugh off the disagreeable things of life. . . . 'Everybody has troubles but father, he never has any!' " Martha once
told a friend that there was one man in this world with whom
she could live in perfect harmony: " 'Father and I are always en

rapport.'" The friend replied, "'Well, anybody could get along with YOUR father, he's an angel!'"[1]

T. T. Root never talked about his religion, but his life spoke with an eloquence that deeply impressed his children. He was a deacon in the Baptist church, as was his father before him, and his opinions carried a great deal of weight.

Martha's great love and deep respect for her father was evident in her early childhood and continued through the years until his death in 1922. She tells of being too shy at first to go to this "precious father" to thank him for the gift of a doll or a penny. He never punished her. But one day Mattie learned the phrase "'I don't have to'" and could hardly wait to try it on her father.[2]

That evening, following grace, he asked her to close the door. "'I don't have to!'" Mattie replied.[3] Her father was astonished. She was sent to her room without supper, to wait until a punishment could be decided upon. The incident made a deep impression on her. Years later she reflected that it was much worse to have his disapproval than to have a switching by anybody else. She realized how much she wanted to please him and to have his admiration.

As a child, Mattie had golden hair, which later turned a rich brown. She had generous, clearly delineated features, with large blue-gray eyes that drew others to her, and from which she viewed the world with love and curiosity. She had a radiant, beguiling smile, still alive when the girlish features and natural beauty had given way to a face worn and creased with pain.

Because there was always the threat of mortal illness in the years when Mattie was growing up, her mother made her wear a little bag around her neck containing asafetida, a gum of Oriental origin, to ward off disease. When colds were in the air, she wore red flannel around her neck to prevent sore throats.

As did other children, Mattie had her chores: on Saturdays she cleaned the lamps, which would get smoky from the kerosene wicks, and did some ironing. She took piano lessons, enjoyed athletics, and loved parties. Mattie got along well with others and had many good friends; but her best friend was the girl next door. There was a fence dividing the properties, and when the girls had a dispute, it was agreed that the first one who wanted to make up would go sit on the fence. Mattie was always the first one there. Even then her way was toward peace. In later years this friend said of Martha, " 'She was the most perfect person I've ever known.' "[4]

Mrs. Root's domestic talents were not passed down to her daughter. Mattie was not fond of sewing, or knitting, or cooking, although at one time she did manage a culinary creation for friends in Union City, Pennsylvania, when in her twenties. Many years later she reflected on this feat. " 'I *have* made an oyster stew—it was really very good!' "[5]

Mattie preferred the world of books and writing. Her mind was always reaching out for ideas beyond the limits of her known world. By the time she was fourteen, Mattie had earned enough money from writing to pay for a trip to see the spectacular Niagara Falls, straddling New York State and Canada. Most fourteen-year-old girls would have bought a new dress, a pair of shoes, or a piece of jewelry. Mattie chose a trip, a portent of her future.

On 13 June 1889 Martha Louise Root, two months shy of her seventeenth birthday, graduated from the Cambridgeboro High School and received an enormous, grandly decorated diploma for having completed studies in Orthography, Reading, Writing, Mental Arithmetic, Written Arithmetic, Geography, Grammar, History, U.S., Physiology & Hygiene, Theory of Teaching, Rhetoric, Civil Government, Bookkeeping, Literature, Philosophy, General History, Physical Geography, Latin, Algebra, and Geometry, and having sustained a good moral character.

Her formal education could have stopped there. In 1889 few girls went to college, and neither Clarence nor Claude, her brothers, had any desire to further their education. But Mattie wanted and needed more. Her parents consented and selected Allegheny College in nearby Meadville. It was not quite what Mattie had in mind. She chose a time when her mother had gone into town, then sat on her father's knee and coaxed him to let her go to Oberlin College in Ohio, an extremely good liberal arts school, which her cousin, Sidney Hart, was to enter in September. Mattie pointed out that it would then be possible to enter into debating, speaking contests, and story writing if she did not have to come home on weekends. " 'It is your companionship I was thinking of, but you just choose your college and go wherever you think would be best for you.' "[6] As his eyes filled with tears, he kissed her and rushed out of the room. T. T. Root obviously hated the thought of losing the companionship of his daughter, of seeing the bird flying from the nest.

Mattie was at Oberlin College for five years, from September 1889 until June 1894. The first two years she was listed in the preparatory program; the last three she was registered as a freshman, a designation given to a student who did not follow the regular curriculum. Mattie, always a maverick, designed her own program, choosing the courses in which she was most interested. Since languages intrigued her, she worked out a program with variety—Latin, Greek, French, and German. She also took English—literature, elocution, and rhetoric—and found time for psychology, mathematics, and Bible. The broad language training was tremendously helpful in later years for the study of a variety of tongues.

In 1893 Mattie moved into the college's literary environ-

MARTHA ROOT
(front row, left) with members of Ælioian,
a literary society for women students, Oberlin College, 1894

ment, becoming a member of Ælioian, one of the old literary societies for women students. Two pictures of her as a student appeared in *Hi-O-Hi*, a college publication. Her hair is arranged on top of her head, and she is wearing a high-throated dress with leg-o-mutton sleeves. Her expression is pensive, relaxed, introspective.

In 1894 Mattie became Martha in Oberlin's publications and was listed with the class of 1895, the year she would have graduated. But Oberlin was not to have Martha Root among its graduates. She chose to leave her college of five years and go on to the University of Chicago. There she moved into Beecher Hall, a women's residence, pursued her studies, had a couple of literary essays published, and in June 1895 was awarded her baccalaureate degree. Once again she received an imposing sheepskin. It was not quite so large and ornate as the one from Cambridgeboro High School, but it amply testified to Martha's accomplishments.

3 Careers

Within the Root family changes were taking place. Martha's two brothers had moved into Cambridge Springs' business arena; Clarence opened a butcher shop, and Claude went into real estate and insurance. Both were married and raising their own families.

T. T. Root decided it was time to leave the spacious Victorian farmhouse, with its statuesque pines and stone marker, and build a more compact home for his wife and daughter. About three quarters of a mile down the street he built a graceful tan-brick house, a curved porch with white pillars its outstanding feature. Although a much smaller home, it had elegance and charm, commanding the corner of Main and Dale streets. It is still a stunning house, its beauty untouched by the years. Martha did not spend much time there, as she was almost ready to launch her career.

Six years away at school, except for summers and holidays, had set the tone and rhythm for Martha's life. Devoted though she was to her family, she was independent, intensely curious, and loved to travel. She had taken her first trip to Europe in 1889 after graduating from high school and before entering college. With a good education she was ready to try her wings in the world. Cambridge Springs was to be her haven, not the arena for her activities.

Martha's first post was in Union City, Pennsylvania, where she taught school and was also principal of the Union City High School for two years. The first year she lived with the Burts, old and dear friends of the Root family.[1]

The Burts became Martha's second family. Lucy Burt and her brothers were like Martha's siblings. The young Merle Burt she took to New York to show the cosmopolitan wonders; Frank Burt she taught to dance. Years later when Merle was a

The Root home at the corner of Main and Dale
streets in Cambridge Springs, Pennsylvania. It was built
after Martha's brothers had married and she was spending
more and more time away from home.

physician and had learned of Martha's painful back, he would write to her in Europe and say that if she were with him he would roll back the rugs, turn on the phonograph, and dance her around the room, his arm giving her back the strong support it needed. That was his prescription. The Burts would all stay in touch with Martha throughout the years and give her detailed reports of their families' progress.

During this period of principalship Martha was asked to lead the school in morning prayers, a task that was not easy for her. " 'It is difficult for me to lead,' " she told a friend. " 'I never enter the room without praying, but to lead is difficult.' " [2]

The role of teacher, or of academic administrator, was not sufficiently fulfilling for Martha. It was confining and lacked the peculiar variety so necessary to her spirit. She took up residence in Pittsburgh and started to use her classical training more imaginatively and creatively as a lecturer.

Since the works of Shakespeare were popular with the

American public and had always intrigued Martha, she developed and polished a series of dramatic lectures based on the bard's plays. During the winter of 1900, under the aegis of the Empire Lyceum Bureau, Martha began appearing in the cities and suburbs of Pittsburgh and Philadelphia—in auditoriums, clubs, schools, and churches—recognized forums for edifying entertainment. In Cambridge Springs the local newspaper reported that "The [Pittsburg] DISPATCH gives Miss Root a unique place as a platform entertainer. . . ."[3] An advance sale of four hundred tickets was recorded for a lecture on *Othello*, given in the Carnegie Lecture Hall on 16 February. *The Merchant of Venice* was another of Martha's representations that was received with enthusiasm.

Always ready to help her hometown, Martha gave a Shakespearean lecture-performance, in the Baptist church on 10 March, to benefit the library fund. The response was overwhelming as townspeople, and those from surrounding areas, flocked to hear Martha dramatize and discuss *Othello*, emphasizing the theme of jealousy that impelled the tragedy. The hall was filled, and many waited outside the doors unable to be seated. The reviews were ecstatic.

Leaving Cambridge Springs the next day by train and traveling east, Martha went forth to fulfill lecture engagements throughout New York State and New York City. It would be a month before she returned to Pittsburgh. She then planned to spend the summer in Cambridge Springs with her family.

During this time of recital and lecture appearances, Martha was also doing some writing. In May one of her stories appeared in the *Pittsburg Dispatch*.[4] It was a light piece of fiction, possibly masking an element of fact, in which a would-be bride's career takes precedence over marriage within minutes of the ceremony. The story is neatly tied up when years later, after the woman has been successful in her musical career, the couple, still devoted to each other, is wed. The title, "Romance in Cambridge Springs," piques one's interest: Were Martha's affections challenged during this period? Was the idea totally fanciful? Or did a friend experience this division of loyalties? The story remains a provocative stimulus for wonder.

The local newspaper gave Martha high praise for her literary efforts, ending the review, "Miss Root is of charming personality, and we are proud to call her 'Our Martha'. We are proud that Cambridge Springs can boast of such talent."[5] Martha had already won their admiration as a lecturer-performer. Now she won it as a writer.

A career in newspaper work began in 1900 for Martha as a summer replacement for the society editor of the *Pittsburg Chronicle Telegraph*. In the days of a more stratified social system the society section played a prominent part in the make-up of a city newspaper. The comings and goings of the rich and well endowed were noted daily. The Sunday papers had many elaborate pages that were richly illustrated—the roto-gravure—showing estates, polo matches, trips to resorts, and carrying detailed accounts of parties and club activities. Martha, with little if any apprenticeship, took over as editor of the society section. Her family's place in town as leading citizens—albeit of a simpler sort—together with her years at college and a variety of travel, had prepared Martha for this new world. She stayed with the paper through September, returning to the *Pittsburg Dispatch* in the fall to take another temporary position. Her career as a newspaperwoman was launched.

Pittsburgh, Pennsylvania, the arena of Martha's activity, was a throbbing artery in a vigorous land. Here the Allegheny and the Monongahela rivers converge to form the mighty Ohio; these headwaters are surrounded by mountains that harbor rich coal deposits. The city's advantageous position beckoned many who would change the face of America and, by extension, the world. Shipbuilders, miners, industrialists, inventors, bankers settled in Pittsburgh—foremost among them Andrew Carnegie, a giant of finance and industry. Railroads were built, steel mills flourished, and coal was mined to keep them running. The pristine, natural beauty of the area vanished under layers of black dust, and Pittsburgh became known as the "sooty city."

Elsewhere in the country daily living still had its fingertips on the simpler styles and patterns of the past. The mail was delivered by horse and buggy; stagecoaches ran between small towns; hayrides in the summer and sleighrides in the winter,

*A street scene in turn-of-the-century Pittsburgh, Pennsylvania,
where Martha Root began her newspaper career in 1900*

with stops at friends' homes for parties, provided much of the
social fun; large picnics and church suppers were a means of
gathering a mixture of generations. Phone lines were just beginning to appear, and in small towns, such as Cambridge
Springs, *who* had a phone was important news (eleven names
were listed as phone owners in "the Springs").

Pittsburgh, with its energy, enterprise, inventiveness, and
muscle, was representative of America's move away from rural life. Andrew Carnegie, the Mellons, the Frick family,
George Westinghouse with his train brake, Pittsburgh Plate

Glass, Heinz Foods—all started their meteoric careers in this river-bound city. And it was with the vast sums of money from these various enterprises that the cultural life of Pittsburgh became so richly endowed. Schools, colleges, opera and theater houses, museums, and libraries were primarily the fruits of Andrew Carnegie's philanthropy, which surfaced once he had accumulated a gargantuan fortune.

It was a city with industry and banking at its hub, and it attracted others with similar interests from all over the world. Hotels were grand, and they flourished. In December 1909 Allegheny Municipality reluctantly united with Pittsburgh, making the City of Steel the sixth largest city in the United States.

Among the daily headlines that Martha probably saw in Pittsburgh newspapers were announcements of military engagements in the Boer War and notices such as Madame Schumann-Heink's singing *Lohengrin*, Booth Tarkington's engagement to be married, and the Nickel Plate Railroad's taking passengers to South Dakota, Colorado, Arizona, and the oil fields of Texas for inexpensive rates. She may also have read the newly published *The War of the Worlds*, by H. G. Wells, and the first article published by Helen Keller in the *Ladies' Home Journal*.

The theater in Pittsburgh was alive with stars in a wide variety of plays; every newspaper carried several pages of theater news. Among the entertainers were Primrose and Dockstader, the leaders in the field of minstrels, which spawned many of the first-rate comics and musical entertainers that would later gain fame in the early motion pictures. Such entertainment was only one aspect of city living that fascinated Martha, who always found plenty to write about in Pittsburgh.

Not long after joining the staff of the *Pittsburg Dispatch*, Martha moved to the *Pittsburg Press*. In January 1901 she took over the women's page, editing articles of local, national, and international interest. In one issue the literary menu offered articles on "Queen Victoria: The Woman"; "The Secret of Madame Recamier's Charm"; "Miss Pittsburg's Observations" (very much an etiquette guide); "Does the Pittsburg Woman Cultivate Her Voice?"; recipes; and a fine interview, by Martha L. Root, with a scholarly Pittsburgh woman who was writing the nineteenth-century history of the city.[6] It was a handsomely set-up page with clear credit to its editor. Although Martha was surrounded by print and presses and the bristling atmosphere of a big-city newspaper, the reporter's usual assignments of hard-core news were never a part of her life. From the first she was a feature writer and editor.

During this period the *Pittsburg Press* and the *Dispatch* both used Martha's editing and writing. In June 1901 she made yet another move, this time to the *Index of Pittsburg Life*, a weekly magazine of social happenings in Pittsburgh and its suburbs. It provided reports of the grand activities of the rich and the very rich.

The automobile was beginning to be a large part of the lives of the wealthy; one needed money to play with these machines. Every new wrinkle became news, providing a new ingredient for the social columns that was a giant step removed from the more pedestrian social happenings. Martha L. Root became editor of the *Index*'s automobile section and contributed much of the material. Years later Martha recalled that she saw her first automobile in Pittsburgh. She tracked it to its garage, went back to the editor, and suggested that the *Index* start an automobile section, which she would run. She did.

The automobiles of that day had a romance about them. Each model had a distinct personality; they ran by steam, electricity, or gasoline. The names are legendary—Lovejoy, Peerless, Packard, Locomobile, Haynes-Apperson, Pierce-Arrow Motorette, Winton Touring Car, Dos-A-Dos, DeDion-Bouton, Panhard—and there were individual creations with no company name.

Martha was entranced. Her first article appeared in the 29 June issue and concerned stables for automobiles. It was the horseless carriage, still "stabled," not yet "garaged." She did not confine her writing to the shapes and decorative aspects of these machines; she also probed into their mechanical abilities and described the workings of the motors and the differences in their performances. Much space was given to possible routes, road conditions, experiments with tires so that the rubber would not melt, and whatever else contributed to the mythology of the mechanical horse. Fashions, too, for motorists were a lure. Each week handsome pages with stunning illustrations and interesting literature on the motorcar appeared.

Another of Martha's stories, "A Man and a Woman," a short piece of fiction with an imaginative, piquant ending, was published in the *Index*.[7] She wrote a wide variety of feature articles, each spreading over several pages, including a description of the Hunt Club and of the Automobile Show in Madison Square Garden. One of the most interesting was an historical piece, "New York to Buffalo Endurance Test," in which eighty-one machines left Fifth Avenue and 58th Street in New York City on 9 September 1901. It was called the "Greatest Event in the History of Automobilism in America." Signposts had been put up along the way, and a map of each junket of the trip was drawn (there were no published maps of routes). These automobilists were pioneers.

Forty-four of the group made it as far as Rochester, New York, when word reached them of President McKinley's death in Buffalo on 14 September, eight days after being struck by an assassin's bullet. The entry numbers were removed from the cars. What was to have been a grand ceremonial entry into Niagara Square, Buffalo, was abandoned as the motorists courteously took another route into the city. All removed their hats out of respect for the country's departed president, and an air of gravity pervaded the scene: "The coming together of the delegates from Chicago and New York with the Buffalo contingent was solemn beyond all expressing. Man grasped his brother's hand, but no one spoke except in a whispered utterance concerning the great calamity."[8] A grieving Elihu Root, the senior cabinet member present, conducted the swearing-in ceremony of Theodore Roosevelt as McKinley's successor, with Judge John Hazel administering the oath of office. It was an unexpected turn of events for the adventuresome motorists.

The new world of motors and mobility was one that Martha could comfortably share with her father. When T. T. visited his daughter in Pittsburgh, the Automobile Palace placed a De-Dion Motorette at their disposal. A friend drove T. T. along the broad boulevards and escorted him to places of interest. Martha accompanied him to the Carnegie Library and Museum; later they viewed the nearly completed exposition building, the Heinz pickling establishment, and a Chinese church, among other spots. Martha's mother also made occasional visits to Pittsburgh, sometimes spending as long as two weeks in order to survey Martha's world as an editor in a busy city.

The *Index* expressed appreciation to its automobile editor by purchasing a Columbia electric automobile for Martha's use. Martha liked her work but looked around for more interesting ways to appear in print. She approached the Holland American Line and offered publicity—articles in the *Index*—in exchange for passage to Europe. They agreed. She then suggested to her editors that she go to Europe and send back stories from Paris, pointing out the prestige to the paper of having its own correspondent overseas.

On 15 March 1902 Martha sailed on the S.S. *Statendam*, bound for Europe. Her first *Index* report appeared on 19 April; its four pages, with accompanying illustrations, described the crew, the dining saloon, the promenade deck, the accommodations, the cooks, and the mechanical workings of the ship. Martha, along with many others, suffered from *mal de mer*, and spent much time dealing with the monster.

There was a mild flirtation going on between Martha and an American passenger, whom she dubbed "Prince Henry, incog-[nito]" because of his strong resemblance to the German prince, Henry, a recent visitor to America. He was a seasoned passenger and gave Martha advice on ocean travel, saw to her comforts, and added a light-hearted flavor to her trip.

Martha's descriptions of the passengers are colorful:

there was a celebrated pianist returning from an American tour, a Dutch colonel and his wife making a trip around the world, a blue-blooded nobleman, stiff enough to stumble over[,] and next to this noble scion of an ancient family sat a democratic passenger, Prince Henry, incog[nito], whose political discussions kept the lower end of the table always lively. American prominence was represented by a distant relative of "Fighting Bob" Evans [a naval hero], whose genial manners won him many friends.[9]

Her description of the ship contained an open criticism, very personal, of the male world; it was the closest she ever came to barbed comment:

The smoking-room, the furnishing of which leads one to appreciate a comfortable evening of joking and playing by the fireside, is reserved for the gentlemen. The few ladies who are occasionally invited in, envy the men the comforts of this jolly good place, for man is selfish and if ever this truth came home to me it was here, where, as on every ship that ever shot down the guideways, the smoking-room reserved for the lords of creation occupies the steadiest part of this vessel.[10]

Martha arrived in Paris via Boulogne-sur-Mer, a city about which she later wrote, calling it the French Atlantic City. Without advance arrangements she checked into the St. Petersburg Hotel with friends but, leaving familiar company, went alone to seek out living accommodations among the French. Martha wanted to experience the language and culture of Paris. She took a series of omnibuses, and when her French fell short of comprehension, she wrote out her questions and received enlightening answers. Martha decided that, Pittsburgh or Paris, bus drivers were about the same, neither terribly concerned with getting you where you wanted to go. Yet she fared well.

In the Latin quarter, a short distance from the museums, Martha located a *pension*, a private home that took guests and served meals, where only French was spoken. She settled in, with guests from other countries, at 14 Rue Monsieur le Prince, which was run by Madame Alliou. Monsieur Alliou, to Martha's delight, was a librarian who brought home all the newest journals and artistically arranged them in a circle in the salon. They were a key to her learning about the French culture of the day.

From this spot, Martha Louise Root, age twenty-nine, set out to gather information and impressions, which she would write up and send back to America. She wrote in-depth articles on the Tuileries Gardens, on sculpture, on fashions for motorists. There was a moving account of Sarah Bernhardt, whom Martha saw in *La Dame aux Camillas*. It was the most exquisite performance she had ever experienced; she was unnerved and frightened by the death scene. Such was the art of the Divine Sarah.

Being an automobile editor, Martha spent much time observing the motor scene in Paris. She called the Panhard Levasser the "aristocrats of the pavements."[11] Still she wanted entreé to the automotive industry. How to do it? She reported that automobiles and newspapermen have the right of way over everything and everyone in France. It was difficult for Martha because she was a woman, and no woman in France had ever covered sports or the automobile field. But she was a trailblazer.

Martha had letters from important men in the automotive business in America and from a newspaper editor in Pittsburgh, with a note of introduction to Algernon Dougherty, president of the American Journalist Society of Paris. Mr. Dougherty left his work to take Martha around, introducing her to important persons and leading her to sources of information. He gave her several of his personal cards as an introduction to newspaper people and wrote on the back: "She is one of us so I'm sure you will help her in any way you can."[12] They did. Despite bureaucratic red tape and a highly secretive operation, she was able to penetrate the inner sanctum of the automotive repositories of France.

An event similar to the New York to Buffalo Endurance Test was a caravan from Paris to Nice, during which two American machines distinguished themselves. It was written up by Martha, along with other articles on the horseless carriage. She was amused at seeing a policeman stop a cab for careless driving, climb up on the driver's seat, and personally drive the vehicle to the police station.

Her articles reported progress in auto design, noting especially the addition of a windshield, which cut down on wind and bugs in the passenger's face; and she described the temporary tops, some of canvas, some of oilskin, which were a protection to her as the rain poured down. April in Paris is not all sunshine and chestnut blossoms.

The most thrilling event was unquestionably the ride to Versailles in the Berg automobile. Mr. Hart O. Berg, of the Automobile Club of America, had designed a touring carriage of twelve horsepower and had it built in Paris. The day it was put on the road Mr. Berg invited Martha to participate in a speed trial of the vehicle.* They shared the front seat, while the "mechanician rode in the tonneau." They started from the Champs-Élysées at about twenty miles per hour, which Martha thought quite fast enough. Some of her descriptions of the ride are memorable:

> The horse-drawn vehicles gave the motor grey-hound the right of way and immediately the swift machine raced in and out among the thousand [horse-drawn] vehicles like a superb animal sure of its game.
>   First to one side of the pavement and then to the other, just grazing the hub of a coupé, or bearing down close to a refuge place the automobile zigzagged its rapid course. Pedestrians, for the most, stood out of reach, but a few women did not see the machine coming and they invariably stood still for a moment, and as the automobile would swerve aside they too, would turn back; the levers responded instantly to the motorist's steady grasp or a dozen people would have been run down in as many seconds.

Martha described stopping for gasoline, its cost, and the beauty of the route to Versailles, where the cars could go at a pretty fast rate, which, she observed, was far preferable to "pottering through the Bois." "Getting ready for some fun," they put on long coats and the necessary goggles, as there was no windshield. They were to try for fifty miles per hour. "This is sport," wrote Martha. [13]

---

*The speed limit in the United States was between eight and ten miles per hour, and most cars could not go much faster. In the Gordon Bennett International Automobile Races, which would be run in Ireland in July, the winner would average 40¼ miles per hour.

The first grade was taken without effort, and she had time to observe the beauty of the chestnut trees in blossom. But odors of pines and blossoms were forgotten when the machine reached the top of the hill:

> the machine, with one bound, began to leap down the hill; a strong wind followed us closely and we seemed to be running a mad race with the power behind and winning against it. The sense of power and freedom was glorious[;] one thought for an instant of Faust, when his youth was given to him again, or of Santos-Dumont [a Brazilian aeronaut in France] as he rides through the regions of air, the exhilaration is beyond the power of words!

The machine came crashing into Versailles and was brought into a palace courtyard. Something was wrong with a cylinder. It was repaired, and they started off again. She continued:

> This time the wind faced us and as the car lunged down the long grade with the full speed gear in, and accelerated to the utmost, my only sensation was that I was being compressed in air, then in ice. I remember seeing nothing but a streak of air in the vista ahead, until something black [another car] crossed the path and the carriage swerved aside, went over a "thank-you-ma'am," and the end of the world seemed at hand. Nobody spoke until the up-grade was reached, then the motorist said that it took more nerve than he had to ride after somebody else's driving.[14]

The magic fifty miles per hour was reached. Martha had experienced the future. She closed the article with a superb technical description of the Berg creation that he was taking back to America with him.

This is the same Martha who, in later years, despite all her traveling, was afraid to cross a street and was nervous riding in cars going at even a slow rate of speed. Perhaps she envisioned multiple Hart O. Bergs behind the wheels of other cars.

Paris and her French adventures behind her, Martha returned to Pittsburgh at the end of May 1902 and wrote a series of articles on the local homes, mansions really, of the very rich.

Their gardens and architecture were grandly described and illustrated, taking a very large portion of *Index* print. She came to know the drawing rooms and landscaped lawns of some of America's most affluent families, venturing as far as Cuba to describe an island retreat of one Pittsburgh family.

Skipping from houses to autos to sports, she wrote of the Schenley Auto Races, golf, the horse show, and the revival of tennis. She wrote of photography, art collections, and museums and special exhibits. Her education was greatly expanding. These accounts would spread over many illustrated pages, always with a large "Martha L. Root" by-line.

A real piece of adventure appeared in "An Automobile Trip to Cambridge Springs and Return," a trip that Martha shared with Mr. and Mrs. Paul Townsend, their little daughter, and Mr. Edward Hamaker.[15] Going 128 miles in a motorcar in 1902, over bumpy, soft, unpaved roads, often planked, with garages infrequent and ill-prepared, took more courage than most had. They were not attempting a speed record à la Paris to Versailles, but the terrain and the idiosyncrasies of motor and environment made it more risky.

The knowledge of *how* to drive a car was elementary; but one needed additional skills. At one stage part of the automobile was lost; a nearby machine shop was able to make a new part, with the help of the male motorists. Two punctures meant tire repairs, and a broken vaporizer needed fixing. A rainstorm, resulting in slippery, muddy roads, forced the party to spend the night en route. But their mood was one of adventure, and the negative aspects were simply dealt with. They decorated the car with goldenrod and stopped at water springs to wash their faces. At four o'clock on Sunday afternoon they arrived in Cambridge Springs, having left Pittsburgh at nine o'clock on Saturday morning.

Two relaxing days with Martha's family rejuvenated the motorists for the return trip, which was shorter in miles but over much more difficult and dangerous terrain. A bridge had been washed out, and the alternative route cut through primitive mountain passages never designed for autos. There was deep sand on the road, and the car zigzagged from side to side as it plunged down the steep mountain path. The driver "half stood in the car holding the brakes with all his man's strength. No one spoke in the crisis which seemed to lengthen out interminably." The climax of this portion of the ride came

> when a little boy driving alone [in a horse and buggy], suddenly appeared at a turn of the steep pitch and the automobile was almost upon him before any one knew he was there. The horse began to rear backwards and then balked, as the motorist with almost a giant's strength held the machine slowly on the steep pitch, one of the women sprang from the Autocar and coaxed the horse to the side of the road where she and the boy held it until the car leaped forward again.[16]

It was obviously Martha who, jumping from the moving automobile, quieted the horse; otherwise, she would have credited Mrs. Townsend. But it was not over. There was a two-mile climb up the mountain through sand eight inches thick. It scraped against the water cock and loosened it. All the water poured out, leaving the engine red hot. "Quietly but quickly Mr. Townsend told his guests to jump from the machine. . . ."[17] They did. They were delayed for over an hour. Eventually, the tank was filled, after which the motor hummed along, taking the difficult climb.

Martha pointed out that motorists get sunburned and blistered faces, but it was not as bad as the body soreness that occurs until one gets used to riding over rough country roads. She said, "It excels mid-ocean trips for stirring up the liver."[18] Not only were cars without windshields and tops; there were no shock absorbers to cushion the blows.

Pittsburgh was getting closer, but they were not yet there.

> There is an awful strain in fast driving at night, and while the automobile leaped ahead into the darkness going over 13 miles an hour, silence fell upon the little company; the road curves in and out and there are only about 25 feet in which to steer the heavy car. Once a plank [part of the road] flew up and struck the machine and then hit Mr. Townsend. . . .

[His] arm was almost paralyzed and his head hurt violently from the strain of guiding the machine as it careened like a devil into the deep darkness. Teams galore were met on this night ride and the railway crossings . . . threatened the machine at every line. [19]

The difficulties and danger had not diminished Martha's enthusiasm. Her only regret was that the trip was over; her companions, she states, felt the same way. It took stamina and a brave, uncomplaining nature to be an automobilist in 1902. Martha had both. It is difficult to reconcile this daring, adventurous young woman with later descriptions of Martha Root as colorless, timid, mousey, for her early suspenseful experiences remained a part of her until the end of her life.

Martha's writing ability and energy were noted by other publishers, and she was wooed away from the *Index* by the *Pittsburg Gazette*, although she would return in later years. Her first article, "In the Capital of the Philistines," appeared on 28 December 1902. It was an interview with Elbert Hubbard, describing his work in the Roycroft Shops, rather like a self-contained Amish village, where the inhabitants, known as the "Roycrofters," made their own bread, clothes, and food. There was a church, a school, a blacksmith shop, and a printing press on the premises. The story occupied a two-page spread and was elaborately illustrated. In future years the Roycroft Shops would publish some Bahá'í literature, request articles by Martha for their publications, and host Bahá'í speakers.

Once again, through her position on the editorial staff of a newspaper, Martha managed a trip to Europe. On 19 June 1903 she sailed from New York on the S.S. *Cedric* of the White Star Line. [20] She spent two months in England, Ireland, and Scotland, first covering the Gordon Bennett International Automobile Races in Ireland. Martha Root was the only newspaperwoman ever to cover this highly competitive event. She explored the British Isles, reporting in print, and also took time in England to look up the records of her ancestors.

For Martha the early years of her career were a time for discovery and relaxation, expedition and introspection. As she experienced new landscapes and cultures and learned about ways old and new, she stored up information that would enrich the articles yet to appear in the Pittsburgh papers and other publications. These experiences were preparing her for monumental tasks still unborn.

4   Incidents

In 1902 Martha was thirty years old. She had a warm, natural charm, made friends easily, and kept them. There was a quiet strength about her that was not threatening, a determination without aggressiveness; she was adventurous but judicious; and she had an insatiable curiosity. In a tough, male-dominated newspaper environment Martha retained her femininity, accomplished much, and gained the admiration of her peers. She was appealing to men, who always went out of their way to help her in whatever country. An escort was always handy. But no budding relationship was allowed to bloom. Martha kept them all as platonic friendships. Marriage would not be a part of her plans. It seems likely that she discouraged serious suitors because she knew that the normal expectations of marriage could not be realized.

In 1896, when Martha was twenty-four, she was coasting down a hill on her bicycle, going very fast, when she hit a stone, was thrown, and was seriously hurt. She was taken to a hospital, where an operation was performed that rendered Martha unable to have children. It had a profound effect on her and altered the focus of her future. Only her most intimate friends knew of this incident. In the future there would be speculation regarding rumors of Martha's early trouble.

This accident cast a long shadow over her life. She might have lived longer, and with less agonizing pain, had it not been for her early traumatic experience. Her operation was undoubtedly the source of her deep distrust of doctors and her vehement refusal to go to a hospital, in any country, despite severe physical need.

The shock of this accident brought Martha close to a breakdown. But she recovered, and there was no bitterness. She retained her joy of life, but she kept her men friends, of which there were many, as just that—friends. As with every other aspect of her life, once Martha had made the adjustment, she did not look back or waste time commiserating but went ahead to live life at its fullest.

Martha's reputation as a newspaperwoman flourished, and her assignments broadened. In 1904, after two or three brief trips to the St. Louis Fair, which was getting ready to open, Martha was asked to be the special correspondent of the *Gazette* to the fair. Not one to limit herself, Martha also wrote syndicated stories and did some magazine work during her extended stay in St. Louis. As always, her articles were grandly presented and illustrated.

The Root name continued to appear in the local *Cambridge Springs Enterprise*, with T. T. Root president of the Borough Council and Martha's frequent weekend visits always a source of interest. A Society for Civic Improvement was formed, its first order of business being to engage Miss Martha Root of Pittsburgh to give a lecture on "Town Improvement."

> Miss Root is one of our home girls, now located in Pittsburg on the editorial staff of the Gazette. She has been an extensive traveller, and being a keen observer, is in a position to give our people much food for thought on this vital question to the town. . . . Besides this, Miss Root has already visited the grounds of the St. Louis exposition and in her lecture will sandwich in some notes on the big fair. [1]

Regular bulletins appeared in the newspaper concerning Martha's upcoming lecture. She arrived a few days early to look over the conditions in the borough. Originally scheduled in the Baptist church auditorium, the meeting had to be moved to the Methodist-Episcopal church because of flooding. The main auditorium and the Sunday school rooms were crowded. Over five hundred persons came to hear Martha speak.

The talk was widely covered by the press, the band played, and the town took on a new vigor as Martha complimented the worldwide fame of Cambridge Springs and gave valuable advice to its residents. With the lecture completed Martha took off, in April 1904, for her residency at the St. Louis Fair, leaving town and family behind for a six-month assignment.

The simple pioneer Root families were no longer contained within a limited area. The Roots had branched out, so to speak. Sylvester and Daniel had each sired a large family, with a combined offspring of fourteen. Most of them married and had children of their own. These would be Martha's cousins, and she had many. The Root women added new names to the family tree as they assumed the surnames of their spouses—Hopkins, Hotchkiss, Rauf, Rockwell, Sherwood, Stanford, Stetson, Shrubb, Thomas—all part of the original Pennsylvania Roots.

It was decided to gather the clan together and get acquainted, or reacquainted, with old and new members. The first Root reunion was held on 12 July 1905. As some organized method of dealing with the details of such an affair was needed, officers were chosen: president, T. T. Root; vice-president, Morton Root; secretary, Will Root. An executive committee was appointed, comprised of Lucy Root, Mrs. George Stetson, and Miss Ella Stanford. No treasurer was named.

A program of musical entertainment and Root history had been prepared for the reunion. Martha spoke on how important it was for families to chronicle their beginnings before they became lost to posterity. There were doctors and educators, ministers and lawyers among the seventy relatives who came from various parts of the east and midwest. The Roots enjoyed each other. The reunion blossomed into an annual affair, carefully orchestrated and greatly enjoyed.

Part 2 / Gathering the Threads

5   Changes

Martha continued to write and edit in Pittsburgh. The newspapers gave her four-inch by-lines, printed with ornamental Edwardian flourish. She moved from one paper to another as opportunity beckoned, and by mid-1905 she had left the *Dispatch* and settled in at the *Pittsburgh* (now with an "h") *Post*. Once again she was society editor and also religion editor.

But life for Martha Root was not to continue along the path that seemed destined for her. Another path appeared, one barely trodden, new to the world, and scarcely articulated. Martha had arrived at a turning point in life more clearly defined than the ones most people experience, although she did not immediately recognize it.

In 1908 an interdenominational missionary convention was being held in Pittsburgh, which Martha was covering for her paper. She had with her Lucy Burt Steeves, of Union City days; Merle Burt's wife; and two cousins from Cambridge Springs. It was a post-convention crowd that gathered late in the evening at Child's Restaurant, the first of the chain to appear outside of New York City. Martha and her friends were a part of the festivities, seated at a large table.

There was hardly a seat available in the crowded dining room when a Mr. Roy Wilhelm from New York was seated next to Martha's table. He was a coffee broker and a member of the Bahá'í Faith, who had recently returned from a visit to the Bahá'í holy places in Akka and Haifa, Palestine, at the foot of Mount Carmel. He has left a full description of his first meeting with Martha Root:

Arriving [in] Pittsburgh on a business trip, too late for hotel supper, they directed me to a nearby restaurant [Child's] which to my surprise I found crowded even at that hour. . . . The head waitress finally found a seat and escorted me to a table well at the rear, seating me beside four young women, and I soon gathered that I was attending a missionary convention of some sort at which representatives were mostly women. Without intentionally eavesdropping I overheard one of these young ladies remark that it seemed a pity that all of the heathen must be lost, or words to that effect. The one sitting next vigorously took up this matter saying that there was one Creator whom she believed was interested in all human beings, and she doubted if really any souls were "lost." I sensed a coolness following, but I wanted to say a word; I recalled the old saw that a man once got rich attending to his own business, but the pressure was too great, and as they left and I had to arise to let them pass, I said I could not help overhearing their conversation, and would I be permitted a word in connection, which was readily granted. In about two minutes I said that my mother and I had just returned from a visit to the East during which we met those born into other Systems of Religion, and observ-

ROY C. WILHELM
an early Bahá'í who introduced Martha Root
to the Bahá'í Faith in 1908

ing that they also said their prayers, and led kind, helpful lives, we now believed that all humanity were being educated to the recognition of One God and a real "brotherhood of man", or something along that line.

This made an appeal to "Miss Martha Root, Society and Religious Editor of the Pittsburgh Post" who gave me her card, but I did not score with the one who made the first statement. . . . Later when I returned to New York I sent one of our Books with a note which in time brought a polite acknowledgment—I found that she passed it along without reading, however! Some months after, I wrote again that I would be passing through the city, and if she would be interested, she could call me in care of my Broker and I might see her after business hours and before the leaving of my train West. This resulted in meeting her at the "Farmer's Restaurant" where we had maybe two hours; she listened attentively, asked intelligent questions, which led me to send another book, which met with better fortune, after my return to New York. If my memory is correct, she then came to a Convention in N.Y. bringing her very fine old father, and possibly another friend. From which time her interest grew and later I met some folks she gathered together in Pittsburgh, followed eventually by Baha'i meetings.[1]

After the meeting with Roy Wilhelm and listening to his discussion of the Bahá'í Faith, Martha did begin to read the books he sent, though, initially, she did not want to be seen with a Bahá'í book. She left the first one on the counter in a drugstore; the druggist's wife found it, read it, and became a Bahá'í.

Reflecting on those days, Martha later recalled:

For nearly a year Mr. Wilhelm sent me Bahai literature, which I never looked at at all, but rather than waste any thing, I mailed it on to Theosophist leaders, New Thought people and anybody who was known here in Pittsburgh for "queer" religious notions.[2]

Despite her earlier resistance Martha eventually began a serious investigation of the Faith, its teachings, its claims, its promises.

Many of the early Bahá'ís in America seemed to share the same attributes—the ability for independent thinking, the willingness to explore new ideas, a fearlessness of reactions by those insisting on the established beliefs, and the financial ability to travel, seeking the truth of the new message. Martha had all these qualities. One of the first things she did was to travel to New York, Washington, and Chicago, where there were Bahá'ís with whom she could discuss the new revelation and its implications. As a newspaperwoman she wanted to have all the facts before embracing an idea of such magnitude.

The first American Bahá'í was Thornton Chase, born in Springfield, Massachusetts, in 1847; he had been a captain in the Civil War and had attended Brown University. A tall, handsome man with a fine baritone voice and an imposing presence, he was a successful insurance executive and traveled throughout the country. He heard about the Bahá'í Faith in Chicago, where his company had offices; it was there that he became a Bahá'í in 1894.

Thornton Chase and Arthur Agnew, another early believer, used to meet in Kimball's Restaurant, Monroe and La Salle streets, Chicago, where they and others gathered at a particular table to discuss the Faith. It was their table between 11:30 and 12:30, when it was taken over by a group of lawyers, who called the Bahá'ís "the Saints" and themselves "the Sinners." The spot became known as the place of the Saints and the Sinners.

According to Mr. Agnew, Miss Gertrude Buikema, a Bahá'í from Chicago, brought Martha Root to this table to meet Thornton Chase. They talked for several hours, no doubt moving on from the noted table when the Sinners moved in. Years later Martha told Arthur Agnew that her talk with Thornton Chase that day was the stepping stone in her acceptance of the Bahá'í Faith.[3] After months of concentrated research and sober thought Martha Root became a Bahá'í in Pittsburgh in 1909. The precise date is not known, but her commitment was probably made late in the spring.

What did the Bahá'í message hold that stopped Martha Louise Root in mid-career and caused her to change her course? What mysterious force opened new pathways into Martha's mind? She had embarked on an intense period of search, employing methods learned during her six years in college and perfected in her newspaper career. She looked at the basic message of the Bahá'í Faith and set out to prove its truth or falseness, a process that she urged others to use as well.

An extensive article, which Martha wrote for the *Pittsburgh Post*, 26 September 1909, set out the history and teachings of the Bahá'í Faith. The news story holds a clue to the attraction that the Bahá'í teachings held for her, particularly their stress on unity, which was the predominant theme of Martha's for the rest of her life. She quoted Bahá'u'lláh: " ' "We desire but the good of the world and the happiness of the nations. . . . That all nations should become one in faith and all men as brothers; that the bonds of affection and unity between the sons of men should be strengthened; that diversity of religion should cease and differences of race be annulled. . . ." ' "[4]

The unity of religion had a strong appeal to Martha, and her article noted that the "Bahai revelation recognizes every [earlier] religion as equally divine in origin . . . all rays from the same 'Sun'. . . ."[5] Writing of progressive revelation, she explained that a messenger from God is sent at intervals in time to renew the eternal, unchanging spiritual message and to bring new social teachings for the age to come. These divine teachers live among mankind and bring directives by which human beings should live. Each comes with a new name, and history has shown that they are rejected by the majority of the people, are reviled and persecuted. Their earthly existence is a continual trial of accusation, distortion, and misrepresentation by religious and secular rulers, whose positions in government and church, they believe, are threatened by the divine teacher proclaiming His special station. However, persecution and death do not obliterate the teachings that flourish after each one has departed, as was the case with Zoroaster, Abraham, Moses, Buddha, Muḥammad, and Christ, whose teachings have been spread by a handful of disciples and sustained through the revealed words of each one. Christ had said to beware of false prophets, but He had also said that one would know a true Prophet by His fruits. Martha studied the writings of the Báb, the Prophet-Forerunner of the Bahá'í Faith, and of Bahá'u'-lláh, the Prophet-Founder of the Faith, and judged their claims to be true.

In 1844, the year that biblical scholars had set for the return of Christ, a young man of unusual spiritual and intellectual capacity, claiming to be the Báb, an Arabic word meaning "gate," had appeared in Shiraz, Iran. His mission was to prepare the world for "Him Whom God will make manifest." The year of _Ghars_, 1260 (1844 A.D.), in the Muslim calendar was the designated year for the return of the Twelfth Imám of Islam. Each of the other revealed religions had also prophesied the coming of the Promised One, in a year that coincided with 1844.

Looking for clues, Martha had explored the Old and New Testaments, which were alive with prophecies about the return of Christ. She had read of the time of the end and the dawn of the Age of Fulfillment and had immersed herself in the history of the Bahá'í Faith.[6] In her article she wrote that one named Bahá'u'lláh had fulfilled the Báb's prediction of the coming of "One Whom God will make manifest." The title _Bahá'u'lláh_ ("Glory of God"), given to Him by the Báb, had fulfilled a biblical prophecy. This latest of God's Prophets had been imprisoned in a black pit, the Síyáh-Chál, in Tehran. After being stoned, bastinadoed, and put in irons, He was banished from His country—first to Baghdad, where He produced the first of His holy books; then to Constantinople and Adrianople; and, finally, to the pestilential prison city of Akka on the coast of Palestine. In Akka, the Most Great Prison, it was thought His voice would be stilled; yet it was from Akka that letters were sent to the monarchs of the world.

Quoting from an account of the early history of the Bahá'í Faith, Martha chronicled the ingeniously creative persecutions of more than twenty thousand followers of the young Faith in Iran. The Bahá'ís were still dying for their beliefs at the hands of fanatic Muslims; their plight was identical to that of the early Christians.

In her article Martha answered some frequently asked questions about the Faith, which may have been questions of her own at one time: Why have Americans not heard of the religion earlier? Do Bahá'ís believe in Jesus Christ? Being a Bahá'í, Martha explained, meant recognizing the truth of all the divinely revealed religions of the past and their Prophets. " 'Most certainly the Bahais believe in Jesus Christ,' " Martha quoted another Bahá'í. " 'One cannot be a Bahai and not accept Christ.' " The Bahá'í Faith was not a new religion, Martha added, but " 'religion renewed.' " [7] The spiritual guidelines that Bahá'u'lláh provided were the same as those given by the divine Prophets of the past. They charted the path to love of God and humanity.

Martha was struck with the simplicity and grandeur of the Bahá'í teachings. The events were historically provable, her logical mind latched on to their practicality, and her spirit was touched by the beauty and divine essence of the writings. To show her readers how practical the Faith is, Martha further discussed some of Bahá'u'lláh's social teachings—educational opportunity for all people, the creation of an international auxiliary language, the establishment of a world commonwealth of nations—all teachings designed to create unity, oneness, and universality. As Martha would write and lecture over the next three decades, she would tell people in every corner of the world about many of the other Bahá'í teachings—the elimination of all forms of prejudice; the equality of men and women; the implementation of a universal monetary system; the harmony of science and religion; the elimination of extremes of wealth and poverty; disarmament and prevention of war—all guides for living that mankind now needed at its present stage of maturity. When Bahá'u'lláh proclaimed these principles, He said they would eventually be fostered by humanitarian groups and governments, but would not be initiated by religious institutions. The writings of Bahá'u'lláh, Bahá'ís believe, are the steps to a unified planet and will establish the foundation for the kingdom of God on earth, promised since the beginning of recorded religious history. Utopian though they seem, the steps outlined for such actions are ultimately practical and possible.

The Bahá'í principles, the history, the writings of Bahá'u'-lláh—all grasped Martha's imagination, and she was eager to share the revelation with her readers, just as Roy Wilhelm and

Thornton Chase had opened new spiritual vistas for her. But beyond their guiding influence was an even more articulate mentor, 'Abdu'l-Bahá.

After the death of Bahá'u'lláh in 1892, His son, 'Abbás Effendi—who took the name 'Abdu'l-Bahá, meaning "Servant of the Glory"—became the Center of the Covenant, to whom the Bahá'í world would look for guidance and interpretation of the vast writings left by Bahá'u'lláh. He had shared the exiles of His Father and had been imprisoned in Akka.

After many years as a political prisoner of the Ottoman Empire, 'Abdu'l-Bahá was still living in Akka in 1909 (the year Martha Root embraced the Bahá'í Faith). The Western press, especially in England and France, had reported on His station and His work, just as they had been reporting for years about the persecutions and successive occurrences connected with the Bahá'ís, and earlier with the Bábís (followers of the Báb). Accounts had been printed of the Báb's banishments and His martyrdom in Tabriz, Iran, and of the imprisonment of Bahá'u'lláh, His claims, and the extraordinary love of His followers, the Bahá'ís, who risked their lives to make pilgrimages to Akka in hope of obtaining a glimpse of the Messenger of God on earth.[8]

Within a few years after the first public mention of the Bahá'í Faith in America in 1893, there were Bahá'ís living in several American cities; and in 1898 the first group of pilgrims from the West made its way to Akka, having received permission to meet 'Abdu'l-Bahá. Once in the prison city they became technical prisoners, but they basked in the light of 'Abdu'l-Bahá's love and the spiritual environment, which was far removed from the climate of the rest of the world.

They returned to their homes and passed on their experiences to searching friends, some of whom simply accepted the new Faith, and some of whom made their way to the East to discover for themselves the validity of the claims and to absorb the wonders of that spiritual fragrance, which in itself proclaimed the Bahá'í Faith's truth.

It was Martha Root's good fortune to have as her mentors in the United States two persons, Roy Wilhelm and Thornton Chase, who had seen 'Abdu'l-Bahá, had shared His table, and had learned first hand the glorious and impeccable message transmitted by the greatest exemplar, the son of a Prophet of God. When Martha met Roy Wilhelm in Child's Restaurant in Pittsburgh in 1908, he had recently been to Akka. He had gone, not as a Bahá'í, but as a companion to his Bahá'í mother. He had thought it too dangerous for her to be in the exotic, predatory atmosphere of a Middle Eastern city without his protection. A conservative, schedule-oriented businessman, Roy Wilhelm went to Akka with no pretensions of favoring the renegade ideas of his mother. But he returned a confirmed believer in the teachings of the Bahá'í Faith. Thornton Chase, the first American Bahá'í, had also gone to meet 'Abdu'l-Bahá in 1907, where any questions he had had were satisfactorily answered, and any misconceptions rectified.

These men, Roy Wilhelm and Thornton Chase, were not only spiritually alert, but they were highly successful businessmen in a competitive world. They maintained this level of accomplishment through integrity and ethical practices, and without seeking to manipulate or denigrate others in their fields. They were industrious and managed to incorporate a high level of business activity with work for the Bahá'í Faith. Following their example for the harmonious integration of secular and spiritual accomplishment, Martha Root would set standards of her own that seemed beyond the ken of ordinary mortals. She viewed with awe and wonder the spiritual guidance she had so recently come upon and shifted the focus of her life. Her romance with religion had begun.

News gathering occupied Martha's professional hours, but her time away from the paper became more involved with the Bahá'í Faith. A glimpse into her activity can be gauged from a letter to Helen Goodall in Sacramento, California. Mrs. Goodall, with her daughter, Ella Goodall Cooper, had visited the holy places of the Bahá'í Faith in Palestine in 1908 and had written about the experience. Martha's message was sent on 19 September 1909 from 223 Coltart Square, Pittsburgh, the first record of communication from Martha as a Bahá'í:

My dear Mrs. Goodall,
    I am a Bahai. Mr. Roy C. Wilhelm of 104 Wall St. N. Y.

gave me the Message, Jan. 23, '09 [this date refers to the long meeting in Farmer's Restaurant]. We organized an Assembly in Pittsburgh Aug. 29, '09. Our secretary is Miss Ethel Hanna, 432 Rebecca St., Wilkinsburg, Pa.

Martha went on to ask Mrs. Goodall to look up one of Miss Hanna's friends, just married and living in Beverly, California. Miss Hanna thought her friend would be interested in the Faith. As Roy had told Martha that Mrs. Goodall was blessed with earthly goods, Martha suggested that Mrs. Goodall call on the friend since, if poor, she might hesitate to come to a wealthy home. Miss Hanna, Martha continued, was from Jamaica, as were two of the five other members of the Pittsburgh Bahá'í "Assembly." "I know you will [be] lovely to Mrs. Miller," Martha wrote, "because you are a Bahai." Martha also informed Mrs. Goodall about her article in the *Pittsburgh Post* on the Bahá'í revelation, a copy of which she would send to Mrs. Goodall. The letter was handwritten on blue notepaper and was signed, "Martha L. Root (Editorial Staff, Ptgb. Post)."[9] She had already started her cross-pollination in the Bahá'í Faith—that process of putting Bahá'ís in touch with other individuals around the world, a process that would continue almost to the day of her very last letter thirty years later.

As soon as the *Pittsburgh Post* article came off the press, Martha got several hundred copies and, with the help of three friends, mailed off the article to people throughout the country and the world. Some copies went to her Bahá'í friends, presenting them with the sort of publicity that they could use in their localities; copies also went to 'Abdu'l-Bahá in Akka and to individuals she thought might be curious enough to investigate this exciting event on earth.

Another chapter had been opened. Martha's first article on the Bahá'í Faith had appeared in print, an accomplishment that would be repeated in one form or another for the rest of her life.

As in the past, whenever a new revelation appeared, the guards of the established faiths—not exploring to see if the new is indeed the fulfillment of the old, as promised—tried to thwart the spread of its teachings. Martha became sensitive very early to the situation and was diplomatic in handling such problems. On one occasion, when Roy Wilhelm was to give a talk in a Pittsburgh hotel, a missionary, who had recently returned from Iran, arrived and asked to speak to Miss Root. Martha took him into an adjacent room, recognized his antagonism, and learned that he intended to disrupt the meeting. She firmly asked him to leave. The meeting went on as scheduled, without interference.

During the year that Martha became a Bahá'í, members of the Faith from the United States and Canada organized their first national convention, which was held in Chicago. Martha, always drawn to centers of activity, soon became involved in preparations for the annual conventions, and from 1911 on was either the delegate or alternate delegate from Pittsburgh whenever she was in the country. In 1914 there was no Pittsburgh delegate, but the convention sent special greetings to Martha.

The Root family was mildly aware of Martha's "new religion." Her father attended a convention with her in New York in 1910, and he made no strenuous opposition to his daughter's attachment to the Bahá'í Faith. The rest of the family was unimpressed. None had the least inclination to join Martha in exploring the claims of Bahá'u'lláh.

Perhaps the event that had the greatest impact on Martha Root's earliest years as a Bahá'í was the visit to the United States of 'Abdu'l-Bahá. In 1908 the Young Turk Revolution had forced Sulṭán 'Abdu'l-Ḥamíd of the Ottoman Empire to free all religious and political prisoners, among them 'Abdu'l-Bahá. After almost forty years of persecution and imprisonment He was free. The sulṭán was dethroned in 1909, and the reign of the "Great Assassin" was at an end.

During that year 'Abdu'l-Bahá laid to rest the remains of the Báb in the newly erected mausoleum on Mount Carmel, bringing to an end the constant removal of His remains from one hiding place to another, and opening to the Bahá'ís a new point of pilgrimage—the Shrine of the Báb—where visitors from all parts of the globe would gather.

The Master, as 'Abdu'l-Bahá was affectionately called by Bahá'ís, then turned His attention westward. From Egypt He went to London and Paris, commanding great attention from religious and secular groups. On 25 March 1912 he sailed from Naples on the S.S. *Cedric*, arriving in New York on 11 April. His entrance into the country did not go unnoticed. Word of His coming had spread, and reporters and photographers surrounded Him for interviews and statements. Headlines blazoned His arrival. One newspaper reported that He had two reasons for being in the country: to view the country as an ordinary tourist and to persuade as many people as possible to work for the establishment of worldwide peace; He was not in America to make converts to the Bahá'í Faith.[10]

As the days followed, however, it became clear that 'Abdu'l-Bahá, whose every living moment was a dedication to Bahá'u'lláh's message of unity, had no intention of abandoning His goal, even briefly, to travel anywhere as a tourist. As He traversed the continent and spoke to audiences, vast and small, on social, political, economic, and religious topics, the clarity and lucidity of the issues and their solutions drew attention to the basis of the Bahá'í Faith, and many were moved to investigate further. In a Unitarian church He declared that the purpose of His trip was that "a bond of unity and agreement may be established between the East and the West, that divine love may encompass all nations. . . ." To the Bahá'ís He "set forth . . . the fundamental principles of the revelation and teachings of Bahá'u'lláh." He expected them, in turn, to disseminate those teachings to reach the "minds, hearts and lives of the people" of America.[11]

The hardened newspaper reporters, for the most part, set aside their flippancy and distrust and responded to 'Abdu'l-Bahá's intelligence, wit, spirituality, and compassion. They searched and probed and found nothing phony. They liked Him, and He was marvelous copy. His every appearance was subsequently reported with headlines as He spoke in the Bowery and in churches, clubs, universities, and auditoriums throughout the country. An editorial in the *New York City Evening Mail* read:

Don't laugh at Abdul Abbas. He has an idea. . . . people
with ideas generally are laughed at. But after the world has
laughed long enough, it turns around and eats the
idea . . . , digests it, and makes it part of its bone and fiber.
Abdul's idea is that all religions are actually the same, and
absolutely one. . . .
A side idea of Abdul's is that things modern are just as
good as things ancient. This notion makes the white-beard-
ed and snowy-turbaned leader exactly as much at home on
Broadway as he was in the lonely cell at Acre. . . .
. . . Another religious teacher, who had some points of
resemblance to Abdul, once went so far as to say that there is
"neither Jew nor Greek, nor bond nor free, nor male nor female." . . . he is the strange anomaly of an oriental mystic
who believes in woman suffrage and in Broadway. He is
worth his picture in the papers.[12]

Beyond the reporters were the Bahá'ís waiting for His presence. They were not disappointed. His being manifested the
beauty of His soul, His enormous, unqualified love for humanity and the world.
Martha was there among them. She also wanted to meet
'Abdu'l-Bahá, to test her own response to the reports from
those who had traveled to Akka. She attended every possible
meeting in the New York and Washington areas, and with her
friend Lucy Burt, followed Him to Chicago, where He laid the
cornerstone for the Bahá'í House of Worship on 1 May. Like
the others, Bahá'í and non-Bahá'í, Martha was deeply affected by His words, His manner, His spirituality, His message.
With it all there was a dynamic vibrancy, an ebullient energy,
displacing all thoughts of the docile passivism that is usually
attached to persons of a deeply spiritual nature. Here was enthusiastic energy expressing logical, uplifting ideas, carving
the road to a universal peace.
The Master was scheduled to speak in Philadelphia, where
the Revell family lived and worked for the Bahá'í Faith. Yet
Martha wanted His presence also on the other side of Pennsylvania, in Pittsburgh. She arranged a meeting, and on 7 May,
less than a month after His coming to the country, 'Abdu'l-

Bahá arrived at the Hotel Schenley, where He received friends in His room. In the evening about four hundred persons gathered in the Hotel Schenley auditorium to hear Him speak. Later He met with doctors and educators.

In contrast to the banner headlines and in-depth interviews with 'Abdul-Bahá in other cities, the *Pittsburgh Post* carried only a modest report of the talk, with His picture, and mistakenly named Tehran, Persia, as His residence. The summary did emphasize His work for universal peace, the equality of men and women, and the oneness of humanity.

Pittsburgh was Andrew Carnegie's town. His millions had presented the city with its cultural blessings—schools, libraries, museums, and an abundance of philanthropic deeds. He saw in the Bahá'í teachings the moral and peaceful solutions to the world's problems and responded by offering large sums of money to further the erection of the Bahá'í House of Worship near Chicago. The funds could not be accepted since only members of the Bahá'í Faith are privileged to contribute financially to the Faith, whether it be for a building or any other activity. Mr. Carnegie did receive a letter and a visit from the Master at a later date.

'Abdu'l-Bahá left Pittsburgh the following morning, 8 May, to carry on His astonishing journey in America. By the time of His departure from the United States on 5 December 1912 He had traveled from coast to coast, from New York to California, stopping at most of the major cities and hamlets along the way, speaking in cathedrals and to welfare societies, in auditoriums and parlors, in synagogues and universities, everywhere spreading the message of unity and peace. He discussed the equality of men and women, economics, history, religion, and language, always demonstrating how each topic was applicable to one's life.

During this time Martha had two private interviews with 'Abdu'l-Bahá. At the one in Pittsburgh, the Master presented her with a white rose, forever after her favorite flower, and blessed her with attar of rose. As He put her head on His shoulder and infused her spirit with His love, He must have sensed her spirituality and her gargantuan capacity for teaching the Bahá'í Faith.

'Abdu'l-Bahá's was also the role of comforter and doctor. Martha told Him that she had discovered a physical problem—a lump, perhaps two, in her breast—and that she was not willing to see a doctor. The Master suggested using alum (aluminum sulfate), a compound that would shrink the lumps. He did not give her directions for applying it; instead of rubbing the alum on the affected area, Martha dissolved it in water and drank it. Her method was not the most efficacious way, and it could not have been pleasant. How long this treatment was kept up is not known, but the problem was held in remission for quite a few years. At forty Martha's life had been a continual process of absorbing information and gaining experience that would serve her in the years to come. Her second career was in its infancy. The Master's visit, His tender strength and wisdom, which touched every aspect of living and predicted the unity of the world of the future, set the stage for Martha's growing commitment.

Martha attended as many of the gatherings with 'Abdu'l-Bahá as her professional life would allow, all contributing to an awareness of the Bahá'í message and how to live by it. One of the most memorable gatherings was a picnic, the Unity Feast, given by Roy Wilhelm at his home in West Englewood, New Jersey, on 29 June, to which the Wilhelms had especially invited Martha Root. This was a significant event, which would be annually commemorated in subsequent years as the "Souvenir Picnic," and was a high point in Martha's life. Wherever she found herself in future years, she always set aside that day, 29 June, to do something particularly attractive to renew the special flavor of the 1912 event. She often wrote to Roy Wilhelm and his mother, remembering the picnic with 'Abdu'l-Bahá and expressing her gratitude to them for having included her.

One other event that made a deep impression on Martha was a gathering with 'Abdu'l-Bahá on one of His last nights in New York. With Him was Valí'u'lláh Varqá, the son of 'Alí-Muḥammad Varqá and brother of little Rúh'u'lláh Varqá. Father and son were martyred together in Iran, each refusing to recant his faith, and each accepting death, leaving a poignant example of Bahá'í devotion. 'Abdu'l-Bahá told the story of these martyrs to His assembled friends, and He singled out Valí'u'lláh to sit near Him. So moving was the story of the father and young son, so strongly etched was the memory of those events, that when the Master finished, He "ascended the stairs to his room where the silent guests could hear him weeping." Twenty years later, after visiting Iran, Martha wrote a moving account of the Varqá family, calling it "White Roses of Persia."[13]

'Abdu'l-Bahá would soon leave New York, sailing for Europe, where He would spend several weeks sharing His message before returning to Haifa. His last days in New York were spent with the Bahá'ís, and He accepted only one or two outside invitations. He was teaching the Bahá'ís how to *be*, how to teach, how to live lovingly—not just tolerating, but loving all. His words invoked understanding, eliminated pettiness, broadened the humanitarian aspects of His message, and encouraged the Bahá'ís to develop the spirituality dormant in most of mankind. He demonstrated the behavior necessary to pave the road to peace and urged all to follow. Among His last words, as He was about to sail on the S.S. *Celtic*, were these: "Your efforts must be lofty. Exert yourselves with heart and soul so that, perchance, through your efforts the light of universal peace may shine. . . ."[14]

On 5 December 1912 'Abdu'l-Bahá sailed out of New York Harbor, leaving His Bahá'í friends feeling bereft. All had been deeply touched. Among those whose lives had been profoundly changed by His visit was Martha Root.

The loss she felt after the departure of 'Abdu'l-Bahá was alleviated by resuming a full schedule of work and increased Bahá'í activities. She covered events for her newspaper stories, wrote articles, visited her family, comforted her father with his asthma attacks, and spent as much time as possible with her mother, whose bad heart had restricted her activities. During the months that followed Martha developed many close relationships among the Bahá'ís, and she also taught the Faith.

Roy Wilhelm became one of Martha's closest friends. She loved his mother and father as well, and they became almost extensions of her own parents. Mrs. Wilhelm was a spirited woman with an inquiring mind and an independent, adventurous outlook, in some ways an older version of Martha.

ROY WILHELM (right) with his parents,
J. O. and LAURIE WILHELM,
whom Martha called her second parents

In August 1913 the four of them, after much planning, took a month-long auto and camping trip through New England. Each was appointed an officer in charge of certain duties: Roy was chief engineer; Mr. J. O. Wilhelm was in charge of the commissary; Mrs. Wilhelm was the poet-cook. Martha was the pilot, called the "Peelot," and the car they drove was dubbed "The Lady." The experience was one of undiluted happiness. It was a time to abandon city trials and responsibilities, enabling the four to immerse their souls in the beauties of nature, which completely surrounded them, to enjoy nighttime swims and morning feasting, visiting friends, and learning to know and appreciate each other.

Roy's laconic humor infected them all. The occasional problems became the source of adventure. Perhaps no four persons ever spent thirty days together with such joy and good humor, with an absence of rancor and pettiness, as Martha, Roy, and his parents. The experience deepened their attachment to each other, which continued to the end of their lives. So pleased were they with the experience that Martha and Roy wrote an article about the trip, which appeared in *Collier's*, one of the country's most popular weekly magazines, and included pictures of loaded car, set-up tent, and views of participants.[15]

Such happy experiences enriched Martha's earliest years as a Bahá'í. She had found a set of beliefs that caused her to widen the arena of her activity and at the same time challenged her to use her talents in new and unpredicted ways. Now the task remained to test those talents to their limits.

6 Shifting Winds

'Abdu'l-Bahá's visit had greatly affected Martha. She probed more deeply into the Bahá'í writings to absorb the guidelines by which one should live. But that was not enough. From her earliest days as a Bahá'í the idea of traveling to new lands to spread the message of the Bahá'í Faith intrigued Martha. In 1911 she had proposed an extended journey, which 'Abdu'l-Bahá discouraged. A woman traveling alone, especially in the Middle East, was more vulnerable than most. Again in 1912, during the Master's visit to America, an outline for a world teaching trip was submitted to Him through Roy Wilhelm. After a lengthy discussion the Master reluctantly agreed as long as Martha could have her salary continued during her travels, for He did not want her to suffer financial hardship. Nevertheless, it was a tepid agreement; He really wished her to stay for the time being in Pittsburgh. Roy reported to Martha that

> From the way he spoke I gathered that he thought some of the conditions of traveling after you got beyond the beaten path, such as over in Persia for instance, would be extremely difficult and perhaps unsafe. He also gave me to understand that the expense over there might be greater than you anticipate, possibly due to the changed conditions now.

Roy's friendship with Martha gave him the privilege of offering his own advice, which he laced with humor to soften the disappointment:

> I think too, Martha, it is a mistake to strain too hard to *create conditions*. I believe in trying to be in shape to grasp op-

57

portunities *when* they come and then to lay low for the arrival of the when, and I doubt if your whenly for this big jaunt has yet arrived, though I some how feel in my bloomin' bones that it *will come.*[1]

By 1914 Martha seemed to feel that her time had come. She decided to see for herself whether Bahá'ís in other parts of the world actually lived as 'Abdu'l-Bahá demonstrated—to see whether the precepts of the Bahá'í Faith made any difference in the way they conducted their lives. She resigned from the newspaper, made arrangements for publications to use her articles, and prepared for a trip around the world. It was a dangerous time. Many nations were bristling with antagonism, and the threat of war hung heavily over the world.

It was not usual for a woman to travel alone, especially in the Eastern countries, but even Europe looked askance at a solitary female exploring the modern and antediluvean spots.

Passports were a new requirement. Martha secured hers along with a number of visas for countries that she expected to visit. The passport was issued on 18 January 1915, #47702, and signed by then Secretary of State William Jennings Bryan. It noted her physical description as: "Age 42; Height, 5 ft. 3 in.; Forehead, high; Eyes, gray-blue; Nose, normal; Mouth, firm, large; Chin, square; Hair, brown-gray; Complexion, medium; Face, long."[2] The passport further indicated Martha's intended visits, as a newspaper and magazine writer, to Spain, Italy, Greece, Egypt, Syria (Haifa, Akka, Jerusalem), India, China, Japan, Australia, and Ceylon.

Never one to wait for balmy weather, although she loved warmth, Martha sailed from New York on her first round-the-world trip, 30 January 1915, in the dead of winter.

Not much is known of this trip, especially the European leg of the journey, although Martha wrote to friends from every stopping point. No accounts have appeared of her visits in Genoa, Milan, Athens, or Madrid, except for a few incidents that have come to light. Only letters from the Middle East and Far East seem to have survived. Her journey took her through Italy, Greece, and Spain, through the Strait of Gibraltar, the

Mediterranean and the Tyrrhenian seas to Naples, and then to Genoa; from there she continued down to the islands of Sardinia and on to Port Said, where she landed in March. Along the way Martha reported on the ravages of an earthquake in Italy. Her stay in Egypt was the longest of any during her journey.

Martha took photographs of her trip and had slides made, a luxury in 1915, for use with a lantern. For years to come the slides would prove useful during lecture tours.[3]

The high point of Martha's journey was to have been her stay in Haifa and Akka, where she would visit the holy places associated with the Báb and Bahá'u'lláh and spend some time in the presence of 'Abdu'l-Bahá. She was also acting in the role of courier, having with her two thousand dollars in gold from Roy Wilhelm, which she was bringing to 'Abdu'l-Bahá. He had been raising wheat, donating it, and caring for the sick and the needy from His own funds.

Martha reached Port Said, Egypt, but could go no farther because Palestine was in a state of war and was occupied by German and Turkish troops. The authorities would not permit her, nor any other traveler, to enter Palestine. People were being sent out from Haifa and Syria, and 'Abdu'l-Bahá insisted that all Bahá'ís leave the area. He would stay. (Lua Getsinger, a well-known Bahá'í teacher, would eventually be among those to arrive in Egypt from Haifa, but not until the summer.)

Martha moved heaven and earth but could not see 'Abdu'l-Bahá. However, she was determined to see her mission fulfilled. She enlisted the aid of Arthur Garrels, the American consul general in Egypt, who pulled the necessary strings, and the gold went through, unaccompanied by its courier. Mr. Garrels proved to be an island of help in later years, both in Greece and in Japan, where his diplomatic career posted him. Her mission was accomplished, but she experienced deep disappointment and frustration by the object of her journey's being so tantalizingly near, yet out of reach.

Although the plum was unattainable, the visit to Egypt was not without its benefits. Martha arrived in Alexandria on 13 March 1915, where she met the first Bahá'í she had encountered since she had left America. Muḥammad Sa'íd, a teacher in the handsome government school, soon to be closed by the war, was able to give Martha firsthand news of 'Abdu'l-Bahá. He had seen the Master briefly during the previous summer vacation; 'Abdu'l-Bahá had sent him back after two days, cutting short his stay. Deeply disappointed, he left Haifa. The next day the archduke of Austria was shot, and war quickly followed. Only then did Muḥammad Sa'íd understand the wisdom and insight of 'Abdu'l-Bahá's instructions. Had he not left then, he would have been unable to return to his home and his work.

Martha also met Muḥammad Sa'íd's wife and friends and shared a special time with them. She was delighted at the thought that she, an American, and he, of ancient Egyptian heritage, could come together with a Bahá'í greeting and know, through the Faith, the aims and ideals of each other. They strongly sensed the historic significance of the exchange of the two cultures. She gave him all the books and letters that she had with her, which he promised to read, study, and return.

He told Martha of the pressure put on 'Abdu'l-Bahá by the Bahá'ís not to return to Haifa after His journey to America and, subsequently, to Europe. They feared for His life or, at least, His imprisonment. The Master told them that He had known such suffering and strife during His numerous years of imprisonment with Bahá'u'lláh that nothing His enemies could inflict upon Him now would compare to those times. In response to their pleas that the Faith needed His personal presence, He replied, " 'The Cause has a Defender who will defend it.' "[4]

The country was still under the yoke of the Turkish government, and its commander in chief, the unscrupulous Jamál Páshá, had threatened to crucify 'Abdu'l-Bahá and kill His followers. It was not until the British were victorious in banishing the Turks and Germans that the Master's safety was ensured and the Faith was given official and appreciative recognition. 'Abdu'l-Bahá was knighted for His service in raising wheat and feeding the populace during the war years.

In the meantime Martha learned that, although there were famine and distress in Haifa and danger of massacres, 'Abdu'l-Bahá was safe. A refugee from Haifa, not a Bahá'í, said that the Master went down from Mount Carmel into Haifa each day to cheer and assist the people. The refugee also told Martha, " 'They love Abdul-Baha in Haifa so much they would go on their hands and knees to get food to him if he was in need. He helps them all and is not in fear of any danger.' " [5]

Martha stayed about six weeks in Egypt, hoping that the political climate would change and that she would be allowed entry into Haifa. She kept busy observing and documenting the scene around her. The world was in turmoil, and Martha was no longer writing about society and automobiles, about museums and horse shows. She was reporting on the vital issues and occurrences of the day.

In Egypt she not only met the Bahá'ís and exchanged experiences, but she worked as a newspaperwoman. She viewed the preparation and trappings of war and once witnessed fifty thousand Colonial, forty thousand French, and thousands of British troops march through the streets of Egypt on their way to embark for the Dardanelles. She was astonished to find no mention of this activity in the newspapers.

It was not only military preparation that World War I created but also the displacement of people because of religious beliefs. Martha wrote about the four to six thousand Jews, expelled from Palestine by the Ottoman Empire of Turkey, who were rescued by an American vessel. Evacuated from Jaffa and Haifa, they were brought to Alexandria, an errand of mercy by the American vessel. Martha quipped, "Moses became renowned for taking the children of Israel up out of Egypt, but the U.S.S. Tennessee has gained celebrity in bringing them back." [6]

She interviewed these Jewish refugees and reported the intolerable conditions imposed upon them preceding their flight from Palestine. She learned of the political situation that had developed in Palestine over the years regarding the Jewish people vis-à-vis their tormentors. One businessman's report to Martha is especially interesting in light of the recent history of Israel:

"The Turks, who did not until recently hate the Jews, do so now because they fear their latent power as a nation. The

Germans foresee the menace of the Jews in a commercial way. . . . They have migrated to Jerusalem for two main purposes,—to establish the center of Jewish life in Palestine and to assert Jewish national individuality in the dispersed communities. They wish to bring the land without a people to the people without a land."

"It is a national movement of an essentially spiritual kind," Martha discovered. "To become Ottomanized would kill these Jews nationally and spiritually."[7] She also reported the distressing economic situation in Jerusalem, partly due to the failure of vast orange crops because there was no petroleum to run the necessary irrigation. The article was sent to a prestigious American magazine and was published while Martha was still traveling.

After visiting many towns and cities in Egypt and talking with persons of all levels of society and of other Faiths, as well as Bahá'ís, Martha realized that there was no hope of seeing 'Abdu'l-Bahá. On 24 April she sailed for India without knowing that two letters from 'Abdu'l-Bahá, dated 20 and 21 April, were on their way. One letter stated:

Praise be to God, all of us are safe and enjoy good health. Up to the present time roads were blocked but now someone is setting forth on a journey and this letter is being sent through him.

Communicate the news of our health and safety to all the friends. Moreover make every effort to come to Haifa and bring with thyself Wilhelm's donation. I earnestly hope that through divine bestowals thou mayest be protected and safeguarded. Should it prove impossible to come to Haifa, then deliver Mr. Wilhelm's donation in Port Sa'íd to Siyyid Javád or Áqá Aḥmad Yazdí and return to America.

The second letter, which came with the same courier, revealed the tensions in the country:

If thou comest to Haifa do not bring with thyself even one written page, though it be a note-book of accounts. Also do not bring any books or pamphlets, because they are extremely suspicious of anything in writing, even an account-book. Go thou first to Port Sa'íd, meet Áqá Aḥmad Yazdí there and from Port Sa'íd come to Haifa.[8]

With such a vestige of hope, Martha would have stayed. She never knew of these two letters of encouragement until after she had set out for India.

Martha's journey took her down the Red Sea, through the Gulf of Aden, and across the Arabian Sea to the west coast of India, where she stopped at Bombay. Little is known of this visit to India, but Martha left an indelible impression on at least one person—Merwan Khosrove of Belgaum, India—who has never forgotten the effect she made on all who met her:

> In 1915 Bombay was honoured by the visit of Miss Martha Root. I was in my teens at school in Poona and my father went to Bombay and accompanied her to Poona where after a short stay, she again left for Bombay. Although now it is over 65 years, I still remember, while waiting on the platform for the train to start, I saw Miss Root take out a comb and begin arranging my father's dishevelled hair. India was at that time under British rule and the 'whites' looked down on Indians as inferior. There were two Indians in the compartment and both looked pleased at this sight; but the Anglo-Indian conductor of the train was shocked—he stood there staring and staring as if struck dumb.
>
> When my father returned from Bombay, he told me to go and attend to Miss Root as she required a translator. I went to Bombay and accompanied Miss Root on her visits to friends, but as soon as any believer saw her, he would concentrate respectfully on her; and if I ever spoke, I was ignored. Heart spoke to heart and there was no need of translation. I had never before witnessed such spiritual communion.
>
> I always felt an aura of spiritual fragrance whenever I saw her meeting a believer—she was altogether unconscious of conversation, just a pure soul in a very frail body, and one whose memory can never fade.[9]

The First World War raged on. The turbulence was reflected throughout the world, and Martha was often unsure whether she could actually continue her trip. But she left Bombay and went on to Burma, her ship landing at Rangoon, where she stopped long enough to read the war bulletins before traveling up to Mandalay. It was a rich experience, for the energy and dedication of the Bahá'ís of Mandalay impressed her deeply. She wrote to Roy Wilhelm, "If you think I work people hard in Pittsburgh, you ought to see how they do in Mandalay." [10]

She was up at 5:00 A.M., sometimes not getting to bed until one o'clock the following morning. Martha was the first American Bahá'í woman to visit Burma. She was staying, and being entertained, in a Muslim home, friends of the Bahá'ís, and "the richest family in Mandalay." Martha spoke in many places, and as a result there was a continual stream of visitors calling on her, not only Bahá'ís but Hindus, Muslims, Parsis, and Buddhists. She wrote that an Austrian countess came, and "we are the only two women. Am having a wonderful time." [11] When she returned home, a fuller account of her sojourn in Mandalay appeared in the *New York Evening Sun:*

> In order that she might see real Burmese life and that she might be more comfortable than in a public inn, they arranged for her entertainment at Mandalay, in the harem of the wealthiest citizen, where she was installed with the family of the favorite wife. Her host explained that his plan was to have her spend a few days with each of his various spouses.
>
> Understanding, however, the very natural jealousy which pervades Oriental households, Miss Root refrained from moving from one wife to another and lingered on in the luxurious quarters to which she was first assigned. [12]

One can understand Martha's reluctance to write home that she was spending ten days in a harem in Mandalay.

Her host was described as a philanthropic man who spent one-third of his income on charitable causes. Enjoying the unique situation, he brought many distinguished officials home to meet his American guest. Although she had no time for writing and no time to be alone, something she longed for, she loved Burma and the people. She thought of her time there as a bit of paradise.

A telegram arrived from a jungle district where there were

Martha Root (standing, center) with the Bahá'ís of Mandalay, Burma, 23 May 1915. Siyyid Muṣṭafá Rúmí, dressed in black, is standing next to Martha.

five hundred Bahá'ís, very poor people, which read, "'Send the American to us.'"[13] Plans were made, and a man was to arrive from the jungle to lead Martha, with Siyyid Muṣṭafá Rúmí, to this remote spot. However, because of the adamant opposition of the American consul in Rangoon, who pointed out the dangers of wartime travel to the district, the expedition was canceled.

Later, when she returned to Rangoon, there was an interesting sidelight to this incident: "A blind photographer who had journeyed from the jungle colony to Rangoon to hear her speak made 500 copies of a photograph he had borrowed of her, which he said he would take back to the jungle to console them for their disappointment."[14]

Siyyid Muṣṭafá lived at the Bahá'í Center of Mandalay, Burma. Most of the building was used as a school where English and Persian were taught and where translation of the Bahá'í writings was ongoing. The first floor was used as a home for orphans and a few very old Bahá'í women. There was a fund maintained by members to aid those who were sick, out of work, or had other needs. Here Martha experienced what she had set out to discover—the Bahá'í way of life in practice.

She called on 'Abbás 'Alí, the man who had built and engraved the stone coffins for the Báb and Bahá'u'lláh. He, his mother, and his wife were all in bed, stricken with malaria. His eyes filled with tears when they met; he had always been the first at the station to meet and interpret for Western visitors. Now he lay ill and was greatly disturbed that he did not greet the first American Bahá'í woman to visit Burma. He died the day after Martha left.

Because of the numerous visitors, as many as forty a day, and of her many speaking engagements, including a talk before the Theosophists, her plan to learn Persian from Muṣṭafá was aborted. But she did find time to show her love for the Burmese. She gave and helped to plant three little trees for the grounds at the new Bahá'í Center. She also gave ten dollars—then a goodly sum in Burma and to Martha's purse—to 'Abbás 'Alí's mother to ameliorate the family's distress. The Burmese friends responded to Martha's almost tangible love. Every day her bed was strewn with jasmine flowers, and when she left Mandalay, seventy-five new friends, Bahá'í and non-Bahá'í, accompanied her ten miles out of Mandalay on her journey.

Martha was still searching for a ray of hope to satisfy her strongest desire, a visit to Akka and Haifa. If the war made the Atlantic Ocean too dangerous for travel, she would go via the Pacific; by one oceanic body or another Martha would do her utmost. Perhaps, she thought, she could go through India and back to Port Said by August. It was rare that Martha, employing a variety of devices, did not get to the place or person on which she had fixed her sights. But this time nothing worked. Akka was not to be won.

Martha went on to Rangoon, where she bought telegrams twice each day to learn of the war news. Dreading the monsoons and another seasickness, she left for Calcutta, on the east coast of India, and sailed via that "terrible Bay of Bengal." "But it only lasts two days," she wrote of the trip.[15]

Even in the midst of the pervasive Oriental culture, Martha's thoughts turned to home and family. She had heard nothing from Cambridge Springs. Her itinerary had changed so often that, even in the best of times, letters would have an irregular course trying to catch up with her. She wrote, "I long to hear if my parents are all right. I may send a cable just to comfort my heart."[16]

Martha arrived in Calcutta the first week in June 1915 and traveled inland to Delhi and Agra, among other spots. Unable to get back to Port Said because the war was worsening, she headed toward Japan. She had written ahead to Agnes Alexander, an American Bahá'í teacher there, and when Martha arrived in Yokohama, a letter from Miss Alexander invited her to come at once to Tokyo.

Martha and Agnes, those two early lights of the Bahá'í Faith, had never met, but she knew that Agnes had arrived in Japan the preceding November to spread the word of Bahá'u'lláh. After an exchange of letters Agnes Alexander was expecting a Miss Root to arrive in Japan. Agnes had gone to the seashore for a few days, and when she returned, Martha Root was there waiting for her, having arrived a short time before. It was the beginning of a long and spirited friendship.

Arrangements were made for Martha to have a room in the same house in which Agnes Alexander lived. Here she had dedicated a room to 'Abdu'l-Bahá, which became the Bahá'í Center in Tokyo, and which was the location of Bahá'í discussion groups every Friday night. The house was called *Kudan Ue*, meaning "above nine steps."

AGNES B. ALEXANDER
an early Bahá'í from Honolulu and later a Hand of the Cause
of God. Martha Root shared many teaching adventures
with her in Japan and China.

Together these two trailblazers covered a great deal of ground. Martha urged Agnes to write about the Faith and place articles in the papers or magazines, and she impressed upon her the vitality of the written word. Agnes asked her friends and acquaintances to arrange talks by Martha. One of Agnes' friends, a Miss Tanaka, was a reporter who had been educated in English schools, had already written about the Bahá'í Faith, and was the first to publish 'Abdu'l-Bahá's picture in Japan. Agnes felt that it was a sign of a new day because a woman was the first to write about the Faith in that country. Miss Tanaka interviewed Martha and published a long article about her journalistic journey around the world and about her being a Bahá'í.

Both Agnes and Martha appeared in the first picture of Bahá'ís taken in Japan. With them is Mr. Fukuta, the first Japanese to accept the Faith in Japan.

Being a journalist opened many doors for Martha, and being a woman in some cases may have been an advantage. In Ja-

MARTHA ROOT (seated, front row), with MR. FUKUTA the first Bahá'í in Japan (front row, far left). AGNES ALEXANDER, Martha's co-worker, is standing in the back row. This photograph, taken in July 1915, was the first taken of Bahá'ís in Japan.

pan she made her first attempt at interviewing the leading government official, Premier Okuma, and was successful. She
quite neatly sidestepped any criticism of the Japanese while
still giving a picture of growing aggressiveness. Her description of the premier is graphic:

> Although a man seventy-eight years of age, Count
> Okuma does not appear to be more than fifty-five. His phy-
> sique is wonderful for his age, particularly when it is remem-
> bered that he has a wooden leg resulting from a bomb explo-
> sion. He practices fencing and Swedish gymnastics for an
> hour every morning, and is president of a society which ad-
> vocates living to be 125 years old.
>   . . . The Count is a brilliant conversationalist, and the
> moment he became interested in his subject my inter-
> preter,—whom I had supposed to be the best in Tokio,—
> passed me a note saying, "His thoughts are so lofty that I
> cannot interpret rapidly enough to give you his idea."[17]

Fortunately, a professor who was present offered to interpret.
   The second portion of the article was devoted to the upcoming coronation of Emperor Yoshihito and Empress Sadako, to
take place from 7 to 29 November. Martha was loaned dia-
grams from the royal collection of some of the numerous apparel that would be worn; these had been drawn and colored in
the royal palace. She gave precise and elaborate descriptions of
the ceremonies that would be enacted and traditionally arranged. It was a fashion scoop for Martha and an inside story
on an international event; the article and pictures were published in the United States. Once again Martha was experiencing, writing, and earning, finding the way historical, provocative, and challenging.
   On 31 July she sailed out of Yokohama, with a brief stopover at Manchuria before the ship set its prow for Hawaii. It
was Martha's first visit to this gem of the Pacific.
   During her three days in Hawaii Martha had several interviews as a world-traveling journalist, spoke at length on the
flight of the Jews, and praised the newspapers of Hawaii for
their balanced reporting of world events. She lamented that

nowhere, since she had left America, had she seen an objective presentation of the news until Hawaii.

On 29 August 1915 Martha sailed into San Francisco, where she was warmly welcomed by the Bahá'ís, among them Dr. Frederick D'Evelyn and Helen Goodall. Martha's father had hoped to meet her in San Francisco if his wife's health was stable. It was a difficult journey from coast to coast in 1915 for a man of seventy-seven. But he was Martha's father, undaunted by the great beyond. He had missed his daughter. As it had been their longest separation, Timothy T. packed up, crossed the country, and greeted Martha on the West Coast. The Bahá'ís warmly welcomed them both. Martha, ever after, had a special spot in her heart for the Californians because of their generous response to her parent.

At the end of this most ambitious journey, Martha began to feel the breadth of her new faith and to recognize how it could work for world peace. She had met Bahá'ís in the Occident and in the Orient, had seen their unity of purpose, their strivings toward the oneness of mankind. In Burma she had witnessed the perfect pattern of living when based on the Bahá'í beliefs; such a discovery had been the goal of her trip, and she felt her questions had been answered. Back on American soil she internalized her experiences, which spurred her to carry on her activities with renewed vigor.

7 New Challenges at Home

On her return to Pittsburgh after having encircled the globe, Martha again became an editor on the *Index of Pittsburgh Life*, the scene of her early adventures in writing and travel. She also took time to teach foreign students in the Department of Industries at the Carnegie Institute of Technology.

The experiences accrued on round-the-world travel became a part of the fabric of Martha's existence, and she maintained communication with her new friends, Bahá'í and non-Bahá'í, via letters to places all over the world. These missives contained news of persons and activities in places where she had visited.

She also stepped up her own Bahá'í teaching. She held weekly meetings on Tuesdays at the Fort Pitt Hotel, and she wrote letters to all women's groups in the city and to the pastors of "some of the broader churches, asking them if they would care to give me a place on their programs to speak upon the Bahai Movement." Twenty of the largest organizations responded favorably, and Martha spoke. Many wanted a return engagement. "Whatever comes to us," she noted, "we can always be happy and we can always serve: we serve sometimes by our very courage in great trials." She also wrote of renunciation: "The Disciples of Christ could resuscitate the world only after obtaining perfect renunciation. You must keep yourselves constantly engaged in praying to God and in spreading the Teaching."[1] Martha was developing a philosophy of life that would be with her until her last moment on earth.

Most major holidays Martha spent with her family. Christmas was still a special time, with the gathering together of the Root relatives; she loved especially sharing time with her brothers' children. Thanksgiving was more demanding professionally, and she stayed in Pittsburgh, though she spent the preceding weekend in Cambridge Springs. The presence of Martha was a joy to her parents, still devoted to each other after forty-eight years of marriage. They blossomed under the attentions that Martha gave them as she administered to the physical limitations of their waning years.

On Thanksgiving morning, 30 November 1916, Timothy Root made breakfast for his wife and brought it to her on a tray. She sipped the hot drink while he attended the fireplace in their room. Then she drew a blanket around her shoulders and quietly slipped from this sphere. Nancy Hart Root, beloved mother of Martha Louise, had moved on to another world. Another chapter for Martha had ended, and a new one would start.

Over her father's protests, perhaps not very vigorous, Martha L. Root, then forty-four, resigned her post at the *Index,* wound up her affairs in Pittsburgh, and returned to Cambridge Springs to care for her father. She reasoned that he should not be left alone, that all his activities were centered around Cambridge Springs, that it would be unwise to uproot him. In a long editorial the *Pittsburgh Sunday Press* paid tribute to Martha's sixteen years on Pittsburgh newspapers—to her as a writer of ability, as a world traveler, as a Bahá'í, and as a person. The closing paragraphs observed that:

> She has helped innumerable philanthropic causes by her expert publicity. Entirely at her own expense, she sends out each month a letter which reaches [100,000] women in the orient. With it are enclosed religious clippings, paragraphs on the feminist movement and on universal peace. These clippings are copied in newspapers and magazines all through the orient. . . . She is a woman of the broadest sympathies, and most altruistic in character. Her friends hope that her resignation from local newspaper work will not be permanent.[2]

Life in Cambridge Springs was different but not static. Her two primary concerns were the Bahá'í Faith and her father. She continued to write and to prepare publicity for the Faith; she was also involved in committee work for the annual convention of the Bahá'ís of the United States and Canada. Among other commitments Martha taught Sunday school in the Baptist church where her family had always been involved. She was passing on to a younger generation the teachings and the example of the life of Christ. She saw no conflict between enriching their lives with the Christian ethic and with her belief in Bahá'u'lláh. Christ was a Prophet of God who lived, suffered, and died for His message, which is accepted and revered by all Bahá'ís. One Cambridge Springs resident remembers that "Martha was a wonderful teacher, clear, patient—wonderful. I really learned from her and so did the others. We all thought a great deal of her."[3]

Martha believed that she was in possession of a gem, a prize—the message of Bahá'u'lláh—and felt she must share it with these friends whom she loved. The best place to communicate these ideas would be in the Baptist church, where so many times before Martha had appeared on behalf of a variety of causes. T. T. Root agreed and went forth to make arrangements, but he was refused. Neither the church nor its auditorium were available to Miss Root and her message. But T. T., like his daughter on so many occasions, would not be put off. He contributed not only his energy and wisdom to the Baptist church, in his role as deacon and adviser to many, but he was also one of the largest contributors to the support of the church. He threatened to hire the largest hall available and to withdraw his financial support unless Martha could be heard. He told them that his daughter had something to say, and she should be allowed to speak.

The minister and the deacons finally agreed, and the meeting was arranged. The church was filled as Martha offered her gift of the Faith to these people. But the meeting was a fiasco. As she told them about the Bahá'í belief that spiritual truth was revealed by a succession of God's messengers, from Noah, through Christ and Muḥammad, to the present revelation of Bahá'u'lláh, one person stood up and violently opposed her, stamping down the aisle and shouting her down as a "perfect blasphemer."[4] She was displacing Christ as the Prophet of Christian truth with an unknown, a foreigner. The church members were outraged. Martha's name was removed from the church records.

Martha ached for the sorrow the incident had caused her father. When they returned home, she put her arms around his neck and wept, not for herself, she later said, but because she felt sorry for him.

Many years later when she returned to Cambridge Springs and was visiting in her old home, now belonging to others, there were friends gathered there to meet her, among them a deacon of the church. She told him that he was sitting in the exact spot where her father was sitting when she embraced him and wept for the cruelty of others, which had so deeply hurt the father she loved. The deacon felt that perhaps the people were not quite ready then for those ideas.

Martha's brothers, their wives, and other relatives were embarrassed by the ideas that Martha taught, and tried to convince T. T. Root that his daughter needed help and should be prevented from mentioning these outrageous teachings. Martha immersed herself in prayer and activity and demonstrated only greater love and tolerance to those who scoffed at her.

There was plenty to do. Among other activities Martha turned to teaching part time at Alliance College, the Polish school for young men. She cherished her friendships with students and faculty. Later, when she returned to Cambridge Springs, she would always walk up the hill to the college, approaching it through the wooded trails, taking visiting friends to this spot she loved. A Bahá'í friend remembers being taken there in 1936:

> early the first morning Martha came to take me to the Polish College where she used to teach English. . . . The buildings were in a wooded, hilly area approached by a wooden bridge over a ravine.* Martha was welcomed by her friend, the bearded Principal, who explained the weekend [absence] of the teachers and students. It was a dreamy and unlikely environment with the portraits of Polish [heroes] staring at us from the walls of the long halls.[5]

---

*This approach was via a footpath behind the college and was not the usual approach.

Despite the adverse temperament of the townspeople, Martha piled good deed upon good deed. Every Saturday night she tended her father's feet, bathed and massaged them, clipped the nails, and nursed any troublesome spots. She did the same for her Aunt Martha, after whom she was named. When this aunt had cancer, it was Martha who took time to bathe her and tend to her once a week.

Martha visited the sick, bringing them gifts of food or little presents. Even those she barely knew, Martha comforted. She seemed to have a sixth sense about where a need existed and appeared with exactly the right word or act to benefit the burdened one. These recipients of Martha's love were among the group that championed her, and some were astute enough to sense the grandeur and mystery that was growing in her. One later said, " 'Where did Martha come from, really?' "[6]

But there was no loving support within her own immediate family, other than her father. Only her niece, Ruth, and later Claude's daughter, Anna, responded to their aunt with warmth. One branch of the family tried to have her institutionalized. Her father's outrage counteracted such ideas.

If a cloud hung over Cambridge Springs, the sky in other places was growing brighter. It was a period of rich, personal satisfaction for Martha. During this time she made some of her deepest and most rewarding friendships with Bahá'ís—Harry Randall and his family and Agnes Parsons, among others. It was also a time of excitement and anticipation in the Bahá'í Faith. The Bahá'ís in the United States and Canada were anxious to get started with the building of the House of Worship in Wilmette, Illinois. The receipt of funds from all over the world indicated that the work might start in the fall of 1917.

The ninth annual Bahá'í convention opened in Boston on 30 April 1917. It was a landmark gathering, the effects of which would shape the history of the Faith, and would touch the world. Martha L. Root was the reporter for the convention.

At the Hotel Brunswick in Boston five of the Tablets of the Divine Plan, 'Abdu'l-Bahá's instructions to the American Bahá'ís for teaching the Faith, were read to those gathered at the convention. Four geographical areas of the United States (the

Northeastern, Southern, Central, and Western states) and Canada were involved. Spirited discussion followed, and it was evident that dedication and enthusiasm were going to spark implementation and teaching the Faith, or as Martha reported, "Action was taken to translate that vision into enduring form in firm and permanent action."[7]

Another notable event at the ninth convention was the appearance of small, blue teaching booklets put out by Roy Wilhelm. There were two sizes, one miniscule (less than two inches square) and the other somewhat larger. They were quickly dubbed "Big Ben" and "Little Ben"; their success was immediate. Originally given as favors at the Feast of Riḍván* before the convention, the first edition of fifteen thousand was quickly sold and another seventy-five thousand printed. These, too, were soon gone. They were constantly reprinted.

Roy Wilhelm's blue booklets became Martha's standby, her best friends, when she started teaching trips throughout the world. They were translated into several languages and found their way into rich and humble, large and small, homes all over the globe. Big Ben and Little Ben were like a pair of wondrous stars appearing in the sky, taking on personalities of their own while helping others to accomplish their missions. For Martha they were indispensable.[8]

It was perhaps at the Boston convention that Martha Root and William Henry (Harry) Randall first worked together. Harry Randall was a patrician Boston gentleman, a lawyer and a dedicated Bahá'í, who maintained one office for his steamship line and another for Bahá'í work, where Roushan Wilkinson acted as secretary. He was a superb speaker whose logic and eloquence moved minds and hearts. He and his wife, Ruth, and their two children, Margaret and William (Bill)— later named Bahiyyih and Baha'i by 'Abdu'l-Bahá—were to Martha a perfect expression of a family living the Bahá'í life. Harry was also the cousin of Loulie Mathews, who has written

---

*The Feast of Riḍván, 21 April, is the first day of a twelve-day commemoration of Bahá'u'lláh's sojourn in the Garden of Riḍván (Paradise), Baghdad, in 1863. It was there that He announced His mission to His companions.

*LITTLE BEN, a pamphlet less than two inches square,
and BIG BEN, a pamphlet somewhat larger, were basic
teaching booklets introduced by Roy Wilhelm at the Ninth
Annual Mashrak-el-Azkar Convention in 1917. Martha Root had
them translated into many languages and used them
constantly in her travels around the world.*

about her severe injuries in an automobile accident near Harry's summer home, where she rediscovered the Bahá'í Faith and was encouraged eventually to become a Bahá'í.[9]

Martha and Harry worked together on many Bahá'í projects, a perfect matching of talents and personalities. Sparks flew, but not in argument, only in excitement and energy to accomplish the goal. There was intensity and understanding between two whose minds and hearts were beautifully attuned. Friends who worked with them called them "soul-mates."[10] This relationship was one of the deepest and most significant in Martha's life. Martha later said of Harry that he taught people much when he was well and rich; but he taught them more in his last days of illness and material poverty.

Her admiration was not limited to Harry. Martha loved the entire Randall family, loved Ruth and her gentleness, cherished the children, and later would bless Bahíyyih with the gift of friendship; Bishop Brown, whose father was killed in the First World War, later became a part of the family, and Martha would include him in her letters to the family.[11]

Working with Bahá'í committees gave Martha the opportunity to serve with Bahá'ís in other cities as well. When the one hundredth anniversary of the birth of Bahá'u'lláh was to be commemorated on 12 November 1917, Martha was appointed to the publicity committee, where she would be working with Agnes Parsons and Joseph Hannen, chairman, both of Washington, D.C. Although Martha had met them many times before, it was her first experience working closely with them. Another deep and lasting friendship developed with Mrs. Parsons.

No one could have been better suited to carry out publicity assignments for the special occasion than Martha, who, apart from her familiarity with newspapers and the wire services, wrote as easily as a bird wings its way across the meadows. If an idea came to her, she would write it, make copies on her neostyle—not in very good shape, but adequate—and send them to Spiritual Assemblies and to individual Bahá'ís throughout the United States and Canada.

The telephone seems never to have been used. If there was an urgency in communicating, a telegram was sent; a Western

Union boy, hurrying through town on his bicycle, would appear at the door with a yellow envelope containing the message. Casual long distance calls were a wave of the future.

Martha sent to Agnes Parsons a model news release of a general nature about the birth of Bahá'u'lláh, the Bahá'í Faith, and the significance of these events in the world. She separately included a list of steps to be taken by each community to gain the utmost exposure for the Faith through this commemoration. There was nothing hazy or tentative about her ideas:

> You could go direct to the managing editor and say you are a friend of Abdul Baha and ask him if he or one of his reporters could take some data regarding the event. Tell him if he takes a good story you will not go to see the other editors. If one leading paper takes it, the others will be alert to follow it up and get something about the affair when it comes off. Explain exactly what your Assembly is going to have—or have it written out, all typed. Then you could give him "Big Ben," one of Roy's blue booklets, and any other information you may have which explains what the Cause is. Also you could give him this general story [which Martha had enclosed]. In this way each paper will have the local cover and the stories will be different.
>
> The [Associated] Press will send out something but they cannot send a very long story. . . .

She closed with a final recommendation: "'Turn your face to Baha-o-llah' and pray for His help—do your utmost and this anniversary will be the means of getting glorious publicity of the Cause before millions of eyes."[12] Martha realized that the more people knew about the Bahá'í Faith and its message for unifying the world, the sooner peace would come to the planet.

In addition to assisting Bahá'ís with press coverage, Martha's attention was drawn to another matter of great interest to the Bahá'í community—the building, as quickly as possible, of the House of Worship in Wilmette, Illinois. As did other Bahá'ís, Martha looked around for new ways to contribute to the fund. Albert Heath Hall, a lawyer from Minneapolis, had been president (1909–14) of the Executive Board of the Bahai Temple Unity, whose purpose was to oversee the business of the building of the House of Worship, commonly called at that time the "Temple." In 1916 he was treasurer of the board and a friend and admirer of Martha's.

She sent him a check for fifty dollars with instructions to purchase fifty shares of Golden Bell Mining stock and put it in the name of the corporation holding title to the House of Worship. If it succeeded, the profits were to go to the "Temple Fund." He responded:

> Your two letters bursting with the faith that "moves mountains" and blind to all save the Cause, received. . . .
>
> I shall follow your instructions, throw no cold water, offer no advice, but send my prayers with yours after the Mezuma. . . .
>
> Are you going to be at Green Acre during the first week of August? If so, I shall see you there. If not, will try to stop off either coming or going and look into your face and grip your hand.[13]

Albert Hall was also seeking to improve his fortune in order to benefit the Bahá'í Faith. He had made an investment in Montana lands, which he sold a few months later at a handsome profit. These funds, he wrote Martha, meant that a few more bricks and pylons would be placed on the House of Worship.

During this period in Cambridge Springs, Martha also took time to study Esperanto, the international language developed by Dr. Ludwik Lazarus Zamenhof, of Poland. The idea of an international language began to be expressed before the dawn of the twentieth century. From the day that Annie Ellsworth sent the first telegraph message, "What hath God wrought?" on 24 May 1844—the day following the Báb's declaration of His mission—the need for a universal code of communication became increasingly clear.[14] In 1900 there were strong suggestions, frightening to many, that the Chinese language be adopted because it used symbols, which would be preferable to the language invented by Johann Martin Schleyer and called, unhappily, Volapük. Bahá'u'lláh had stated that a universal language must be chosen, but that it could be a new language or one selected from those already in existence. For years the arduous process of selection has been ongoing.

In 1887 Dr. Zamenhof had introduced Esperanto, meaning "one who hopes," to advance the cause of international understanding and peace. The language was euphonious; the spelling was phonetic; the grammar, it was claimed, could be grasped in half an hour, and there were no exceptions to the rules. Yet Esperanto had precision, flexibility, literary power and beauty, and the capacity for growth. It soon attracted many advocates, and by the early part of the century its students were scattered throughout the world.

Martha's interest in an international language was heightened when she became a Bahá'í. Her first knowledge of Esperanto came in 1910, but she took her first lesson in 1912, when 'Abdu'l-Bahá was still in the country. He had encouraged Bahá'ís to study the new language, seeing in it, if not the ultimate language solution, at least a source for the message of world peace to spread.

A ten-year-old budding genius was Martha's first teacher. Winifred Sackville Stoner, of Pittsburgh, had written six books, two in Esperanto, and spoke eight languages, which she learned through a game devised by her mother; the Esperanto game was called Ĉio (which means "everything"). Martha was so enthusiastic with the process that, after one lesson, she typed out the game, listing the steps to be taken, the equipment necessary (a pack of Esperanto cards), a page of vocabulary, and a pronunciation guide. Then she made many copies and sent them off to friends throughout the country and in Akka.[15]

Agnes Alexander, who was quite adept in the language, had visited the Esperantists in Tokyo with Martha. In 1918, following the Bahá'í convention, Agnes, who was visiting in the United States, spent some time with Martha in Cambridge Springs. An Esperanto conference was being held in mid-July at Green Acre, in Eliot, Maine, and Martha wanted to be prepared for it. Agnes Alexander's memories of those days centered on Martha's energy, discipline, and enterprise. Every morning at 6:30, regardless of Agnes' desire to remain abed, Martha routed her. "'Time to get up, time to get up,'" she would say. "'You have to teach me Esperanto.'"[16] Agnes was not enchanted. She was dedicated to the Faith, but she also responded to her bodily needs. Martha acknowledged, but ignored, the signals that her body, too, needed rest. Eventually, Martha became an adept Esperantist. But before becoming an expert, she had written over one hundred articles proclaiming its virtues.

With the demands on Martha's time increasing, she began to feel that the large house on Main Street needed more care than her time allowed. Mrs. Root, until her health failed, devoted her days to maintaining the home, preparing food, and entertaining. These had little part in Martha's life, which was occupied with writing, teaching, and being a companion to her father. The decision was made to sell the brick house that T. T. Root had built and move to a flat in the Arcade Block in the center of town, farther down Main Street.

Although she was not an enthusiastic homemaker, Martha was extremely neat and tidy, with a sense of organization, basic to any well-run home or successful venture. The American Legion had meeting rooms in the Arcade Block, and when they became untidy, Martha hired a cleaning woman so that the place would be sparkling for the veterans. These gestures of friendship and generosity were deeply appreciated by the Legionnaires, who offered their space to Martha if she wished to have large gatherings.

At home Martha would make breakfast. Her father loved pancakes, and she became adept at making these circular satisfiers. They took other meals in a restaurant. Friends remember Martha escorting her father, often wearing Nancy Root's handsome shawl around his shoulders for added warmth.

T. T. Root was aging, had asthma, but was generally in good health and good spirits. He was still an enthusiastic sportsman, and Martha accompanied him often to Sheffield, Pennsylvania, where two families of relatives lived. Here T. T. did some of his best fishing. They also went to the theater, to baseball games, to the circus, and to whatever else intrigued her lively pater. Many of these entertainments had been put aside during Nancy Root's illness. Now with his daughter as a companion, the colors sharpened, and life took on a pinwheel effect of activity.

Although Martha was not making public statements in Cambridge Springs regarding the Bahá'í Faith, she invited to her home a few carefully chosen friends for discussions of the writings and principles of the Faith. She could no more stop offering this gift than she could stop breathing. She also maintained very close ties to the Bahá'ís in Pittsburgh.

The early Bahá'ís, as well as later ones, were persons of independent thought and often strong personalities. They came into the Faith after recognizing the station of Bahá'u'lláh; but they often retained their old postures in dealing with one another and openly criticized that which displeased them. They had not yet learned the process of consultation. Often the approach to problems came from the world of argument, hurt feelings, and a reluctance, or inability, to deal with conflicting ideas with moderation, grace, and spirituality.

Spiritual Assemblies had not yet evolved the art of mature consultation, and fissures in the community developed, not over religious questions but through the inability to deal with problems when strong and thorny personalities were involved. Pride, centered on unshakable belief in one's own ideas and opinions, was usually the culprit.

In 1918 the Bahá'í Faith in America was a fledgling; 'Abdu'l-Bahá had been in the United States less than six years before. The Pittsburgh community was experiencing dissension, and Martha was turning her spiritual consciousness toward dissipating the lack of harmony through prayer. She had discovered a prayer, the "Súrat 'ul Hykl," which she felt held the key to unity.[17] For nineteen days she arose and prayed from 3:00 until 6:00 A.M. for peace and harmony within the Pittsburgh Bahá'í community. The prisms of the gem were beginning to appear.

There was also disunity on the national level. A problem had arisen, was vociferously championed on opposite sides, and was threatening the harmony at the upcoming national convention. Martha, working on the convention plans and programs, felt the vibrations of disharmony and sought to change the atmosphere before it poisoned the spirit when the Bahá'ís met. She suggested to Mrs. Parsons and other friends that Bahá'u'lláh's Tablet "Surat 'ul Hykl"

> has the solution for unity at the coming Chicago Bahai convention, April 27–30. Perhaps friends individually in each Assembly could read it and the prayers for two hours each morning for nine mornings beginning 5:00 A.M., April 16–24. This very unity of seeking might make of us empty vessels in which Baha'u'llah could place the treasure of KNOWLEDGE and he could teach us that of which "one letter will encompass the whole world."

She wrote out the "Surat 'ul Hykl" and mailed it to ninety-five Spiritual Assemblies. "These morning hours have been wonderful ones," she told Agnes Parsons. "If we can, all of us, only become immersed in the sea of evanescence, we shall have no problems."[18]

How many of those to whom Martha wrote actually made the effort at early rising and prayer is not known, but tranquillity was not the mood at the convention. Tempers were hot, and cracklings of verbal fireworks were heard all around. The Bahá'ís were to meet at the commodious home of Mrs. Corinne True. This site was unacceptable to one faction and yet was exactly what the other faction wanted. In the name of unity Martha Root recommended that the meeting take place at some neutral spot, which would not compromise either group. Outrage was the response by some. One person in particular was extremely vocal. How could Mrs. True's home not be considered the most sacred spot for the convention, since 'Abdu'l-Bahá's presence had sanctified this home? How could Martha Root be so blind? So insensitive? No place could substitute, couldn't she know that? It was a volatile atmosphere that was not quickly abated. Hot, stinging words of Martha's proposal swelled letters to those who were not present.

But the state of enmity was hard to cling to where Martha was concerned. Her most virulent critic, Claudia Coles, became her protective friend and compassionate helper in London a few years later.

Such were the experiences that brought spiritual growth to Martha and other adherents of the Bahá'í Faith. With the Faith's emergence from obscurity, an awareness of the grandeur of its teachings was beginning to appear. The Faith was more than a belief in a Prophet and a system of laws; it called for a change of hearts, for putting into practice the lessons of living and working together harmoniously. Peace in the world would start with individuals such as Martha Root, who would continue to radiate the lessons of unity to others for many years to come.

8 South America

There was about Martha Root a literalness that translated the writings of Bahá'u'lláh and the messages to the Bahá'ís from 'Abdu'l-Bahá into directives for action. This is exactly what they were meant to do. Most people agreed with the ideas and hoped that someone would follow them. Martha took them personally. She tried to fit into her life as much of the proposed programs as her circumstances would allow. But she was restless and felt that she could not wait until the perfect arrangements could be made to begin the work of spreading the Bahá'í Faith.

Martha committed her thoughts to paper as easily as most humans breathe and frequently sent them off to 'Abdu'l-Bahá in Haifa. On 7 November 1918 she wrote to Him of her desire to travel the world on behalf of the Faith. This was a source of joy to 'Abdu'l-Bahá. In His response He replied, "My hope from the blessings of His Holiness Baha'o'llah is that thou mayest forget rest and composure and like unto a swift-flying bird, thou mayest reproduce the melody of the Kingdom and engage in songs and music in the best of tunes." If Martha needed incitement or additional stimulus for her already strong desires to travel and teach, the Master provided it with His colorful directives. It was like a clarion call, a trumpet blast, for He added: "As ears are awaiting the summons for Universal Peace, it is therefore advisable for thee to travel . . . to the different parts of the globe, and roar like unto a lion the Kingdom of God.* Wide-reaching consequences thou

---

*The words "like unto a lion" are not found in 'Abdu'l-Bahá's original letter but are implied by the word for "roar." The authorized translation for this quotation is "All ears are alert for the summons to the Most Great Peace. It is therefore better for thee to travel now around the world, if this is conveniently possible, and roar out the call of the Divine Kingdom. Thou shalt witness great results and extraordinary confirmations."

shalt witness and extraordinary confirmations shall be exhibited unto thee."[1] General statements had been turned into a personal summons with promises of divine help and success. Martha was on fire.

The war in Europe was ending. The eleventh day of November 1918, the eve of Bahá'u'lláh's birthday, saw the cessation of hostilities. The armistice was signed on the day of the Unity Feast at Evergreen Cabin, West Englewood, New Jersey, 28 June 1919, the event that still annually commemorates 'Abdu'l-Bahá's memorable visit there in 1912. Martha wrote of the spirit of unity and rejoicing that permeated the gathering in 1919.[2]

The annual Bahá'í convention in 1919 had been held at the Hotel McAlpin in New York, where the Tablets of the Divine Plan, written by 'Abdu'l-Bahá, were presented. These Tablets were the charter for all future national and international teaching plans and delineated in specific terms the work the Bahá'ís were to achieve for centuries to come. For many Bahá'ís the 1919 convention was their first opportunity to hear 'Abdu'l-Bahá's directives for America's spiritual mission. The Tablets were potent, and Martha, especially, felt their force. The story persists that when the session was over Martha Root was nowhere to be found. She was upstairs packing her bag to leave, losing not an hour before acting on the instructions of 'Abdu'l-Bahá to teach the Bahá'í Faith.

When a few of the Tablets were first read in Boston two years earlier, Martha's mother had died only a few months before. Martha was comforting a grieving father at the time and was not in a position to act. Now she felt that she must respond to this overwhelming desire to spread the word of Bahá'u'lláh. Apart from the United States and Canada, 'Abdu'l-Bahá also urged that South America receive the Bahá'í message.

Which area should she choose? How could she leave her father? Martha was in Pittsburgh when she was seized with the idea of making travel arrangements at once: Go to South America. Uncertain, unhappy, trembling, she nevertheless committed herself to sail on the *Albah*, Lamport & Holt Lines, from New York to South America on 21 June 1919.

Martha was torn between duties, each as demanding of her

love and time as the other. She suffered violent pangs of conscience on both levels. She could not go and leave her elderly, ailing father. She must go. She must follow 'Abdu'l-Bahá's instructions.

Although Cambridge Springs was populated with Root relatives, brothers and sisters of T. T. Root, his two sons and their families, plus scores of cousins, the responsibility and care of her father was squarely on Martha's shoulders. Nevertheless, prodded by the certainty that she was doing the right thing, and with her father urging her to do what she must, with tears streaming down her face, Martha started to pack. The doorbell rang, and there at the door was a neighbor wanting to rent the flat for relatives from Philadelphia during the months when Martha would be gone. They would be happy to take care of Mr. Root. He would retain his own room and bath, and in all other ways they would live as a family. Martha's prayers had been answered.

In 1915 Martha had circled the globe to discover how Bahá'ís lived in other countries and to ply her trade as a reporter. Now, four years later, Martha Root was about to begin the first of her historic journeys for the Bahá'í Faith. Here she set the style for her future trips; and the blueprint, which would develop over the next twenty years, was being drawn.

Martha arrived in New York several days before her ship was to sail and spoke on the Bahá'í Faith every day or evening. On the second night she met the head of a newspaper syndicate who was interested in her South American venture, and he arranged to buy her articles, which he would send to more than one hundred newspapers. He also offered to publish a short article on the Faith, which would be syndicated. The doors were opening.

But tests were on the threshold, too. A seamen's strike delayed the 21 June sailing. The problem had its advantages, for it enabled Martha to go to West Englewood, New Jersey, and attend the Unity Feast commemorating 'Abdu'l-Bahá's visit in 1912. While there, she visited the home of architect Louis Bourgeois, near Evergreen Cabin, and viewed his model of the Bahá'í House of Worship to be constructed in Wilmette, Illinois.

On the *Albah* the tensions mounted as the ship lay in port, passengers aboard. Week followed week, and the situation was stagnant. Then Chinese sailors were brought out to replace the strikers, and a threatening climate resulted as antagonisms mounted. On board Martha described the scene:

> The ship stood out at the Statue of Liberty. . . . The seamen who refused to sail were given the Message. Abdul Baha's views of the economic situation were explained to them, so there was a little feeling of love and sympathy and blue booklets taken back to the union men through the sailors who did not go.[3]

Strikebreakers took over, for which Martha was grateful. A longer delay would have made the trip impossible because of her commitments in Cambridge Springs, but "in her heart she *KNEW* they would sail, for the guidance had been so clear at every step."[4] After a month's delay, the *Albah* sailed out of New York on 22 July.

But the strike had taken its toll. Martha was ill and over-come with an intense fatigue, partly induced by apprehensions of her own limitations for the tasks she had undertaken and by the vast differences in life-style between her and the other passengers, who smoked, drank, and gambled; she did none of these, nor did she harbor any enthusiasm for sports. For two days pain took over, but she read and was revived by words of 'Abdu'l-Bahá:

> Let not conventionality cause you to seem cold and unsympathetic when you meet strange people from other countries. . . . Be kind to the strangers. . . . Help to make them feel at home; . . . ask if you may render them any service; try to make their lives a little happier. Let those who meet you know, without your proclaiming the fact, that you are indeed a Bahá'í.[5]

As it was written, so Martha responded. All the bon voyage gifts that she had received were distributed for the comfort of others. She prayed for greater capacity to serve more intelligently and lovingly. Again the doors opened.

The men had given money to buy prizes for the sports events aboard the ship. Martha took "the best small article of her apparel," perhaps a scarf, wrapped it in the artistic Japanese style, and took it to the sports committee to be used as a prize. It was the only woman's gift. She told them she did not know much about sports, but in order to join in the " 'family party' " she was going in for all "except the heavy weight contests."[6]

Two days after the ship left New York, Martha asked the captain's permission to speak in the evening, since it was a Sunday, on the Bahá'í Faith. A large notice was put on the bulletin board. Although no one had ever heard of the Bahá'í Faith, all came except a few Catholics. The first to enter the room where the talk was being held were the men of the sports committee; they had done much to make the event popular by talking about it and by bringing their friends. The captain, purser, and several officers were there.

The sea was not calm; and as Martha spoke, the ship pitched and rolled so that she had to hold on to a pillar to keep herself upright. She spoke for over an hour. Then a bishop, who had never heard of the Bahá'í Faith, got up and spoke against it. "He said," Martha wrote, "one could never be a Christian and believe in these other religions too. M* replied to him point by point and from that evening they have been friendly—his very arguments against the movement later made friends for it."[7] The lecture, so early in the voyage, created questions, which were answered, and generated an atmosphere of trust. There were many quiet talks on deck as a result.

Martha used other latent skills. She had once studied palmistry, and "just in fun" she read a passenger's hand.[8] Once again the right note was struck. It was an instant success. So many rushed over to have their palms read that the captain lined them all up to take turns, he first, with both palms up. She made many friends. Three days later the captain questioned her skills before the crowd. He was sure that Martha could not read his hand exactly the same a second time. " 'If

---

*This diary is written in the third person, with Martha referring to herself as "M."

you prove you can,'" he challenged her, "'I'll put it on the records of the [*Albah*] . . . among the distinguished passengers that you are the first Bahai ever to ride over these lines and that they can find out all about what a Bahai is by reading the book you put in the ship's library.'"⁹ The second reading was identical to the first. It was a triumph for Martha and for her mission.

The drinking on the ship was great and constant. The bar, which was next to Martha's room, was open from 6:00 A.M. until 2:00 A.M. in order to be as accommodating to drinkers as possible. Martha's roommate was the champion poker player and stayed up half the night proving it. She also owned two monkeys, which shared the cabin. Now Martha understood what 'Abdu'l-Bahá meant in a letter to her when He wrote, "Thou mayest forget rest and composure. . . ."¹⁰

When Martha went to the smoking room one night, as usual, to say good night to her card-playing roommate, one of the businessmen wanted her to drink a champagne toast for his birthday. She wished him many happy returns but declined the drink. He offered a toast to the Bahá'í Faith, asked for a blue booklet, and later had several conversations with Martha about the Faith.

Martha Root never sidestepped her own principles or her way of life. Yet in the midst of sophistication and questionable behavior she was the most popular, and surely the most unique, woman on board. And she shared in the gala festivities. At a fancy dress ball she went as a Persian woman and was chosen by the captain to present the prizes.

The chief steward suggested that Martha tell the help about her religion, which she did. The Chinese seamen had the message, including 'Abdu'l-Bahá's letter "China, China, China, China-ward," sent down to them since the captain did not permit Martha to go where they worked.¹¹ With the time growing closer for her to give the message to the South Americans as well, she found time during the voyage to study the Catholic religion, which was predominant in South America, so that she could present the Bahá'í teachings from the Catholic point of view.

After two weeks at sea the first South American city on the
northern tip of Brazil came into view: Pará (now Belém), with
175,000 residents. Martha's unusual and fortuitous experiences began to occur. Most of the cities along the coast were
stopping-off points for the passengers, who left the ship for
two-hour jaunts or sometimes full-day excursions. Martha's
plan was to leave the ship at Bahia, on the eastern shore of Brazil, which had been especially mentioned by 'Abdu'l-Bahá as a
place where "its efficacy will be most potent."[12] Her other
main goal was Panama, also singled out by the Master, which
lay on the other side of South America. Access to both places
was to present great difficulties, but Martha loved a challenge.

In Pará Martha left her companions and made her way to a
newspaper office. This was not easy since she did not speak the
language, but by using sign language and props she reached her
destination. After conversing "badly" in French, she tried to
explain the Bahá'í Faith to the editor and staff.[13] They asked
her to write about it in one thousand words, in English, and
they would have it translated.

Then the newspaper people "jumped up in excitement" as a
man entered whom they introduced as the best lawyer in Pará,
who spoke English.[14] She discovered that he had entertained a
relative, Elihu Root, a few years earlier. He translated her article into Portuguese, the language of Brazil, and the paper
agreed to run it and to print any future articles of hers. Blue
booklets were given out to the newspapermen, and Martha
Root became the first Bahá'í to visit Pará. As the attorney
brought her back to the ship in his motorcar, she discovered
that he was the lawyer for the line on which she was traveling.
Martha and the Bahá'í Faith had a new friend. Thus had Martha spent her first day on South American soil.

Some of the stopovers were brief and difficult to negotiate.
In Ceará (now Fortaleza), those passengers who wanted to go
ashore had to jump into small sailboats, pitching wildly in the
rough ocean, presenting the large possibility of involuntary
immersion. Martha risked it. Wearing the long dresses of the
period, carrying her blue booklets, the light fading, she
jumped from the *Albah* into the bobbing sailboat, lamenting

that she had only two hours in the gathering dusk to present her booklets and the message.

Martha was going about the cities as a woman alone, which was frowned upon by South Americans, although they did make some exceptions for women from the United States. She compared these social restrictions and niceties with the behavior of the South American women on shipboard, which she found shocking. Yet, although a solitary female traveler might have provoked a social taboo, Martha pursued her mission.

The *Albah* stopped at Pernambuco (now Recife), the fourth largest commercially important city in South America, from where the ship would sail down the coast to Bahia. But in Pernambuco it was learned that Bahia was closed because of yellow fever. If Martha left the ship and made her own way to Bahia, her goal city, despite the yellow fever, it meant the loss of the ticket from Pernambuco to Rio de Janeiro, several hundred miles away. And there were other problems. "Added to all this," she said, "there were four cases of yellow fever developed that day in Pernambuco and a revolution started in which several were killed, street cars burned, bridges bombed. . . ."[15]

Four American businessmen who had planned to stay in Pernambuco changed their minds. Martha was advised to stay with her ship. But 'Abdu'l-Bahá's mention of Bahia stayed with her. Her diary reported:

> Throwing herself down on the bunk in the stateroom after this perplexing day, M could look through the port hole into the darkness where Jupiter alone shone brightly, steadily, unmoved in his course. She rose up, ordered her bags ashore, where she had made reservations with two steamship companies, in hope of getting a passage to Bahia on a Brazilian ship. She took the chance, insane as it looked to other passengers.[16]

Although only Portuguese was spoken, Martha learned that an American businesswoman was staying at the Hotel Parque. Martha sent in her card, "with the right hand corner turned down which means less formality in South America," and prayed that if it were right for her to go to Bahia she would meet this American woman who might help her. They met, and almost the first words to come from Martha were, " 'I am a Bahai.' " The American woman asked, " 'Did you ever know my cousin, Lua Getsinger?' " [17] A new friendship was begun.

Martha's new friend, Lillyan Vegas, to whom she refers as "Mrs. Z.," had a cot brought in so that Martha could share her quarters, for there were no rooms available at the Hotel Parque. When Martha went back to say good-bye to her shipboard family, she discovered that Mrs. Z. was well known among the passengers as an astute and successful business person. The businessmen were impressed by Martha's good fortune. Some of the passengers gave her gifts and escorted her back to the hotel, along empty streets guarded by soldiers. Before she left, the captain asked for more blue booklets.

The friendship of Mrs. Z. was a boon to Martha for several reasons, but especially because she spoke Portuguese fluently. After conversing haltingly in French with the press, Martha was writing an article about the Bahá'í Faith for the largest newspaper in Pernambuco; but when Mrs. Z. came on the scene, she took Martha to the editors of five leading newspapers and conversed with them in their native language, giving the message as Martha directed. The light of understanding in their faces and attitudes forcibly brought home to Martha the need for an international language. They all took articles that Martha had prepared, and they promised cooperation with her work.

On 16 August Martha and Mrs. Z. sailed from Pernambuco bound for Bahia on the *Itapuhy*. Martha's first goal was within sight. The passengers represented many nations, and in this two-day voyage they heard about Bahá'u'lláh, the latest messenger from God, and about the road to universal peace. Those bound for America were given letters of introduction to Roy Wilhelm.

One morning the cadences of an Oriental chant reached Martha's ears. She followed the sound, and when the Arab had finished chanting his prayers, she introduced herself. Through an interpreter she learned that he lived in Akka and had often shared meals in 'Abdu'l-Bahá's home. His father had actually known Bahá'u'lláh. She gave him a blue booklet, and he promised to carry a gift from Martha to 'Abdu'l-Bahá.

A six-hour stop in Maceió, a city of seventy thousand, was blessed by meeting a merchant friend of Mrs. Z.'s, who transported them in a sailboat to a car and then showed them the city. Like others he responded to Martha's mission and drove them to all the newspaper editors. Those who were not in the office were called on at home. Martha wrote an article on two international thefts, as she felt, rightly, that this work would bring her in closer touch with the commercial world.

Because of yellow fever raging in Bahia, Lua Getsinger's cousin decided against stopping there but would go on to Rio. Martha, undaunted, left the ship, engulfed by a violent rainstorm. It had been a stormy trip throughout, and Martha was one of the few to escape seasickness. Once again she braved the enormous waves, almost eclipsing the little boats, bobbing like corks in the ocean, waiting to take the passengers ashore.

As if she had waved a magic wand, two young English-speaking missionaries appeared, who took Martha to a hotel in Bahia "as easily as violets spring up in spring."[18] They also took her to call on friends from the *Albah*, who lived only four doors from where Martha was staying.

Having arrived in Bahia, which in 1919 had a population of some 280,000, Martha set about studying facets of both the city and the state of the same name, later sending a report of several hundred pages, not brief, to 'Abdu'l-Bahá. She learned of their commerce (one of the richest states in Brazil), their religious views and tendencies, their intellectual pursuits. This information would be used not only for Martha's benefit during her visit but to aid Bahá'ís in other places to know the needs of the area and the opportunities available in this young giant of a country. Among her observations were that

The Portuguese and Brazilians are born aristocrats. If Bahais come to Brazil they must learn the Portuguese language (not hard to learn) and learn the customs of these Latin peoples. South Americans meet strangers socially before they do any business. "Paciencia amanha!" (Patience, tomorrow! . . .) is the first lesson to be learned, Brazilians do everything slowly and with ceremony.[19]

Like others, the missionaries were drawn to Martha, and they came to call on her at the Hotel Sul Americano before they left for the vast interior of Brazil. She learned from them about the high rate of illiteracy (90 percent) among the indigenous people and about their lack of medical care. One missionary, she was told, rode six days to reach a doctor.

Martha was still concerned about disregarding the social rules by going about alone. She continued to seek opinions in support of her mode of travel and welcomed those that were favorable. One American businessman, a Mr. S., approved and assured her, regarding females from the United States, that "she would be shown fine respect if she is a good woman. . . ."[20]

There was in Martha Root an indefinable quality that made others eager to lend assistance. One of her shipmates who lived in Bahia took part of each day to introduce Martha to distinguished and influential friends, and Mr. S. made appointments with newspaper editors, escorted her, and interpreted for her.

She placed books, given to her by American Bahá'ís, in the local library, where the books were immediately sought after. Articles began to appear in the newspapers, together with pictures of 'Abdu'l-Bahá and of Martha; a friend had taken her picture, which was made available to the papers. She carried twelve pictures of the Master but once remarked, "One ought to carry two hundred."[21]

People came to Martha, asked for literature, offered to help teach the Faith, gave her dinners, flowers, gifts, and when she was leaving, escorted her to the ship. "Abdul Baha did it all," she would say.[22] Mr. S. also wrote letters of introduction for Martha to his wife and sister in Rio de Janeiro. Before her departure he had requested a variety of Bahá'í literature and had become another staunch friend for Martha and the Faith.

The charmed atmosphere stayed with Martha, and to everyone's surprise she was able to leave Bahia after six days, upsetting predictions of her being marooned there for months. She sailed on the *Itassuce*, a highly disinfected ship, after being examined and allowed to leave. Passengers' baggage was also disinfected. Martha quipped, "It was heroic—quite brimstone enough for this world and the next!"[23]

The small Brazilian ship rolled incessantly during the four-day voyage from Bahia to Rio de Janeiro, and almost everyone was seasick. Martha was the only woman in the dining room. These were the winter months in Brazil, and the rough seas reflected the less benign climate, which was wet and cold. Martha used her now well-practiced French and was able to talk about the Faith. One friend she made was a Curitiba resident, who was given six books to place in his city library.

Finally, they arrived in Rio, which proved to be a gem. Martha, responding like a runner whose course is laid out, moved from consulate to newspapers, to acquaintances, to libraries, donating books, always making friends, and enjoying their offers of translation, transportation, and introductions. The articles flowed; their publication in newspapers and magazines opened the way for future conversations and discussions because the word *Bahá'í* had already been seen in print. The relatives of her American business friend in Pernambuco were a valuable link to the Rio de Janeiro community, and they entertained and assisted Martha throughout her stay.

The Esperantists were especially active in Rio, both as individuals and groups and as publishers of Esperanto periodicals. Like most South Americans, they enjoyed entertaining and hosted a gathering for Martha as well as a lecture by her. She discovered that the language was greatly respected in Rio and that a street was named "Dr. Zamenhof."[24] While in Rio Martha also spoke at the Brazilian School of Naval Aviation and the Brazilian Army School of Aviation.

The worldliness of the city was an ever-present factor, but Martha looked askance at it. Nevertheless, she saw in this worldliness the means of employment for pioneers. She compiled a list of possibilities; in the midst of more esoteric recommendations she wrote, "A catsup maker could do well, good canning establishments are needed. . . ."[25]

She also recommended printing the blue booklets in Portuguese, not Spanish. She would use Spanish booklets in Argentina, where Harry Randall was sending five thousand, which she hoped would be waiting when she arrived.

On 5 September Martha left Rio for São Paulo, which she called the Chicago of South America. The journey by train was "like riding 12 hours in a Paradise whose wealth is not yet discovered. . . ."[26] Despite its commercial orientation the beauty of São Paulo touched Martha's soul. The business block was nestled in gardens. The exotic plants, the concerts, the violinist playing in a grocery store—all these plucked at Martha's aesthetic sensibilities.

But São Paulo was expensive. Martha shopped for a hotel where she would be among people other than North Americans. She found one with a room on the fifth floor, no elevator, and had to pay New York prices. Still having no knowledge of Portuguese, she was able to get by once again with her French. The libraries were always a focal point for Martha, where she presented gifts of Bahá'í literature. She had been especially impressed by the one in Rio.

The vitality of São Paulo was left behind as Martha took the train, heading for Santos. She was struck by the enormous feat of engineering that created a railroad through almost impenetrable forest. The skill and the beauty equally commanded her praise: "The train hovers like a bird around the mountain sides, and one is thrilled, awed by the grandeur of millions upon millions of forest trees, above and below."[27]

In Santos Martha again chose a small hotel where only Portuguese was spoken. She relied not on language but on her ability to read character to accomplish her tasks. She loved the Brazilians, loved their courtesy, their manners, their thoughtfulness of her needs as a woman traveling alone.

The Theosophists of Santos, having seen an article by Martha Root in a local paper, a speedy accomplishment, were excited by the implications of the Bahá'í message and wanted her to address their society. A talk was impossible because her ship was sailing on the day they contacted her, but they sent a committee to call on her. One of the members had heard briefly about the Faith in 1914 and had been seeking further information ever since. He had written an article and had made a presentation on the Bahá'í revelation for his society, using his limited history. Martha's article opened up new vistas for him. He was a waiting soul and wanted to write about the Faith, translate its literature, and travel around the world to spread the teachings.

The three-day visit to Santos, and Martha's publicity on the Bahá'í Faith, had uncovered this gem in a mine of stones. All those she met were extremely interested in the teachings, which emphasized the oneness of humanity, and they completed plans to publish five thousand blue booklets, translated into Portuguese, with several Theosophists participating to ensure a perfect translation.

Following this fruitful meeting Martha's new friends put her aboard the ship sailing for Argentina. She seems never to have synchronized her love of warm weather with her voyages. The Brazilian winter was not kind, and ocean travel was extremely unpleasant. The cold, the sleet, the mountainous, raging seas made seasickness a normal state of health, and Martha found herself "a little laggard in giving the Message."[28] But the memory of 'Abdu'l-Bahá's unfulfilled desire to travel the world and endure hardships to spread the word spurred Martha on. A shipboard conference grew out of the interest of a few. Almost everyone on board attended, and the interest was high.

The Bahá'í literature that Martha carried with her was almost gone, but the "gift of love to South America," in the form of several thousand booklets that Harry Randall had printed and was sending to Argentina, would fill the response to Martha's presentation. Names and addresses were taken, and literature would be sent. One Frenchman said, "'I have not always understood well ze words you speak me but I understand ze life you have and it is for that I am interested.'"[29]

The ship made a twelve-hour stop in Montevideo, Uruguay, where Martha's card-playing roommate of the *Albah* lived. Martha stopped at the family business address, and a touring car was sent to bring her to the family home. They, too, after entertaining Martha, helped to put Bahá'í books in English clubs and libraries and took her to a newspaper editor, who used an article on the Faith. Then she was off again.

The ship arrived in Buenos Aires, Argentina's capital, on 20 September. Martha settled into this Spanish city, where she stayed until 4 October. She used every contact that came her way—chambermaids, doctors, teachers, translators, newspaper editors—all embracing a variety of religions from Christian Science to Catholicism.

That mysterious element in Martha's personality that made others want to serve her greatly aided her work in new places. One of the most prominent magazine editors offered to go to all of the Italian newspapers with Martha's articles, during two days of torrential rains, while she visited all the English papers. There were four hundred newspapers and magazines in Buenos Aires. How many of these were actually visited is not known, but, in Martha's words, all those contacted responded favorably to the Faith and used her articles. She had a good press, and her stories were everywhere.

The Theosophists in Buenos Aires as well were enamoured with the Bahá'í Faith and its disciple. She was elaborately entertained with dinners and receptions, and letters of introduction to influential persons were given to Martha. They sent to her *pension* "beautiful books, flowers, candy, [and] clippings of articles."[30] She, in turn, wrote letters of introduction to those soon to visit the United States.

As she had done in other parts of South America, Martha gave many talks. Before leaving home she had prepared well for presentations on some of the principles of the Faith and had researched her topics and canvassed friends, especially for material on the economic solution. This and the equality of men and women, a universal language, and universal education, were all magnetic ideas for the mentally alert and seeking friends of South America.

So impressed was one person with these teachings that he had an office outfitted with furniture and a telephone for Martha to use during her stay. She was touched by such a display of faith and generosity; but she could not accept, as many persons were calling at the address first given in the newspaper. He also offered to pay for a hall for three years, as a meeting place, if a Spiritual Assembly could be formed. Such was the ardent response of some who heard about the Bahá'í Faith through Martha Root.

9   *The Other Side of the Mountain*

In the weeks since Martha had left New York Harbor, she had accomplished much of what she had set out to do. She had spoken about the Bahá'í Faith to hundreds of persons, made friends, given public talks, supplied individuals with literature about the Faith, written articles, put books in libraries, and gone to Bahia. Her second goal, traveling to Panama, still lay ahead, and it threatened to be a more difficult accomplishment than that of reaching Bahia.

But Martha was never one to sacrifice a destination because of troublesome obstacles, inconvenient weather, or mode of traveling. She would leave Buenos Aires and cross the Andes to reach the west coast of South America, where she would make her way north to Panama. The journey was always hazardous, but in the winter the risk and dangers mounted alarmingly. Martha's friends tried unsuccessfully to dissuade her. A newspaper article described the journey she was about to take: "'If you would consider riding around the edge of the Woolworth building [then one of the world's tallest buildings] (when it is covered with ice and snow) on a gentle mule a safe pastime, then have no fears regarding the inconveniences in crossing the Andes in winter.'"[1] Stories of frozen faces, fingers, and toes reached Martha, but she was adamant, determined to fulfill 'Abdu'l-Bahá's hope of taking the message up the west coast of South America and into Panama.

The friends Martha had made showered her with gifts of books, fruit, flowers, lunches, dinners, and candy. Some brought heavy underwear, woolen garments, even a fur coat that could be passed on to a New York relative, and additional food from friends of all nationalities.

Inevitably, a protector appeared, a New York "business diplomat" who was crossing in the same group, who said "he would do anything he could for M."[2] She seemed to touch a well-spring in people, and they wanted to shield and comfort her.

The trip would begin by train, then shift to mule-back. Martha was fortunate in having as her roommate in the *camorata*, or sleeping compartment, a young, intelligent Italian woman who spoke French and Spanish fluently. Martha's Buenos Aires friends, still thinking of her comfort, had wired ahead to friends that she would be coming through. Even brief stops had a contingent to meet Miss Root, who in turn gave them her finest gift, the Bahá'í message in print.

Although a landslide had washed out the route that Martha was to have driven, other means of transportation were found. Seventeen years after Martha Root was setting a speed record through French villages in Mr. Berg's automobile, she climbed on a mule to cross the snowcapped Andes. She recorded the experience in her diary:

> The trip by mule back over the "top of the world", for the Andes are among the highest ranges, the Aconcagua rising to a height of 23,300 feet, was thrilling enough for the most sensational. To pray the Greatest Name among these minarets of God was to glimpse the glory of the Eternal, Unknowable. The ancient trail led 10,400 ft. above sea level. The people on mule back were infinitesimal specks clinging to mighty terraces that bear no other appearance of humanity except the cavalcade. As "ants in an endless and boundless forest" so they huddled on the edge of jagged peaks, frozen chasms, and stiffened mountain torrents. Everybody felt very small and a wonderful feeling of camaraderie sprang up. Fortunately the sun shone brightly and the acute cold was not so terrible as all had expected. . . .
>
> A detour through one dark tunnel took over an hour in stumbling, slipping blackness in which the frightened mules shied and fell. M, as her mule plunged downward into the mouth of the tunnel gripped the pommel, threw her body far back, closed her eyes and prayed the "Ya Allah El-Mostaghos"* for all. Over and over again in that black uncer-

---

*O God, the Refuge.

MARTHA ROOT
on the left, as she crossed the Andes in 1919. Martha's historic trip to
South America was a whole-hearted response to 'Abdu'l-Bahá's
teaching directives in His Tablets of the Divine Plan.

tainty, the clear, vibrant voice of the Italian girl would ring
down the line of mules: "Mademoiselle, are you all right?"
Then and even now to write about it, tears of deepest tender-
ness spring to the eyes at the thought of such a friend. . . .

Later, out from the tunnel, when the procession came to
precipitous downward slopes towards Chile, M could not
even see that "one inch" margin that had been promised by
the man in his newspaper account—to her this was by far the
most dangerous part of the journey. So it was with tremendous joy she saw the men getting off their mules and walking
farther in down the mountain side. She did the same, for the
mules would sometimes slip a yard in this perpendicular
path and they were frightened also. Taking the guide's hand
they made the descent together and when they could not
walk they could run! The warm sun had melted the crisp
snow just enough that they could get a foothold. They
stopped every few minutes to breathe as one's breath is very
short in this altitude. Some fainted, some had "puna",
which is bleeding of the nose and ears. Everything given M
was passed along to those who needed it.[3]

The descent was finally complete, and the other side of the Andes was a victorious reality. Martha, her Italian friend, and her New York businessman counted it as one of the happiest events of their lives. Later, in describing this Andean crossing in winter, Martha said, "I wore three suits of woolen underwear, two sweaters, two coats and a steamer rug, and then nearly froze to death."[4]

Martha gave Bahá'í booklets to the guides and customs officials and then boarded a train. From icy mountain peaks she now rode into the tropical gardens and orchards of Valparaiso. Once again she was absorbed into others' lives. The quality that had drawn the Buenos Aires friends was felt in this new city:

> The New Yorker's firm in Valparaiso treated M as a sister. They put her bags through the customs, had them taken by their own porters to the ship, called a messenger boy to escort her to the Theosophists, later took her to lunch with the New York guest of honor, and all three men took her in a launch to her ship. She explained the Bahai Cause.[5]

The scheduled four-day stopover in Valparaiso had been whittled down to four hours, because of the violent storm that had resulted in the tunnel detour in the Andes. After the strenuous physical and emotional stress of the Andean adventure and the flirtations with danger, it would have been natural to use the brief respite relaxing and gathering strength for the next leg of the journey. But this was not Martha's way. These hours were used to call on the president of the Theosophical Society, whom Martha presented with a letter of introduction. Martha left articles with him to be given to the newspapers, both in Valparaiso and in Santiago, another schedule victim, with no time at all for a visit.

Martha described cities, apart from their physical and commercial attributes, by population and the number of newspapers published. Santiago was a city of three hundred thousand and eleven daily papers. She translated these figures into the number of publications that could carry the Bahá'í message to them, and she felt she was the instrument to create the occurrence. Therefore, she could not, must not, rest those four hours in Valparaiso, nor anywhere else. She might miss an opportunity. Someone who could become a vibrant apostle of the Faith might be waiting while she rested. Everyone was a vessel waiting to be filled with the Water of Life, and Martha was the handmaiden ready to pour the Supreme Elixir. That mission was the source of the fire, the radiance, the love, that emanated from her being; it was the magnet that drew her fellow travelers to her. "Every friend met on this trip," she felt, "is just the beginning of a long friendship. Letters and literature can be exchanged and other Bahais traveling to South America or the friends coming to North America will be joyfully received."[6]

The trip, with its variety of temperatures and experiences, had taken its toll, and Martha came down with a severe case of grippe while on shipboard. But she did not allow herself the luxury of resting and healing. She was off telling about Bahá'-u'lláh and His teachings.

> Grippe had to be the shadow to make one appreciate the sunshine, so the first few places are but memories of trying to get ashore to the newspaper offices to explain the Bahai Message, then leaning against the friendly lamp posts for strength to drag one's self back to the boat. . . . The paper in Coquimbo is "El Longitudinal"; the newspaper in Antafogasta is "El Mercurio."[7]

New friends from Chile went ashore with Martha to act as interpreters. And so it went in city after city along the coastal route when the ship put in to port—Iquique, Arica, and other places where articles would be used. Passengers themselves acted as peace doves, carrying the message for newspapers back to their native lands—New Zealand, Australia, Mexico, Venezuela, Spain, Panama.

The passengers were making mostly short junkets via the ship, and there was not enough time for Martha to give a talk; but one told the other, and another, and so the grapevine carried the message throughout the ship. As she had given away all of her Bahá'í books and pamphlets, she spent fifty dollars, a small fortune in 1919, on South American newspapers and periodicals that carried her articles, and most of those were gone.

It was on this ship, sailing up the west coast of South America, that Martha started to learn the basic principles and pronunciation of Spanish, which she felt to be a better tool for communication in South America than French or Esperanto, still in its infancy. She urged Bahá'ís to learn as many languages as possible until a universal auxiliary language took over.

With a three-hour stop near Lima, Peru, Martha wanted to use her introductory letters to a newspaper owner, a senator, and two physicians. It was a thirty-minute ride to Lima from the port of Callao, in addition to the time it would take to get to the train, make contacts, and reverse the process. How was she to get there, find these men, and get back on time?

Full of faith, Martha got on the electric tram. Almost as if she had rubbed a magic lamp, two young English-Spanish-speaking men appeared who took her to the leading hotel to find out how to reach these persons. The hotel manager led her to a chair and suggested that she write out a message to each one. He took these, along with her letters of introduction, Bahá'í booklets, and the newspaper articles, saved for this use, and assured her that he would take them personally to the individuals and that they would be used. The two young men became interested and mailed the Bahá'í message to their families in Australia and New Zealand. It was neatness and heavenly dispatch all the way.

The very last day on the ship Martha was asked to give a lecture. It was translated by a Mexican passenger so that both English and Spanish heard the words of hope. "There was such a warmth of love and interest, everybody seemed happy." It was a cosmopolitan gathering, and they would take these seeds back to Japan, Spain, France, Germany, Panama, Venezuela, Iowa, California, Oklahoma, and New York. "Each one has a clipping or something which explains a little of the Cause to carry with him."[8]

The ship sailed into Panama on 25 October 1919. As Martha set foot on its soil, that link between the North and the South, between the Orient and the Occident, her second goal was reached.

There was a pattern in Martha's visits to a new spot: her credentials were presented, letters of introduction were shown, interpreters appeared, resistance melted away, and the message of the dawn of a new day was welcomed. Speaking opportunities opened up, and magnanimous acts by eager hosts followed in the wake of Martha's message and her outpouring of love.

Panama was no exception. In one week the measure of Panama was taken and Bahá'u'lláh's message given. She used her professional credentials to visit sites and persons otherwise out-of-reach, such as the heads of all the government works, and medical authorities. Her Esperanto and her sense of spiritual mission worked to reach other groups. As a result, practically every publication, group, or association became a channel for Martha's presentation of the Bahá'í Faith.

The one place Martha could not land was the leper colony at Palasaco, near Panama. Because the high winds had sent some passengers plunging into the sea when they were attempting to land the little boats, all others were ordered back. But Martha's spirit reached them through two books and four boxes of candy.

She saw and appreciated the unique aspects of Panama and predicted that "Some day, some one will build a mighty university on the heights of the Panama Canal Zone, how glorious if it could be a Bahai seat of learning!"[9] Today, on one of those heights, is the Bahá'í House of Worship, dedicated on 29 April 1972, its architectural brilliance a beacon of spirituality and hope overlooking the region. One day there will be a seat of learning on the mountain, which will fulfill the wish of this first Bahá'í to carry the hope of Bahá'u'lláh's revelation to Panama.

Martha made the five-day voyage to Havana, received the captain's permission to lecture on the Bahá'í Faith, and presented the only program on board during the entire trip. She did not wait for opportunity to knock but rather took the first step:

If any one feels timid about asking [for] opportunities to speak let him remember that no day comes twice to any ser-

vant in the Cause and Abdul Baha has said to "roar like a
lion the Words of God" and "sing like a bird the Melodies of
the Kingdom". The great heart will not falter—and the
world is ready![10]

One day and two nights in Havana gave Martha time to sow
seeds. Every minute was used to make contacts and give lectures. Near the end of her stay she had just a few hours of rest,
which she took, fully clothed, before the ship would sail early
in the morning. But the brief sleep was "very sweet for the singing of her heart told her the Holy Spirit had wafted Fragrances
over Havana."[11]

Martha was soon back in the United States. From Key West,
Florida, to Washington, D.C., where she spent three days,
Martha visited every major city and its newspaper editors
along the coast. Eventually, she headed toward home, and on
15 November 1919, five months after leaving Cambridge
Springs, she returned.

T. T. Root, now eighty-two, had been sitting at the window
watching for the first glimpse of Martha. He shared the joy of
reunion with his daughter, whose absence had left its striations
on the days and weeks as they moved on to this time of homecoming.

Martha Root, apostle of the Bahá'í Faith, had completed
her first major journey for the sole purpose of spreading the
teachings; her response to the Tablets of the Divine Plan of
'Abdu'l-Bahá was absolute. South America was a pod, and
Martha had deposited the seed. Tens of thousands of minds
were now aware of the spirit that would permeate the planet
when human hearts would respond to the teachings.

Her journey was singular. She had set a pattern for herself,
and for others, if they chose to follow. One Bahá'í later lamented that although she and her husband had gone for several months to teach in South America, they could point to little
progress when compared to the achievements of Martha—a lament that would be repeated in later years from other souls in
all parts of the globe.

Martha did not settle down and take time to internalize the
spectrum of adventures that had occurred on her trip—the

trains, the ships, the high seas, the mules, the mountains, the gardens, the articles, the lectures, the new friends. The morning after her return to Cambridge Springs she went to the high school and started classes to master Spanish. She felt that she must make the most of her new friends and contacts and reach them in their own language.

Within a short time she was reading their letters in Spanish, although still writing to them in English. She had left their shores but did not leave them to fend for themselves in a spiritual desert. She considered their needs and responded:

> One thousand Spanish Bahai booklets have been mailed to South America. M has written four hundred letters. The Spanish speaking friends are getting out booklets in their own country now and the Portuguese speaking friends have published five thousand in their own language. Over $500 worth of Bahai books have been sent by Bahai friends who have read part of these Pilgrimage letters. Two or more souls are going to teach. One thousand sets of addresses have been entrusted to steadfast Bahais who will write to the new friends.[12]

Like her forebears Martha had opened up a new territory, which she infused with the spirit of Bahá'u'lláh. It was the first time that the Bahá'í Faith had been carried to South America; it was also the first time that a Bahá'í, totally selfless, detached, and with only the promulgation of Bahá'u'lláh's message the motivating factor, had undertaken a voyage of such magnitude and with such a plethora of physical risks.

During her tour Martha sent 'Abdu'l-Bahá detailed accounts of the states and cities visited; the geographical and cultural settings; the newspapers, libraries, and schools that received Bahá'í literature; the individuals she met; and the places where she spoke. 'Abdu'l-Bahá was deeply moved. In a letter to Martha He wrote:

> It is clear and evident that the power of the Kingdom is aiding thee, that the glances of the eye of His loving kindness are turned toward thee, the hosts of the Supreme Concourse are helping thee, and the power of the Holy Spirit is support-

ing thee. Before long the results of this mighty undertaking will be uncovered and laid bare before the eyes of all men.

Therefore be thou assured that this call to the Manifestation of Bahá'u'lláh, this proclamation of the Word of God and the promulgation of His Covenant shall influence stone and clay, how much more the children of men. . . .

In brief, thou art really a herald of the Kingdom, a harbinger of the Covenant. Thou art self-sacrificing, and showing kindness to all the peoples of the earth. Thou art now sowing a seed that in the long run will yield thousands of harvests. Thou art now planting a tree that shall everlastingly put forth leaves, blossoms and fruit and whose shadow shall grow in magnitude day by day.[13]

10   Home Again

Cambridge Springs' residents, with a few exceptions, still viewed T. T. Root's daughter with suspicion, but her South American adventure had brought her a new celebrity. The town was cautiously proud of her journalistic and lecturing achievements and her broad range of travel. Since she had not simply visited one or two spots in South America as a tourist, but had participated in the life, had written and lectured in most of the major cities on both coasts, and had talked to editors, business people, and administrators, Martha's views were sought and respected. She was invited to speak at the Chamber of Commerce, the first woman to achieve this distinction, a fact noted in headlines on page one of the local newspaper.

At the meeting the businessmen were made aware of the reason for her trip—to spread the news of the Bahá'í Faith—citing the principles of the equality of men and women and a universal language. She entertained them with stories of amusing incidents that had occurred relating to these ideas. But intertwined with facts about Bahá'í principles, Martha also gave them solid, practical information regarding the cultural and commercial facets of life. As businessmen, with a few entrepreneurs among them, it could be helpful to know that England controlled the only passenger line down the east coast of South America and had raised fares to discourage would-be developers from the United States. Referring to communication, on which modern business depends, she observed:

The only cable line to the east coast is also controlled by England and runs from New York City by way of London. Messages that should get through with an answer in a day

are purposely slowed up . . . for six to seven days, and then
are badly garbled. London knows all of America's business
in the great new country before New York does. . . . The
United States does, however, have a cable line down the west
coast and expects soon to have one down the east coast,
since the highest courts of Brazil have recently decided that
England should not have a monopoly if Brazil is to be
served.[1]

Martha also mentioned mining activities, noting the particular success of a local entrepreneur who had bought a vana-
dium mine for a relatively small sum because he conducted the
transaction with bags of gold rather than figures on paper.
Moreover, she stressed the need for more railroads and, above
all, the patience, good manners, and lack of criticism that are
needed to succeed with the South Americans on all levels.

The *Enterprise* reported that "more than ever, local residents realized that we have a townswoman who is one of the
most traveled and enlightened people in the world."[2] Maybe
so, but the residents of Cambridge Springs did not equate this
enlightenment with spiritual perception. If anything, it was genius gone wrong.

There was one person in town, however, who was listening.
Lucy Wilson was the widow of Dr. Alphonse Wilson, a school-
mate of Martha's, whose sudden illness and death cut short his
promising medical career in Wilkes-Barre, Pennsylvania.
After exploring other avenues, Lucy settled down in Cambridge Springs, in the Wilson family home, and gave music lessons. She was a pure soul, spiritually awake, a loving and sympathetic being. She became Martha's friend and ally—and a
Bahá'í.

Martha wanted to make the most of her recent South American experience. Her written account of the journey was reproduced, mimeographed, in 1920. Carrie (Vaffa) Kinney in New
York devoted her time, helping to turn out hundreds of copies
that would go to Spiritual Assemblies where they existed in the
world, to traveling teachers, to interested friends in the Orient
and in South America, and to the national convention in the

spring where they would be sold for a nominal sum. Martha paid all expenses, but she was beholden to Carrie for her tremendous efforts. Still, Martha did not have ten copies left when Ella Goodall Cooper wrote from California, hoping to take some with her to Akka.

If spring was a busy time for Martha, it was also a time of illness. Martha was struck with a severe case of influenza that brought all activities to a halt, except those she could manage through letters. T. T. Root's bad health kept Martha in Cambridge Springs at convention time in 1920. A delegate proposed that a telegram of love and sympathy be sent to her, which helped ease her sadness at not being able to be present. But there would continue to be new challenges to tax her abilities.

11 Excursions

A brilliant Persian teacher, Jináb-i-Fáḍil-i-Mázindaráni, had arrived in the United States during the last week in April 1920; he had a deep knowledge of the history and teachings of the Bahá'í Faith. The National Teaching Committee decided to use his talents in as broad an area as possible for the duration of his year-long stay. The first trip was to be made to the upper New York State region, with the particular goal of speaking at Chautauqua, a dynamic center of cultural, educational, and religious thought, where thousands gathered over the summer months.

For a Middle Easterner, simply to arrive in a city and contact those groups who might be interested in a Persian speaker had distinct limitations. An advance person was needed to schedule talks and publicize the event. Harry Randall thought Martha would be perfect for the task; moreover, it was the kind of activity she loved. A train from Boston took her to the Buffalo area, which was at least a full day's journey in those days. She met with success in most places, got the publicity rolling, and then went to the southwestern tip of New York State to reach Chautauqua, beautifully situated on a large lake. But here success was elusive. There was absolutely no possibility of scheduling a Bahá'í talk.

Harry Randall, with Jináb-i-Fáḍil and two other Persian friends, arrived at the Iroquois Hotel in Buffalo on 13 August. The talk was a huge success and opened up more possibilities to tell about the new Faith. A minister offered his pulpit, and the Rotarians invited them to address their club.

In East Aurora, New York, Martha had arranged for a presentation with her old friends from her newspaper days, the Roycrofters. The talk was held in the Roycroft Chapel and was

HARRY (WILLIAM H.) RANDALL
an early Bahá'í and Martha Root's co-worker
and dear friend

so successful that they were invited back to speak at a Sunday service. The Roycrofters' magazine, with a circulation of fifty thousand, carried an account of both talks.

That Sunday was a busy day because arrangements had already been made for the Bahá'ís to give the morning service at Lily Dale, the largest Spiritualist camp in the United States. The Spiritualists were very active and seeking in those years. Their two magazines, *The National Spiritualist* and *The Progressive Thinker*, had publicized the event, and three thousand filled the auditorium. Jináb-i-Fáḍil spoke on "The Bahai Vision of Immortality."[1] Martha, who took down his talk verbatim, felt it should be studied by every Bahá'í.

Harry Randall also spoke, and the audience cheered both of them. They wanted more. The afternoon program was changed to allow a second presentation on the Faith. Outside, in a beautiful, natural amphitheater called the Forest Temple, a talk was given on "New Evidences of Life After Death."[2] Together Harry Randall and Jináb-i-Fáḍil were magnets, drawing people into their sphere of thought, with their dynamic and lucid qualities. Jináb-i-Fáḍil was invited to sing a hymn, but instead he chanted a Bahá'í prayer in his native tongue, amidst the hushed gathering.

A second overture to Chautauqua, which Martha dubbed "the new 'Jericho,'" was again resisted.[3] A talk was simply not possible. Harry Randall, too, spoke to the directors. Impossible. The speaker's program was filled up for weeks. Over Harry's protests, Martha insisted they all make the trip to Chautauqua, regardless of the decision. Jináb-i-Fáḍil *would* speak. She felt 'Abdu'l-Bahá's spirit urging they go.

On arrival, Martha went to the hotel to call on Dr. Vincent, head of the committee that arranged for the speakers. As he was not in, Martha went for a walk, praying every step of the way. Suddenly, there on the path in front of her was Dr. Vincent; it was the same Dr. Vincent who had taught her at the University of Chicago. She explained her errand, resistance vanished, and a time was arranged. Jináb-i-Fáḍil and Harry Randall spoke in the great auditorium at Chautauqua at the best hour of the day, addressing a gathering of four thousand. It was an unqualified success; "the Chautauqua audience cheered again and again."[4] The newspaper reports were glowing. Martha thought it was the most significant event in American Bahá'í history, except for 'Abdu'l-Bahá's visit in 1912.

In Jamestown, "one hour's ride by trolley from Chautauqua," an inspiring talk was made by Harry Randall to a club made up of lawyers and newspapermen.[5] They had wanted political, not religious, fare; but Harry was brilliant, answering all questions, completely winning them as he explained the solution to the world's problems with Bahá'u'lláh's spiritual teachings. The numerous requests for follow-up material was a confirmation of the impact of the ideas.

The teaching trip, so finely orchestrated by Martha, was an enormous success, due not only to the desire of each one to serve but to the blending of personalities. Harry Randall's daughter, Bahíyyih Winckler, once reminisced about the deep bond between her father and Martha and their respect and admiration for each other:

It was amusing to see them together because both were organizers, both had tremendous willpower and ability and they would laugh at each other, then Martha would proceed about what she wanted to do and Father would say, "Well, let her do it. She's going to do it anyway, you might as well let her do it."[6]

It was Harry Randall who, seeing the fire in Martha's eye, realized that she wanted to arrange Jináb-i-Fáḍil's itinerary and to prepare the publicity. He suggested that she go on three days ahead. He would follow with Jináb-i and the others. The arrangement proved to be perfect for the two strong-minded individuals.

The excursion into the northern and western regions of New York State proved to be rewarding for all involved. It revealed the readiness and enthusiasm of countless persons for the message of the Bahá'í Faith. Martha derived much pleasure from her part in the project, and she would soon have a new opportunity for that pleasure to be rekindled.

12 Confusion and Confirmation

In 1920 the Bahá'ís decided, following 'Abdu'l-Bahá's instructions to Agnes Parsons, to hold a "'Convention for unity of the colored and white races'" in Washington, D.C.[1] It would be the first of its kind in the United States and in the world, and would address one of the earliest concerns of the Bahá'í community—the elimination of prejudice.

Perhaps the most pervasive prejudice, the Bahá'ís felt, was that of race. Bahá'u'lláh had told the world that universal peace would come only through unity, not through the seeds of disunity sown by prejudice. His son 'Abdu'l-Bahá also stressed the necessity of bringing the white and colored races together, to be as the waves of one ocean, the flowers of one garden.[2]

The amity convention was tentatively scheduled for December 1920. Unfortunately, Martha's membership on the arrangements committee became the cause of one of the few personal misunderstandings in Martha's Bahá'í life, and it stemmed directly from her eagerness to serve all to the utmost.

On 1 October 1920 Martha wrote Mrs. Parsons of her plans to be in Washington in a few days to help prepare for the amity convention. T. T. Root was ill, but she hoped that he would be sufficiently improved for her to leave him. Aunt Lucy, who lived in town, was also ill, and Martha was seeing to the comfort of both. Yet her confidence in 'Abdu'l-Bahá was absolute, and she was sure that He would arrange an improvement in parental health. She was equally certain that "illness is just a test of faith."[3]

Martha was aware of the time and energy that Mrs. Parsons was putting into the convention preparations. She also had two children, one severely handicapped, a husband, and a large house to oversee. Being in the diplomatic and social spotlight of the nation's capital added to her social responsibilities. Martha longed to be of service, to make a substantial difference, "to be 'hands and feet and anything'" in order to give Mrs. Parsons the freedom to do the necessary work for the amity convention.[4]

The next dated communication to Mrs. Parsons was a telegram that arrived, astonishingly, from Saint John, New Brunswick, Canada, on 11 October. It read: "Love I can come Washington immediately or shall I continue help Fazel. Reply Hotel Royal. Martha Root."[5] The response was that Martha should stay to help Jináb-i-Fáḍil.

Between these communications was a world of misunderstanding resulting from incomplete communication on the part of others about plans that rerouted Martha, leaving Mrs. Parsons believing that she had been deserted and would have to carry on alone, which she knew was totally impossible. The misunderstanding began in Montreal when May Maxwell, one of the earliest Bahá'ís living in Canada and a woman of deep spiritual sensibilities, asked Martha to begin a teaching trip with Jináb-i-Fáḍil as speaker. The plan would be similar to that undertaken in August, but with Canada as the arena of activities. Jináb-i-Fáḍil and Harry Randall urged Martha to do it, and Harry phoned Mrs. Parsons to get her agreement.

She agreed but did not reveal then her profound disturbance at the turn of events. Martha wrote to Mrs. Parsons from New York, en route to Canada, and expressed concern at being taken from one urgent task to do another; but she promised to "come the earliest possible moment & meantime will do what I can in preparation. I was very sad to disappoint you & not to begin *at once* but am doing all I can & we will rush it next w[ee]k. I pray to do 'whatsoever He willeth!'" In a subsequent letter of explanation, which she enclosed with part of a letter from May Maxwell, Martha sadly admitted, "I cried & cried in New York . . . because I was so sorry to leave you & come to Canada, but Abdul Baha has said unity above everything else. . . ."[6]

Martha's attempts at doing each one's bidding for the sake of unity had backfired, resulting in upset and confusion. May

MAY BOWLES MAXWELL
one of the earliest Canadian Bahá'ís. By asking Martha Root to begin
a teaching trip in Canada with Jináb-i-Fáḍil, she inadvertently
caused the rescheduling of the first Bahá'í race amity convention,
which was held in Washington, D.C., in 1921.

Maxwell, in Montreal, had been unaware of the great plans under way for the amity convention when the Canadian trip was proposed. On learning of the difficulties that ensued, of Mrs. Parsons' aborted plans, and of the postponing of the convention, she wrote an anguished letter to Martha:

> Now just for a moment I must relieve my heart on the subject of Mrs Parsons and the Inter-Racial Convention. I repeated to you her night letter, although you make no allusion to it in your letter, yet I hope you received it.* As I read her words, it came to me very strongly that your having disappointed her and my being the cause of it, had become a test, and I only hope and pray that I am wrong. I know that you and Harry and all the Members of the Teaching Com-

---

*Martha wrote on the letter: "I had not recv'd it when I wrote my card."

mittee feel as I do, that this Convention is the most important thing in America at this time. I believe that if it is not carried into effect, bloodshed will follow, because the Master has fore warned us of this in a Tablet, the relations between the colored and the white were never so acute, the spirit of revolution was never so strong, and the Bahais alone can set the power of the Covenant in motion which will quench this world consuming fire. . . . We know that He has told us that nothing will be changed until the Bahais change it, and if I have been in any way, even so much as by one jot, responsible for the postponement of this Convention, I do not know how I can bear such a burden of guilt. I beg and implore of you and Harry and others . . . to look into this matter before you decide to change all your plans and see whether there are insuperable obstacles to the holding of this Convention now, because it is self evident when the greatest Bahai events and Divine forces are about to be released in the world of existence the dark forces set up every opposition, and advance every plausible excuse.[7]

Despite the intensity of feeling regarding the amity convention, it was postponed until spring 1921, which seems to have been a positive change. By the time Mrs. Maxwell's letter was received, Martha had already gone on to Saint John, Montreal, London, and Saint Thomas, Canada, to arrange programs.

It was a whirlwind teaching trip but successful beyond all hopes. Martha stayed in Saint John and arranged a dinner before the Canadian Club, which never allowed religion or politics to be discussed on its platform. Martha had arranged the talk as an educational lecture, and "never was the Message given more thoroughly, but every one cheered and there was such *love* & joy and unity. . . ."[8] And so it went with Martha at the helm, arranging and publicizing. In Montreal she wrote a different article for every paper before leaving for Saint John, so that early publicity could seep in, before the Bahá'ís came back to present the programs.

Everywhere the Bahá'í speakers met with receptive audiences, due largely to Martha's preparation and the high quality of intelligence and compassion of the speakers. Mrs. Maxwell said of Jináb-i-Fáḍil:

> He never disagreed with anyone no matter how false the theory advanced . . . never tried to show anyone they were wrong or mistaken. . . . individually or collectively, he first created the point of contact and sympathetic understanding with his hearer.[9]

Mrs. Parsons obviously forgave Martha, sending along a check for fifty dollars to defray her expenses, which were numerous—all the railroads and buses and overnight accommodations, plus meals. Martha worried about accepting any help. But Harry Randall convinced her that it was perfectly proper, since her means were extremely limited, and the ongoing cost of maintaining contacts in South America and the Orient were great.

Wherever she went on her Canadian trip, Martha informed the press of the upcoming amity convention and sought contacts for the program. Elihu Root, who had been invited to participate, was sympathetic to the situation, but his diplomatic schedule made it impossible; however, he did suggest a friend, Mr. C. Lee Cook. Martha sent her relative in Clinton, New York, a copy of *Some Answered Questions* and *Paris Talks*.

In one city after another the Bahá'ís managed to speak before the most influential persons, to Theosophists, Esperantists, and members of other faiths. Of the entire adventure Martha felt that the visit to Saint John was the greatest miracle, with the power of the Holy Spirit strongly present. She felt they were like days in heaven; it was the love extended from the people at Saint John, Harry Randall added, that made it seem like paradise.

May Maxwell realized Martha's innocence in the awkward arrangements and looked to the qualities that made her service unique:

> Martha Root is too well known and loved, as well as too evanescent to eulogize, but the Canadian believers wish to

pay her their tribute of love and gratitude for her inspired
and indefatigable services, for her genius in pioneer and
press work, through which she obtains such remarkable and
universal response from the Press. Through her love, service
and sacrifice the spoken word to hundreds became the written and published word to thousands.[10]

Martha stopped back in Cambridge Springs long enough to
see that her father was doing well before heading out to Dayton
and Cincinnati, Ohio; St. Louis, Missouri; Louisville, Ken-
tucky; and other points. In each city she set up meetings and
lectures and did the publicity work, which seemed to infect the
area spiritually and to prepare the ground for the speakers. As
a result, not one but several forums were made available at
each stop. Everywhere Jináb-i-Fáḍil spoke, success was met.
Although he went on to speak in many of the major cities in
Minnesota, Martha returned to Cambridge Springs during the
last week in November 1920.

She was home when she received the letter from Alfred Lunt
on behalf of the Executive Board of the Bahai Temple Unity
appointing her chairman of the Ideas Committee. She would
be assisted by Horace Holley, D. J. Hanko, Barbara Fitting,
and Edward (Saffa) Kinney; in addition, there were eleven other members scattered throughout the country. Martha's duty
was to inspire them to come up with suitable and creative ideas
to raise money for beginning construction of the Bahá'í House
of Worship in Wilmette.

Not one ever to take an assignment lightly, the responsibility
really weighed on Martha. She was working constantly as it
was; when Mr. Lunt's letter arrived, she was in the midst of
writing four articles on the Bahá'í Faith and was forced to can-
cel a trip to Topeka, Kansas, because of her father's health.
She told Mrs. Parsons:

Alfred Lunt's letter has just come announcing the Ideas
Committee, it takes my breath but if Abdul Baha thinks this
servant can assist I pledge it my utmost endeavor—can one
individual do all that and the convention work with you and
the Southern teaching trip to help Janabe? Whatever seems
best I promise every utmost endeavor.[11]

Martha dug in her heels, got out her Corona typewriter, made use of her very old neostyle, and after many prayers, sent letters to each member of the Ideas Committee. Some of the letters were literary compositions, one in particular assuring great results:

> If every Bahai would "wrestle with God" for one IDEA every day for the Temple [the Bahá'í House of Worship], and try to sacrifice as the Bab, Baha'o'llah and Abdul Baha "lived sacrifice" to bring Their Heavenly Ideals into Reality on this earth, lo, two miracles would be wrought! Not only would the Temple be speedily built in time for Abdul Baha to come . . . but of the "City of the Heart" of each Bahai it would be said: "And the city had no need of the sun[,] neither of the moon to shine in it: for Baha'o'llah (the Glory of God) did lighten it and the Lamb is the light thereof."

Reflecting on her own habits, she added, "If you begin tomorrow it may be too late." [12] Another letter closed with:

> Several papers are asking for Mashrakel-Azkar and other Bahai articles so I do not spend much time on this letter to you—for Abdul Baha will give you the Guidance. Please overlook it if I do not do the work in your way and know that like you, my "head is in my hands" to serve the Kingdom of El-Abha. Yours in His Love and Covenant,
>   Joyfully,
>   Martha [13]

She drew their attention to an article that appeared in the *Great Falls (Montana) Daily Tribune*, 26 December 1920, which she considered perfect and which she urged all to use as a model for their regional papers. She also recommended including a picture of the Bahá'í House of Worship design.

The Ideas Committee work necessitated Martha's spending much time in New York and traveling between home and the city. When T. T. Root was able, he accompanied her, and they would stay in the city for two or three days. To do the job well took long periods of concentration, and Martha questioned her ability: "I should be frightened did I not trust Abdul Baha to adjust the weight to the back."[14] Yet her persistence began to yield results. Throughout the country the committee members, looking for spiritual approaches to the task of raising money, began to put their creative energies to work. They were spurred on by Martha's challenge: "Living in such a maelstrom of materialism we sometimes almost forget the glory of our calling." Further encouragement, laced with promises, prodded the Ideas Committee into action:

> You do not know how much you can do until you begin and do everything through prayer. You may be given spiritual insight, second sight, until your own capacity will astonish you. If your purpose is pure and your heart absolutely severed the Supreme Concourse and Abdul Baha CAN DO THE WORK through you.

Martha was speaking through the power of experience. Leaving no possible source of help untapped, she sent a registered letter to 'Abdu'l-Bahá asking His "Blessing and Confirmations" for each one's part in the House of Worship work.[15]

The U.S. post office was being used to its fullest as the blossoming Ideas Committee information was sent forth to all sections of the country. Martha urged that the committee's report be ready before the annual Bahá'í convention, 23–27 April 1921. Ella Cooper's brother was making a seal; artist Victoria Bedekian was creating art work that would be reproduced and sold at the convention. During this time Martha was also busy helping a committee arrange the program for the race amity convention, which would be held 19–21 May 1921 in Washington, D.C.

The days were filled. Martha was in New York to work on the Ideas Committee correspondence, to meet with friends from South America, to see Leonora Holsapple (Armstrong) off to her pioneer post in South America, and to delight in working with her close friends—"Isn't it a joy to work with Harry!"[16] In February she was off to Chicago to meet with the Executive Board of Bahai Temple Unity. By 18 March the

Ideas Committee work was complete, and she was in Washington for a week to help with arrangements for the amity convention. This first interracial convention was beginning to take shape, as Martha Root and Agnes Parsons, together with Mariam Haney, Mrs. Boyle, Gabrielle Pelham, and especially Louis Gregory, set the plans in motion.

Sparse and economical in most ways, Martha was prodigal when it came to luggage. There was always that piece of literature or that reference book that might be needed, and who could tell which one it would be? When she arrived in Washington in March, she brought a lantern with slides (1,500) weighing nearly fifty pounds, her Corona typewriter (nine pounds), and a suitcase, plus a few other odds and ends. She had previously left a trunk at Mrs. Parsons' home. "You will think it looks like lots of baggage for a week or so," she predicted to Mrs. Parsons, "but wished you to see the Bahai slides and I felt we needed the typewriter."[17]

In early April when Martha was needed back in Washington, she combined the trip with a lecture series. While in Atlanta, Georgia, she visited Eugene Debs, a social democrat and labor spokesman who was in prison. She was an ardent supporter of Mr. Debs and brought him books of Bahá'í views on business and labor. He and his brother received letters from Martha regularly, and she urged other Bahá'ís to write to them as well. His was a new, strong voice urging justice toward laborers; drastic measures, which led to his imprisonment, were used to stifle his message.[18] Martha was reaching out a caring heart and hand. During that trip she also gave three talks in Augusta, Georgia, and, in response to persistent requests, presented an evening lecture in Petersburg, Virginia.

On a trip such as this, Martha would take a sleeper, or overnight train, to a particular point, rise early, and then change to a day coach at a lower fare. Meals were usually simple snacks. Although it was early April, "it is very hot and nice. . . ."[19] She liked warm weather, and for once the weather and her traveling plans coincided.

Martha was eager to work hard and do a good job for the race amity convention, not only because of the past confusion but because of her growing appreciation of Agnes Parsons.

AGNES S. PARSONS
a wealthy and prominent Bahá'í in Washington, D.C.,
whom 'Abdu'l-Bahá asked to arrange the first Bahá'í amity convention
for blacks and whites. Mrs. Parsons' diplomatic ties in the
nation's capital opened doors for Martha Root.

She became increasingly aware of her extraordinary ability, her generous spirit and harmonious attitudes. A closing sentence in a letter to Mrs. Parsons reflected her feelings: "You are so dear, so sweet, so kind, it has been the bounty of Abdul Baha to work with you." [20] In keeping with the formality of the day, Martha still addressed her friend, co-worker, and hostess as "Mrs. Parsons." Not until 'Abdu'l-Bahá named her "Núr," meaning light, did Martha use this more familiar form.

There was some time spent at home between the April committee work in Washington and the annual Bahá'í convention in Chicago. But not much. After a few days Martha was on her way to Chicago, where she was to give a major talk on Saturday, 23 April 1921, opening night of the Bahá'í convention.

Lucy Wilson, who accompanied her friend to Chicago, has left an intimate picture of the physical preparations:

> Martha always wore white when she spoke in public. The first Baha'i Convention I attended was held in . . . Chicago. I recall Martha's asking me to come to her room and help her dress—someone had sent her beautiful pink roses (she was to speak that evening). Already she was dressed in a simple white gown and told me just where to tack those roses on the drapery of her dress—one or two on the shoulder, then a rose in her hair—such lovely soft light brown hair that she wore in coronet braids about her head.[21]

In Martha's talk she gave highlights of her South American adventure, which thrilled the Bahá'ís of Canada and the United States. She captivated them, not only because of the audacity of her decisions along the numerous and hazardous routes but because of the implications of the trip. All could live differently when in the service of Bahá'u'lláh. And here was Martha Root to prove it, through fever, plague, revolutions, torrential storms and tempestuous seas, giddy mountain ranges, lack of friends, lack of language, a lone woman with limited physical and material resources. Yet she returned home rich in friendships, rich in experience, having fulfilled the goals intended.

Illness settled on Martha during the Chicago activities, and rest was necessary. But resting meant not looking up anyone between sessions, staying in the hotel, writing articles for newspapers, talking with reporters, and getting new people in touch with Bahá'ís.

An extra day was required in Chicago to give the Ideas Committee report. Returning home at 5:00 A.M., 29 April, Martha found her father alone and ill. He had the grippe, and his neck had to be lanced. Martha ached to see her aging parent unattended and in pain. He had not wanted to concern her while she was in Chicago, and he intensely disliked being the cause of worry and of taking Martha from her work. She responded with the loving care that she had given him all her adult life.

The fact that Martha was due back in Washington on 5 May did not create a carefree mood. A cousin, who had lived with the Root family when she was attending Allegheny College, and who had been given a grand wedding by Martha's parents, had invited her uncle to visit in Sheffield and do some trout fishing while Martha was involved in the race amity convention in Washington. But his health was seriously impaired. Although his bag was packed, day after day the trip was postponed.

Martha's bags were also packed and ready. Meanwhile, she wrote publicity for daily and Sunday newspapers everywhere, and she prayed. She was waiting for the sun to shine, literally and figuratively, certain that 'Abdu'l-Bahá would see to it.

George Latimer, from Seattle, Washington, visited Cambridge Springs, and Martha arranged for him to give a lecture at Alliance College; she gave her slide show. In a letter to Agnes Parsons she asked, "O Mrs. Parsons, please pray the healing prayer for father and for his happiness. . . . If this is the most important convention I am sure the doors will open for me to come in good time and that everything will go just as Abdul Baha wishes." [22]

The weather was not cooperating. Martha was certain that if the rain stopped and the sun shone, her father would improve, his asthma attacks would lessen, and he would be able to get some sleep. She mailed an article special delivery and urged Louis Gregory to help as much as possible. Noting Harry Randall's excellent talk in Chicago, she suggested that he chair one of the opening-day sessions of the amity convention.

Obstacles increased. T. T. Root's health did not improve. Another letter to Agnes Parsons described the scene at Cambridge Springs:

> Father . . . was very ill with spasmodic [asthma] and high temperature. It seems a crime to leave him alone. But I prayed very hard last night and he slept. . . . He is not able to go to my cousin's [in Sheffield]. I have arranged for some one to come and stay nights with him. My relatives and the [neighbors] criticize me very severely for leaving father as I do, but I feel if the convention is the most important Abdul Baha is going to make father comfortable and happy while I am away. . . . My cousin [in Cambridge Springs] was near-

ly killed, run over by an automobile last night. I am just going to the hospital now. The Doctors say they cannot tell until night whether she can live. . . .

Notwithstanding all these things I am coming to Washington leaving here Friday afternoon and doing it with father's permission. I will do all I can for my cousin's family
until then. Father is so kind, he says I must go—and for his
very [sacrifice] I feel Abdul Baha will bless him and make
him well and happy during the two weeks.

There was a penned postscript: "I will *surely come & work like
a trojan* when [I] get there."[23]

Despite the problems, Friday afternoon saw her on the train
heading for Washington, determined to support completely
the convention that had been proposed by 'Abdu'l-Bahá to
Mrs. Parsons.

The problems, the postponements, the confusion, and the
misunderstanding all served to heighten the sweetness of success at the first amity convention between the races, a landmark in the building of unity in the Bahá'í Faith and in the
world. The program opened on Thursday night, 19 May 1921,
with morning and evening sessions on Friday and Saturday.
Participating in this feast of goodwill were senators and educators, clergy and businessmen. Black soloists and choral groups
provided the music, including a violinist who was the grandson
of American scholar Frederick Douglass. The most extravagant hopes for success were fulfilled. It was a brilliant event, a
blueprint for future gatherings and a sign for America to begin
a rearrangement of values and attitudes. Responses from both
races were rewarding.[24]

These three days of concord between the races in the nation's capital saw the beginning of a concerted effort on the
part of Bahá'ís to carry amity conventions to other parts of the
United States. The goal was clear: to alert all people to the necessity for harmony among the earth's residents, if a peaceful
planet was to become a reality.

Shortly after the Washington convention Zia Bagdadi, a Bahá'í from Chicago, was visiting 'Abdu'l-Bahá in Haifa. 'Abd-
u'l-Bahá expressed His happiness to Mr. Bagdadi at the success

of this unity effort and showed His guest a newspaper article. Mr. Bagdadi responded:

> "My Lord, this is an article written by Miss Martha Root which appeared in a Cleveland newspaper; it contains a Tablet from Abdul-Baha, the contents of which are to the effect that unless the white and colored races become united, there will be bloodshed; that through the Bahai teachings only can racial, political and religious prejudices pass away. . . ."

'Abdu'l-Bahá's response, as recorded by Mr. Bagdadi, was that He feared that much more than bloodshed would occur. Continuing racial disharmony could mean the destruction of America, as the country's enemies agitated one race against the other, creating extraordinary crises. He urged the concentration of the Bahá'ís on the elimination of racial prejudice in order to prevent the devastation and destruction He foresaw.[25]

Before returning home from Washington, Martha stopped in Harrisburg, the capital of Pennsylvania. There she spoke to a member of the governor's staff, a good friend of hers, about Eugene Debs and the possibility of doing something about his situation, which to her was flagrantly unjust.

At home T. T. Root had been well cared for. Martha had arranged for a woman to come during the day; Claude spent the nights with his father, and Clarence took him to his home for meals. He was "better, and yet not really better."[26] Once back, Martha filled his days with conversation and read to him by the hour, lifting his spirits as his strength waned.

The eighteen months since her return from South America was probably a tremendous test of endurance for Martha as she strove to balance filial responsibility with Bahá'í service. Yet uppermost in her mind was her commitment, told to 'Abdu'l-Bahá in late 1919, that the rest of her life would be dedicated to working for the universal awareness of the Faith of Bahá'u'lláh, to the exclusion of all else except family responsibilities. She had already tested a variety of approaches to teaching. But in the months to come her search would continue in order to find new and more effective methods for reaching all people.

13 Creating Opportunities

In 1921, while enjoying the warmth of being home again in Cambridge Springs, Martha decided to write a book, or large pamphlet, about the Bahá'í Faith.[1] Addressing letters to famous individuals all over the world, she gave a brief history of the Faith, stated its principles, mentioned the plans for building the Bahá'í House of Worship, and asked for their response to the Bahá'í teachings:

> The object is to show what you and other successful men of affairs think of this Bahai Cause as a means to bring the spiritual emancipation of the races.
>
> Would you not consider it a privilege to send me a few lines telling what these principles are doing? Your word, united to the tremendous power of the great ocean of Creative Thought will help the multitudes. GOD gives you opportunity to be a means through whom this Universal plan can come into operation.
>
> Yours for humanity whom we love,
> Martha Root.

This communication was also sent to friends throughout the country, asking that the letter be taken to distinguished persons in their areas. "You will be guided by the Holy Spirit," she promised.[2]

It is not known how many answered the summons for pronouncing the value and effect of the Bahá'í principles, but hundreds read the letter and absorbed some knowledge of the Faith. Some interesting responses did appear, one from a highly placed individual, the Reverend Alton H. Cowles of Buffalo, who wrote:

> If the Bahai faith can promote a condition of civilization such that

One religion will do
For Catholic, Protestant and Jew,
And bring men to accept one faith,
One God, One Upward Path:
'twill hold the right to sway
The hearts of all in U. S. A.[3]

This work was being done as she cared for her father and battled her own physical frailties. The breast cancer that had earlier troubled her had been in remission for nine years, probably aided by the unique prescription of 'Abdu'l-Bahá. But it was creating painful symptoms as the focus of the malady moved from the original spot to other areas, affecting both the chest and the stomach. Again, Martha consulted no doctor. She was often forced to reduce her work schedule greatly as she dealt with the pain. She was like a runner, temporarily on the sidelines but running in place while she waited.

In September 1921 Martha traveled to the Midwest to confer with Bahá'ís about a race amity convention in Cleveland, where racial conditions were serious. She lectured in several cities and used her slides, which she found extremely helpful in her talks.

After arriving back home, Martha spent her nights caring for her ill and delirious Aunt Martha, until sidetracked once again with her own intense pain. "It teaches me," she noted, "that if we are going to do anything for the Cause, these 'great days are swiftly passing'."[4]

Agnes Parsons, aware of Martha's physical suffering, though not knowing the cause, wrote to 'Abdu'l-Bahá in Haifa and asked for His prayers. Martha's gratitude and improved condition were reflected in a letter to Mrs. Parsons:

My Dear, how can I thank you for writing Abdul Baha to heal me! I have had such a hard summer, ill four times with this acute pain. . . . Now I feel I am Cured and I am going to have perfect faith in Abdul Baha; life looks entirely different to me now and I feel I shall be well and travel to many parts of the world to give the Message before I pass on.[5]

During this period Martha, with the help of Lucy Wilson,

gave a benefit entertainment for a Cambridge Springs man who was ill and destitute. The editor of the newspaper had brought the unfortunate predicament to the attention of the readers and had asked for donations, hoping to raise fifty dollars. When there was little response, Martha and Lucy took on the role of fund raisers in their own way. They secured the Chamber of Commerce rooms and transformed this utilitarian space into a place of beauty. The public was invited, and many came. Martha showed "a travelogue with gay and serious scenes, and gay and spiritual songs thrown on the screen for everybody to join in. Lucy . . . is an excellent accompanist and we had a fine leader to direct the voices in the audience."[6]

It was, of course, a teaching effort, yet subtle, with some Bahá'í scenes and principles interspersed with a Christian motif. Martha had learned from Mrs. Parsons how to " 'fire the cannon noiselessly.' " The target sum was doubled, and friends were made for the Bahá'í Faith. Martha recalled that "The Catholics were very pleased with this entertainment the other night and the Presbyterian clergyman spoke of the wonderful spirit and commended the benefit highly in his sermon last Sunday."[7] Everywhere gratitude was expressed for Martha's efforts, which produced a purse and a brighter outlook for the invalid.

The period in Cambridge Springs had opened up new doors for spiritual exploration and had alerted hundreds more to the Bahá'í Faith. Nevertheless, Martha needed resourcefulness and patience, especially in coping with her physical limitations. She prayed for opportunities to be of greater service even as she gave unstintingly of her time and energy in a circumscribed geographical area.

14 Mexico and Guatemala

Martha was as restless as an explorer marooned on placid waters waiting for the winds to change. She felt she was harboring a gift that should be dispersed to waiting souls in other regions. With an improvement in her own health and a brighter outlook for her father's well-being, Martha was ready to venture forth. She chose Mexico and Central America, of which 'Abdu'l-Bahá had said, "If one breath of life be blown over them, great results will issue therefrom."[1] Martha was determined to provide that breath of life.

On 25 October 1921 she boarded a train for Washington, D.C., where, with the help of Mason Remey, she took care of passport requirements. She also spent a few days with Agnes Parsons, Mariam Haney, and other friends before starting on her multistate junket.

She could not pass Atlanta, Georgia, without a visit with Eugene Debs at the federal prison. But she had to promise the authorities that she would not write anything about her interview. Martha referred to Mr. Debs as "one of the great souls that I have met." She had been writing to him every week for at least a year and had sent him Bahá'í books. Her hope was

> that every Bahai will LOVE Mr. Debs and extend to him every courtesy—people believe in the Bahai Cause through deeds, not words. Mr. Debs is giving his life for the oneness of humanity. Lincoln could not have been more sincere, more thoughtful, more kind, more strong than is this beautiful soul. I love his character and look upon him as one of my dearest brothers.[2]

The following afternoon, 30 October, Martha addressed a group in one of the local hotels before leaving for Memphis,

Tennessee. There she spoke several times at the Henderson
Business College, a forward-looking school devoted to educating black students in professional skills, as well as arts and sci-
ences. It was the same institution that Louis Gregory had spoken at a few years earlier. The college was the fruit of Professor
George Henderson, its director, a multifaceted man, a gifted
speaker, a musician, and a Bahá'í. 'Abdu'l-Bahá was aware of
his work and had sent him a letter praising his vision and effort.

The westward trip was resumed, and Martha arrived around
the first of November in Austin, Texas, where she was welcomed with open arms by Anna Reinke. This former shepherd-
ess of a thousand sheep had been living in Austin for nine
years, where she actively taught the Faith and had established
herself as a dressmaker. She had a large clientele, handsomely
turned out through her tailoring skills, and was as "smiling and
lovely as the great blue morning-glories . . . adorning her
unique bungalow."[3]

With Anna's help, Martha took the now familiar steps to inform the city's residents about the Bahá'í Faith. Articles were
written for the daily and Sunday newspapers, and each day was
devoted to lectures in clubs, schools, and colleges. The most
exciting of these took place at the University of Texas, where
Martha spoke on " 'Opportunities in South America.' "[4] So enthusiastic was the reception that the head of the World Politics
Department invited her to stay and give another lecture to his
department. The second lecture was also a great success; the
hall was filled. The Theosophists also arranged for two lectures, and even the Confederate Old Ladies' Home wanted a
talk.

Adventure always accompanied Martha, this time to a small
area called Bee Cave, twenty-five miles from Austin in the Texas mountains where Anna Reinke was raised. There, at a Sat-
urday-night dance, cowboys were told about the Bahá'í Faith.
Martha reported that

At 10.30 o'clock after the Texas jigs and a rousing good
time, everybody sat down and Miss Root gave the history of

the Bahai Cause and all the vital Principles. Miss Reinke passed around the blue booklets. The cowboys were IN-TERESTED and showed their appreciation. A lecture had never before been given in those regions. . . .[5]

Martha felt those cowboys would be fearless in proclaiming the Faith since in that region their courage was honed on rough, western trails. Describing the road to Bee Cave she observed that it was

scattered over with Gibraltar rocks as common as cedar brush. The path was like going up to the top of the world and coasting down. The party from Austin went in a motor truck nicely padded with hay. The men pushed the truck where it couldn't go it alone and several times Anna ordered every one off to walk up the 'accident' bends. Everything is BIG in Texas and the dangers, when there are any, are BIG too.[6]

After six days in Austin Martha left for Mexico City. She wrote that the state of unrest in Mexico need not deter any Bahá'í from going there to work and to teach. " 'Dost thou prefer to die upon thy bed?' " she quoted.[7] Martha, surely, did not. She had been brushing up on her language skills for Mexico. Her Spanish was not letter perfect, but she could converse and conduct her affairs reasonably well with it. When perfection was needed, she used a translator to avoid misinterpretation.

Martha knew no one—not a soul—in Mexico. She began her rounds, starting at the top. Her first call was made to President Alvara Obregon. She wrote, referring to herself in the third person:

More than a hundred soldiers stood around the palace office building which extended the entire length of the Cathedral Plaza. She explained she was bringing the President of the Republic of Mexico Baha'o'llah's Solution of the Economic Problem. She showed several introductory letters of recommendation. . . . The soldiers ushered her from one official to another until she reached the private secretary of the

President. He spoke English perfectly. She explained and gave through him to the President, Baha'o'llah's Economic Solution as discussed in the Star of the West, December 31, 1919, in the article by Mr. Alfred E. Lunt. She also gave the Compilation on War and Peace, the Hague Tablet, a blue booklet and the Covenant photograph of Abdul Baha; she arranged to send other books.[8]

During the three weeks in Mexico, Martha contacted editors of magazines and newspapers and spoke in churches (Catholic and Protestant), private and public schools, and colleges. Especially receptive were the Theosophists. In Mexico City she addressed their first annual convention and was invited to speak a second time. She had an additional thousand blue booklets printed, as the supply she had brought with her had already melted away. And she supplied libraries with books on the Faith.

In traveling to all parts of Mexico, Martha continued to contact editors, to address various organizations, including women's groups, and to make friends. She was the houseguest of a congressman's wife in Puebla and the governor's wife in Veracruz. The British vice-consul in Guadalajara was a former captain of the British forces in Palestine and had met 'Abdu'l-Bahá.

She discovered that there was one Bahá'í in Mexico, a Mr. C. P. Forest, who had seen one of Martha's articles in a newspaper and came to call the day before she left. It was a touching visit. He was from Palestine but had heard of the Faith in New York about five years earlier, become a Bahá'í, and set up a business in Mexico. He had had no further contact with the Bahá'ís. Her visit and the ensuing publicity were a feast for one isolated from spiritual sharing.

Martha's travel plans called for leaving Mexico from Veracruz and going by rail to the southern Mexican frontier into Central America. Because of the smoldering political situation, with a revolution imminent, the officials told her not to go. It was too dangerous, especially for a woman; if anything happened, it was impossible to send aid quickly. But Martha had had a vision in which 'Abdu'l-Bahá assured her that He would send someone with her. The decision was never in doubt. The official in Veracruz told her, " 'You may be the only one on that car, but I'll send a man over with you to help you buy your ticket.' "[9]

At 9:00 P.M. Martha crossed the station platform, which was deserted except for the conductor, and boarded the unlit, empty train. Soon another woman arrived and sat directly opposite Martha. She was German but spoke English perfectly; she, too, was headed for Guatemala. She became not only a delightful companion, but enormously helpful to Martha as well. Others began boarding the train, and soon every seat was filled, contrary to the eerie emptiness predicted. The passengers were Mexican, Spanish, German, and French. Forty soldiers rode with them for protection. Because of the unrest the train did not travel at night but spent that time silent in cities.

The German woman's son met them at the border. Because of his friendship with the Central American consul, that official arose at 6:00 A.M. to validate Martha's passport, which would otherwise have cost her four days and a solitary trip into Central America. When they reached Guatemala, these new friends saw to her baggage, got her through customs, brought her to a good hotel in Guatemala City, and invited her to their home. The promise of 'Abdu'l-Bahá had been fulfilled.

The paradisical climate and panoramic quality of Guatemala delighted Martha, whose fondness of warmer temperatures was briefly indulged. Political unrest seeped through the ordinary activities, but Martha saw a brighter future through the initiation of the Bahá'í Faith for the "ancient, intelligent Indians and the Spanish," and for the immigrants that would flock to this metropolis when political stability appeared.[10]

Her first sortie was to arrange an interview with the president of the republic, Carlos Herrera. She spoke with the secretary of the minister of foreign relations, explained the Bahá'í teachings, and left several Bahá'í booklets. An interview with the president was arranged for Monday or Tuesday at 2:30 P.M. Appearing on Monday, Martha was asked to come back on Tuesday. By Tuesday he was ex-President Herrera. Martha chronicled the events leading to capitulation:

Monday night came the revolution! Machine guns were in action over the city all night. The palace was surrounded by 500 soldiers, President Herrera was kept a prisoner there and his Cabinet imprisoned in the fortress.

But the Bahai Message had also been given to the Liberals, some of the very men who next day went into office under the new government.[11]

The schools were not in session, eliminating that source for lectures, but Martha felt that all important avenues of communication had been covered. "People of calibre from every party were met, the library visited, also interviews with altruistic women, and the business men."[12]

Thursday morning, after two nights of steady bombarding, Martha left for the coast and sailed for New Orleans, where she completed a month's teaching (10 November–9 December 1921) in this Spanish-oriented city. She felt satisfied that her goals had been realized. In New Orleans, a southern reflection of European life, Martha visited every newspaper and library, gave every city editor and managing editor a blue booklet, which, she reported, each one read. French and Italian translations of Bahá'í literature were put in the libraries to accommodate this cosmopolitan culture. As a result, a lengthy article about Martha's travels and the Faith appeared in a prominent daily newspaper, *New Orleans States.* It was later picked up and reproduced on page one in Cambridge Springs.[13]

Making contacts and friends Martha viewed as only the first step; nurturing them followed. A list of Mexican and Guatemalan friends was compiled, with brief biographical sketches, and was sent to Bahá'í friends asking that each " 'adopt' " one and write to that person, rather like a pen pal, sending along Bahá'í ideas and information.[14]

Looking back on the trip, Martha remembered that "The most dangerous part of the journey had been the night of November 27 and day of November 28." This time of unrest seemed especially significant when Martha learned on reaching home, 15 December, that 'Abdu'l-Bahá's earthly existence had terminated on 28 November. Her deep sense of personal loss was tempered by the largess of guidance He left behind, by His example, and by His written and spoken words. In a letter to the National Teaching Committee she commented:

"Precious friends, the same Beloved who spoke to us from Acca to the United States, to Mexico and to all other parts of the world speaks to us now just as tenderly from the fair Kingdom of Abha. He has told us how we may always commune with Him—through the Power of Ya Baha El-Abha!—. There is one beautiful way to tell Him and the people of this world how much we love Abdul Baha, our Center of the Covenant—it is to try to love as He loved, try to serve as He served, sacrifice as He sacrificed, be happy as He was Happy. . . . O we can delight Abdul Baha, we can bring joy to the Supreme Concourse. He has told us: [']His Ancient Graces are universal and His Spiritual Favors world-encircling. All that He hath given to others, He will confer upon you a [thousandfold]. . . . Do ye not look upon your own shortcomings and capacity. Behold His All-Embracing Love and Clemency! [']"[15]

15   Tests and Vital Changes

Cambridge Springs welcomed back its itinerant daughter, offered the usual front-page publicity, and took note of the dangers risked and overcome. There was appreciation mixed with a touch of awe at the courage and energy exhibited by Miss Root. But the residents were not rushing to her door to share the spiritual message she had taken to Mexico and Central America. There were no dramatic changes.

The end of 1921 held a particularly sweet note for Martha. On Christmas Day President Harding pardoned Eugene Debs. He was free to leave the federal prison. It is uncertain whether Martha's urging of help from influential friends and prominent governmental persons was instrumental in his release, but her assistance certainly was a noticeable addition to the body of protest waging war on injustice. And Martha had sent many potent prayers heavenward. It was a day to rejoice. Mr. Debs, in the months following his release, called attention to the Bahá'í Faith and its teachings. His was a strong voice in the country, and Martha believed he would one day embrace the Faith.

Nineteen twenty-two ushered in a year of profound change. In His Will and Testament 'Abdu'l-Bahá had left the leadership of the Bahá'í Faith on the youthful shoulders of His grandson, Shoghi Effendi, who would become known to Bahá'ís as the Guardian. The overwhelming responsibility was awesome. Mountfort Mills, who with Roy Wilhelm had been summoned to Haifa to confer with Shoghi Effendi, spoke about the scope of his work: " 'All the complex problems of the great statesmen of the world are as child's play in comparison with the great problems of this youth, before whom are the problems of the entire world. . . . No one can form any conception of his difficulties, which are overwhelming.' " [1]

144

Nineteen twenty-two would also be Martha Root's last year in Cambridge Springs and would bring about a complete change in her mode of living. The early months were spent caring for her father, corresponding with two hundred new friends in Mexico, and maintaining her earlier international bulletins of news and progress. She gave several lectures but confined her travels to the eastern seaboard. Combining friendship with effort, she again worked on the plans for the annual Bahá'í convention, which would be the first assemblage of the Bahá'ís since the passing of 'Abdu'l-Bahá.

At this fourteenth annual convention Martha was one of the main speakers. Her talk was a subject close to her heart— "'Apostles of the New Day and Their World Journeys.'" She chose examples of the steadfast, from Ṭáhirih, the Persian poetess who had secured her place in history as an emancipator of women, to Agnes Alexander, who, as a Bahá'í teacher, was leading the way in Japan and Korea. She spoke of Mírzá Ḥaydar-'Alí (known to Bahá'ís as the Delight of Hearts) and the sufferings he underwent, which were merely an accompaniment to the message of his life. Bahá'u'lláh had written to him:

"I have heard thy cries and am conscious of thy tears. Remember in all times and in all places that God is faithful and do not doubt this. Be patient, even though great calamities come upon thee. Fear not! Be firm in the path of the Lord, as a mountain unmoved, unchanging in thy steadfastness. God has made afflictions as a morning shower to His green pastures and as a wick for His lamp, whereby earth and heaven are illumined."[2]

It was as if Martha were preparing herself for the years to come, setting her goals, raising her standard. She closed her talk by reminding those Bahá'ís gathered in Chicago of 'Abdu'l-Bahá's strong desire that someone arise and take the message to China. God's assistance was assured.

That gathering, the fourteenth annual Bahá'í convention, was a special time, and all attending felt it. Martha wrote to Harry Randall, "The convention was the greatest miracle of

the Power of the Bahai Cause to unite that I have ever witnessed. It seemed as if I lived ten thousand years in those few
days." [3]

Martha's sense of humor had not diminished under her
spiritual raptures. Homeward bound, she met and described a
fellow traveler:

> On train rode all day with typical Texan gentleman, six or
> seven feet tall, ranch hat and etc. He corraled this Bahai
> Cause feeling it possessed the spirit—the spiritualized some-
> thing that materially he demands in "temperament" from
> his polo ponies. He is going to buy books in N. Y. and when
> he gets these—well, you all will just be saved a trip to Texas,
> for unless am mistaken he is the kind of man who will
> "round up" his state. He did not say this, but I felt it. [4]

Back in Cambridge Springs the first order of duty, apart
from filial attention, was to prepare an article about happiness
for her friends in upstate New York, the Roycrofters. Martha
decided, except for a lead-in paragraph, to use only quotations
from the Bahá'í writings. The article was a sampling of positive Bahá'í thought, which radiated an acceptance and joy,
while treading this path on earth. One passage promised that

> "When the divine message is understood all troubles will
> vanish. Shadows disappear when the universal lamp is
> lighted, for whosoever becomes illumined thereby no longer
> knows grief. He realizes that his stay on this planet is tempo-
> rary and that life is eternal. When once he has found reality
> he will no longer retreat into darkness." [5]

In May, Martha initiated a series of talks in Cambridge
Springs on certain universal principles, aspects of the Bahá'í
teachings. The Chamber of Commerce, the finest place in
Cambridge Springs, was to be the setting for these Saturday-
night presentations. The press, always friendly to Martha,
gave her front-page publicity for each of the lectures. "The
Harmony of Science and Religion," "New Evidences of Life
After Death," and "Universal Education—Four Ways of Ac-

quiring Knowledge" attracted many and piqued their interest in the teachings.[6] The talks were prompt, brief, and the discussions lively. Finding some help with decorating, Martha transformed the functional meeting rooms into a space of visual delight.

Her joy in holding these public discussions was short-lived. Discontent over her activities arose, and her lofty ideas were not to be given free reign. When the president of the Chamber of Commerce and some of its most important members were out of town, the Presbyterian minister met with the board, several of whom were his parishioners, and discussed Miss Root's religious views, which they said were penetrating the talks. As a result the board passed a vote to stop the lectures.

Martha was devastated. It was a deep, personal blow aimed at the Faith through her. She wrote to friends:

> Of course I know the talks had caused a spiritual revolution. The town was agog, for and against. You who do not live in a small town could not understand it. My sister-in-law and even my brother just plead with father to make me stop those talks. So much criticism just made me ill, I won't describe it—but all Saturday afternoon I prayed . . . that all the Hosts of the Supreme Concourse . . . would just focus on this town and demonstrate the Power of the Holy Spirit. Every nerve was just crying out in agony. Suddenly Baha'o'llah took me in His Arms and said not to pray any more, the prayer was answered. They would demonstrate the Power of the Holy Spirit. I was better, calm, poised. (the Secretary had said I could go ahead and speak that night but not to announce any more) I dressed in white with the garden white narcissi in my hair and on the gown. The Chamber of Commerce was a dream of loveliness—my friends brought bouquets of white narcissi and branches of white bridal wreath. Each week I had taken rugs, screen, drapery and decorated the place. These meetings in every minutest detail were artistic so that everybody loved them—and we gave the flowers away at the close, one to each individual. They were not just "meetings"[;] they were the home for the descent of the Holy Spirit. I studied those subjects hard every day—took more energy than to write a dozen articles.

Martha felt that Bahá'u'lláh's promise had been fulfilled, and that her words were inspired. She continued, "The Holy Spirit dazzled—I could never speak again those living, creative inspirations, everybody was happy. . . . Every chord was love. . . ."[7]

Even though the talks were stopped, interest was heightened. Scores of persons asked about the Bahá'í Faith, many were reading books about it, and individuals proposed other meetings. One of the richest women in town, whose interests seemed far from spiritual matters, "the kind Roy calls a 'highstepper,'" initiated weekly discussions on selections from the Hidden Words of Bahá'u'lláh. A few other spiritual seekers emerged. One person said, "If it's the truth the churches can't hold it back."[8]

But it was discussed adversely in the Bible classes on Sunday, and from the pulpit the clergymen were not kind. Also, on the street was heard:

> "Say, are you a convert to Miss Root's religion?". . . "Not yet, but my wife and my two daughters are converts!"

Loud laughter followed. To Martha it was not a source of laughter but of deep hurt. She crossed the Chamber of Commerce off her list; "better never to ask for it again—for any Bahai speaker."[9]

Small gatherings in her home or the homes of friends became the pattern. At least one group felt that she was not too dangerous; she was asked to address the Girl Scouts.

Martha, perhaps because of constant prayer, seemed to have a heightened intuition and a closer relationship than most with the world beyond. When she was wracked with frustration and unhappiness at the Cambridge Springs incident, she dreamt of Helen Goodall, who had passed away shortly after the death of 'Abdu'l-Bahá. Martha described the dream to Mrs. Goodall's daughter, Ella Goodall Cooper:

> I drew the white scarf over my face to hide the tears & someone beside me saw it & she drew the white scarf away & said very gently but very *firmly* that humanity must never see me

weep. I must always be *happy.* It was your precious Mother but I could not speak quickly enough, she was gone and I became wide awake. . . . her face was transcendent and she was so gloriously happy—she was living what she told me to do. . . . it made me ashamed that I felt so sad over the C. of C. affair, and it made me happy to feel her presence. . . . Isn't life strange . . . these spiritual births are sometimes full of pain. This Camb. matter has been like that. . . ."[10]

One of the highlights of the summer was Martha's attendance at the Swedenborgian convention in Urbana, Ohio, in June. She was deeply impressed with the spirit of the gathering and felt its possibility for being fertile ground for teaching the Faith.

But the place of peace to Martha was Green Acre, the Bahá'í school in Eliot, Maine. She had gone there whenever possible since 'Abdu'l-Bahá's visit to this spot in New England in 1912. As if absorbing as much of its essence as possible to draw on for future needs, Martha spent seven weeks there in July and August, doing publicity for the numerous programs being presented. This arrangement was feasible because Mr. Root was spending much of the summer with relatives and was indulging in his favorite sport, showing "people in that locality how to catch fish."[11]

Martha traveled from Maine to New Jersey with the Wilhelms at the end of August. "The Cabin," which was formerly their home, had been redesigned and turned over to the Bahá'ís of West Englewood, New Jersey. It had just been finished and was filled with friends for a Bahá'í gathering. As Martha was leaving for home, Roy's father suffered a stroke and lapsed into unconsciousness. He never recovered from the illness and died late in October.

After returning to Cambridge Springs, Martha realized that her own father's health was exceedingly fragile. She stayed close to home, not venturing far from Cambridge Springs, and turning down invitations that would take her far afield. In early October, T. T. Root came down with a severe case of bronchitis, which, within two weeks, developed into pleuresy. Meetings at home were canceled, partly because of her father's health, and partly because of Martha's own fatigue. She was up most of every night responding to his needs. The doctor assured her that he would be better, that there was no cause for alarm. She wrote to friends about her father's condition, adding her nurturing touch of love and reliving the memories of Green Acre. To Alfred Lunt she reminisced: "I often think of our happy hours under the *apple tree* & the feasts in the blessed Annex. How heavenly to meet the friends."[12]

As October gave way to November, T. T. Root did not improve. On the night of 3 November 1922, at age eighty-five, Timothy T. Root passed on. Only his sister Lucy, the youngest of the eight children of Sylvester and Mercy Root, survived. Another sister, Aunt Martha, had passed away during Martha's Guatemalan visit. Martha had a premonition of her father's passing, and when Lucy Wilson called in the afternoon, Martha asked if she would come back later to spend the night. She explained that her father was " 'going tonight.' "[13] He died just before midnight.

Although the burial service was conducted in the Baptist church that T. T. Root had so staunchly supported, Martha invited the other three Protestant ministers in town to participate in the service. She also invited the Catholic priest, who felt he could not be a part of the church service but, at Martha's request, came to the home and offered prayers. The Baptist minister read two Bahá'í prayers and some words chosen by Martha. Lucy Wilson recorded:

> At the grave, after the family and friends had gone, Martha tarried and dropped a rose in the grave—it was as if the deepest bond of earthly ties was loosened.
> Suddenly I knew why I had come to Cambridge Springs to live those years—just to stand beside precious Martha in her grief—as no one else understood her being a Baha'i.
> She came to stay with me that night. The next day Martha said, "I must work hard to finish things here as from now on I serve only the Cause of Baha'u'llah." . . .[14]

The deep love and appreciation that Martha felt for her father were reflected in a moving tribute that she wrote:

He was a wonderful father to live with. He did not take everything for granted. The little courtesies in the home were never forgotten. . . .

. . . What a father means to a son only a son can tell you, but the camraderie between father and daughter is also a holy treasure. . . . He was pure in heart and absolutely selfless. No matter what his daughter's faults were he saw her only as perfect and he was always intensely loyal. And with it all, every day . . . he was just the same, gentle, lovely and lovable. . . . Is it any wonder that when she came back from the cemetary [sic] and stepped into his room she felt she could never again take off her hat there!

But his spirit spoke to her with his same smile and twinkle in his eyes: "You and I still together. I am going with you every day of your journey. You are going to do all that we talked over and I am going to help until I can tell you: "The Master is come and calleth for thee." [15]

Martha had often referred to her father as a wonderful Bahá'í because he was willing to stay alone and because he encouraged her to carry out her Bahá'í work. He was still encouraging her.

Now Martha was ready to start winding up her affairs and gathering her personal belongings together. This would not be difficult, as she did not save any unnecessary articles. "I never keep anything. I believe in keeping everything in motion," she had written to Alfred Lunt. [16]

Legal matters were not so simple. If all had acted honorably, the affairs could have been settled easily. It emerged as a classic case of the older, financially comfortable brother, who, having been left the larger share, used sharp, dishonest pressure tactics on a younger, unsuccessful brother, and who tried to dupe his sister.

Having unwittingly followed Clarence's advice in the beginning and signed over her charge as coexecutor of the estate, ostensibly to simplify matters, Martha soon realized the unwisdom of her act. Shocked by Clarence's duplicity, Martha consulted with her trusted Bahá'í friends via the mails. She was torn between walking out on the whole business and staying to bring about justice and, most important, to help evolve her brother's soul. She did not want his life here, and in the next world, to be besmirched by this unscrupulous act. The sum at stake was not large, but it would mean funds for Martha's travels and money for the education of Claude's daughter.

Understandably, her first recourse was prayer, deep and ardent prayer. She also had friends in town who came to her aid, including people at the bank and in positions that handle information involving estates.

At this crucial period she was disabled by a severe case of grippe. Running a high temperature, she was forbidden by the doctor to leave her room. But it allowed other relationships to flourish: "my brother Claude always comes with every meal[;] through all eternity I shall remember Claude's love to me!" Anna, Claude's seventeen-year-old daughter, also helped to serve her aunt and displayed detachment and young wisdom. Referring to the inheritance she said, " 'We can get along without as well as Uncle Clarence can get along with it.' " [17]

As Martha lay in bed and dealt with the material unpleasantness, travel plans began to take shape. China loomed large in the future. When Harry Randall wrote that she should rest before starting off, she responded, "I do not rest here. I 'rest in action' and my most perfect rest and joy would be to teach." [18]

Her deepest attachments of love and friendship were communicated to her friends, for she knew she might not see them for a long time. "I love you all so devotedly," she wrote to them. "I lean upon your strength—it is you who will really do the work, I am only your 'Andrew'. I thank you for your love, your counsel, your wonderful lives." [19]

Martha's stand for honesty was supported on all sides. Her dear friend, Dr. Logan, who was also an excellent businessman and president of the bank, knew of the discrepancies in Clarence's execution of the will and was willing to impose severe penalties. Clarence, confronted by Martha and Claude with the knowledge of his deed, stormed out of the house. For three days Martha had no idea what avenue his anger would take.

Her prayers, and those of friends, were answered. Clarence was mollified, ready to do the decent thing, and treated Martha with consideration. She felt that in some ways he was trying to shape up to his father's image. "He has been to church . . . ," she observed, "and sat in his father's pew . . . and deposited the sum that his father always used to give. In Clarence's mind that means religion, he has never been touched by the Holy Spirit before, religion is an unknown language to him."[20] Martha felt he had been so used to driving hard bargains that it had become second nature, that he perhaps did not really mean to cheat them.

Whatever his intentions, the matter was settled. Martha got the finest lawyer available, over her brother's protests, to ensure the covering of legal intricacies. All the furniture had been left to her, and she divided it equally between her brothers. All else was absorbed by others—the farm, the boat, the small personal items. Her sadness at her father's passing was heightened by the inordinate display of intemperance and insensitivity by relatives. She had wanted only one article of her father's, a camel's hair sweater. That, too, was taken. Weeping, she unburdened herself to Lucy, " 'Was that too much to ask?' "[21]

Martha now had an inheritance of some money, some property, which would yield mortgage payments, and a vacant lot, which would yield little. She appointed her cousin Sidney Hart, owner of a stereoptican company in nearby Meadville, to represent her ongoing affairs and gave him power of attorney. He was absolutely honest, a wise, cautious, and successful businessman, and he would serve her well in years to come.

Now there was nothing to hold Martha back. She divested herself of all that anchors one to the earth. The restlessness that had for so long been stirring within her to be off and teaching would be put to rest. " 'Now I can begin my real work,' " she said.[22]

It was as if the Cambridge Springs experiences of later years, tainted with prejudice, greed, and injustice, were designed to soften any possible nostalgia that might make Martha's leaving more painful. She felt that with her departure she might never see Cambridge Springs again. This perception was not entirely true, but her visits would be brief and seldom.

In December 1922 Martha Root, age fifty, left her hometown of Cambridge Springs, Pennsylvania, to take up her residency in the world.

Part 3/*Weaving the Tapestry*

16 The Journey Begins

"O that I could travel, even though on foot and in the utmost poverty, to these regions, and, raising the call of 'Yá Bahá'u'l-Abhá' in cities, villages, mountains, deserts and oceans, promote the Divine teachings! This, alas, I cannot do. How intensely I deplore it! Please God ye may achieve it!"[1] These words of 'Abdu'l-Bahá, reflecting both His lament and His supplication to the Bahá'ís, helped set the course for Martha's life. The message was wrapped around her mind, and the words insinuated themselves into her being. They became the prod for her energies and her comfort in distress in lands far from home. She would do for the Bahá'í Faith what circumstances had prevented 'Abdu'l-Bahá from achieving. When Martha Root left her home in Cambridge Springs, her direction was clear.

She had originally envisioned a trip across the southern part of the United States to San Francisco, from where she would sail for Hawaii. Later she would go to Japan and then settle in China for an indefinite period.

In response to the National Teaching Committee, Martha shifted her plans from the warm, southern route to a lecture trip charted along a northern artery of the United States, ending in Seattle, Washington. Because of the climate this rearrangement was not as appealing to Martha, who wrote, "I almost freeze to death every winter." But she would graciously and cheerfully bend to whatever directives would best serve the Bahá'í Faith, explaining that "Abdul-Baha in six Tablets told me to go to all parts of the world—all the continents—the Easts and the Wests . . . to the North and the South—. The aim of my life is to fulfill those Tablets absolutely."[2]

Martha went to Washington, D.C., to secure a round-the-world passport (her other passport had been stolen in Mexico). Along the way she visited friends and filled speaking engagements in Pittsburgh (four talks); Harrisburg; Washington; West Englewood, New Jersey; and New York City. Most of her luggage had already been shipped to Seattle, including her typewriter, lantern unit, and 250 slides.

Over many years Martha had collected portions of the Bahá'í sacred writings from all over the world, the process having involved hundreds of letters and lengthy research. These filled six large, loose-leaf books, bound in leather, which she sent to Roy Wilhelm. They had been arranged alphabetically and indexed, representing perhaps the most definitive collection at that time, and an enormous amount of work.

Her hope was that these books could be sold for about $1ᴐ0, money that she would use to buy Bahá'í literature for use in her travels. To Horace Holley, a member of the National Spiritual Assembly of the Bahá'ís of the United States and Canada, she sent the unorganized originals, among a trunkful of other materials, for use at his discretion.* Her fine collection of books on South America, Mexico, and Central America were sent to Corinne True, to be given to individuals ready to undertake a journey to any one of those countries. For herself, Martha said, "I carry the Creative Word on the basic Principles & Abdul Baha's addresses in this country, that is sufficient for me[.] I concentrate on them & let other people study other points in detail—just as I would study if I were not so busy with this."³

As far back as April Martha had sent money to Agnes Alexander in Japan to have the blue booklets printed in Chinese, little realizing that Martha herself would be the first to use them. The rest of her affairs for this northwest journey were put in the hands of George Latimer in Portland, Oregon, her "impresario."⁴

---

*A National Spiritual Assembly is an elected "body of nine individuals empowered in the Bahá'í writings to direct, unify, coordinate, and stimulate the activities of individuals as well as local assemblies within its jurisdiction" (*The National Spiritual Assembly of the Bahá'ís of the United States* [Wilmette, Ill.: National Spiritual Assembly of the Bahá'ís of the United States, 1975], p. 2).

The dawn of the new year, 1923, shone on Martha in a little hotel room in Akron, Ohio—cost, one dollar per night—where she was writing day and night to get out advance publicity, and preparing summaries of each talk to hand out to reporters who would come to the lectures. These were sent out to friends across the country where she would speak, together with photographs of 'Abdu'l-Bahá, the House of Worship architectural model, and herself. Now Martha's expertise in publicity was turned on her own efforts as it had been for others. It was all for the Faith.

The old year had been closed out with talks in Toronto, Canada, and Buffalo, New York. Now from Akron she would make her way west through the coldest states at the coldest time of the year, through Wisconsin to Duluth, Minnesota. There she gave eleven lectures in four days; it was wise to keep moving in a city where twenty-five degrees below zero was not even commented upon. Before she left, it went down to forty below. Martha then traveled to Butte, Montana, where she lectured at least once a day for a week. After continuing her journey through Helena and Spokane, Washington, to Portland, Oregon, she wound up her cross-country trip with two weeks in Seattle. She had blazed a trail from east to west, spoken in nineteen cities, and addressed a variety of men's and women's clubs, the Theosophists, the Twentieth Century Club, and numerous churches and schools. Every newspaper carried an account of each presentation, usually accompanied by a picture of Martha, the House of Worship model, or 'Abdu'l-Bahá. The publicity was extraordinary. The fruits of her Akron diligence were evident as she visited city after city across the northern belt of the United States.

Rouhanieh (Mrs. J. W.) Latimer accompanied Martha from Portland to Seattle and spent two weeks with her while Martha completed her traveling plans and gave fourteen lectures. Martha wrote to the National Teaching Committee that "The days in Seattle were days in heaven. They do things in such a BIG way. They are original." [5]

Illness prevented Martha's going to Vancouver, but she asked the Bahá'ís to write to the Vancouver Spiritual Assembly, thus completing her trip through the medium of letters. Of this time Mrs. Latimer felt

> that the friends have received something from Martha that will be lasting and out of her trip will come one of the great spiritual awakenings. . . . Her life of self sacrifice, her untiring efforts in the Cause of GOD, have made us all realize the true meaning of sacrifice. It is not what she said on the subject, but the doing! . . . . There has been the greatest awakening of the colored people in Seattle, and it is our longing wish that our beautiful friend, Louis Gregory, will soon return to the Coast. . . . Through his efforts the people of Portland and Seattle opened their doors for our blessed sister, and in her they found the spirit of humility and love. . . . One distinct feature of Martha's talks was that during her stay in both Portland and Seattle, the people who came once, continued to come again and again. . . . May a universal prayer go out for Martha's health, that she may have the strength to do His Will. . . . In all the worlds of GOD we shall be grateful that she came our way.[6]

With economy, rather than comfort, uppermost in her mind, Martha had asked George Latimer to book a third-class passage to Yokohama at $70, rather than $210 for first class; the difference would pay for printing the blue booklets in Esperanto. To her surprise a first-class passage was awaiting her, courtesy of Roy Wilhelm and his mother.

On 22 March 1923 Martha Root, the only American among the Japanese passengers, sailed out of Seattle aboard the *Kaga Maru,* with its prow set toward Yokohama. She seemed to have a talent for choosing the most uncomfortable season in which to sail. The spring storms were rampant, pelting the vessel with rain, sleet, wind, and raging seas, and reminded Martha of the tempestous journey to South America she had taken in 1919. During the three-week voyage there was one remarkable day of sunshine.

The intemperate ocean sent Martha to bed, where she stayed four days, fighting headaches, chills, and fever. Even so, she was beginning to rest, commenting, "Roy says the Lord has to break some people's legs to give them a rest. The hostess of the deep is even more thorough. If passengers did not stay in bed, she didn't hesitate to hit them with part of the library. Of course too she did not mind banging the whole table full of dishes right at them."[7]

In the dining room the captain seated Martha next to him, and he took the time to teach her a few words in Japanese. Of course, the blue booklets in Japanese, courtesy of Roy Wilhelm, were handed round and questions arose: "'Who 'Abdul Baha, who Baha'u'llah?'"[8] But a vocabulary of approximately fifty words was limiting. Only the captain spoke English, and he and Martha had many talks. She had given him *Divine Philosophy,* which he was reading.

After numerous postponements because of the rough ocean, a time was finally set for a lantern-slide presentation. On 7 April all the passengers and crew, "excepting the man on the bridge and the sleeping babes," came to view Martha's slides.

> The engineer set up the lantern and ran the slides. The Captain and I stood on the stage. He has read the blue booklet carefully and most of "Divine Philosophy". So he explained the Bahai Cause first and [then] interpreted as I spoke. The talk lasted one hour and everybody cheered the pictures. There are thirty fine boys and girls in the Third Class and I'm sure they will never forget who Abdu'l-Baha is. More than one hundred were present. . . .
>
> I realized how significant these slides are for foreign countries. The Oriental people love pictures, and with the pictures I could make them understand the life of Abdu'l-Baha and Baha'o'llah. Am very thankful I brought them.[9]

The weather reverted to chilling sleet and raging winds. The violent storm tore off the ship's railing near Martha's cabin, banged open the porthole, and deluged her and all her belongings, inconveniently at 2:00 A.M. She got up, dressed in wet clothes, and sat in the music room, while her coat and other things were put on a radiator to dry. A pot of tea was brought, and it was sent spinning across the room. Martha did not lose her sense of humor, commenting, "We were 'real movies.'"[10]

Discomfort or not, Martha was full of praise for the efficient captain and his crew. She was pleased, also, with her ability to use chopsticks and with her progress in Japanese, however slight. The cabin boy complimented her, "'Every day, every time, your Japanese language improving itself.'" Limited though her vocabulary was, the language inadequacy drew people to her. "Everybody laughs at it," she admitted. "I do too—but it has helped to make us friends."[11]

Her spirit must have pleased the captain. In the officers' dining room he gave a special Japanese dinner for her, called "Guy-na-be," prepared on a little Japanese stove with meats and vegetables. Many of the officers were present.

With it all, she was resting, taking a spiritual journey through the Bahá'í writings, and preparing herself for the work ahead. She dreamt of her father and saw him led by a child into the next world to his waiting wife and friends.

Because of the season and the violent storms she was doubly grateful to the Wilhelms for her first-class accommodations, as there was little or no heat in third class. Even so, she wore two sweaters and a winter coat when she sat down to do her writing.

On the morning of 10 April 1923 the *Kaga Maru* sailed into Yokohama Harbor. It had been almost a three-week adventure on the misnamed Pacific Ocean. Using her modestly expanded Japanese language, Martha parted from her shipboard friends and happily set her feet again on Oriental soil.

17   Back in Japan

After the cold, grim, and dismal weather, and the intemperate tossing about on the ocean, the stability and beauty of Japan in April was like paradise. It was cherry-blossom time, and the floral beauty and fragrance transported Martha to poetic heights. She likened the blossoms to "a caravan of drifted ivory which had marched with silver feet from some far sphere."[1]

There were two smiling faces waiting to greet Martha at the port of Yokohama—Agnes Alexander and Ida Finch, from Seattle. Excited about Martha's visit, they extended her a warm welcome to the country. Her luggage was collected, and the three friends headed for Tokyo.

Agnes had made many friends since Martha's first visit six years earlier and thus had a broad base of contacts that would spur the teaching. She had learned braille and worked with the blind; her skill in Esperanto opened many doors; and her university contacts were abundant. Talks had been arranged in many groups and clubs, and a full schedule was awaiting Martha.

After having been violently rocked in the ocean's cradle for almost three weeks, Martha took no time out for rest. She arrived in Tokyo at 6:00 in the evening and at 7:00 P.M. gave her first talk before two hundred students at Waseda University.* And so it went. From schools to clubs, to Theosophists and Esperantists, for ten days in Tokyo before going on to Kyoto, she talked about the new revelation and the principles it es-

_____
*Agnes Alexander, in her *History of the Baha'i Faith in Japan 1914–1938* (Tokyo: Baha'i Publishing Trust Japan, 1977), p. 46, seems to be incorrect in stating that Martha Root spoke "The first evening after she arrived."

poused. Martha loved the pace and the work. She called it "Bahai Sky Larking in Japan"![2]

One of the high points of Martha's visit was a talk given at the Chinese YMCA before a large group of Chinese students studying at the universities in Tokyo. She was impressed by their intelligence and earnestness, their bent toward brotherhood movements and away from the military. They represented to her the "'Renaissance of China.'" A student from Wuchang and Hangchow in China was particularly attracted to Martha; he acted as her interpreter and gave her letters of introduction to friends in those cities. Along with his friends, he attended almost all of Martha's lectures in Tokyo. "Because of Martha's selflessness and devotion," Agnes observed, "her presence brought confirmations wherever she went."[3]

But Martha soon realized that there were thistles among the

MARTHA ROOT
Canton, China, 1930

cherry blossoms. The Tokyo police suspected Martha Root of being a " 'Red,' " or Communist, and had her tailed for more than a week. All persons connected with her were questioned. The source of this suspicion stemmed from a remark made in a lecture to the Esperantists of Yokohama, when she stated that the Bahá'í movement was spreading to Russia. A conservative Japanese newspaper published a scare-producing headline and a story revealing a " 'communistic plot' " and stating that Miss Root was preaching " 'a doctrine practically the same as communism which is inconsistent with the Japanese Government's policy.' " A wire service picked up on the story, identifying Martha Root as a relative of Elihu Root, and elaborating on the situation:

> The police today visited the Tokio home of Miss Agnes Alexander, a relative of the famous family of missionaries and traders in Hawaii, who is entertaining Miss Root. They questioned the servants at great length. . . .
> Miss Alexander has been suspected since entertaining the Russian poet Eroshenko, who was deported from Japan a year ago as the result of a charge of Soviet conspiracy in connection with the Bahai movement.
> Miss Root . . . today appealed to the United States Embassy for protection. She had no intention of offending Japanese officials, she declared, and hopes to succeed in explaining to them why Bahaism does not menace Japan politically or religiously.[4]

The above excerpts from a news story appeared in Pittsburgh under a two-column headline, "Pittsburgh Girl Trailed by Tokio Police as 'Red,' " with a prominent subhead mentioning Martha, the Bahá'í Faith, and Soviet propaganda.

The police incident threatened to disrupt Martha's plans, but she was finally permitted to leave Tokyo after ten days. She was philosophical about the incident, but she did not relish the negative headlines in the Japanese newspaper involving the Bahá'í Faith. She felt that any new idea that the Japanese government did not understand was put down under the heading of dangerous thought. The event resulted finally in more positive coverage for the Faith than could otherwise have been achieved, as the more moderate Japanese newspapers came to the rescue with articles of explanation.

There were others in Japan who also had friendly feelings toward the Bahá'í Faith. The founder of Waseda University, Count Okuma, whom Martha had interviewed in 1915, had said to her, "'What the young men of Japan need more than anything else today is the pure Teaching of Christ or the pure Teaching of Buddha, but not the creeds of the Christians or the dogmas of the Buddhists. Perhaps this Bahai movement will offer this. I will read your book.'" When Agnes Alexander called on him later, she found that he had read the books Martha gave him and that his response was positive: "'I am glad you have come to my country to spread these noble principles.'"[5]

With her friends Martha left Tokyo and went to Kyoto and Kobe, where she spoke in each place to large gatherings of Esperantists. Martha took a little side trip to Ayabe before the three headed for Osaka to take Martha to the harbor. On 25 April 1923 she embarked on a steamer for China, her dream—one of them—about to be fulfilled.

18 China

China, China, China, China-ward the Cause of Baha'o'-
llah must march! Where is that holy, sanctified Bahai to become the teacher of China! China has most great capability.
The Chinese people are most simple-hearted and truth-seek-
ing. The Bahai teacher of the Chinese people must first be
imbued with their spirit, know their sacred literature, study
their national customs and speak to them from their own
standpoint, and their own terminologies. He must entertain
no thought of his own, but ever think of their spiritual welfare. In China one can teach many souls and train and edu-
cate divine personages, each one of whom may become a
bright candle of the world of humanity. Truly, I say they are
free from any deceit and hypocrisies and are prompted with
ideal motives.

Had I been feeling well, I would have taken a journey to
China myself! China is the country of the future. I hope the
right kind of teacher will be inspired to go to that vast empire
to lay the foundation of the Kingdom of God, to promote
the principles of divine civilization, to unfurl the banner of
the Cause of Baha'o'llah and to invite the people to the banquet of the Lord![1]

The challenge in this statement attributed to 'Abdu'l-Bahá
had long been a guiding element in Martha's life. Years before
events made it possible for her to go to China, she had eight
thousand copies of the passage made and sent to friends all
over the world. She hoped that someone, somewhere, would
respond to the summons of the Master. But, in the end, Martha
Root was the "holy, sanctified Bahai" who would take up residency in China. She had read and studied everything she could
about the country, the people, its customs and culture. Now
she was ready to settle down among them, learn from them,

and alert them to the spiritual dawn on the horizon. It was the beginning of her year in China.

Everything fell into place for Martha in this ancient land. On the train ride into Peking she learned of a language school, where she could enroll. At the school she heard about a British doctor, a woman, who had a rest house, or a small hotel, that needed a hostess. Martha called on her and was engaged. In exchange for a few courtesies she was given a lovely room, her meals, and laundry. Martha sat at the head of the table during meals, conversed with the guests, all Europeans, collected the money from them, and turned it over to the doctor. The residence was aptly called Ping an Fang, "House of Peace." Years later she recalled that

> "It was a beautiful house, with a centre courtyard. . . .
> "The meals and house were looked after by Chinese. All the cooking was done at the front of the house, and our rooms looked on to the courtyard, which was most picturesque. Sometimes in the moonlight we had dinner served there."[2]

The social graces did not take all of Martha's time. Within three weeks she had started tutoring a young boy three times a week, had met the head priest at the largest Muslim mosque and told him about Bahá'u'lláh, and had taught twice in the Yenching Women's College, where she was also invited to speak on universal peace and what the girls of China could do to further it. To friends back home she wrote that "I came home and wrote an account of this talk and mailed it to nine newspapers and newsbureaus. . . . The 'Chinese Standard' telephoned for my picture and sent a boy out for it, so I think the papers will use something."[3]

Her study of language occupied much time, and the method of teaching intrigued her. " 'We sat down,' " she explained during a newspaper interview, " 'and the teacher pointed at three of us, and uttered sounds until it dawned on me he was saying, "I," "You," "He," and that was how I was taught Chinese.' "[4]

Martha was entertained in Chinese homes where there were

other guests of interest. Among these was an artist whose work was currently being exhibited in a Peking museum. The painter, a Chinese woman, knew very little English but wanted to learn more since she was going to New York within a year. She offered Martha a wing in her home, with meals provided, in exchange for English lessons; she also promised to secure other pupils for Martha.

Since the House of Peace had only Europeans as guests, and as Martha longed to be with the people of China, she was tempted by the offer. She arranged to have Ida Finch, still with Agnes Alexander in Japan, come to Peking and take over the duties as hostess, while Martha moved farther out of the city to begin her new arrangement.

In the country Martha engaged a Chinese teacher to come each day to give her a language lesson, which she did not find easy:

the language is very hard to learn, one has to "sing" the sounds five different ways—it is not wise to trust to "picking it up" but it is important to have a very good teacher. If I speak correct Mandarin, it is respected everywhere and while language differs in different cities I will always be able to get around. . . . People here coming from other provinces can understand each other—only some words are pronounced differently.[5]

Although willing, if necessary, to pay for the language lessons, Martha was able to exchange her tutoring in English for Chinese.

Peking was, to Martha, the center of civilization in China, and the National University, with three thousand students, was the great center of Peking. She offered to teach an English course when it appeared that their Harvard-educated appointee, a Chinese, might not arrive. But he did appear, and Martha was greatly disappointed at the loss of such an opportunity. However, the magic of China held. A large, sealed envelope arrived, containing an invitation for Martha to write for an English-Chinese newspaper syndicate and also do articles for them in Esperanto. She accepted.

During her stay in China the political situation was a tangled web, infinitely complicated both in national government and within the provinces. On 12 February 1912, after the Ch'ing dynasty had come to an end, the Republic of China was inaugurated; but it was under warlord domination until 1928 and was plagued by constant fighting throughout the country.

In 1920 there was an attempt to combine nationalism with the strongly emerging force of communism in order to stay within the boundaries of the Versailles Treaty. Three years later, in June 1923, shortly after Martha Root's arrival in China, the Third Congress of the Chinese Communist Party became involved, under pressure, with the Russian system of communism. In addition, part of China was under Japanese domination. The multiple forces at work caused one political split after another.

Adhering firmly to the Bahá'í principle of noninvolvement in politics, Martha sidestepped those stories that could be compromising and resisted the urging by the owner of the syndicate to write political news. When the pressure increased, Martha wrote a letter of resignation, which she forgot to enclose with her newspaper copy. She prayed for guidance, for 'Abdu'l-Bahá to "SHOW me." To friends she wrote:

> He did show me. This morning came a beautiful letter that this syndicate hears from editors they are delighted with the news and several papers have used my stories on the front page—that is sure they are "news". (my name is never used, only the name of the syndicate and am glad because of political conditions in China). Also he wrote that the President of the Far Eastern Railway will give me a pass to Mukden in October when the corn harvests are on, that is most interesting time to write. So Abdul Baha put that journey off till cooler weather![6]

Martha was seeking for ways to get news of the Faith in print. A new avenue occurred to her:

> Yesterday I took a chance on sending in with my other copy, nearly a column about the Houses of Justice and used the

Name of Baha'o'llah.* It went to every English and Chinese paper in China and Philippines. Will try to send you copy of "The North China Standard" which has it tonight. That one story alone was worth the whole summer's effort. Perhaps others can follow from time to time. . . .[7]

For the Chinese editions Martha would get an article to the editors two hours earlier than she would for an article written for the English edition. This would allow enough time for a translation to be done.

Life continued to be full. There were talks to English-speaking groups and many calls on persons of rank to speak about the Faith, among them the adviser of President Li Yuan-hung. Martha interviewed the heads of corporations from Russia, the United States, and China for syndicate stories and spent time in libraries studying Chinese history and culture. But she slighted her study of language, as she could no longer do it daily and keep up with her newspaper assignments, which kept her on the move. Martha's teacher, whom she named "Dearest," was a strong Confucian with a beautiful spirit—"the finest spirit of any man I have met in China or any woman." Yet she lamented, "I WISH to study Chinese, of course I have no time to STUDY, I just pick it up from listening to my teacher. Probably he would like a pupil who would STUDY! Anyway, we may be meeting only for him to get the Message, he has the booklet."[8]

Even with a full schedule Martha took time to write to several individuals in the United States, with copies sent to Shoghi Effendi. She urged them to come to Peking, advised them of employment possibilities, and assured them of the beauty of the city and its people:

---

*Houses of Justice are the administrative institutions of the Bahá'í Faith, which are elected by the international, national, and local Bahá'í communities. At present, only The Universal House of Justice, which governs the affairs of the worldwide Bahá'í community, is referred to as a "House of Justice." The national and local administrative institutions are known, respectively, as National Spiritual Assemblies and Local Spiritual Assemblies.

> There is so much that is radiant, so much that is beautiful.
> I wish I could send you the charm, the old-time magic, the
> lovely art and the picturesqueness of Peking! It is glorious
> here, no one need ask for any greater favor than to live and
> die in China. I love China. . . . You will find the Chinese
> perfectly beautiful souls. Am wonderfully happy here.[9]

Martha also gave them clues on how to prepare at home for the
possible journey to nurture the seeds she had sown. It was her
hope to have the nucleus of a Bahá'í community in Peking before she left to travel to other parts of China. She had fallen in
love with China and its people and wanted them to be touched
by the Bahá'í revelation.

Although her life was busy, Martha missed her friends, but
she could feel their spirits near her, sustaining her when weariness washed over her. "I love China," she wrote to them, "but
I love you and China would not be so dear to me if your
love, your prayers, your letters, your spirit did not touch me
close."[10]

Inserting itself into the positive, enterprising glow was the
ugly spectre of illness, which haunted her hours. Martha became concerned lest her health fail and no one would be
spreading the Faith in China. There were days when she felt
that "only the Power of the Holy Spirit kept me on this plane."
At times she was in great pain, but she wrote, "The pain may be
to teach me that the Power of the Holy Spirit is the only
Strength that carries any of us forward."[11]

Despite it all, she continued tutoring. A friend helped by
projecting on his movie screen a complimentary advertisement
that she wished pupils. One of her favorite students was a nine-
year-old boy.

> "His parents were very wealthy and I had to call at their
> house. As soon as I entered, I was met by a servant with a
> bowl and a towel rung out in very hot water, so hot that there
> was no necessity to dry the hands.
> "I was then received by his mother, who could not speak a
> word of English, and my small pupil. We first were served
> with cakes, candy, and tea, and then the lesson commenced.

At first it was about the cat and the dog, and I said the words and then we played cat and dog. This was interrupted with gymnastics as a relaxation from the brain work, and then once again it was back to the cat and dog. Once a month they entertained me in a restaurant. Before I left I gave a tea party, and they both came with two servants. I had four servants, and mine stood behind the guests and their servants stood behind me."[12]

The child loved his American teacher, whom he called "Miss Loot," as did the other Chinese. His distress when he learned she was leaving was acute: "Such a thought had never entered his head, and he refused to eat anything. . . . The tears streamed down his cheeks, and he refused to wipe them away. It took nearly an hour to calm him."[13]

Children loved Martha. They seemed to sense her love, the purity of her spirit, and the absence of anything threatening or manipulative. During her visit in China she wrote a story about China for children and a "how to" article about talking, breathing, and memorizing the Bahá'í writings. Both appeared in the Bahá'í children's periodical *Magazine of The Children of the Kingdom.*[14]

Adults, too, were drawn to Martha. In the process of calling on persons of stature who might be friendly to the Bahá'í Faith, Martha made many friends who often invited her to dinner, where she could share her mission with their other guests. She, in turn, often invited her Chinese friends to dine with her. One of her calls was made on the President and Mrs. Y. S. Tsao, of Tsing Hua University. Dr. Tsao, a 1911 graduate of Yale University, and his Swedish-born wife, an American citizen, were married in London, where Dr. Tsao was serving his government. The friendship with Dr. and Mrs. Tsao, both broad-minded, thoughtful individuals, resulted in their later becoming Bahá'ís and giving years of open support and friendship for the Faith. Dr. Tsao arranged a lecture at the university and through the social door invited others on a spiritual quest.

Martha was sowing the seeds, opening the doors, begging for more literature, writing, and studying. She would not travel until she had a grasp of the language. By early fall she was also teaching as an assistant in an Esperanto school.

On 1 September 1923 a violent earthquake struck Japan and caused a major catastrophe. Two-thirds of Tokyo burned, thousands lost their lives, and more than a million were homeless. Ida Finch had left Martha on 19 August and was back in Tokyo, where she was talking to Agnes Alexander when the quake struck:

> without the slightest warning the house began to shake most violently. Miss Alexander escaped to the street, but it seemed impossible for me, so after it was over I joined her in the street, unharmed. We read the prayer of protection and remained on the street most of the afternoon for the quaking and shaking continued at intervals all day and for many days after. The house . . . was damaged and must be repaired that it may be an adequate shelter. I jumped into the little front garden and while repeating the Greatest Name saw the earth open around me and the house-front falling toward me. But I felt perfectly secure in His love.[15]

Ida had been in Tokyo making arrangements for her return to Seattle. She had planned to visit a friend in a neighboring district, but her intuition urged her to go back home. Half an hour later that entire area was demolished, its residents gone.

For days Agnes and Ida worked to clean up as best they could, slept in their clothes because of continued quakes and possible fires, and viewed with incredulity the streams of dazed and wounded survivors. Agnes recalled that four days

> "after the great quake and fire masses of humanity passed along the broad roadway near home, coming, coming, coming from the burning district below . . . scarcely anything to be found to eat . . . food was brought in from the outer provinces . . . there was no running water and the fires could not be put out; the trains and tramways, the gas, electric lights and telephones all ceased operating . . . with the help of a kind student friend I found my way to what had been the American Embassy; but only a few pillars re-

mained. The only center remaining at Tokyo was the New Imperial Hotel [especially designed by American architect Frank Lloyd Wright to withstand the earth's upheavals]. On the tenth of September Mrs. Finch left Tokyo to be taken by the United States Government on the steamer to Seattle." [16]

Miraculously, none of the Bahá'ís was injured. An incredible set of circumstances had either removed them from the affected area or had protected them in the midst of destruction.

With devastation everywhere and her house too fragile for habitation, Agnes Alexander succumbed to Martha's glowing word-pictures of Peking and its people. She decided to spend some time with her friend in China before returning home to Hawaii. By mid-October these two pioneers of the Faith were again working together. Agnes had many contacts in China with individuals who had been students in Japan; some of these were teachers or administrators in schools throughout China. Many were Esperantists.

The first to offer a forum for the Faith was Mr. Pao, who had visited Agnes in Japan with the editor of the *Canton Times*. He was working in Peking as a secretary to General Feng, who ran a school for children of army officers. Mr. Pao was delighted to find his American friend from Tokyo in Peking, and he arranged for Martha Root and Agnes Alexander to speak at the school. The idea of reaching the children of military officers with the spiritual message of peace delighted Martha and Agnes, who wrote years later, "Thus they became torch bearers of the Message of Baha'u'llah to General Feng's army of 10,000 men." [17]

One friend led to another in a chain reaction spreading the Bahá'í Faith. Martha had met a Mr. P. W. Chen, who was inspired by her lecture. Of him, Agnes said:

From the day Martha met Mr. P. W. Chen, he became a devoted friend and assisted us. It was he who saw the Baha'i books which Mr. Pao had brought from Japan, in Shanghai in 1920, and at Mr. Pao's request translated from them for a newspaper in Shanghai. In Peiping [Peking] he was a

teacher of a middle school. Through him Martha and I were
invited to speak in a large gathering on the Cause. He introduced us to a Mr. Deng Chieh-Ming, who became an ardent
friend to the Cause.[18]

Deng Chieh-Ming began an intensive study of the Bahá'í
Faith, felt the need for instilling these principles into the world,
and searched for a way to further the Faith. He would find a
means to do this before Martha left China.

By mid-November Martha was ready to do some traveling
outside Peking. With Agnes an itinerary was worked out. They
would visit three cities where Agnes had friends from Tokyo
and three others where letters of introduction from Peking
friends would open the way to speak in schools. So eager was
Deng Chieh-Ming to learn more about the Faith and to be helpful to the American ladies that he went along on the teaching
trip.

Lecture times did not always coincide with travel schedules.
They spent a night in Tientsin, where Martha had two scheduled talks the next day. The second talk was moved to the evening, forcing them to take a midnight train for Ginanfu (now
Chin-ch'eng). There was a special compartment for women. It
is hard to imagine the benign Martha Root and Agnes Alexander being a source of fear to anyone; but these Occidental ladies, perhaps because of their foreignness, frightened the Chinese women. Deng Chieh-Ming mollified their fears by
explaining that they were friends of the Chinese people and
were harmless. The women were calmed. After arriving at Ginanfu, Martha and Agnes found an Esperantist friend who arranged for them to speak in the Shantung Christian College.
During the lecture he translated their message into Chinese.

Martha had arranged the trip to include a visit to the town of
Chefoo (now Yentai), home of Confucius, Chinese philosopher and moralist, whose wisdom still permeates the Orient.
Martha and Mary Alexander, Agnes' sister, who was making
part of the journey with them, took a day's journey to visit the
sacred mountain before stopping in Chefoo.

To speak to the students in this town had a special meaning.
Here the descendants of Confucius, perhaps the seventy-sixth

generation, still lived. One of these descendants, a five year old, came with his mother and little servant to meet them. Martha, never without a token, gave the little boy a pocketknife that Roy Wilhelm had thought might come in handy. He had not realized that it would find its way into the hand of a little Confucian on the other side of the world.

Every location housing a friend was not necessarily a metropolis situated on a well-traveled route. Tsuchowfu (now Tsechowfu) was such a place. Agnes told about the experience in a history that was published several years later:

> On the way to Nanking, Martha and I dropped off the train at Tsuchowfu, where Miss Chien Yung Ho, whom I met in Tokyo . . . , had become principal of a school. She had invited us to stop there and tell her pupils of the Baha'i Cause. . . . It was very early on a cold morning that our train reached Tsuchowfu. Just as Martha and I stepped from the train, two American men were boarding it and asked where we were going. We found that the Chinese city of Tsuchowfu was distant from the railroad stop. They had come to the train in rickshaws and told us to take them and go to the house they had just left where a warm fire was burning. We were certainly protected and cared for by the Hand of God. The owner of the house where we were taken was an American who was in the Standard Oil business and was accustomed to taking in guests. When we told him of the school we wished to visit, he offered to go with us to the Chinese city, several miles distant, and inquire at the American Mission hospital where to find it. The school was near the hospital, and within an hour . . . we were telling the Glad Tidings to the pupils in that far away school. Then Miss Chien and other teachers arranged a gathering for us in the afternoon and we remained with them until evening, when we returned to the home of our kind host, and left early the next morning on our way to Nanking. . . .[19]

Nanking, a metropolis on the Yangtze River, had an abundance of schools. Again, a Tokyo friend arranged for talks in schools on all scholastic levels, where the teachers of English were interpreters for the message of Bahá'u'lláh. The same procedure was followed in the several schools in Soochow (now Wuhsien), and later in Shanghai, which would be the last city on their tour and from where Agnes and her sister would sail for Hawaii. Several hundred blue booklets, part of the luggage from Peking, had all been dispersed and were now part of the literature of China.

When they reached Shanghai, Martha was ill for several days and had to rest. She bid Agnes and her sister bon voyage at the end of December and settled in for a two-and-a-half-month stay in Shanghai. Feeling too ill to make her rounds of contacts with schools and societies, she occupied her time with writing articles about the Faith. By the second week in January she felt strong enough to take them to editors of newspapers. She was amazed at the results.

> Well, today nine papers have Bahai articles. In no city have I had such success in the publicity part in such a short time. . . . Coming to Shanghai I was not well for so long and yet I could write articles when I did not feel able to go out and make engagements and lecture, so that is why there have been so many articles just at first. But these articles have helped me in getting engagements to speak, so it has in reality done just as much good. O, Abdul Baha has blessed every move and am so grateful today. Have not time or money to go out and buy all the newspapers (some of them are 20¢ a copy too*). . . .[20]

The Confucian Association and the Theosophists contacted Martha requesting public presentations. The Esperantists quickly scheduled a lecture and brought followers from several cities to hear her; the lecture was being translated into Chinese, which would be gone over the day before with an interpreter. Martha had enough knowledge of Chinese to handle her everyday affairs but always used an interpreter for lectures to avoid any subtle intonations that would alter the meaning of her talk.

In preparing publicity about the Bahá'í Faith, Martha found that a picture of the model of the House of Worship in

---

*In 1924 newspapers in America cost two or three cents each.

Wilmette excited great interest wherever it was used. In this new city a prominent architect contacted the owner of the *Shanghai Times*, who had become a friend of Martha's, to get more information about the House of Worship, and he was directed to Miss Root. His excitement about the architectural originality was enhanced as he learned about the Faith and the model, which reflected beauty and unity.

Martha's health was improving, and inevitably the public pace resumed. She wrote to her friends:

> I leave many things undone, and every day I lie down for two hours to get the strength to do the most important work—I mean in Shanghai I have done this and thus the strength has come. Abdul Baha knows I have done my utmost. The test of the year is if the Message has been spread in China, it isn't a question of health or how much or how little work, but only if the Holy Spirit has poured over China. . . .

And she added, "Roy, the 'two miles of bad roads' as we used to say, are over for Shanghai, I think."[21]

Many newspaper editors had become Martha's friends, and she was asked to write articles for the *Shanghai Times*. She happily accepted the assignment, once again moved in the tide of people, and became part of her adopted region. Her writing was also a useful tool in reaching out to the people of the area, and her circle of friends broadened daily, nurtured by a lecture schedule that continued to be full.

As the time for her stay in northern China diminished, Martha felt the need to travel to the heart of the country. True to form, she chose February, the coldest time of the year, to embark on a nineteen-day trip. Third-class travel was cold and cheerless, and the least costly hotels chosen by Martha yielded little in the way of warmth and comfort. She was hardly coddling a recuperating body.

Internal wars prevented her going to many of the places she had planned to visit, but she managed to get to a number of towns and cities, among them Wuchang and Hangchow, home base of her interpreter in Japan. She was seeing China, and she was staggered, awed, by the immensity of the country. "There is no end to China!" she discovered. "On beyond Changsha, out in the West is Szechuan Province with a population greater than that in the United States!" The vast numbers of people challenged her imagination to find comparisons: "If the populations of Austria and Hungary, Belgium, France and Germany, Italy, England, Scotland, Ireland, Wales, Japan, Mexico, and Spain were wiped out, these countries could be . . . repeopled by Chinese and leave enough people in China to give it a population as dense as that of the United States."[22]

Martha had sprinkled a part of that vast heartland of China with a small portion of the teachings of Bahá'u'lláh. Moved by the modesty, humility, and gentleness of the Chinese, her love for them deepened. "It is a Favor and a Bounty of God to have the privilege to do anything for China. I do not think one of you will ever come who will not love the Chinese people."[23]

The trip, despite its being an extraordinary experience, was arduous and debilitating and had taken its toll. Once again Martha was struggling with the perversity of her physical frailties. She hated the thought of being weak, of having to rest. As she reported her situation, a note of defensiveness crept in, a response to those friends who felt she should greatly modify her activities.

> If any of you took these trips, you would be just as likely to be ill as I. I have not spent the money to go first class and to stay in the steam-heated, expensive foreign hotels. I have gone as economically as possible, for I have very far to go. It was the worst season of the year to go to Central China, but none of us ever stop for weather. All are ill sometimes and nothing matters if in the time we are well, we have faithfully sowed the seeds for a divine civilization.[24]

Yet the state of her health did not prevent her from fulfilling an intensive ten-day series of lectures in schools and clubs before leaving Shanghai.

She was desperately unhappy about her capricious health, but her sagging spirits soared when she received a letter from

'Abdu'l-Bahá's sister, Bahíyyih K̲hánum, known to Bahá'ís as the Greatest Holy Leaf. It was a simple note, written in English by a visitor in Haifa, but it vaulted Martha to the skies. There, in the heart of China, came love and encouragement and welcome news of prayers being said at the holy shrines for Martha's health and for her work in China. It transformed an aura of gloom into one of radiance.

Before leaving Shanghai, Martha fulfilled another task she had set out for herself: to have the blue booklets, Big Ben and Little Ben, translated into Russian, in anticipation of a visit to that other vast country. With such last minute details addressed, she packed her bags and, on 27 March 1924, sailed down the east coast of China to Hong Kong, where new goals waited to challenge her.

19 Hong Kong

Hong Kong was a beehive of activity and enterprise, a British crown colony with a large English population, located southeast of China at the mouth of the Pearl River, and at the conjunction of the Formosa Strait and the South China Sea. The city was as intriguing as its situation and was one of the liveliest and most colorful places in the world.

The bustle and frenetic energy did not deter Martha Root from her single objective—to get out the message of Bahá'u'lláh. After arriving in Hong Kong at the beginning of April 1924, she made her calls on editors, university presidents, librarians, to whom she described the Faith and left literature. She had already visited nineteen of the leading cities in China, had lectured in all of them, and had come to Hong Kong with her credentials of accomplishment.

Speaking invitations rolled in, articles were written, talks were given, and the Bahá'í Faith and its devotee became known throughout the area. With it all she made friends and warmed the hearts of those she met. So exceptional were Martha and her work that the *Hongkong Telegraph* paid her a special tribute—an editorial, highly laudatory to both Miss Root and her religion. It stated in part: "we can all the more readily admire the effort to sow the good seed; and however much might fall on stony ground, some is sure to find fertile soil in which to take root." [1]

One of her most important lectures was given at the Hong Kong University, and exceptional coverage appeared in another of the most prominent morning papers. The account included a reference to the Indian poet, educator, and humanist Rabindranath Tagore. Martha noted that one of the questions asked by Mr. Tagore on the first day he arrived in Hong Kong

was " 'How is the Bahai Cause progressing?' "[2] It was an item
not to be overlooked in this multicultural, cosmopolitan city of
the Orient.

From Hong Kong Martha managed to take a brief trip to
Canton, where conditions were explosive. At least one person
was deeply moved by one of her lectures and wrote a lengthy
letter expressing a change that had occurred: "Although I had
read of the Bahai movement before, it was not until I saw the
Bahai principles as lived out in your life of unselfishness, kindness, and simplicity that I began to comprehend their fuller
meaning."[3] He then set about studying the Bahá'í Faith in earnest.

Martha's talks were not scholarly, but simple, direct, un-
adorned statements with concentration on one or another aspect of the Bahá'í Faith, including its principles and the lives of
the central figures of the Faith. But when Martha spoke, her
plainness was transformed. She glowed with a spiritual light,
and the purity of her message and motives made her a compel-
ling presence. There was no ego involved, only the need to tell
people of the oneness of mankind and the route to achieve it.
There was no aggression, no stridency, only love—a deep,
penetrating love that made itself felt wherever she went.

Martha did not limit her efforts to the more obvious seed-
sowing activities; she became a part of the community of China and tried to enrich lives in other ways. She loved working
with students and admired their intelligence, their demeanor,
and, especially, their lack of vanity. In a newspaper article she
recounted an incident that demonstrated their self-effacement:

> "One student was to play the flute at a club concert. Instead
> of facing his audience, he went and stood in one dark corner
> of the platform, with his face to the wall, that the beautiful
> melody might float out without a sight of the human agent.
> The Chinese have absolutely no egotism in their makeup."[4]

It was probably in Hong Kong that Martha started a public
questions club, which reflected her journalistic interests, and,
surprisingly, a musical club, which was most likely devoted to

Western classical music. Where she found the time and strength to be involved in such additional activities is a source of mystery.

Before giving five scheduled lectures in Hong Kong at the end of May, Martha took a four-day sea trip in a cargo boat down the China Sea to Saigon and Cambodia. She apparently was the only passenger, at least in a stateroom, on an immaculate, beautiful little boat named *Lorestan*. The voyage was blessed with calm seas, an uncharacteristic situation for Martha. She luxuriated in reading, relaxing, making friends, and eating with the officers on the veranda of the cargo-yacht. It was an experience of undiluted joy.

She spent a week in the Saigon area of French Indochina, then an idyllic spot with superb roads and railroads, and traveled about in an "atmosphere of infinite purity and softness," which fed her aesthetic sensibilities.[5] She went on into Cambodia and, as always in the Orient, fell under the spell of the culture, the unmatched architecture, the enigmatic ruins, and the loving, gentle people, whom she loved as well. She sampled all types of transportation, including the rickshas and elephants, and was captivated by the sampans.

Of course, Martha went to the newspapers, including those published in French. She made friends with the only female editor in Indochina, a dynamic French woman, who published a succession of Martha's articles with pictures. The Chinese and Annamite (now Vietnamese) papers were equally receptive and published several articles. However, a public lecture could not be given without the permission of the governor. In an account published in *Bahá'í Magazine: Star of the West* she explained:

> After a call upon the Governor and presentation of credentials—also a copy of the lecture written out specially to show him—the Governor himself telephoned the President of the largest school, giving his approval of a lecture. The students represented all the different religions, and there was a true spiritual bond between students and speaker, for all were the friends of God![6]

Martha felt a strong chord of harmony with all the Southeast Asians and reluctantly left them to return to Hong Kong. On the ship, the same *Lorestan,* the captain jokingly feared that with the large amount of cargo, plus many more passengers, they would all go down to watery graves. " 'You see this Bahá'í business has got into our veins,' " he admitted. " 'We can't force them off, we are brotherly!' " [7] Those who had come aboard with their food and basins were camping out on the lower deck. Soon they were all reading Bahá'í booklets.

Returning to Hong Kong at the end of May, with the lectures over and the work done, Martha's goal was fulfilled. During more than a year in China, she had brought the Chinese people her greatest gift, the word of Bahá'u'lláh. Before she left, Deng Chieh-Ming had started a Bahá'í university. It was set up along the usual lines, but it also had daily lectures in Esperanto, and was permeated with a spirit of tolerance, and grounded in the religious unity of mankind.

Because of Martha Root's efforts with lectures and in print, she reached millions of people in China who had not heard about the Bahá'í Faith. Many more people read about the Faith in Chinese newspapers sent to the Philippines. Although she was leaving, she carried the love of the Chinese in her heart. Now Martha Root strapped her bags, tallied her luggage, and set her sights on Australia.

20 Australia, New Zealand, and Tasmania

Having left the burning heat of Saigon in May 1924, "as hot as India at its hottest," and the comfortable warmth of Hong Kong, the ship sailed to Australia, "down and under," with the perversity of having its winter when most other spots were enjoying summer.[1] Although the seas were not the gargantuan displays experienced on the *Kaga Maru,* it was a stormy twenty-eight-day voyage, and Martha was desperately ill much of the time. The ship sailed the length of Australia, with Martha disembarking at the southeastern tip in Melbourne.

Unlike her arrival in China as a solitary figure, unknown, with no one to greet her, and with no accessories to make decisions and arrangements, she was given an elaborate welcome in Melbourne. There were dozens of bouquets, baskets of fruit, and gifts of every kind. Martha was overwhelmed. There were not many Bahá'ís in Melbourne and vicinity, but the spirit of love and warmth infused a weary Martha with renewed vigor and gratitude for the Bahá'ís. They had some knowledge of her work in China and of her earlier journeys on behalf of the Faith, and their extravagant welcome was in appreciation for past efforts and anticipation for help to spread the message in their vigorous land.

Also waiting for her was a railway ticket, enclosed in a letter from Clara and Hyde Dunn, asking that she join them in Perth, on the other side of Australia. Later they would spend time traveling with Martha back toward the eastern part of the continent.

After two days' rest and a winnowing out of her belongings, some of which she sold to replenish diminishing funds, Martha was once again on the move. She boarded a train that would take her from the east coast to the west, across the entire Aus-

MARTHA ROOT
July 1924, in the western port city of Perth, Australia,
where she was the guest of Hyde and Clara Dunn.

tralian continent to Perth, on the shores of the Indian Ocean. Again the open-hearted hospitality of the Australians and their appreciation was shown by the masses of bouquets and gifts for Martha. Special among them was a necklace, ornamented with her name. In a letter to some friends she recalled, "I sold everything I could part with, beads, necklaces, clothes, etc., in Melbourne and then come up here and get this exquisite necklace! Their financial gifts of money have been a wonderful help so my expenses in Australia will be easy."[2] It was a welcome to melt her heart. And there were the Dunns.

Clara and Hyde Dunn of California were described by Martha as "two Bahá'ís, with beautiful grey hair and sweet young faces . . . filled with Light and Love. . . ."[3] They had come to Australia in 1920 in response to 'Abdu'l-Bahá's Tablets of the

Divine Plan. Not young, they had given up everything and sailed to Australia, practically out of funds. They struggled against vicissitude, became successful in business, and were a model of love and unity. Wherever they went, they sowed the seeds of the oneness of humanity. There was an energy about them, and they were a powerful example to all they met. The Faith began to spread, not in vast numbers, but modestly and consistently. During a vacation they had taken the message to New Zealand, and the nucleus of a Bahá'í community was formed.

Martha stayed with the Dunns, and they did everything for her comfort. Clara massaged Martha's back to ease the nagging pain and, with Effie Baker from Melbourne, set about restoring her physical well-being.

But Martha's purpose never flagged. Reporters came for interviews, and her rhythm of teaching fell into place. Australia had a large, diversified group of clubs and societies, all of which she addressed. She spent the month of July in Perth, lec-

HYDE AND CLARA DUNN
who, in response to 'Abdu'l-Bahá's Tablets of the Divine Plan, left
California to bring the Bahá'í Faith to Australia. The photograph
was taken before Clara, with Martha Root, bobbed her hair.

turing thirty-eight times. A special event, with admission charge, was a lecture on "The Great Renaissance of China," held in the Literary Institute.[4] On the stage was a map of China and immense flags of every country. The Chinese of Perth came in a body, the American consul sat on the platform with Martha, and she was introduced by the mayor.

A new teaching tool appeared. The West Australia Wireless invited Martha to broadcast a talk on the Faith. Arranged for 28 July 1924, the broadcast gave Martha her radio debut. With such a successful teaching event behind them, the Dunns, Martha, and Effie Baker, whom Martha referred to as "the sweet toymaker," left Perth, where the Bahá'í community had swelled from two to thirty-six, and traveled back across Australia.[5] Hyde Dunn often was able to combine teaching with his business trips.

Martha and Effie left the Dunns at Adelaide and went on to Melbourne, where she gave twenty-five lectures. The publicity was extraordinary, and everywhere she was showered with attention. Receptions were given before or after talks; there were teas with Martha as guest of honor; announcements of open houses were made for the discussion of the Faith. Officialdom welcomed her, and an admirer presented her with five thousand Bahá'í booklets that he had had printed.

In Melbourne, after a lecture to the Esperantists, Martha was again invited to broadcast. She had a perfect radio voice—clear, firm, mellow—and her spirit reflected in her tones. The new communication medium was still in its infancy, but its implications for spreading the word excited Martha. "The Words of Baha'u'llah about an international auxiliary language went out three thousand miles," she remarked. "Ships on the ocean sent back wireless of approval and a telegram of congratulations was sent from Queensland, the far North."[6]

Months later, after a talk in Adelaide, Australia, a newspaper account appeared under the headline "Miss Martha Root on the Wireless." A portion of the story reported one listener's response:

Seated in my dining room at Malvern on Thursday night I heard on the wireless, as clearly as if the lady were next to

*Martha Root (front row, right) with a group of Bahá'ís in
Melbourne during her first trip to Australia in 1924*

me, Miss Martha L. Root, the American journalist and
traveller. . . . We were trying to pick up music at the time,
and this fine, carrying voice, of charming accent, broke in
surprisingly. So engaging were the tone and style of the visitor that there was no resisting hearing her to the very end.

"It is as easy to have universal peace as war," were the
first words which came through. "We must teach universal
peace in all the public schools." Then Miss Root proceeded
to advocate the formation of a world-wide committee of the
best linguists, because there could never be universal peace
without some kind of universal language.[7]

There followed a summary of the principles that she advo-
cated, a report on the numerous clubs and groups where Martha had spoken, and an expression of admiration for her work.
The modern technology was a miracle to Martha, and she
would use it to its fullest.

Although surrounded by loving friends and a receptive, ad-
miring public, the strain of the lecture schedule in Perth and
Melbourne in July and August had affected Martha's health.
She decided against any further lectures because "it seemed

humanly impossible to take it" and made arrangements to sail on 4 September, weeks earlier than originally planned. With the temperature changes and the lack of rest, Martha had another attack of grippe: "in Melbourne . . . I kept going—I did not miss a lecture—it hurt my heart and gave me a pain in the back of the neck that would not go away."[8] Here was the onset of a physical problem, the neck pain, that would subside at times but would torment her for the rest of her life.

Although it seemed best, Martha hated leaving Australia so soon without going to New Zealand and Tasmania when she was so near. The decision became a burden. Another burden was her inability to maintain correspondence with her newly made friends in China; it aggravated her, and she chided herself for not doing things properly. Torn between her desire to serve and her physical need to rest, Martha cabled for guidance to Bahíyyih Khánum, who was administrating the affairs of the Faith at the Bahá'í World Center in Shoghi Effendi's absence. She wired back, "'Your wish.'" So the decision was squarely with Martha. In a letter to friends she revealed her feelings:

> I just could not come to the ends of the earth and then give up raising the call in Sydney, this important capital[,] and New Zealand. . . . So I decided to come forward and since then Abdu'l Baha has showered me with greater strength and love and gifts of money for my passage and steamer rug and woolens.

Martha prayed all the healing prayers and admitted, "I might go and take a 'rest cure' and die, and I might go faithfully forward to raise this Call in New Zealand and get well doing it."[9] The humanly impossible was accomplished. In mid-September Martha and Effie sailed from Sydney to New Zealand, which was "my ideal of Heaven," and spent twelve lecture-packed days in Auckland, and two days in Wellington.[10]

The labor groups were strong and active in this part of the world, and many of Martha's talks were based on Bahá'u'-lláh's solutions to the economic problems and His teachings on

*Martha Root (on the right) in Auckland in 1924. With her is
Margaret Stevenson, the first Bahá'í in New Zealand.*

labor and management. Her audiences numbered usually four
to five hundred, sometimes more. Of one she noted:

> Universality of the Bahai Cause is shown in the fact
> that . . . a lecture on "A New Phase of the Economic Prob-
> lem" was given . . . before . . . [a] large audience of social-
> ists, Bolshevists, I.W.W.s, atheists and agnostics. So enthu-
> siastic was the response that she was invited to return and
> lecture before the Women's Labor Group.[11]

In Auckland she addressed the Labor Party at the Strand
Theatre, with two thousand persons attending, and had tea
with the labor leaders. In Wellington she spoke to the Labor
Party for Men and separately to the Labor Party for Women,
who gave her a large reception that was well covered by the
press.

These talks were but a small segment among others given to

churches of every sort, to Boys' Clubs, Girls' Clubs, Esperantists, Theosophists, teachers' groups, the Spiritualists, the Rotary Club. In Wellington Martha gave five major lectures in one day, the most she had ever done. Everywhere the press turned out and gave Martha Root a celebrity's coverage. There were long stories with pictures and summaries of her life and of the Bahá'í Faith. She was also interviewed by several magazines.

During her two weeks in New Zealand there was not an idle moment. The Call had been raised, letters of introduction exchanged, and friends made for the Faith. In early October Martha and Effie left heavenly New Zealand to return to Sydney. Of the sea trip Martha later quipped, "If I were a sun-dial and only recounted the hours of 'sunshine' I would not tell you that the [Tasman] sea between Australia and New Zealand, at least in the equinoctial season is more indescribable than Hades—it is one of those little purgatories with a Heaven on each side." [12]

Martha and Effie arrived back in Sydney, the site of one of the world's most beautiful harbors, on 7 October. Staying again at the Salvation Army hotel, "very plain but clean," Martha notified no one of her arrival and took two days' rest. [13] Here she also found an opportunity to write, thus modifying one of her pressing burdens. This coming into a city unannounced would become a trait of Martha's, as successive journeys to successive countries became a way of life, and the accretion of unfinished work demanded solitude. Sometimes she did it because of health.

In Sydney, Australia's capital, Martha's appearances ran the gamut from the high world of officialdom, where every other person seemed to be a lord or lady, to the more modest levels of society. Friends received a short account of her visit:

My first talk was at a tea given before the English Speaking Union, two hundred guests, in the Astor tea room. The guests of honor were Sir Keith Smith (the aviator who made the first flight from London to Australia), Lady Smith and myself. . . . Sunday afternoon a talk was given in the open air, in the Domain Park, before the Labor Party. I stood on a big auto truck and "shouted"—There was an immense crowd, at least a thousand. The same evening a lecture was given in the New Thought Centre and the hall was crowded.[14]

It is difficult to conjure up the image of Martha Root, dignified lady, speaker at literary clubs and genteel forums, standing up in a truck to be seen and shouting to be heard, in order to give the message to a thousand Australians gathered in the park. It was the quality of detachment from a self-image that lifted her above the ordinary.

Martha spent nine days in Sydney, giving a minimum of two lectures per day. The Psychological Club, the New Civilization Center, the Women's League for Peace and Freedom, all were part of her schedule. And everywhere she spoke to the Chinese, with whom she seemed to have a special affinity. While still in Australia, shé learned that Deng Chieh-Ming in China was giving examinations for the opening of his new Baha'u'llah—Glory of God—University. He had found a way to instill the Bahá'í teachings into the Chinese culture.

After another busy nine days of teaching in Hobart and Launceston, Tasmania, and four more days in Melbourne, Martha sailed to Adelaide for a brief reunion with the Dunns. It was to be her last stop in Australia before visiting South Africa. Her travels had not allowed for a time of rest or even a modified program; all of her talents were being taxed to new limits. During the course of five months, June–November 1924, Martha had blazed a trail, meteor-like, that would be hard to equal. In appreciation the people had sent her gifts of woolens and a thousand useful things. The Bahá'ís, aware of Martha's continual expenses, gave her gifts of money; for they realized that her life was a mission for the betterment of the world, but supported by her own limited means. She spent nothing on herself—there were no frivolities—and they wanted to share in some way, however small, the work she was doing.

Of the success in Australia and New Zealand, Martha said it

was due entirely to the unselfish work of the Dunns, the foundation they laid, and their exemplary lives, which created a unity and spread beauty and energy along their path. Her praise of their work was boundless, her admiration infinite.

21   South Africa

The *Balranald,* a third-class, one-class ship, which Martha boarded in Melbourne, sailed out of Adelaide on 13 November 1924, bound for Cape Town, South Africa, and carrying a very tired, ill Martha Root. She would not be restored to warm spirits and good health until after getting around the bight—that area of roiling water at the mouth of Australia.

In Adelaide the Dunns had brought gifts of tea and oranges, chocolate and crackers; Effie Baker had made Martha some summer dresses in anticipation of the South African heat; the head of the Nestle's Milk Chocolate firm sent a large box of chocolates for Martha to share with the children on board; and there was an abundance of gifts from other friends expressing their thanks and wishing her bon voyage.

The three-week trip was a time of rest and recuperation. At the early stages Martha was too sick with a deep-seated cold and exhaustion to be involved with activities on the ship. She was steeped in kindness and treated with the greatest care and solicitude. The purser moved her out of a cabin shared with others and into a four-room suite, without extra charge, where she enjoyed the solitary splendor. He sent in baskets of fruit and offered to satisfy any culinary desires her stomach could handle. The stewardess, too, "has just spoiled me."[1] As a result, Martha soon overcame her indisposition and shared with other passengers the gifts from the horn of plenty. She also shared with them the Bahá'í Faith, giving two lectures with nearly everyone present. The aura of kindness and friendliness made it the best ocean experience she had ever had.

In Durban, South Africa, there was a three-day stopover, which she used to lecture and to make contacts for a return visit. She arrived on Tuesday at noon and gave three lectures on Wednesday, being introduced and entertained by the mayor of Durban. Again, the press was responsive and looked forward to her return. Despite the oppressive heat, she loved South Africa, "because it is bathed in sunshine."[2]

On the last leg of her voyage from Durban to Cape Town, at the confluence of the Indian and Atlantic oceans, the seas were so rough that Martha had to leave her cabin, take her steamer rug, and lie down in the air to control the seasickness. The heavy seas limited the number of talks, but the passengers knew of the Faith and of Martha's mission.

Fanny Knobloch, who was pioneering in South Africa and was one of three sisters who were all dedicated Bahá'ís, was waiting on the dock to greet Martha when the *Balranald* nosed its way into Cape Town Harbor on 8 December.[3]

These two pioneers—Fanny and Martha—worked together perfectly. Fanny's home on Camberwell Road was the hub from which messages and plans emanated. From there Martha, with Fanny at her side, embarked on the familiar round of lectures, receptions, and radio talks.

Describing Martha as a lecturer, Fanny wrote to her sisters:

she arose—all in white, like a Spirit come to us on the sunbeam, which might suddenly cause her to vanish from before our eyes. . . . How wonderfully she presented the Teachings. Surely, surely, she is filled with the spirit of our Glorious Lord.

His presence with us . . . was felt by all and we were happy beyond words.[4]

As in Australia and New Zealand, Martha was again treated like a celebrity. The mayor and leading citizens introduced her to the lecture audiences and entertained her in their homes. One ardent admirer of both Martha and the Bahá'í Faith was the former mayor of Cape Town. He sought to make her stay in South Africa as comfortable and attractive as possible; among other amenities, he changed her third-class rail ticket to first class. Martha later recalled that she "rode right through South Africa in a little private room! It certainly was a great blessing to have that rest on the train."[5]

Fanny was stunned by the mountains of correspondence that Martha tried to maintain, even while traveling: "Martha's

FANNY KNOBLOCH and MARTHA ROOT
in Cape Town, South Africa, December 1924.
Martha had bobbed her hair in Australia.

correspondence calls for a typist but we can't afford it so we just 'keep on, keeping on. . . .' "[6]

The month in Cape Town must have seemed like a grand example of American energy at work. Even in the intense heat, in the days before air conditioning, Martha gave thirty lectures, four of which were broadcast. In addition, there were small gatherings, individual meetings, and receptions. She was sowing seeds in the garden that Fanny had furrowed and would leave them for others to nurture.

On 10 January 1925 Martha started on the two-day journey into the Transvaal. Her plan was to visit the major cities in South Africa—Cape Town, Johannesburg, and Pretoria in the Transvaal—and then travel back to Durban, from where she would sail to England. She had considered going on to Haifa; but because it would cost an extra $230, and because no teaching by Bahá'ís was allowed in the Holy Land, she looked upon it as a luxury that would be sacrificed on the altar of economy.

Having booked passage to England, her plans changed magically. The work of an American Aladdin, the gift of a trip to Haifa appeared before Martha. As she sat in her private railroad room heading toward the Transvaal, she could contemplate the prize, the jewel, waiting in the near future.

But first there was Johannesburg. Here the reception to Martha and the Bahá'í message was exceptional, more than she could have hoped for. Every door opened, and again four of her lectures were broadcast. "Both Australia and South Africa say that God has gifted this servant with a voice that is heard very distinctly in broadcasting," she noted. "It is a wonderful way to promote the Bahai Cause."[7]

But the altitude in Johannesburg was a factor that had to be reckoned with. The heart is a barometer, and Martha's was affected. She had difficulty breathing and found that she could do "nothing except the lectures twice a day." She felt she had never worked so hard as she did in "Joburg."[8] Even though she turned down numerous dinner invitations, there seemed to be no shortage of social activities.

Everywhere the red carpet was rolled out, and Martha was received, entertained, and helped by friends and administrators. In a letter to her friends she told them that "The broadcasters, the Theosophists, the Spiritualists, the Esperantists, the Women's Clubs, and some of the Churches pass me on from one city to another, give me letters of introduction, or they themselves wire ahead."[9] The Chinese in every city were also among the sponsors of Martha's lectures. In Johannesburg she spoke to several hundred Orientals, and the Chinese consulate gave a reception in her honor.

When Martha reached Pretoria, the capital of South Africa, the mayor's wife came to call almost before luggage was opened and took Martha to visit various clubs, arranging talks. During her five days' stay an Esperantist, who knew the Zamenhof family, drove Martha to all her engagements. A Bahá'í from East Transvaal arrived in Pretoria to help during Martha's visit and was of great service in a city without Bahá'ís.

On the last stretch of her South African visit Martha went

back to Durban. There her days were filled with prearranged lectures, which were extended as she waited out a late sailing. She made several broadcasts, and numerous friends smoothed the way. The hospitality throughout South Africa deeply impressed Martha, who was struck by the immense kindness of the people. "They are beautiful," she observed, "and the sunshine of South Africa makes it one of the most lovely countries in the world."[10] One more area of the world had been enriched by 'Abdu'l-Bahá's courier. Martha was fulfilling His wishes.

22   The Approach to Palestine

During the first week in February 1925, traveling third class on the *Lanstephan Castle,* Martha sailed from Durban, up Africa's east coast, and through the Red Sea toward its destination, Port Said, Egypt. Even during this journey the ship became a vehicle for delivering the Bahá'í teachings. At the stops along the way Martha visited eight African coastal cities and delivered books to each of their libraries. In Zanzibar this modern-day spiritual courier brought booklets to the sulṭán.

While en route Martha also picked up a touch of malaria, which replaced the more usual and pedestrian seasickness and brought on chills, fever, and severe headaches. She recovered, however, and managed to enjoy the companionship of the other passengers. Although she was in third class, several persons who had heard of her work came to call from first class, offering their assistance in any way possible. Lady Rose-Innes and her husband, Brigadier General James Rose-Innes, were particularly helpful; they were friends of the Cape Town mayor who had been so touched by Martha's spirit.

For some reason Martha felt it took more courage to request permission to lecture on the *Lanstephan Castle* than on other ships on which she had sailed. But her Cape Town friends lent strong support, the captain was agreeable, and she gave a talk on the Bahá'í Faith as the ship sailed up the Red Sea.

Several hundred people were present. . . . We were going up the Red Sea—on the one side was the Land of Mecca, on the other the Land of Moses and to the North of us the Land of all the Prophets and Messengers of God, Palestine, the . . . New Promised Land! I told them the story of Baha'u'llah and Abdu'l Baha. Officers on the deck were from Khartoum [a city west of the Red Sea], and they heard the

201

story of Abdu'l Baha's and Hader Ali's imprisonment in the dungeon in Khartoum. The setting sun flooded us with its glory, then the lecture was over. There was a silent hush over the five hundred listeners and then a big applause.[1]

Martha's knack for friendship served her well during the trip. When she took time out from studying Esperanto "and rested my brains," she made a dress with material given her, a white wash satin.[2] A friend in first class cut it out and basted it, while Martha added the finishing touches. It would serve her for her talks, for which she always dressed in white. Other friends invited her to their homes in Scotland, England, and various spots on the globe.

After sailing for more than a month, the *Lanstephan Castle* was in sight of Port Said. Martha's fondest dream would soon be realized. To loved ones she confessed:

> You can never know what it means to be going to Haifa and Acca. I keep the fast and pray to be worthy to go.* Everything is packed and everything is as clean and shining as it can possibly be. . . . Ten years ago this month I moved heaven and earth and could not get from Port Said to Haifa, now Abdu'l Baha, my mother and my father have passed to the Kingdom of Light, and I a pilgrim feel I am going "home" in going there.[3]

Martha was enthralled at the prospect of meeting 'Abdu'l-Bahá's family, descendants of the Báb and Bahá'u'lláh. That included 'Abdu'l-Bahá's sister, the Greatest Holy Leaf, Bahíyyih <u>Kh</u>ánum; His daughters; and His grandson Shoghi Effendi.† The latter, a gifted and spiritual young man, had been plucked from his studies at Oxford in England to advise and administer the affairs of the Bahá'í world religion.

The awesome assignment bequeathed to him, together with the irreplaceable loss of His grandfather, 'Abdu'l-Bahá, in

---

*Each year Bahá'ís fast from sunrise to sunset for nineteen days from 2 to 20 March.

†*Effendi* is a title of respect, meaning mister or sir. <u>Kh</u>ánum means madam or lady. Shoghi Effendi's surname was Rabbaní.

whose shadow and love he had been reared, and with whom there was a mysterious, indissoluble bond, had for a time a crippling effect on Shoghi Effendi. He knew, better than any, the scope of his legacy. For almost two years before going to Oxford he had acted as 'Abdu'l-Bahá's secretary, had framed and translated letters, and had gained some familiarity with the needs of the Bahá'í community throughout the world. His deeply spiritual training and his sense of detachment left no room for ego; and as the enormity of his task struck him, a sense of unworthiness and inadequacy darkened his days.

During the difficult early period of Shoghi Effendi's ministry, the Greatest Holy Leaf administered the affairs of the Faith until he was able to assume his responsibilities as Guardian of the Bahá'í Cause. Gentle, retiring, compassionate, permeated with spiritual endowments and a wisdom born of innate talent and sobering experience, she guided the infant Faith through those troublesome days.

Her life had been tempered by more than forty years of imprisonment, deprivation, and cruelty. As a child she had been banished in 1853 from Tehran to Baghdad with Bahá'u'lláh and His family and forced to embark upon a grueling winter journey across the frozen, snow-encrusted mountains. They had only light, inadequate clothing for the difficult trip and barely lived on the insufficient food. In 1863 they were banished still farther from their homeland to the Turkish city of Adrianople. The final expulsion took the exiles out of Adrianople in 1868 to the prison city of Akka, where the Greatest Holy Leaf fainted from the suffocating stench of their noxious quarters. It was an incarceration that the authorities did not expect the exiles to survive. Bahíyyih Khánum had seen Bahá'ís tortured and martyred and had survived it all. Now in her mid-seventies she stood at the helm of the Bahá'í world community and served Shoghi Effendi, as she had served her Father and her brother, until this great-grandson of Bahá'u'lláh could devote his energies to the task that awaited him.

Gradually, Shoghi Effendi, whom 'Abdu'l-Bahá had called the "priceless pearl," assumed the Guardianship of the Bahá'í Faith. His was not a divine station, as was that of the Báb and Bahá'u'lláh, nor the special station bestowed on 'Abdu'l-Bahá as the Exemplar of the Faith. Yet Shoghi Effendi's station was unique and exalted. In His Will and Testament 'Abdu'l-Bahá designated Shoghi Effendi as "the blest and sacred bough that hath branched out from the Twin Holy Trees," whose shade "shadoweth all mankind"; he was also "the sign of God, the chosen branch, the guardian of the Cause of God," to whom all Bahá'ís must turn. He was also entrusted by his grandfather with the interpretation of the Bahá'í writings, the growth in the number of Bahá'ís throughout the world, and the creation of the divinely ordained world order of Bahá'u'lláh.[4] Such was the spiritual inheritance of this young man in a secular world.

Shoghi Effendi's days as the Guardian were filled with tribulation. The staunch Bahá'ís of the East and West wrote to him, assuring him of their love, loyalty, and support, which filled him with gratitude. But in other quarters he met envy, hostility, and acts of malice by those intending to put themselves in prominent and powerful positions. There was an absence of trustworthy souls to assist with the work. The world was still largely unaware of the message that was necessary to bring about global unity and peace, and there was a paucity of believers to spread that message. Some spiritually motivated Bahá'ís had left their homes and taken up residence in far-off places; others served on committees, gave talks, and spread the teachings as best they could. But the efforts were minuscule compared to the greatness of the task.

And then there was Martha Root.

Not only did Martha travel and teach; she wrote, and she saw to it that what she wrote was printed. She acted as a public-relations firm, in motion for the Bahá'í Faith throughout the United States and then in whatever country she appeared. Under 'Abdu'l-Bahá's tutelage she had turned her sights on the world. But she recognized and responded to authority. When the earthly leadership of the Bahá'í Faith was transferred by 'Abdu'l-Bahá's demise, at seventy-seven, to a twenty-four-year-old descendant, Martha unquestioningly submitted to the youthful head.

Newspaper clippings and accounts of her travels—lectures, receptions, interviews, itineraries—all began to find their way to Shoghi Effendi at the World Center of the Bahá'í Faith. He learned not of an occasional talk, but of several daily appearances; not of a handful of listeners, but of audiences of hundreds, occasionally one or two thousand; not of an isolated newspaper notice reporting a talk, but of numerous accounts with headlines and summaries of lectures and comments, pictures of the Wilmette House of Worship model, of 'Abdu'l-Bahá, and of the speaker. Martha's coverage of the principles of the Bahá'í Faith and their application to modern issues and developments, including radio broadcasts radiating to distant listeners, was all-encompassing and gargantuan.

Her accounts appeared in city after city across the United States, and in Yokohama, Tokyo, Kyoto; in Peking, Canton, Shanghai, Hong Kong; in Saigon and Cambodia; in Perth, Adelaide, Melbourne, Sydney; in Auckland, Wellington, Hobart; in Cape Town, Johannesburg, Pretoria, Durban. There, in print, were the evidences of a dedicated individual with a single purpose—to travel to every country in the world, to speak, to write, to inform as many persons as possible about the Bahá'í Faith and its message of universal peace.

To a beleaguered Guardian, Martha Root appeared as a torch, a resplendent light in a world of shadows, another Joan of Arc. Here was one whose devotion to a task set out by 'Abdu'l-Bahá would match his own, although performed on another level. Shoghi Effendi's letters successively revealed pleasure, amazement, gratitude, and awe at the unfolding accomplishments of this herald of the Faith. One of his earliest responses to her work, in which he expressed his admiration for her unparalleled services, reached Martha in Peking, December 1923. Another went to Shanghai in 1924:

My dearest Bahá'í sister:—
Your letters laden with the perfume of love & service revive & invigorate our souls & cheer our spirits. We thirst for more. You are always guided, inspired & sustained by the spirit of 'Abdu'l-Bahá. Go forth therefore confident & unafraid proclaiming far & wide the Divine Message of Bahá'u'lláh. You have my prayers & you may ever rely upon my boundless affection, my high esteem, my wholehearted & undiminished support.
Shoghi[5]

Martha's travels were already beginning to challenge would-be correspondents as to where letters should be sent. To eliminate confusion Martha used the American consulate as an address in whatever country she was visiting, and she always left a little money with the consulate to cover the additional postage of forwarding mail. Hence there was never a problem with undelivered mail. But a secretary to the Guardian wrote, early in Martha's wanderings, "Your restless activities in the service of the Cause have carried you so far and wide that it has already become quite a difficult matter to locate your whereabouts on any map." Shoghi Effendi added to this letter:

> My dearest most precious sister:—
> I am always anxious to hear from you as I deeply realize the signal service you are rendering to the Cause as well as the unsatisfactory state of your health. I pray for you from the bottom of my heart & I assure you that you are never never forgotten. . . . You are under His wings. He will surely guide you and lead you to success. I indeed have nothing to add, for your work is perfect, your efforts magnificent, your achievements glorious. I pray you may achieve your heart's desire.[6]

Martha's heart's desire—to go to Akka and Haifa, to meet Bahíyyih Khánum, and to confer with Shoghi Effendi—was about to be achieved, a positive answer to his prayer.

The *Lanstephan Castle* arrived early in Port Said, and Martha had to strap her bags and disembark about 10:00 P.M. But she had given a lecture and had spread the blue booklets among the passengers. Her heart was singing. It was 8 March 1925. Egypt was at hand; Haifa and Akka were near.

It took a few days to deal with the cumbersome necessities before the brief journey across the bay could be realized. Friends had also arrived from Australia and New Zealand, among them Effie Baker; from the United States, Corinne True joined the pilgrims. Together they arrived in Haifa on 13 March and were brought to the Western Pilgrim House, where they would stay during their long-awaited visit to the holiest places of the Bahá'í Faith.[7]

23   Haifa: The Spiritual Center

Perhaps no traveler before or since has more deeply appreciated the history and the significance of the hallowed region at which Martha Root had finally arrived. Here in Haifa rose Mount Carmel, the holy mountain, " 'the Hill of God and His Vineyard,' " sanctified by Isaiah as the "mountain of the Lord" to which "all nations shall flow," and the ancient home of Elijah.[1] Here on this mountain, praised by Bahá'u'lláh in His Tablet of Carmel, were entombed the sacred remains of the Báb, martyred in Tabriz, Iran, in 1850. The Báb's bullet-ridden form, except for the untouched face, had been secretly rescued and hidden, had been moved over the years from one hiding place to another, until, on 21 March 1909, 'Abdu'l-Bahá poignantly laid Him to rest in the shrine built on a spot designated by Bahá'u'lláh. Here, too, in a separate room was entombed 'Abdu'l-Bahá, Martha's mentor, Who brought love, joy, and wisdom to the world.

Lucy Wilson wrote that Martha seemed very close to the Master, that even after His passing she would carry on conversations with Him, as she did the last night of her father's life, seeming to know it was a terminal point. On other matters she seemed to have intimate knowledge, after communing with Him, of just where to go, what to do, how to carry on. Now she was within His special precincts—His home, His shrine, His land.

The approaches to the shrines and surrounding areas were still in a primitive condition, all of which would change under Shoghi Effendi's direction. Martha described going, on the second day, with the others past the beautiful new Western Pilgrim House, given by Ruth and Harry Randall: "up the ascending stony road, standing to rest and looking back one saw the ribbon road stretching down to the blue Mediterranean and beyond, like a gift from Heaven, nestled the little white city of Acca." The first moments at the Shrine of the Báb were vivid ones for Martha:

> The stately Persian Bahai caretaker took us to a bench[.] He took off his shoes. We did the same and then he led us to the door & into the Tomb of the Bab. Upon the floor were soft, rich red rugs. Going to the threshold of the shrine he knelt in sublime devotion. One by one, our group of pilgrims bowed the forehead to the threshold and poured out a prayer of deepest gratitude. How it flashed upon that inner eye that His Holiness, the Bab, shot against the walls in Tabriz had heralded in the Coming of the Promised One of all the ages! With what difficulty and danger had his precious

THE SHRINE OF THE BÁB
the resting place of the Prophet-Herald of the Bahá'í Faith, Haifa,
Palestine, as it looked in 1925 when Martha Root first visited it, and
before the superstructure and dome were added. 'Abdu'l-Bahá
was laid to rest in a separate room in the Shrine.

remains been hid for years and then brought secretly to this holy mountain[,] the . . . home of the exiles! The millions who kneel and pray at this Tomb of the Bab will go forth to be heralds of this Bahai Cause and some, like Him, will be Martyrs to promote these Teachings.[2]

Martha Root, pilgrim from the other side of the world, was drinking in the essence of this spiritual journey.

But a totally different experience awaited her when the pilgrims moved on to the adjacent tomb:

> Then going to the other room in this divine house, the pilgrims bowed with foreheads at the threshold of Abdu'l Baha's shrine. But He stood beside the pilgrims. This one heard Him say: "Be happy! Be happy! Be happy!" And again "Ye can always communicate with me through . . . [']Ya Baha El-Abha[.']" And again came His words, "Remember I am with you always, whether living or dead, I am with you to the end!"[3]

It is doubtful whether anyone but Martha Root heard those words of 'Abdu'l-Bahá, as she seemed to have a private line of communication. Her response was unique:

> In those moments of prayer at His Threshold the Beauty of the Holy Spirit swept the heart clean and empty. The Bab, Baha'u'llah and Abdu'l Baha stood together to answer the petition for Shoghi Effendi, for one's friends, for one's world work. The whole future was silhouetted in that memorable moment. The Hosts of the Supreme Concourse are directing. It will all come perfectly.[4]

There is no account of Martha's visit to Bahjí, the Tomb of Bahá'u'lláh, outside the city of Akka. Knowing Martha's spiritual capacity and depth of feeling, one can only sense the ecstacy and the reaffirmation of mission that this holiest of holy spots must have created.

During these jeweled days in Haifa there were several special visits with Shoghi Effendi. One day he invited her to the shrines to pray with him. At other times they conferred on her work, his aims, the teaching—they were all one. But her heart was burdened to see how hard he worked, often right through meals. It was a familiar story: an enormous amount of work, too few hours, too few hands and minds to help. One bright mind and noble soul, the Scotsman Dr. John Esslemont, was offering all he could. He had come from England to help the Guardian as a secretary, assisting with writing and translations; but the doctor's strength was waning:

> Dr. Esslemont helps him a great deal, but Dr. has been very ill, he came out of the hospital to his room last week and could walk out a little each day. Then he had a relapse and is now in bed. His health is very frail but he is so precious to the Cause with his writing, his Persian, his help in translating. Please let us pray for him strength to serve longer.[5]

If there could be no physical help for the Guardian, Martha felt there must at least be a show of love, of support. She wrote to friends, "After praying about it . . . I thought if we could each write him a little note of love and appreciation and urge him to take a little change just during the hottest weather, we would be remembering what 'Abdu'l-Baha told us about Shoghi." She described the Guardian as

> so spiritually beautiful. Every time I am with him I am so HAPPY! He radiates joy and love to everybody. His mind seems all comprehensive, he grasps the big problems and always knows just what to do; his translations are great—but he tries to dictate letters and perhaps add a few lines and doing this for all the world is taking his strength just terribly. . . . it is not giving him time for the other big questions which are crowding. You have no idea how many letters come asking questions. He wishes all to write, his joy is to hear the news of the Cause, but it is the ANSWERING that is going to kill him. . . .[6]

Martha stayed in this rarefied atmosphere more than a month, gathering physical strength and spiritual sustenance.

Martha Root (front row, second from right) with Bahá'ís in
Haifa, Palestine, spring 1925, during her first pilgrimage
to the World Center of the Bahá'í Faith

One of the richest experiences of this sublime visit was the time spent with Bahíyyih Khánum. From her Martha drank in the history of the Faith, the days in exile, the terrible days in the Akka prison, and her memories of Bahá'u'lláh, her Father— His unspeakable sufferings, His divine patience and courage. There were stories of 'Abdu'l-Bahá, His sacrifices, His generosity and selflessness, His concern for the poor, and their response to Him.

Bahíyyih Khánum told of 'Abdu'l-Bahá's return from His three-year trip to Europe and America and of His spending fifteen days visiting His friends and the poor people of Akka, told of their excitement, of their spreading the news of His return. They thronged to His house congratulating Him and themselves, saying, "'Where did you go & leave us without a friend and brother? Did you not know you mean everything to us?'" He had brought presents from Europe for them all, and warm overcoats for the poor old men of Akka. "This is what

BAHÍYYIH KHÁNUM, THE GREATEST HOLY LEAF
daughter of Bahá'u'lláh

he always did," Martha explained, drawing on Bahíyyih Khánum's account,

> if he had two cloaks he gave the best one & the warmest one
> to whomsoever needed it most—much to the disappoint-
> ment of his wife who wished her beautiful husband to be
> warm & to look well. His clothing was always immaculately
> clean, an example to the rich and a comfort to the poor.[7]

The beauty and benignity of Bahíyyih Khánum touched
Martha; she saw how one could overcome the gravest difficul-
ties and live without bitterness or anger, suffused with love.
Among her papers she noted:

> There is no detail even for your physical comfort too
> small for her to provide for and as for your spirit, almost un-
> consciously she trains you to meet your life with joy and

courage. You suddenly feel what a wonderful gift she has given you—the treasure of seeing how one can live a heavenly life on an earth plane full of troubles.[8]

Three doctors in consultation had advised Bahíyyih Khánum against getting out of bed, but she did not want to miss meeting with the pilgrims, and especially Martha, whose spreading of the revelation brought by her Father had captured her imagination and admiration, and who was daily in her prayers. Martha wrote of a special gift from her, recalling that she "put on our finger a little gold ring set with a soft red, glowing stone engraved with the symbol 'The Glory of God.'"[9]

Most impressive were the traits that added an Olympian grandeur to her presence. Martha noted her patience, her equanimity in the face of continuing problems in Haifa, and her infinite pity, love, and joy: "How truly expressive is her name, for Bahiyyih in Persian means 'full of light'!"[10]

Prayer beads given to Martha Root
by the Greatest Holy Leaf

More history of the family was gathered at the home of Rúḥá Khánum, 'Abdu'l-Bahá's daughter, who lived next to His home. She spoke of her father's teaching irrigation to the poor people, of His planting lentils and wheat, grains, beans, and barley during the war to feed the poor, as no government agency was concerned with them. She spoke, too, of the Master's almost prodigal unselfishness. A friend had sent some fur so that the Master could have a good warm coat; He had it cut up and made into twenty caps for the elderly men of the town.[11] Such stories became precious additions to Martha's memories of the Master's life.

Although Dr. Esslemont lay seriously ill in bed with tuberculosis, Martha was a welcome visitor to this brilliant medical scholar and linguist. They spent precious time studying Esperanto, of which he was a master. Later Martha would write to him urging him to teach Esperanto to 'Abdu'l-Bahá's youngest daughter. The doctor responded, "I shall be very pleased to take on Monaver Khanum as an Esperanto pupil if she cares to start. . . . I hope Monaver will turn out as satisfactory a pupil as yourself! I am proud of you."[12]

Another topic for their conversations in Haifa may have been Dr. Esslemont's recently published book *Bahá'u'lláh and the New Era*. Martha found the book to be an excellent teaching tool to supplement Big Ben and Little Ben, as it provided an extensive history of the Bahá'í Faith and a summary and explanation of its principles and teachings.[13] Three and a half of the early chapters had been read by 'Abdu'l-Bahá, Who had suggested some improvements before He passed away in 1921. The success of the book would confirm Martha's opinion of Dr. Esslemont as a great scholar. "Everything he did bore the mark of extreme efficiency. . . . ," Martha would write a few years later. "In our Esperanto work he was not satisfied with just any word, but sometimes we would discuss a dozen words and search their exact meanings in several dictionaries to find the word that would most brilliantly express the spirit of each thought."[14]

Several months after Martha had left Haifa, Dr. Esslemont would reciprocate her concern for his health by urging her to take time off from her taxing schedule. "I hope you will stick to your pious intention of resting a few days when you get to Budapest," he would write to Martha on 21 October 1925, "but Effie Baker has just been telling me about the way you carried out your plan of resting for a few days when you got to Sydney, and so I 'ha'e ma doots'!"[15] Although Dr. Esslemont would die on 22 November 1925, he had set the tone for perfection in language, a standard that Martha intended to reach, and he would forever be helpful in her teaching work with his book on the Bahá'í Faith.

Between visits with the Bahá'í residents in the Holy Land, there were opportunities for more meetings and conferences with Shoghi Effendi. He emphasized the need for Martha to concentrate all her energies on teaching the Faith—rather like urging William Shakespeare to stick to his writing. He shared with her some writings of 'Abdu'l-Bahá that he had discovered, containing predictions for Iran's future. He emphasized the use of Esperanto and urged her to publicize the current persecutions of Bahá'ís in Iran, a purge that foreshadowed another that would occur in the 1980s. And he opened up a new field of endeavor, one that would increase the stature of the Bahá'í

DR. JOHN E. ESSLEMONT
Esperantist and author of Bahá'u'lláh and the New Era,
the first comprehensive book on the Bahá'í Faith

Faith and put it in the center of world events. An International Bahá'í Bureau was to be established in Geneva, Switzerland, which Martha Root would open with the help of Mrs. J. Stannard of London and India. It would eventually draw on the abilities of other capable Bahá'ís as well. There was no hesitation on Martha's part. This new project simply meant a change of plans. Martha would again postpone her trip to England, and Switzerland would shift into primary focus. It was her first assignment as an emissary of Shoghi Effendi.

Of those last days in the Holy Land, Martha recalled that "All the sweet incidents of the visit to Haifa and Acca are just like the fragrance of the rose attar, Mary Magdalene used in her love for Christ—every day we still inhale that marvelous perfume!"[16] But this special time, this time with its ethereal overtones, was at an end. Haifa and the Holy Land were woven into the tapestry of experience as Martha left the spiritual womb and headed back to Egypt. She felt renewed, restored, blessed.

In Port Said she took a room in a small hotel, the Hotel de la Porte, where she could prepare her own meals and where friends could come to call. Among the visitors was Siegfried (Fred) Schopflocher of Montreal, who had come through China and Australia. It cheered Martha to know that the seeds she had sown were being watered. She also relished firsthand news of Harry Randall, Roy Wilhelm, and her other friends.

The last four days in Port Said were a special treat. She spent them at the home of 'Abdu'l-Bahá's youngest daughter, Munavvar, and Aḥmad Yazdí, her husband. There was mutual admiration for each other's lives and a joy in sharing time together. It was a rich experience for Martha and for her hostess, who wished to emulate Martha and to serve as she was serving; but Munavvar's duties lay in other directions.

Before Martha left, a letter arrived at Port Said from Dr. Esslemont in which the plans for Martha's work in Geneva were reiterated. Shoghi Effendi appended a note, which must have pleased Martha immensely. It was written, as he often did, at the bottom and around the sides of the letter in order to save space:

My dearest & most precious Martha

The fragrance of your visit has overpowered us all & as the days go by we feel more & more the penetrating power of your sublime love for & devotion to this mighty Cause. On behalf of the Family who love you dearly, & myself whose heart has drawn of late so close to you I wish to assure you again of our deepest gratitude for your stupendous efforts, our heartfelt appreciation of your magnificent achievements & our increasing prayers for your good health, happiness, prosperity & spiritual success. You are always with us wherever you go.[17]

On 5 May 1925 Martha boarded a ship of the Union Castle Line, which would sail from Egypt into the Mediterranean Sea, out of the Orient and into the West. Mr. Schopflocher, who was sailing later in the day, came on board with a box of chocolates and a beautiful letter containing twenty pounds sterling (a little less than one hundred dollars) to be used by Martha for her "comforts." Martha wrote to the Wilhelms:

it will be such a big help in the publicity work I so long to do—my "comfort" is to promote the Cause. I will use it very carefully and I think I shall later write Mr. Schopflocher and tell him just how every £ was spent. There is so much to do and everything costs so much.[18]

This friend, in turn, carried back presents from Martha. She sent perfume and a white woolen shawl to Roy's mother, some Egyptian-patterned cushion covers, suitable, Martha thought, for some niche in the West Englewood cabin, along with several other tokens from the Middle East. Her close friends were always lodged in the choice areas of her mind, right next to the work being done or about to be launched. She missed them greatly.

As the ship carried her toward Switzerland, Martha was preparing herself for her first stint in Europe, and she looked forward to the end of the voyage. Her stateroom, which was simple, neat, and clean, was unhappily right over the throbbing propellers. "Am traveling 3d. class," she told Lucy Wilson, "but 3d. class or first or any class I am always happy to leave a boat. I love train travel but am not fond of ship traveling."[19] Unhappily, most of Martha's highways were necessarily the oceans' arteries of the world.

Soon the vessel would dock in Genoa, Italy, and Martha would make her way via rail to Geneva. As she wrote letters and arranged her personal affairs, she felt a sense of peace and enrichment resulting from her experiences and friendships in the Holy Land. Her visit, which for many years had eluded her, fulfilled all of her hopes. At the same time she was filled with a sense of expectation for her work in Geneva, especially assigned to her by Shoghi Effendi.

24   Modes and Mores

High style was not a Martha Root hallmark. She did not go forth into the world as an exponent of the last word in fashion. This lack was not by design because Martha cared about how she looked. She gave more than a passing thought to what she would wear, what she had worn, and what her own perception of her appearance was—which was far different from the observations of others.

When it became evident that Martha would be making numerous public appearances, friends with good taste and the financial means to maintain a varied wardrobe would turn over to Martha clothes of fine quality, along with occasional pieces of lingerie, hoisery, gloves, scarves, and hats. It was rarely necessary for her to spend money on clothes.

Some women have an intuitive fashion sense and, with two or three dresses and a few accessories, will always turn up looking superb. This was not the case with Martha. She was always neat and clean, clothes washed, well pressed, and mended. But style escaped her, and her sense of dress was usually described as dowdy or eccentric.

If she received a fine coat, she would shorten or lengthen it, add a belt or a collar, changing a simple, elegant line into something unrecognizable from the original creation. These gifts of clothing, however, were deeply appreciated:

My clothes are just like the manna from Heaven, when I need something it just seems to come and I just thank God— what I do not spend on clothes goes a long way in the Cause. Monover [Yazdí] gave me a serge dress and it looks so smart. . . . The other is the dark brown velvet dress Amy Stevenson of Auckland, New Zealand, gave me. . . . [We]

219

shortened it and I will wear it with a piece of lace Mrs. Parsons gave me when I went to Atlanta. . . . Katherine [Nourse] gave me a little hat to match this dress.[1]

Her sense of the perfect dress for a particular occasion was unique. In a period when fashion was more circumscribed than it has become, Martha's tastes were whimsical. When rich materials and certain cuts and hemlines were limited to formal wear, a full-length velvet dress would seem perfectly fine apparel in which to address a winter-afternoon session of the Theosophical Society in Belgrade. In order not to appear overly casual she would top it off with a brown straw hat. Certainly individual, certainly unusual. Did it matter? It seems not. After the first surprised moments, appearance was forgotten once Martha Root started to talk. And she was always asked back.

When she was requested to address a group of fashionable young college women in Montreal at the home of May Maxwell, Martha added a white velvet jacket, suitable for a formal evening event, over the dress she was wearing. Bahiyyih Winckler recalled the scene:

I was upstairs with Martha and she was dressing for the occasion and she put on a white velvet jacket . . . and I said, "Martha! You don't want to wear that, it's noon! That's for evening!". . . "No, no Bahiyyih," she said, "I'm going to wear this." And really, she looked so, sort of, strange. She just hadn't dressed the way I would think you'd dress for the middle of the day. And I thought, "Oh, dear, she's going down to this very sophisticated crowd of young people and they'll just snicker when they see this little woman, frail little thing, come into the room dressed in a white velvet jacket in the middle of the day—and Oh, I had all these foolish thoughts.

There was a long flight of stairs in the Maxwell house and down the stairs went Martha into the living room where there was a good crowd of these young people. . . . I could not see Martha, but I could look into the living room . . . and . . . see the faces of a good many of the students. . . .

They looked Martha over, and then Martha began to talk; and Martha gave such a simple talk—always her talks were very simple, it seemed to me; . . . and I would think, "Here is an intellectual group, or there is an intellectual group, and why doesn't Martha really get down to brass tacks and do something that is a little more scholarly?" No, Martha spoke in this simple way.

Well, that day she enchanted those students, and as she talked more and more they came under the spell of her love, and of a power that came from her spirit.

When she spoke she was transformed. . . . she became a different person—she was giving the Faith. And these students were enchanted, and it didn't matter whether she had on a scarlet, or a white, or a black garment—it didn't matter what she had on—I think if she'd had a bathing suit on it wouldn't have made any difference to them. They loved her and they absorbed what she had to say. They *felt* her, as well as receiving the message in a simple . . . way.[2]

The first mention of apparel appeared in a letter to Agnes Parsons, who had given Martha a gift of white lace. "I tried the lace on the dress this morning," she wrote to Mrs. Parsons, "and it is very pretty. I faste[ne]d it into the form of a collar and little cascade vest effect and it is exquisite. I will only wear it for the 'call' and perhaps when I speak tonight in Atlanta."[3]

The more traditional residents of Cambridge Springs did not know quite how to react to Martha's sartorial originality. Lucy Wilson, reflecting on the beauty of her friend's life, said, "The only criticism I heard was bluntly made to me, 'Isn't Miss Root eccentric about her dressing?' I could only say, 'If I could have half her shining radiant spirit the outer would mean little to me.'"[4]

Over the years Lucy Wilson would knit sweaters for Martha. It was a work of love, as Lucy later developed arthritis, and certain activities were difficult for her. Sailing to Japan, Martha wrote to her:

I just *love* the sweater you made for me. . . . The color is so *my* color that I wish I never need wear anything except my

own colors. I wear it with pretty white cuffs & collar . . .
and black chiffon bow. . . . I wear the black patent leather
belt with it & the black satin skirt and it looks very
sweet. . . . I wish you were always with me to help me decide about my clothes. Your judgment is always just perfect.[5]

Another sort of story came from Agnes Alexander, who had
given Martha some handsome white material that was being
made into a dress for her public appearances. Martha wanted
the dress short; Agnes, who was probably also not the last
word in fashion, told her that dresses were no longer being
worn short; Martha said in Europe they were short; Agnes asserted *that* time had passed; Martha said, "Well, I want my
dress short."[6] So, short the dress was made. The strong will
that carried Martha through seasons of difficulty was also
present in decisions of not very great moment.

Martha's cutting and snipping of clothes was not limited to
her own needs. She once had a white petticoat, in which she
saw the possibilities of a new creation, and

took that skirt & cut off that very wide hem & am giving the
cloth to make a baby-dress for a dear little young wife whom
I think will be a sweet Bahai. Little Simeon will have a dress
and I shall still have a hem in the petticoat.[7]

Martha was aware of trends, and if they could be useful,
they were adopted. During the 1920s—the Jazz Age—wom-
en's locks were snipped and shortened, and bobbed hairstyles
swept the land. When Martha arrived in Perth, Australia, she
and Clara Dunn followed the fashion and had their hair cut,
which was quite a bold step for older women. A letter from
Perth brought the news to her friends:

What will you say when I tell you Clara and I have our
hair bobbed? Hers is beautiful. I wear mine curled just a little and as it is very fine, it is fluffy and really looks just as
well as before. I love it short, easy to keep clean and shining,
and it is more restful to have it short. This is a new age—

MARTHA ROOT
Sydney, Australia, 14 October 1924, with newly bobbed hair.
She called this her "glamour" picture.

equality of the sexes. Please do not "paddle" me till you see
me. You might decide it is becoming.[8]

The change was probably not a total visual success, but for
convenience when traveling it was a boon to Martha. The coro-
net braids were gone, replaced by a modern hairdo.
    Some pictures of Martha taken during this early period of
shorning look totally unlike those images that have become familiar to the Bahá'í world. Martha called them her "glamour
pictures." She wrote to Harry Randall, with pictures enclosed,
"They really don't look like me, but aren't they glamorous?"[9]
    Because of numerous public appearances many photo-
graphs were taken of her, often by the media, and others by individuals who wanted to preserve the memory of a visit. One of
these picture-taking incidents upset Martha. She alerted
friends that a picture would arrive from her niece, sent by the
admiring former mayor of Cape Town:

He telephoned the last day and said he would send out the
motor car at 11 A.M. for Fanny and me to come in to have

our pictures in a group. It was terribly hot, my bags had
gone to the train and I had put on a dress of Fanny's to go in
town because her dress was cooler than my traveling one.
The car came a half hour too early, I had just started to curl
my hair (I always have my hair curled and take pride in having it just right) but that morning I was so TIRED and des-
perate, I thought that nothing mattered and I put on my hat
and ran down stairs not to keep them waiting—I thought we
were just going to a picture post card place. In the studio the
wind blew, it was impossible to keep our hair in place. They
took the group and then Sir Frederick said for the man to
take one of me, so that in the years ahead South Africa
would have a picture. He suddenly snapped it for he said I
was too nervous to sit for a picture—had spoiled a group
plate a minute before by moving. My hair looked terrible,
the dress isn't mine, if you cut out the picture and just make
a little head, it looks more like me than the other one. I feel
sorry I did not take time—and let them wait—while I curled
my hair and put on my traveling dress. . . .

A cheerful note concluded her account: "but nothing for the
Cause has gone wrong." [10]
Meherangiz Munsiff, a Bahá'í who would meet Martha in
India in 1938, was with her when one of the last formal photographs of Martha was taken.* Of that day in Bombay she remembered "the amber necklace, the light brown dainty dress
of pure silk and how I helped her curl her hair. . . . Neatness in
personal appearance including the filing of the fingernails
which she taught me, seemed to her quite important and necessary." [11]
Martha felt strongly that it indeed was important as a Bahá'í
teacher to be "very neatly and carefully dressed." [12] But that
did not mean spending a lot of money on apparel. When Martha visited Munavvar Khánum in Port Said, she observed not
only Munavvar's spirituality, as Martha's was also observed,
but she noted that it was possible to get along with very few
clothes. A person only had to be creative with what little was on
hand.

*See p. 490.

Being well dressed always meant choosing carefully an important accessory—it was an era of hats. Only in the most casual circumstances would a woman go hatless. This millinery was often heavily adorned with feathers, plumes, birds, ribbons, and flowers. The Jazz Age did usher in simplicity, but many of the older women adhered to the ornamentation of yore. Since Martha inherited most of her headgear, there was an interesting process of addition and subtraction, of borrowing and lending, from hat to hat to fit the occasion, as perceived by Martha. She recounted this process in a letter to Ella Cooper:

> Ella, I took the little wings from your hat & put on to my own little hat to wear in Zurich & Stuttgart & thus put the larger hat flat into the suitcase—I did not want to take a hat box & a lot of things to Stuttgart when those people have so little. . . . it will not smash it the way it is packed. . . . I will wear your hat in Budapest & in London. It is a beautiful hat, but I am going to make it smaller in the crown. . . . It is so beautiful. I shall use it a great deal. (But I do not want to wear it on trains, but just as a dress hat).[13]

Style was even more elusive in the cold months. During a moderate spell in Budapest Martha described her attire: "I have come back to *one* pair of stockings, *one* shirt, & *one* sweater. . . . When the weather is moderate, I weigh just 100 lbs. But when I get on all my wool paraphanalia I look to weigh 152 lbs. I bought the golashes . . . and one wool undergarment but nothing else to wear. . . ."[14]

While traveling through foreign countries with a variety of monetary exchanges, Martha generally relied on American traveler's checks; but in some places where these were not acceptable, American currency was welcome. She wore a little white-linen, envelope-shaped bag around her neck, a gift from Roy Wilhelm, which contained some American money for emergencies and several times had been a simple solution to a knotty problem. The bag was reminiscent of the red-flannel-wrapped asafetida that had hung round her neck as a child.

Initially, Martha often refused clothes from friends; but she usually succumbed, as it was necessary to maintain appearances, and her other costs were a constant drain. In a relatively brief period she had spent more than one thousand dollars on traveling and literature to be given to those she met. Her expenses made quite a dent in extremely limited funds, yet the value of those expenses in 1924 and 1925 was many times greater than it is today.

Despite a limited purse, it never kept Martha from paying her obligations. Roy Wilhelm, who was a millionaire, would often take care of a need when he learned of its existence; but Martha insisted that he accept her reimbursement, which was handled through her cousin Sidney Hart. When a sum of ninety dollars was involved, Roy demurred, and Sidney notified Martha. She insisted:

> My cousin Sidney has just written me about that $90 . . . I want you to take it and I will write you and Sidney a joint letter from Geneva. . . . I shall never feel I can write you for anything if you do not take the money—and I know you are doing far too much for me. I do not want you to go "broke" and all worried about money affairs. Shoghi told me about the lights you sent . . . and . . . told me about the land. . . . You are an ideal Bahai, Roy, and I want you to be careful and not give more than you can. I don't want you to be harrassed about finances. . . . What you have done for me has helped me so much that I could go forward without stopping one day. This trip to Haifa and Acca and the four days with Monover [Munavvar Khánum] have been the most wonderful trip of my life.[15]

It was Martha's desire not only to alert the world to the Bahá'í Faith, but in the process to try as much as possible to follow in the footsteps of 'Abdu'l-Bahá—to live as He did, simply, frugally; to accept a minimum of help, and that only when necessary; to grow spiritually; to suffuse the world with the spirit of love; to be detached; to be generous; to love all. She would go to every city visited by 'Abdu'l-Bahá, and to those He yearned to visit, and would fulfill His dream. In Budapest her hope to stay in the same hotel where the Master stayed was threatened when she found that the price had soared. She could not bring herself to spend that much money on creature comforts.

Detached though Martha was, she nevertheless traveled with mountains of luggage. Her trunks and suitcases were her attic, her basement, her office, her library. They were home and often doubled as furniture. Separately containing her kitchen, writing materials, current seasonal clothing, and accessible Bahá'í literature, her luggage was identified usually by place of origin—such as, New York black bag, Port Said straw, and yellow Bombay. Each would be checked off a list on arrival and departure. When departure was looming, there would be several lists as packing proceeded, and check-offs were made on completion. Martha's luggage was legendary; but, then, she carried with her all her earthly possessions.

When calling on an individual, whether king or servant, infant or elder, Martha always brought a gift, humble though it might be, as a token of love. With the material gift she brought the spiritual, and she traveled the globe to deliver it. She felt that everyone in the world had the right to this gift, and she was the courier.

25 Switzerland and Its Neighbors

Geneva was at the heart of international hopes—for peace, for justice, for education in its broadest sense. It was an intellectual center and the home of the League of Nations. Here, on Lake Geneva, most of the international congresses gathered to map out plans that would be brought back to various global points.

In mid-May 1925 Martha traveled up from Genoa, through Italy and France, through the Swiss Alps, and expected to arrive in Geneva in the middle of the night. But due to a fluke at customs she arrived in broad daylight. Her luggage was a factor:

> One cannot ride third class and go through without changing. . . . I changed cars six times and missed the train in Moudaine—because it is a border place and there were so many people and so much baggage they could not get it inspected in time, but by missing the train and waiting from 2 a.m. to 5 a.m. in the station I traveled through this beautiful Switzerland in the daylight—the inspector was from BROOKLYN! He took me into the first class waiting room and made me very comfortable.[1]

For fifty-four dollars a month Martha found living quarters where she could get room and board and do her own washing and ironing. It was a tiny room, but that did not dampen Martha's enthusiasm. She enjoyed dipping briefly into domesticity. The bedstead was taken out, so the bed looked like a low divan. Her luggage formed a window seat, which she covered, along with some pillows and table tops, with a coarse Egyptian handwoven cotton cloth, a "warm, sunshiny yellow," purchased for a few cents a yard.[2] Bahá'ís in Egypt had given her a brass coffee pot with six little cups and saucers; the Australians had given her a tea pot. With a wood-alcohol outfit, which she said cooked her food perfectly, Martha was ready to receive guests. If people sat close together, nine could fit in her room. 'Abdu'l-Bahá had his *biruni*, or drawing room, where He received guests, served them tea, and spoke of the Faith. This was to be Martha Root's biruni.

The room was near the Esperantists in the heart of the city, eliminating carfare. It looked out onto the Rhone River and a little park, with trees of every spring shade of green, and white-peaked mountains beyond. "I am happy every time I lift my eyes," she wrote. "It's a beautiful room to pray in, feeling near to God."[3]

The sterling qualities of the Swiss, which seemed to reflect John Calvin's years among them, had a certain appeal to Martha. She noted that the Red Cross was started in Switzerland and that "Geneva is a very scholastic city, not large and very *clean*[—]that sounds good to me."[4] After the less disciplined cities of the Middle East the contrast was welcome.

Within a few days Martha had contacted friends and some Esperantists and had traveled to Lausanne with Mrs. Katherine Nourse, a Bahá'í living in Switzerland with her young son and daughter, Philip and Katherine. The plan was to stay in Geneva and its environs for five months and then go to London for four months, before moving on to other parts of Europe.

In Geneva the Arms Congress was in progress, and the International Labor Congress would soon start. Martha felt that her past talks with labor groups, documented with newspaper clippings, and her friendship with Eugene Debs would prove a useful bridge with the Laborites. The Esperanto congress would meet in August, and the League of Nations would be in session during September. Martha felt there was "a great mystery, a great purpose in our coming here."[5]

Mrs. J. Stannard arrived in Geneva shortly after Martha to head the International Bahá'í Bureau. Rooms were rented that included a large area seating sixty (Bahá'í Hall), with big doors opening into Mrs. Stannard's office, which could accommo-

*Martha Root (standing second from left) with Bahá'ís at the
International Bahá'í Bureau, Geneva, Switzerland*

date another forty persons. A little office on the far side of the
hall Martha decided to rent for nine dollars a month. This was
done for two reasons: to add income to the enterprise and to
enable her to pursue her own work while being available to
greet visitors and help in a minor way to launch the project.
The decision was a concession on Martha's part, as she could
more easily have done her writing, uninterrupted, in her own
room, obviously getting more done: "But I am just praying to
put the Cause first & not think whether it will be hard or easy,
but whether it will attract souls."[6]

Martha, who had resumed her study of Esperanto a few
days after arriving in Geneva, worried whether she should use
all of her time teaching the Bahá'í Faith rather than sharing it
with language study. But she felt once Esperanto was mastered
it would be a powerful force in meeting people all through Europe, and thus her study would achieve both goals. She hoped
to be fluent in the language by August when the conference
would open.

The Swiss were vigorous walkers, and within the first week

the Esperantists invited Martha to walk with them up Mont Blanc. When she discovered that it would be a ten-hour jaunt, she demurred. "I did not dare attempt it because of my heart."[7] But in June she accepted a second invitation from the Esperantists, this time to go up Mont Salève. It was to be an experiment in stamina, and if it seemed too difficult, she would turn back. To Roy Wilhelm she wrote wistfully, "Wish you could go along. You could sit on Mother's shawl up in the clouds and eat all my lunch."[8]

As early as June Martha began making arrangements to have two Bahá'í sessions at the forthcoming Esperanto congress. Every word had to be in Esperanto—presentations, questions, and discussions. Shoghi Effendi asked Julia Culver of the United States to join Martha in preparing for the congress; between them a highly successful program emerged.

It was the Seventeenth Universal Esperanto Congress, with eight hundred delegates—Martha Root and Julia Culver representing the Bahá'í Faith—and several thousand Esperantists filling Victoria Hall. The two Bahá'í sessions were held at the International Esperanto Bureau, 19 Boulevard Georges-Favon. Both sessions were crowded, with twenty-five countries represented.

Since this congress marked the first public melding of the Bahá'í Faith and Esperanto, the reports have an historic value reflected in the following excerpts:

> Miss Martha Root spoke on the subject "What Is The Bahà'i Movement?", giving its [principles], its history and how it has spread in eighty years. Prof. Charles Baudouin of Geneva University, author of "Contemporary Studies" and other books world renowned, was the other speaker, his subject being, "The Bahà'i Movement And Esperanto".* These addresses will be printed. An open forum followed, Miss Root replying to the questions. Prof. Peter Stojan of Petrograd, member of the International Esperanto Committee, began the discussion by speaking on the principle of

---

*Professor Baudouin was not a Bahá'í.

the harmony of science and religion. One delegate told of her interview with 'Abdu'l Bahà in Paris. Often two or three were on their feet at the same time, trying to ask questions. . . . Perhaps never has there been such a Bahà'i opportunity to reach the thinkers of so many different lands at the same moment, as in these two sessions—for the COMMON LANGUAGE made every thought clear to the representatives of each country.[9]

The portraits of 'Abdu'l-Bahá and Dr. Zamenhof, creator of Esperanto, hung in the huge Esperanto Hall, decorated with filmy white flowers, Swiss violets, and branches of green, the Esperanto color.

It was at this congress that Martha met Lydia Zamenhof, and another strong friendship was born. Martha wrote that

The two daughters of the late Dr. L. L. Zamenhof, inventor of the Esperanto Language[,] were present at the second session. They are Dr[.] Sophia and Miss Lydia Zamenhof of Warsaw, Poland. Dr[.] Sophia Zamenhof read what her father had said about the need of a universal religion, in his paper written for the Universal Races Congress in London, July 26–29, 1911. Miss Root followed with the exact words of Dr. Zamenhof concerning 'Abdu'l Bahà and an interview in London when Dr. Zamenhof gave his views concerning the Bahà'i Movement. Mrs. Oumansky from Russia and Czechoslovakia gave the words of 'Abdu'l Bahà to Esperantists. . . . Dr[.] Adelbert Mühlschlegel, a fine Bahà'i Esperantist from Stuttgart, gave a beautiful address on the Teachings of Bahà'u'llah about a universal auxiliary language. . . . several delegates said they would give lectures to their home groups explaining all they had learned. Miss Root received many invitations to give Esperanto lectures in England, Germany, Rumania, Poland and Czechoslovakia.

The report concluded: "The President of one of Europe's best known Peace Societies and a noted Esperantist, summed the whole matter when she said in the open forum: 'Let us work that all Bahàis may become Esperantists and all Esperantists become Bahàis!' "[10] No words could have been more endearing to Martha's heart. The Bahá'í sessions at the congress were a success.

Another source of happiness was the presence of Ella Cooper at the congress. When she gave a talk that had been arranged by Martha, Ella captivated those present with her beauty, intelligence, and grace. Martha remarked to her later, "I wish your husband could have seen how radiant & beautiful you were & with what fire you spoke to our Esperantists that night in Geneva. They were all so delighted."[11]

Ella Cooper also observed Martha in action, noted her unceasing activity, and viewed the toll being exacted from so much work and so little rest. She had a serious talk with Martha and approached her in the only way she thought would be

ELLA GOODALL COOPER
daughter of Helen Goodall, and one of the first Bahá'ís
in the San Francisco/Oakland area of California,
was a friend and confidante of Martha Root's.

effective: if her health were impaired, if she spoke when she was tired and worn, and in pain, she would hurt, not help, the Bahá'í Faith. In her gentle way she demanded that Martha take time out to rest, with a little pampering, the costs to be assumed by Ella.

Martha was genuinely touched and wanted to do as she was told. In a letter to Ella she wrote:

> I love you and appreciate your splendid qualities & I want you to know I *thank* you for speaking to me exactly as you did. I think it is so dear of you to want to help me to *rest*, I need it so, and I do appreciate your kind offer. I may take the two weeks before Budapest, if I cannot keep going, but I have a great longing to take the rest there in the hotel where He stayed. So I kiss you and thank you, Ella. [12]

Even as she wrote, Martha was in bed dealing with her nemesis—the recurrent pain from her cancer and a debilitating weariness. Nevertheless, she prepared a talk to be given that evening with a Swiss interpreter.

She wired the Bahá'ís and the Esperantists in Zurich and postponed her visit for a week due to illness. In the same letter to Ella she added, "I was not able to go—when I go I want to go with spiritual fire & enthusiasm and am praying for strength to go *properly*. They (Esperantists) have yesterday announced a big lecture on the 'Bahai Movement', Oct. 31, in a public hall. I am to speak in Esperanto & the President interpreting into German." [13]

The Geneva period was drawing to a close. Once again the visit to England was postponed as Martha's energies were directed to other parts of Europe.

The scheduled lecture in Zurich loomed large in Martha's consciousness. Her weakness continued, but she *had* to be there; she could not let the opportunity pass. Gathering together all her possessions after the six months in Geneva, she went on to Zurich, where she arrived at the end of October 1925. Uncharacteristically, she spent most of the time in bed, getting up only for the lectures. She spent three hours with Mr. Karl Yost, going over the talk so that his translation into German was perfect. He also took care of all arrangements, unburdening Martha of these necessary details. The lecture was an enormous success. The hall was crowded, many stood, and Martha felt that her Esperanto went very well, the best ever. There was a second, follow-up meeting on Sunday, studded with many university professors and students, a "splendid audience," immensely grateful for Martha's presentation.[14]

Referring to her health, Martha insisted to Julia Culver that "Baha'u'llah will help me, and you will see that I will not hurt His Cause. I couldn't when every breath is a prayer."[15] Her role, her destiny, it seemed, was not only to perform but to overcome. Yet in Zurich it did occur to her that she might never get back home. She asked Julia if she would wrap more sturdily a package that had been left behind in Geneva. The letter to Julia is also a glimpse into Martha's generosity and deep feelings for her family: "There is nothing new," she explained, "except the watch, and I did not pay any money for anything except the $3. for the watch & my relatives sent me $4. I am so thankful to send them these things as a sign of love for I may not get back to America and I want my relatives to love the Cause." She asked Julia to say nothing to them about Martha's health, adding, "I am going to be better."[16]

For the next several months Martha's life took on a kaleidoscopic character as she traveled back and forth through Germany, Austria, Holland, and the several Balkan countries, luggage in tow. Everywhere she used contacts made in a variety of countries and at numerous gatherings embracing a variety of interests.

Leaving Switzerland, Martha went from Geneva in the south to Zurich in the north, then into Germany, visiting Stuttgart, Frankfurt am Main, and Karlsruhe. She also traveled east to Vienna, Austria, for a month's teaching, where she spoke every evening of her stay, and often during the day. At every stop she was entertained by intellectuals, bankers, business people, and the now familiar groups who sought her lectures. One particular source of happiness was meeting with people who had known 'Abdu'l-Bahá, and speaking in places where He had spoken.

Perhaps the most significant event was the interview granted by Madame Marianne Hainisch, mother of Austria's president. She was a most unusual woman, an active supporter of human rights, who did special work to improve the status of women and initiated ideas far ahead of her time. She had first heard of the Bahá'í Faith through the poems of Ṭáhirih (Qurratu'l-'Ayn), a Bahá'í martyr and the first Persian woman to lay aside the veil. It was a memorable meeting, the highlights of which were preserved in an article published in *The Bahá'í World*.[17]

On the other end of the scale, it was in Vienna that she met Franz Pöllinger, whom she considered the most selfless, humble, generous, self-effacing individual that she had ever known. Going without food himself, he would bring her sandwiches and insist that she eat them because she was denying herself the necessities. He would direct her everywhere, stay with her, protect her, because she was telling the world about Bahá'u'lláh. "No princess," she wrote, "was ever more devotedly served."[18]

She felt blessed—blessed in her contacts, and blessed by her friends. Later, in referring to the time in Vienna, she recalled, "I would have thought [after] the first day of Bahai work in Vienna, the prospect was not so very encouraging, but wonderful things came, so I look for miracles in every city."[19]

Although most of the stops were relatively brief, Martha felt a spiritual wave surge over her when traveling and teaching:

When I once get started in a city I do not even stop to write a postcard to my relatives. Everything goes like the rushing sweep of the Holy Spirit. Then nothing material matters. 'Abdu'l Bahá and Baha'u'llah help me . . . & the people of the city help, rather they do it all, I just pray, listen to the Guidance & act. But it is a very *happy* time.[20]

The work in all the cities went well; to Martha it seemed like a miracle. Everywhere the Esperantists provided a forum for talks, women's clubs were receptive, and university professors would embark on a study of the Bahá'í teachings, with one professor committed to lecture before the Science Club of Vienna.

Martha reached Budapest, Hungary, near Christmastime and was forced to shop for hotels when she realized that she could not afford the rates at the one where 'Abdu'l-Bahá had stayed. On arrival she was beset by a series of small problems, all creating demands on her budget. She broke a corner of her front tooth, and that would mean a soaring dentist's bill; the porter handling her luggage pulled the handle, and out came the top of one of her suitcases; her flatiron broke; she discovered, to her great distress, that passport visas to all the countries she hoped to visit would total two hundred dollars. She was also plagued by the Hungarian currency:

> The money in Budapest is *awful*. A banana cost 30,000 crowns (I did not buy one), 60,000 crowns to get my flat iron repaired etc. It is hard to figure in such soaring terms—one dollar is about 70,000 crowns. I went to six hotels and looked at rooms and chose the cheapest of the six and the cheapest room in this. But even so, everything here is three times more expensive than in Vienna. . . .[21]

It was also unsettling to have to pay seven different kinds of taxes in a hotel, in addition to the cost of the room.

Martha thought she was lucky to get along at all in such a place. She was following her usual spartan diet—"a few apples, bread & butter, a little cheese or figs"—and making her meals in her room.[22]

The Christmas holidays were a special time for Martha, and she cherished the memories of those sparkling days in years gone by. There was no one to share them with her in 1925, as she was alone in Budapest, a complete stranger to the land and its people. As always, she turned to prayer and work. The first week would be devoted to getting the writing done and then exploring possibilities for Bahá'í work. For all its problems Martha felt that Budapest was probably a better area for teaching than the upcoming Bulgaria, Rumania, and some of the other small Balkan countries.

Because of the questionable tone of the chosen hotel, Martha felt she must leave, but it led her to the place of her dreams. Of the experience she remembered:

> I stayed in that hotel for over a week. . . . But that hotel was terrible morally. . . . Something happened and I knew I had to move, but I stayed & prayed one night for them—thought I wouldn't run away from hell without praying for them first. . . . Then after looking at 9 hotels, I went again to the one where Abdu'l Bahá stayed, the man (after I told him about Abdu'l Bahá) made me a very good rate & I went to that nice hotel for nine days. How the Cause spread! It was as if I were not there, just Baha'u'llah & Abdu'l Bahá in Budapest.[23]

The change of residence had turned a dark experience into a spiritual adventure, and Budapest became a light in her chain of cities.

> The places where I spoke were crowded, many stood, people called & many are deeply interested. The last day people called from 11 A.M. to 11 P.M. (I had announced I would be in that day) I ate no lunch or dinner, & sometimes nine were there at one time. Many people invited me to their homes. I only went twice, I couldn't, not able, but every day people called at the hotel.[24]

The train, cold and crowded, took Martha in mid-January 1926 through Hungary and into Belgrade, Serbia (now Yugoslavia). It was a brief visit, only two nights, because Martha learned that no teaching could be done without full permission from the minister of cults, who was on a two-week vacation. But the trip was not wasted. She took steps for future work, placed a book in the National Library, and met the managing editor of the largest newspaper, who became interested and used an article on the Faith. She also met the Esperantists, the American minister, and the presidents of three women's clubs; and, surprisingly, she was asked to give a lecture on the principles of the Faith at the YMCA.

Luggage intact, Martha boarded a train amidst the cold January air, rode through the Carpathian Mountains, and, after skirting the Danube, stopped in Bucharest, Rumania. There her efforts would create more than a ripple in Bahá'í history and would bring world attention to the Faith of Bahá'u'lláh.

26 Royalty

Rumania was a monarchy ruled by King Ferdinand I and
Queen Marie. Ferdinand had come to the throne in 1914 and
was crowned king of Greater Rumania in 1922. He was a scholarly and impartial ruler who initiated many reforms but whose
kingdom was experiencing serious political strife in the 1920s.
Queen Marie, daughter of English royalty, was a beautiful
woman, intelligent, gifted, with a flair for the dramatic and artistic. She worked to improve the lives of the people of Rumania, sought to raise the level of education and human values,
and was a tremendous asset to the throne. Both she and her
husband were held in affectionate esteem by the Rumanian
people.

Queen Marie was the granddaughter of Queen Victoria of
England and, on her mother's side, of Czar Alexander II of
Russia, two monarchs who had not turned away from Ba-
há'u'lláh, and both recipients of letters from Him.[1]

Martha, who believed that even a queen should have the
message of Bahá'u'lláh, had been told that it was impossible to
see Her Majesty, that she was in a period of personal sorrow
and was receiving no one. On 26 January Martha wrote to
Shoghi Effendi from Bucharest:

> I am speaking each day or evening in Bukarest [sic], every-
> thing is going just like a miracle. . . . I have just strength
> enough to do the daily work and the correspondence is utter-
> ly neglected—I cannot do more. In fact I do nothing, other
> people arrange and come for me and take me and Abdu'l
> Bahá blesses each effort, it astonishes even me.

The usual contacts had been made, and Bucharest was responding. But Martha wanted more. In the same letter she told
Shoghi Effendi:

I shall leave here Feb. first or second or third, [as] soon as I can have [an] interview with the Lady in Waiting to the Queen of Rumania, she had promised to see me, but she has grippe these few days, of course I should be very happy if I can meet the Queen, but if I cannot this Lady in Waiting will convey to her my messages and Bahá'i books.[2]

The frailty of Martha's health had not weakened her determination. In a letter reporting several other episodes, Martha slipped in an informal account of events leading to her meeting with Queen Marie:

The Amer[ican] Minister said I could not see the Queen Marie of Rumania, but I wrote her a letter & sent her 'Abdu'l Baha's picture and Dr. Esslemont's book. Next day came a

QUEEN MARIE OF RUMANIA
the first crowned head of state to acknowledge and call attention to
the Bahá'í Faith. Martha Root met with her on eight occasions.

letter from the Palace inviting me to visit her the next day at noon. Next to my visit to the Greatest Holy Leaf, this visit to Queen Marie was one of the most splendid events of my life. I took her the Greatest Name and "Seven Valleys"—and two Esperanto books and my Esperanto pin, a little bottle of perfume, a little box of candy, a branch of white lilacs, and a report of the Education Congress in Edinburgh (She was the Princess of Edinburgh before her marriage). She asked me to tell her about the Bahai Movement & said she had been reading the book I sent and was very interested in the Principles. (She gave me the address of a dear friend of hers in Vienna whom I am to call upon). She asked a number of questions. I loved her and felt more at home with her than with many other people who are not queens—I learned a great deal from her, too. It was such a happy visit, she was so sweet, so gracious—she held the Greatest Name and Shoghi Effendi's [probably 'Abdu'l-Bahá's] picture in her hands while we talked—for most of the hour. I feel I can write & send her books or news.[3]

Martha's audience with the queen took place on 30 January 1926 at Controceni Palace, outside the city of Bucharest. The gates and the doors were opened to her, and she was brought to a lady-in-waiting, who led her up a spiral staircase to the queen's drawing room. Martha was struck by her beauty and spirit:

> Queen Marie of Rumania comes quickly forward, smiling her welcome. How beautiful she is! She looks like a flower herself, in her blue silk morning dress with gold low shoes and hose . . . while from her grave blue eyes flashes the light of a great spirit; she knows, she understands, she loves![4]

After the greeting Queen Marie's first words were, " 'I believe these Teachings are the solution for the world's problems today!' "[5] She had stayed up until 3:00 A.M. reading *Bahá'u'lláh and the New Era* and later in the day sent off her invitation to Martha.

There was much that was personal in the conversation, much on world matters, manners and morals, religions and

CONTROCENI PALACE
Bucharest, Rumania, where Martha Root first
met with Queen Marie

prejudice, Esperanto and education. It was a totally satisfying meeting and the beginning of a friendship, albeit limited, that would last until the queen's death in 1938.

The Bahá'ís in the region were understandably excited by the prospect of Martha Root's meeting with Queen Marie. A well-traveled North American Bahá'í, with much material wealth at her disposal, told of Martha's preparations for the audience, which was to take place within twenty-four hours.

From her small stipend she put aside a certain amount of money to purchase the gifts she would bring. The candy was a small piece of chocolate wrapped in gold foil; the perfume was small and of questionable quality. The well-endowed friend learned that Martha would hire a carriage for the thirty-minute ride to the palace but had no funds for a return trip. She politely refused the offer of a private carriage placed at her disposal for a trip to and from the palace. The offer of a gift of expensive perfume to take to the queen was also refused. Martha did things in her own way and with her own money.

The friend reported with amazement the rejection of these

offers and humorously told of Martha's buying the cheapest perfume—the kind worn by every streetwalker in Paris! Smelly perfume or not, Queen Marie was enchanted. And Martha did not need a carriage for the return trip. The queen sent her back in the royal coach. This modest, plain, unfashionable woman from Cambridge Springs, Pennsylvania, had opened new doors to Queen Marie's mind.

Martha dressed carefully for her audience with the queen— of course, using what she had. She wrote Lucy Wilson that she washed and pressed the long white dress that she had worn to the Bahá'í convention in 1921. To Ella Cooper she wrote:

> Ella, I wore your hat when I called upon the Queen (and the white dress I wore at the Esperanto evening). I have your hat put back now—in the winter sometimes I took the crown (top) off & put it on my little hat, but now I have it back to its original shape & will wear it just as you wore it.[6]

The visit to Queen Marie of Rumania did not go unnoticed in Cambridge Springs. Three-quarters of the editorial page of the *Enterprise-News* was devoted to the event. The opening, double-column paragraph read, "Martha L. Root is the most distinguished individual ever developed in Cambridge Springs. You may not agree with her but you must admire her. She also interests you. She recently visited with Queen Marie. Here is her account of it." A highly descriptive story of the audience with Queen Marie followed, with three double columns taking almost the entire page. It was the same article that would appear in the *Bahá'í Magazine: Star of the West*, probably given to the editor by Lucy Wilson.[7] While Martha Root was not seeking justice and recognition from Cambridge Springs, events were shaping positive sentiments on her behalf.

With the acknowledgment of the Bahá'í Faith by Queen Marie, the Faith had gained another strong proponent of its message, for the queen was a gifted writer. Taking two hours every morning to work at this craft, she produced literature in a variety of forms—essays, articles, short semifictional pieces, biography, autobiography, history, playlets. Her broad experience in grand and unusual settings, her interaction with the Rumanian people, her ties to almost all the royal houses of Europe, all had a romantic fascination for the reading public.

The queen also wrote articles that were syndicated in more than two hundred newspapers in the United States and Canada. Here she made her first public statements on the Bahá'í Faith, inviting readers to examine the teachings that taught love, unity, peace. The first of these statements appeared in May 1926, and others were published soon thereafter. Many of the statements were translated and published in China, Japan, Australasia, and other parts of the world. Portions of the first article follow:

> A woman brought me the other day a Book. I spell it with a capital letter because it is a glorious Book of love and goodness, strength and beauty. . . .
> [The] writings are a great cry toward peace, reaching beyond all limits of frontiers, above all dissension about rites and dogmas. . . . It teaches that all hatreds, intrigues, suspicions, evil words, all aggressive patriotism even, are outside the one essential law of God, and that special beliefs are but surface things whereas the heart that beats with divine love knows no tribe nor race.
> It is a wondrous Message that Bahá'u'lláh and his son 'Abdu'l-Bahá have given us. They have not set it up aggressively knowing that the germ of eternal truth which lies at its core cannot but take root and spread. . . .
> I commend it to you all. If ever the name of Bahá'u'lláh or 'Abdu'l-Bahá comes to your attention, do not put their writings from you. Search out their Books, and let their glorious, peace-bringing, love-creating words and lessons sink into your hearts as they have into mine.
> One's busy day may seem too full for religion. Or one may have a religion that satisfies. But the teachings of these gentle, wise and kindly men are compatible with all religion, and with no religion.
> Seek them, and be the happier.
> By Marie, Queen of Rumania[8]

For a Faith that had struggled to be heard, whose martyrs had died and were even then dying, unnoticed by the world, the public tributes by a reigning monarch were balm to the souls of the Bahá'ís. To Shoghi Effendi, laboring under the undiminished tribulations of the Guardianship, and striving to gain acknowledgment of the Bahá'í Faith as a world religion, they were a source of unexcelled joy.

Martha wrote a note of appreciation to Her Majesty, who responded warmly:

> I received your books & dear letter safely. Having today your address can send loving thanks. The beautiful truth of Baha'u'llah is with me always, a help & inspiration. What I wrote (for the syndicates) was because my heart overflowed with gratitude for the Revelation you brought me. I am happy if you think I helped. I thought it might bring Truth nearer, because my words are read by so many. The books of Abdul Baha are also an immense inspiration to my Ileana. . . .[9]

An appended note by Martha reveals that Her Majesty had given a large order for Bahá'í books at Burnsides, Ltd.; a few days later, Princess Ileana, the sixteen-year-old daughter of the king and queen, had also sent for a large order of books.

The results of Martha's letter to Queen Marie on 28 January 1926 were greater than she ever expected. She was filled with humility and gratitude.

27 Staying on Course

After three years of difficult and exhausting travels—1923–26—the visit with Queen Marie in Rumania was a decided boost to Martha Root's morale. Martha, frail aristocrat of the soul, had met with sympathy and understanding from one of Europe's most noble members of royalty.

Although Martha accepted a few invitations from the queen's ladies-in-waiting—titled and privileged members of society—she turned down an invitation by the Rumanian minister of foreign affairs to address four hundred guests at Foundation Carol University. She could not stay on for another week, as she had her plan of visitation mapped out and was steady on her course. Ingenuously, she suggested to Queen Marie that perhaps the queen would give a lecture on the Bahá'í teachings. Although the suggestion was not carried out, Martha understood, remarking, "I *know* I did wisely *not* to rush it too much for there is much orthodoxy and the Queen is broader than many of her subjects."[1]

Martha went to Sofia, Bulgaria, the first week in February 1926 and stayed twelve days, spending almost all her waking moments with university students, with whom she seemed to communicate easily; she also lectured in Esperanto. Several editors used articles on the Faith, a sign of enlightened awareness that pleased her. She sent a book with a letter to thirty-two-year-old King Boris II and one to his sister. But there was not the dramatic response that she got from Rumanian royalty.

Constantinople and Greece were wisely put on a list for future visits. "I have not the physical strength or the money to do them properly," she explained in a letter to Shoghi Effendi and Roy Wilhelm.[2] She planned her return to Vienna via Budapest, where she had three speaking invitations and a promised meet-

247

ing with Count Apponyi, a member of a noble Hungarian family.

The heavy schedules, the bitter cold, the long, uncomfortable train rides took their toll, and when Martha reached Budapest, Hungary, she was exhausted. As a result, she canceled all engagements. No one knew she was in the city, which allowed her to rest and to write ahead to Vienna and set up talks with the professors contacted earlier.

Slipping out of Budapest, she arrived on 18 February in Vienna, Austria, and went directly to the hotel and to bed, again notifying no one of her arrival. The long shadows of illness and exhaustion enveloped her. She worried about delinquent correspondence and the Esperanto congress work not yet started. "And here I am trying to get rested enough to rest," she quipped to Ella Cooper, "if you know what that means. . . . Am writing this in bed—I know I shall be all right, Ella, and keep on until I get the Bahai Message to every country. . . ." Yet her sense of humor was still lively: "Ella, the work this winter was the best of my life. Bahá'u'lláh didn't have anything the matter with His Heart. . . ." And she added, "I have given my life and what I have. Everyday I make mistakes."[3]

The letter lay unsent. Alone, weak, and sick, in a foreign city, no one aware of her presence in Vienna, unattended by a physician, she lay through long nights and days as she struggled and prayed for strength. "Dearest Ella," she continued the letter a few days later, "here is the fourth day & this not sent. I have been ill. I do not know what to do if I do not feel better—I think I will just stay here longer. The friends do not know that I have come."[4]

Debilitated, miserable in inactivity, Martha languished. Slowly strength returned. She reached the professors, rekindled their interest, and, still recuperating, went on to Berlin. There was an urgency and efficiency in her plan to contact individuals in Germany and Holland to enlist their participation in the Bahá'í sessions, possibly two or three, at the Universal Esperanto Congress in August.

Martha also intended to prepare two "very carefully written papers" that she hoped to be allowed to present at the general sessions or convocations. She chose to write on "Universal Religion and Homaranismo" (the ethics of Dr. Zamenhof) and "The New Call to Universal Education." Although she had received an Esperanto diploma in Geneva, she worried, in a letter to Shoghi Effendi, about her limitations in speaking the language: "I speak before the Esperantists in every city, am not satisfied[;] one ought to be a great Esperanto scholar so that the very perfection would be an asset to the Bahá'í Cause."[5]

The meeting in Geneva with the two Zamenhof daughters—one "seemed so sad"—had stirred Martha's hopes of bringing the message of Bahá'u'lláh more deeply into their lives.[6] She wanted somehow to be able to fit Warsaw into her schedule. As if she had willed events, Martha learned that a monument honoring Dr. Zamenhof, who had died in 1917, was to be unveiled in Warsaw on 18 April. She wired asking for a place on the program.

From Berlin arrangements began to take shape. Martha would go as a representative of Shoghi Effendi and the Bahá'í

LYDIA ZAMENHOF
daughter of Professor Ludwik Lazarus Zamenhof, creator
of Esperanto. A friend and colleague, Martha Root
thought her brilliant and her translations of the Bahá'í
writings superb.

Faith. Additionally, she would spend a two-week period of intensive study of Esperanto with Lydia Zamenhof, the sad one. When Martha arrived at the hotel in Warsaw on 11 April, she was invited to stay with the Zamenhof family, an arrangement that suited her in many ways:

> Lydia, the younger daughter, perhaps 25[,] is studying English, she is home all day, and she will help me with my Esperanto and I help her with her English. I share her room as they have only a flat. Two sisters and brother[,] his wife and babe all live together[;] the flat is on the fifth floor, no lift, but it is very pleasant and they are lovely. . . . It will bring Esperanto and Bahai Movement closer together. I shall pay for my board and room, and I hope pay generously, because their father gave his all to found Esperanto and they are working hard. . . . I feel that 'Abdu'l Baha and Dr. Zamenhof are wishing this closer coming together of the two movements.[7]

Only one suitcase and her typewriter went with Martha; everything else stayed at the hotel. She planned to devote her time totally to study, and the five flights were a deterrent to spontaneous adventures.

The unveiling of the monument, a gift from the Esperantists of the world, took place in the Hebrew cemetery in Warsaw, with friends from Poland and other countries in attendance. Martha brought white roses, similar to those in 'Abdu'l-Bahá's garden, and spoke about the greatness of Dr. Zamenhof, of the love and esteem tendered him by the Bahá'ís of the world. He had not only created Esperanto to bring unity and peace to the world; he was also a poet and humanitarian. It was a solemn and moving ceremony.

Esperanto took precedence during this period, and scholarship in language began to seem possible. But study had to be put aside, and travel once again became a way of life. With London as the target Martha started out by way of Czechoslovakia, a country whose leadership she admired.

Having written ahead to President Masaryk and sent some literature, she called the palace when she arrived early in May. The president and his daughter were out of the city, but instruc-

MARTHA ROOT
during her first visit to Prague, Czechoslovakia, in 1926

tions had been left to send a car to bring Martha Root to the palace, where she had an interview of more than two hours with the secretary of the president and the head of libraries. She spent much of the time calling attention to the persecution of Bahá'ís in Iran and in seeking governmental support to halt the atrocities.

During her eight days in Prague she gave numerous lectures and made plans to have Little Ben published by the Esperantists in the Czech language. Vuk Echtner, a young man who heard Martha speak and was drawn to the Bahá'í Faith, translated some of the writings into Czech and became one of the first Bahá'ís in his country.

To Martha the people of Bulgaria and Czechoslovakia seemed more spiritually awake than anywhere in Europe. Her strong hope that a Bahá'í teacher would go to either of these countries would be answered within a year by Louise Gregory, an English Bahá'í who was married to Louis G. Gregory of the

United States. Later Martha's wish was again answered by Marion Jack, a devoted Canadian Bahá'í teacher.

Another aim of Martha's was fulfilled in Prague—to interview the secretary of the late Count Leo Tolstoy. Valentin Bulgakov, a refugee from Russia, had much to say about the Bahá'í Faith and Leo Tolstoy's admiration for the teachings as a path to peace. In one of his last works Count Tolstoy observed, "'We spend our lives trying to unlock the mystery of the universe, but there was a Turkish Prisoner, Bahá'u'lláh, in 'Akká, Palestine, who had the key!'"[8]

Feeling tremendously uplifted, Martha went to Dresden, Germany, to meet with the Bahá'ís. She was able to speak several times before going on to The Hague. Again, she was forced to her bed by physical infirmities. She gave no lectures, saw no one, and spent the time recuperating and overhauling her things. "Everything I had was broken or worn out."[9] But she did manage to send to the queen of The Netherlands the Bahá'í "Tablet to The Hague" and Dr. Esslemont's book *Bahá'u'lláh and the New Era.*

Illness or not, she prepared to move on. London was at last within sight, and she remained optimistic:

> it seemed impossible to start to London but through the bounty of God when I reached London I felt well. So many times when I think I cannot go another step & I rise up & go forward the health comes to meet the task. . . . I feel it was a wonderful answer to prayer.[10]

Such prayers were often Martha's most potent medicine.

The first half of 1926 had been historic, but it had also been a physically trying time. Although her bouts with sickness were becoming more serious, Martha sent her prayers heavenward, resumed a thoroughly optimistic attitude, and set her sights on the British Isles, the land of her forebears.

28   The British Isles

Martha arrived in England in early June 1926. During the early part of her stay, she was the guest of Annie and Harry Romer, two Bahá'ís formerly of New York. Mr. Romer had been sent to England on an Associated Press assignment, and he and his wife had settled in the outskirts of London, where they were bathed in sweet country air. From there Martha Root and Annie Romer traveled to Manchester and Bournemouth, meeting friends, giving lectures, and carrying on Martha's work.

What was routine for Martha became a source of amazement to those viewing, for the first time, the pace of her activities and accomplishments. She did more than give talks every day or evening. To newspapers and societies she sent out two hundred letters seeking support for the halting of the Persian massacres. These letters would prompt many positive replies before Martha left Britain several months later. Factual accounts of the persecutions were also sent to European rulers who had spoken with Martha about the Faith. One member of royalty living in Geneva, Prince Arfa, sent one of Martha's articles on the persecutions to Tehran, where it appeared in seventy-five Persian newspapers. The British press, too, became well informed about the atrocities, as Martha personally contacted the Press Association of Great Britain, Reuters, and the *London Daily Mail*. Mountfort Mills, who was living in Paris, came over to London to consult with Martha about the Persian afflictions, lending wisdom and moral support to her efforts.

In addition to her activities designed to focus the world's attention on the plight of the Bahá'ís in Iran, Martha was handling the voluminous correspondence necessary to prepare for the smooth running of the Esperanto congress to be held in Edinburgh, 31 July to 7 August. Unfortunately, Julia Culver, who was to have come to London to assist with the congress, was taken ill, and her trip was canceled.

Whether because of a request by the English friends, or because she knew Martha's needs, Julia provided monetary assistance for secretarial help. Miss Pincott, a sensitive, efficient lady, worked for several hours each day to reduce the mountain of writing that faced Martha daily. Claudia Coles, a Bahá'í from Washington, D.C., who had moved to London, wrote to Julia:

> What a God send you are. There is absolutely nothing that you could have thought of that would be more of a help just now to Martha than to provide her with an expert stenographer and typist.
>
> It will make all her work at Edinburgh and here easier and enable her to do a lot of things that she could not have done. . . .
>
> She looked so happy when I gave her your message about getting a Stenographer, and felt it such a help. . . .
>
> . . . [It] is a fairy godmother boon.

She expressed her concern about Martha's very tired wardrobe: "I have said nothing about clothes, but thought when you did come you could get Martha a suit, or Kasha dress to use for speaking &c. later on. . . . Everything will be all right until you come. . . ."[1]

Never idle, juggling her many affairs on behalf of the Faith with both formal and informal appearances, Martha put the finishing touches on preparations for the Esperanto congress. Julia Culver, while not able to be present, shared with Martha the expenses, paying for the programs, slides, and incidental costs. Responding to nudging from London, she also sent Martha a handsome coat and a blouse, or waist, as they were still called in the 1920s.

The Edinburgh Esperanto congress was a gathering of searching, dynamic persons from all over the world, with every movement—religious, political, humanitarian—represented. It was here that Martha deepened a friendship with Abbe Andreo Che, a Catholic priest from Rumania, and one of the world's foremost lecturers and teachers of Esperanto. It was Martha's hope that he would be invited by the scholarly groups in America to lecture and thus demonstrate the advantages of Esperanto as an auxiliary language in the United States, the land of many tongues. He became a great friend of the Bahá'í Faith.

The Bahá'ís were allowed two sessions at the congress, both held in the Free Church of Scotland, where 'Abdu'l-Bahá spoke in 1913. They came off smoothly, a tribute to the time, planning, energy, and care that Martha had given, aiming as always for perfection. The first session was chaired by a member of the Zionist Movement in Great Britain, Dr. Immanuel Olsvanger, who was also one of the world's great Esperantists. Martha spoke on "'The Positive Power of Universal Religion'" and answered questions.[2] Later there was a slide presentation of Akka and Haifa and a musical program. Martha chaired the second session, for which she had arranged a stimulating program with the major talk by Professor Ernest A. Rogers, head of the Montezuma School, Los Gatos, California. Lady Blomfield, a dedicated English Bahá'í who had hosted 'Abdu'l-Bahá in her home in 1911, had come from London to assist with the meetings and conferences. Her contributions continued in many ways throughout the eight days.

Almost all countries were represented, and Martha was particularly pleased that both Lydia and Dr. Sophia Zamenhof were able to attend. But an unattractive note was injected in an otherwise successful and harmonious week. Two persons at the congress attacked the Bahá'í Faith. It was disturbing, though Martha commented, "One has to expect some criticism."[3] To balance the unpleasantness, an individual offered to translate some Bahá'í writings into braille, using Esperanto.

A unique arrangement was introduced on the last afternoon. There was to be an oratorical contest before the congress delegates and guests. Martha was one of nine speakers who drew subjects from a hat and spoke impromptu in Esperanto an hour later. Her language skills had taken a long stride forward.

Happily, the congress was not all work. Martha participated in its festivities—the mayor's ball, the boat excursion through the Firth of Clyde (a deep inlet where the Atlantic Ocean meets the River Clyde) and the Kyles of Bute—using the opportunities for sharing the Faith. Another source of pleasure was a telegram of congratulations from the world-renowned Swiss scientist Auguste Forel, an ardent proponent of Bahá'í principles. It read, "Long live the universal religion of Bahá'u'lláh! Long live the universal auxiliary language, Esperanto!"[4]

The work of the congress finished, Martha returned to England. She was invited to stay with her friend Mrs. Thornburgh-Cropper, one of the early Bahá'ís of London, but Martha felt it would be more advantageous to live among persons as yet unaware of the Faith. She chose the rooming house of two spiritually alert friends who had expressed an interest in the Faith. It was an expensive place, but she took a single room on the top floor. The owner, sensing Martha's need for frugality, offered to make it any price she wished. But in particular circumstances habits of economy were suspended; refusing to jeopardize a potentially rewarding situation with penury, she paid the owner's price.

A whirlwind teaching adventure got under way almost immediately. Shoghi Effendi had cabled Mountfort Mills in Paris to assist Martha with meetings and lectures in London and its environs. However, Martha did not wait for help but got off to a running start, speaking every day and evening. When Mountfort arrived, they worked in tandem, spiritual skylarking, Martha Root fashion. One of the more interesting invitations came from the Spiritualist church, where Sir Arthur Conan Doyle was president. They accepted and conducted a Sunday-morning service. Later they went to Oxford, Shoghi Effendi's university, spoke twice there, in Manchester College, and donated books to the library.

Other Bahá'í friends joined Martha and Mountfort for a spate of talks about the Faith, among them George Townshend, former canon of St. Patrick's Cathedral, Dublin, and Laura and Hippolyte Dreyfus-Barney of Paris, who traveled widely spreading the Bahá'í teachings. They visited Professor

R. A. Nicholson, the Orientalist, of Cambridge University, who had written extensively of the Faith in Persia, its history, the political and religious forces at work to quench its fire, the suffering and persecution of its followers. They also spoke at the Religious and Ethics Committee of the League of Nations and at the National Council of Women. An invitation from the Esperantists of Birmingham took them out of London and its suburbs. In this industrial city, rather like the Pittsburgh of England, Martha was a guest in the home of Quaker friends of Dr. Esslemont's.

Mountfort Mills returned to Paris, but Martha went on to Manchester for a very full eight days. She acted as an anchor person, staying for the entire teaching tour while others came for briefer periods, among them Mrs. Schopflocher of Montreal; Louise Gregory, en route to Budapest and Vienna; Lady Blomfield and Dulcie Turnbull of London; and Aḥmad Yazdí of Port Said.

A vast spectrum of humanity heard these representatives of various cultures, who joined Martha Root for talks on the Faith. There was, for instance, a noon-hour lecture at the Linotype and Machinery Company before seventeen hundred employees, arranged by John Craven, a Bahá'í in Manchester.[5] Later the speakers were luncheon guests of the directors, who encouraged Mr. Craven to show visiting Bahá'ís through the linotype works. Shoghi Effendi was at one time a recipient of the linotype tour.

Manchester was also the home of an acquaintance of Martha's whom she had met in China. Occasionally, when a foreign boat was due to arrive in China, Martha would go to the dock to see if a familiar face might be among the passengers. On one of these excursions a tall, eldery man disembarked who reminded her very much of her father. She offered to help with certain cumbersome landing details and recommended the hotel where she was staying. After they had become friends, he made her promise to be his guest if ever she came to Manchester.

True to her word, Martha arranged to stay at his home, run by a dour, elderly housekeeper. Her host was a highly respected city alderman, who always wore a red tie and was known as "the 'Stormy Petrel.'"[6] All would have been well, except that distinct tensions appeared when the housekeeper became openly jealous of Martha. The housekeeper was certain that the middle-aged female guest was interested in a more permanent relationship with the alderman. Martha found the situation somewhat amusing, but it made her uneasy. She would have preferred staying with Bahá'í friends who were eager to have her, but she tried always to broaden her social contacts and make friends for the Faith. Uncomfortable though it was, she succeeded, and Stormy Petrel became a staunch friend of the Bahá'ís.

Once the tour of the provinces was completed, Martha settled back in London, hoping her mission would change some hearts there. In order not to miss any opportunities, she had a notice printed and delivered to potential forums that announced her availability for lectures and listed eight topics from which sponsors could choose.

BAHÁ'Í, ESPERANTIST, INTERNATIONAL
JOURNALIST & INTERNATIONAL LECTURER

Miss Martha L. Root
will speak in London during September
and until October fifteenth

Her subjects are :—
The Bahá'í Movement.
The Bahá'í Movement in its Relation to Christianity
The Bahá'í Viewpoint of Immortality.
Scientific Proofs of Life after Death.
The New Universal Education.
Universal Peace: How to Bring it.
Esperanto as a Universal Auxiliary Language.
The Harmony of Science and Religion.

HER ADDRESS FOR MAIL IS - C/O AMERICAN CONSULATE, LONDON

*A card Martha Root had printed in London
in 1926 and sent to groups, clubs, and other forums
that might be interested in scheduling her for a talk*

Despite the damp, chilly weather and the constant need for an umbrella, Martha's health was better than it had been on the continent, and she liked London immensely. She felt it a great bounty to spread the teachings among the British. But there was not the warmth and response to the Faith in England that she had experienced in other lands. "The English," she explained, "are very conservative & slow to take these Teachings but when once they get them they make such great Bahais." She added, as if to bolster her feelings, "I will never be discouraged." In another place she wrote, "When the English get these teachings they will take them to China and other lands with the same calibre, stick-to-itiveness, and efficiency with which they have taken Christianity."[7]

In October the British Broadcasting Company invited Martha Root to speak about her impressions of the British dominions and aired the talk during the visit to London of the premiers of those same dominions. Having been to nearly all of England's dominions scattered throughout the world, and having been involved with the people and their modes of living, Martha could speak knowledgeably about these divergent cultures. She was as eloquent in England as in other countries.

During unscheduled moments Martha found time to plan a trip to Spain and Portugal and to study their history, culture, and current political trends. "I shall be happy," she confessed, "when we get to this NEXT WORLD where there is no geography and where we are always working together."[8]

Martha had a clear grasp of the problems created by man in his attempts to use a geographical area for power and control. Such political boundaries often made Martha's tasks more difficult to fulfill. But they rarely stopped her. Rather, they served as a challenge, eagerly met.

29   Iberia and Stuttgart

After five months it was time to leave the familiar and start for other places, with other customs and languages. To Shoghi Effendi she cabled, "'Love do you approve that I continue original plan starting Portugal late November please wire.'" The message was typically dotted with terms of endearment expressing her love and affection for the Guardian. His answer was equally warm: "'Do as Divine guidance inspires you. Tenderest love.'"[1]

Martha's decision was to leave the British Isles at the end of October 1926 and travel to the Iberian Peninsula, where she would visit both Spain and Portugal. This episode is practically a blank page in her adventures; perhaps because of the strong, pervasive religious character of the peninsula, opportunities for speaking did not materialize.

In Madrid, Martha wrote a letter to King Alphonso XIII and called at the palace. There she met the king's secretary, which was quite an achievement, and gave him the letter and a copy of *Bahá'u'lláh and the New Era*. To Martha's delight the secretary promised to present her gift to the king when he returned. She also called upon the military dictator, General Primo de Rivero, again got as far as the secretary, and gave him *The Mysterious Forces of Civilization*, an interesting choice in light of subsequent events that toppled the regime. Martha's expectations for positive results were not very high: "They are very *Catholic*, so I do not know what will happen—but I went & took the Message & they were very polite."[2]

By December Martha was back with friends. Julia Culver invited her to spend Christmas at her apartment in Stuttgart, Germany, along with Emogene Hoagg, who was living in Italy. It was a time of peace, rest, and joy. The apartment, "large and beautiful," was in the city but up on the top of a mountain. In a letter written on Christmas Day Martha described the mood:

> From my window, (I sleep in the library,) I look down over all Stuttgart. My spirit tries to search out where all the beautiful Bahá'ís live, who last year, were so dear and cordial that I shall remember them in all eternity. Emogene . . . plays Chopin's music so it seems celestial. Emogene's laugh is music too.[3]

As a result of Julia's illness, which had kept her from the Edinburgh congress, she learned to bypass the rich and tempting European dishes and became an early champion of natural foods. It was Julia, not her household help, who prepared the meals of fresh vegetables, salads, fruits, and wonderful soups. At least during the holidays Martha would have something besides bread, figs, and apples.

While in Stuttgart a medical consultation was put on Martha's agenda: "Julia takes us to her Doctor and with his new electrical invention, he tells us what is the matter with us and then treats us. He said for me to stay in bed as much as I can and rest and not see people."[4] An impossible prescription. Eventually, there *was* a visit with the Stuttgart Bahá'ís after Julia's firmness melted under Martha's blandishments. She could not bear to leave without seeing her friends.

In the mountaintop apartment Martha had a mystical experience that thrilled her: "I had a vision last night and saw the progress of the Cause so advanced I was astonished, it was far beyond my dreams! It gives me great courage to go forward." It may have been Julia's maternal concerns for Martha that also brought her mother into her world of vision. She was very near, and "she spoke of father and their intercessions for us all. Mother said she prayed for me patience, faithfulness, wisdom, capacity."[5]

The time spent at Julia's was the closest Martha came to the period of rest that she had been promising Ella Cooper she would take, with Ella underwriting the costs. Every letter would contain a promise, along with reasons for not yet fulfilling it, such as, "When I get to a place where I can halt my work," or:

> I did not take the vacation yet, I did not dare use the money to rest, because this trip through the Balkans is so expensive I was afraid I could not manage—but I know that if I would stop and take the little rest I would do better work. It is my heart, Abdu'l Bahá knows I TRY.[6]

So present impossibility became a promise for the future. A rest, she was certain, would be possible in Belfast, or Budapest, or Bucharest, or Warsaw. It never did happen. Martha rested only when forced to bed by a rebelling body. Christmas in Stuttgart was the limit of indulgence.

30 Germany and the North Countries

For the next six months, January–June 1927, Martha would be in Germany, Poland, Czechoslovakia, and the Scandinavian countries. As she mapped out her itinerary for 1927, it took on the flavor of a travel circuit for a professional peace ambassador. She planned to be in Berlin until 25 January:

Then I speak two days in Rostock, then two days in Schwerin, and will be in Hamburg until the 7th of February. Then I go to Brussels to an International Congress for the Elimination of Race Prejudice and to do some speaking in Belgium. From there I go direct to Copenhagen where Miss Johanna Sorensen is arranging my lectures. I leave Copenhagen March 7th for Norway and Sweden.[1]

In her travels Martha learned of an Esperanto peace congress for the teaching of peace in all schools of the world, to be held in Prague, Czechoslovakia, over the Easter holiday, 18 and 19 April. The significance of this congress grew in Martha's consciousness, and participating seemed vital. Hence Prague, too, was built into Martha's plans. She would come down from Copenhagen, stop at Danzig (now Gdańsk), Poland, on the way to make plans for the Universal Esperanto Congress to be held there in July, go to the Prague peace congress, try to meet President Masaryk of Czechoslovakia, do some speaking, and nurture friendships made earlier. "Then," the plan continued, "I would go up again through Latvia, Litvia [sic], Esthonia and then to Helsingfors [Helsinki], Finland, which is only four hours from Petrograd."[2] Martha's grand plan was laid out, and only a more vibrant teaching opportunity, other directives from Shoghi Effendi, or an act of God would deflect her from her course. She followed the counsel of

Bahá'u'lláh in every aspect of her life except one—moderation in all things. Her work, without cessation, on behalf of the Bahá'í Faith was more than a shade immoderate. It was Olympian.

Annie Romer, whose husband had been transferred by the Associated Press from London to Berlin, had started making contacts and exploring possibilities for Martha, preparing the way for her visit. The Romers had taken a large apartment, and Annie was planning teas or "at home[s]," in keeping with the custom, where Martha could meet or entertain friends.[3]

Martha accepted their extended hospitality, but she chose to live by herself, where she could write when not speaking or making contacts. Even sociability after a day of working or an evening of lecturing was not a luxury Martha allowed herself. At one point, after unanswered correspondence mounted, she noted, "In future am going to room alone and do as I did in China—I accomplished more in China than in any other country and it is because I did the writing and speaking . . . and not much talking in between times."[4] Annie Romer urged Martha to put aside her writing until Berlin, when she would help reduce the volume. It was a joy, and a rarity, for Martha to come into a city where there were close friends who knew her needs, her routine, and had the time, energy, and devotion to help with the tasks.

On the way to Berlin, Martha stopped at Gera and Leipzig, where there were some Bahá'ís. In both cities the Bahá'í and Esperanto messages were intertwined, the Esperantists setting up lectures that combined the two, and the Bahá'ís paying more attention to Esperanto. It was Dr. Dietterle in Leipzig, head of the Esperanto Institute of the German Republic, who urged Martha to attend the peace congress in Prague, request a place on the program, and speak about the peace-generating principles of the Bahá'í Faith. He personally introduced Martha at a large meeting of the Esperantists and spoke in glowing terms about the Bahá'í principles and the Bahá'í Esperanto magazine *La Nova Tago*.

During the first week of January 1927 Martha arrived in Berlin, where she spoke on the first evening before the Charlottenburg Esperanto Society, one of thirteen Esperanto clubs in the city. Her lecture was so well received that the other groups got together and sponsored a joint lecture. Both talks were about the Bahá'í Faith, and many listeners requested Bahá'í literature. For Martha, Esperanto continued to be a powerful tool for spreading the Faith.

Besides the familiar round of lectures there was one of a slightly different nature, a joint meeting, given in English, sponsored by three peace societies of Berlin. Martha Root was on the program with a Chinese speaker, a speaker from India, and a black professor from the United States. Five hundred heard words from four different cultures, each speaker motivated by a single goal—world peace.

Because of Martha's work with Esperanto, Berlin's most prestigious newspaper, the *Berliner Tageblatt*, which had a keen interest in this new language, published a lengthy interview with Martha about Esperanto and the Bahá'í Faith.

When Martha met with the Bahá'ís of Berlin, she played a Victrola recording of 'Abdu'l-Bahá chanting in Persian, a Christmas present to her from Mr. and Mrs. Herrigel of Stuttgart. She wanted to share the beauty and richness of His voice and to let them feel the purity and joy latent there.

Vast publicity blanketed the city for Martha's last two lectures in Berlin, where she and Mr. Herrigel would share the platform. Wherever Martha spoke, normally those who heard her responded positively, if not to her message, at least to her spirit, to the love that emanated from her. But Berlin housed dissident voices. Twice in the middle of her talks persons whom Martha termed "Bolshevists" yelled " 'down with religion' " and tried to disrupt the meetings. There were menacing threats of personal danger. It was unsettling and frightening, "but Baha'u'llah protected me," Martha wrote Ella Cooper, adding, "Better not mention this, I did not intend to."[5] In 1927 the Socialist movement was pushing Adolph Hitler into a leadership role; it would try to neutralize the effectiveness of religion, which answered to a higher power. Thus it was probably the Nazis, not the Bolsheviks, who tried to shout Martha down.

Nevertheless, she was happy. The presence of Harry and Annie Romer in Berlin gave a magical quality to her time there, causing her to remark, "It is just like two weeks in Heaven working with Annie in Berlin."[6] The Romers were also a buffer between Martha and the life of a metropolis. "Strangely enough," Annie revealed, "with all of her traveling, she dreads getting around a big city very much."[7]

But this shield, this cushion against the abrasiveness of the city, would no longer be available when Martha traveled alone to the northern countries. She lamented that "It is very sad to leave sweet Annie Romer! She has eyes like Mother's & she is an angel. We have worked day & night here & been so happy doing it."[8]

Between Rostock and Schwerin, Martha added Warne-münde to the roster of cities before going on to Hamburg. Her lecture schedule was full as she visited large places and small, speaking to large groups or intimate gatherings about the reve-lation of Bahá'u'lláh, the path to peace, and Esperanto, the language of peace.

When she arrived in Copenhagen on 28 February, she was met by Johanna Sorensen, a beautiful young Bahá'í, devoted to the Faith, who did not live near any other Bahá'ís. To have Martha Root of America come to that Scandinavian city was an unequaled gift. Johanna had set up lectures, following Mar-tha's advice and guidelines.

To make maximum use of unscheduled hours between arri-val and public performance Martha and Johanna, who was very shy, visited three of the largest newspapers, explained the Faith to the editors, and left 'Abdu'l-Bahá's picture and litera-ture both in English and Danish, which had been skillfully translated by Johanna. Martha then wrote a letter to the king and queen and crown prince of Denmark, which she left at the palace, along with three Bahá'í books. The royal family was not at home. Within hours of coming into Copenhagen, Mar-tha Root had started to spread the message, to raise the call, and the fruits were soon evident. Three very good articles appeared in the Danish newspapers, preparing the residents for the lectures to follow.

The Scandinavian countries were almost entirely Christian, mostly Protestant. On 1 March Martha geared her first public lecture to these sentiments, speaking on " 'The Bahá'í Move-

ment in its Relation to Christianity.'"[9] The interpreter was the
son of a professor of comparative religion at the University of
Copenhagen.

Her campaign on behalf of the Bahá'í Faith was launched.
For one week in Copenhagen and peripheral areas Martha
would speak in Esperanto and English, receive guests, explain
the revelation of Bahá'u'lláh, and further the Faith. The
Esperantists were constant aids and supporters of Martha's
efforts on behalf of the Faith and could be counted on in every
city to publicize lectures, send invitations, and attend the various presentations. Martha's gratitude to them grew as her travels increased, and her reputation among them magnified. Besides the practical, they acknowledged the aesthetic; in
Copenhagen they presented her with a giant bouquet of Danish
pink tulips.

There were frequent coincidences, or unexpected situations,
that added a piquant flavor to Martha's travels. In Copenhagen she looked up the name of a friend of Roy Wilhelm's,
but it was such a common name in Denmark that the telephone
directory had many pages of the equivalent of "Smith." She
picked one and telephoned. The man who answered was the
head of the Vacuum Oil Company of Scandinavia, and he was
delighted to hear from her: "In ten minutes he came over in his
motor car, said he did not have the pleasure of knowing any
Mr. Wilhelm, but that he was interested in spiritual matters
and would do anything he could to serve."[10] Within a short
time he arranged a lecture at the International People's College
in Elsinore (Helsingör), site of Shakespeare's *Hamlet*. He and
his wife would drive Martha to Elsinore, have lunch at the hotel, attend her lecture, and drive her back to their country
house for tea.

After several inquiries her new friend discovered that it was
his youngest brother and wife, and his sister, who had met Mr.
Wilhelm. They, too, wanted to escort Martha Root to Elsinore,
and it became a family affair. On Sunday Martha was invited
to the older brother's home for dinner and explored his library
of rare religious books. She remembered that "'He was so
courteous, so swift to serve the stranger at his city gate and thus

he heard of Baha'u'llah. He said he was expecting a great
World Teacher or Prophet, but he had thought he would come
from Denmark. He said he would read the books.'"[11] Martha
was impressed with his charity and generosity. She learned
from other friends that he had turned over his inherited estate
from his father for an impressive orphan's home and had also
built a Home for Aged Housekeepers and Maids. It had been a
fortuitous and rewarding telephone call.

When one traveled as much as Martha, acquaintances frequently overlapped and often relaxed what might have been a
strained situation. In Denmark there were several friends of
friends. At Elsinore, Martha met a girl who had heard of the
Bahá'í Faith from Jessie Revell, an old friend in Philadelphia.
An American women knew Rouhanieh Latimer of Oregon,
who had seen Martha off on the *Kaga Maru* four years earlier.
The president of the National Council of Danish Women, who
introduced Martha at her lecture, was also an auxiliary delegate of the Danish government to the League of Nations, in
Geneva, where she had met Martha. She, too, was eager to
know more about the Faith.

An interesting woman from Sweden who had spent some
time in Tehran had known Dr. Susan Moody, Elizabeth Stew-
art, Dr. Clock, and Lillian Kappes, four Bahá'ís working in
difficult circumstances at their professions in Iran. Her admiration for their spirit and accomplishment was vast. Martha
brought out a recent copy of *Bahá'í Magazine: Star of the West*
that had their pictures and an article on their work. A bridge of
trust and friendship was built. It was a unifying experience.

The long trip back from Copenhagen to Prague, undertaken
at great expense specifically to attend the peace congress, was
interrupted by a stop in Danzig, where Martha was able to arrange for two Bahá'í sessions at the upcoming Universal
Esperanto Congress in July. From there she went to Berlin to
prepare her talks for Prague, feeling fairly certain that at least
two speaking slots would be made available to her.

These talks were to be in Esperanto, and the utmost care was
given to every word and nuance of the language. She intended
to quote Bahá'u'lláh and 'Abdu'l-Bahá on universal peace, on
the education of children, and on the coming together of the

two. Harry and Annie Romer were of great help, and the talks were polished and refined. Martha's next task, as she saw it, was to memorize them. She carried them everywhere to ensure constant study that would result in a letter-perfect presentation.

While still in Berlin, Martha was notified that she could not speak at the peace congress in Prague. Only those who had made actual experiments on teaching peace in the schools could make presentations. Nevertheless, she traveled to Prague, arriving on 17 April in time for the opening session. When someone said no, Martha firmly believed, that was the time to go to work. She prayed deeply, ardently. Attending the congress, she learned that one of the speakers had fallen and broken a leg. "I went at once to the Director of the Conference," Martha recalled, "and told him I had a speech all prepared and that I [could] speak in ESPERANTO! He was most gracious and while I did not speak that day, he arranged for me to speak on the evening program the following evening. It was like a miracle the way the doors all opened in Prague." [12] To create an impediment to Martha's plans was risky.

Her affairs in Czechoslovakia continued to be charmed. She met Dr. Edvard Beneš, minister of foreign affairs, who had opened the peace congress and had later invited her to the palace. There she learned, among other information, that he was reading the Bahá'í books she had left on her earlier visit.

In Prague she also met Vuk Echtner, a young man who had absorbed the teachings and been enriched by the Bahá'í writings during Martha's first mention of Bahá'u'lláh in Czechoslovakia. He spoke five languages, a gift he was now using to translate the Bahá'í writings. Day and night he helped Martha and, on the evening of her speech, went to the congress an hour early, going up and down the aisles, passing out Bahá'í booklets and discussing the Faith. Before Martha spoke, most had read the material and had some knowledge of her source. She termed this twenty-one year old "the best Esperantist in Prague." [13]

Financing this unexpected conference, a diversion from her original plan, made a large dent in Martha's economy. It meant backtracking, creating double costs for transportation, rooms, meals, and other expenses. But her enterprise and creativity solved the problem: she sold a gift.

In Hamburg she had learned from a letter sent from London that the Bahá'ís of Mashhad, Iran, were sending her a tablet of Bahá'u'lláh, along with a lock of His hair, and a handsome Persian prayer rug, exquisite to the eye, exquisite to the touch.* Martha was suffused with gratitude and humility. On learning of the gifts in transit she addressed a letter to the Mashhad Bahá'ís:

> my heart was touched beyond all words to express it. Nothing in a long time has given me such happiness and such deep confirmation as this letter from the Spiritual Assembly of Meshed. It gives me new courage to go forward. I can never tell you in words how greatly I shall appreciate this Tablet from Baha'u'llah adorned by His Fragrant Hair; I am sure in some mysterious way this Tablet will affect the Bahai Cause throughout Europe. With all my heart I thank you. [14]

Martha sent Harry Randall a carbon copy of her letter to the Persian Bahá'ís, revealing across the top and along the side her feelings regarding the gifts:

> The Meshed friends are sending me a hair from Baha'u'-llah's head, and a Tablet from Baha'u'llah and a Khorassan rug. What wonderful gifts and the *love* that prompted them! I am not worthy, but my heart is deeply touched! They would be worthy gifts to give to Her Majesty, Queen Marie—if I could give them up. Of course I just long to keep them a little while myself. I know they are sent for a great purpose and perhaps Baha'u'llah wishes them for Queen Marie. [15]

Before the letter to Harry was actually mailed, the affair was settled. Martha added another note to this copy: "March 15—I

---

*A tablet is a letter or message sent on fine paper, originally of a specific composition and consistency.

When Bahíyyih Khánum, the Greatest Holy Leaf, would care for Bahá'u'lláh, she would save the clippings of His hair. Over the years they accumulated, and several persons of spiritual depth were rewarded with these remembrances.

am going to give the great Gift of the Hair and Tablet to Queen Marie. I have written her Mar. 13, all about it."[16] Although these gifts of inestimable value, so precious to Martha, had not yet reached her, they were already promised to another, to a queen, in whose possession Martha felt they might affect history.

The rug was another matter. Of this handsome Khorassan prayer rug she noted in a letter two months later:

> How I wish you could have seen that exquisite, soft, lovely in color, lovely [to] touch, rug. It reached me in Prague, and only a Bahai could understand that I sold that glorious gift and used the money. It was like a holy Confirmation that Baha'u'llah blessed my returning back the long distance from Copenhagen to Prague to try to raise the Call at this important Congress. (And it was expensive, but it succeeded.)

Martha also included a lengthy passage for the Persian Bahá'ís, ending with, "I shall always be a better, finer, more noble Bahai because you thought of me and showered your love upon me. Your rug IS my spiritual carpet and my spirit truly pos[s]esses it and enjoys it, for I always remember it."[17]

The road to Prague to speak of Bahá'u'lláh's teachings about peace had obstacles to bolster purpose, and silken threads to smooth the way. Martha accepted both. She overcame the first and blessed, and used, the second.

31 Northward

Uplifted by the events at Prague, her health cooperating, Martha picked up her trail north into the Baltic countries, first responding to an invitation from the Esperantists to lecture in Stettin, Germany (now Szczecin, Poland), during the third week in April 1927. Forty-five persons lingered after the large audience dispersed, discussing the Bahá'í Faith until after midnight.

The next morning Martha began the long trip up through the Baltic countries. Her travel information was usually in a foreign language. Thus Kaunas, Lithuania, was called "Kovno, Litva"; Tallin, Estonia, was known as "Reval"; Helsinki was "Helsingfors"; and Prague was "Praha."

The Baltic countries of Lithuania, Latvia, and Estonia had all been part of Russia until 1918. The twenties was an interim period of independence for them, as they would soon be once again under the arm of the Soviet Union. Martha, noting that it had been a terrific struggle, marveled that they could hold their own against bolshevism. One Latvian told Martha that his country was the crossroads between bolshevism and Western Europe. She thought " 'bulwark' " a more fitting word.[1]

The first stop in Kovno was not very productive. It was a Lithuanian holiday, lectures needed to be announced a good deal in advance, and the country was under military control. But she did see the minister of foreign affairs and through him sent books to the president of the republic. Also visiting the Litva University, she met a young professor who was a graduate of the University of Chicago.

Martha would always write ahead to the Esperantists, notifying them of her schedule and securing their assistance in setting up lectures. Although in most countries they were free to arrange meetings for Martha, the Esperantists in Kovno could only visit her at the hotel.

Martha found a better environment for the Esperantists of Riga, Latvia, and Reval, Estonia. When her train stopped in Riga, the Esperantists were assembled at the station to welcome her, waving the green banner of hope, the Esperanto flag. Newspaper photographers were waiting to take pictures, interviewers came to the hotel, and articles appeared in four papers and three languages—Latvian, German, and Russian. Arrangements were made for Martha to speak at the Anglo-Latvian Club. The Esperantists also arranged a public lecture in the president's palace, where the minister of foreign affairs was presented books that he would pass on to the president. A secretary of Latvia would place two additional books in the university for Martha.

Twenty-five friends accompanied Martha to the train to see her off at midnight. She had known no one in the Baltic countries when she started her trip; but she was like a spiritual Pied Piper, and people followed her song of love. Appreciating the thoughtfulness of the Esperantists in ensuring a comfortable place for her on the train, she reported:

One Esperanto boy left the lecture and went to the train two hours ahead and sat there to hold the best place for me. I had not known it until I walked into the crowded train and there sat the little hero. We all cheered him. Do you wonder that I love the Esperantists and feel grateful to them. In little kindnesses and in big ones they have opened Europe.

There would otherwise have been no reserved seat for Martha. She was traveling third class on old trains that had formerly been used on the Trans-Siberian Railway. They were absolutely devoid of any comfort other than providing space, and Martha wrote that "Heavy plank boards seemed to hang all round the car[;] these could be fastened up, so in tiers were board beds for nearly everybody." Primitive though the accommodations may seem, to Martha they were "the most comfortable cars for poor people I have ever seen."[2]

Nevertheless, it was a long, arduous journey, sitting on plank boards, day and night, over uneven tracks and rough terrain. For Martha it was ameliorated by family attachments: "Dear mother's woollen shawl makes a divan of any place."[3] She looked at all the poor in her company, not with superior, class-conscious eyes, but with love, thinking how kindly 'Abdu'l-Bahá would have treated the passengers if He had been there. Martha sat in their midst in these crude surroundings and communicated love.

Arriving in Reval, Estonia, in early May 1927, four Esperantists called at the hotel for interviews, which she gave in Esperanto, more and more a convenient tool of communication in foreign lands. Two wrote it in Estonian, one in German, and one in Russian. Each of these interviewers was a writer of poetry or short stories, so they took the time to compare their articles in order that each would vary in some degree from the others. That sense of creativity and originality delighted Martha's professional sense.

One characteristic of the press that astonished her was its efficiency. When another journalist came by for an interview, this time in English, Martha wrote:

> It was remarkable, five hours later they were selling the paper with the interview. It was one of the best articles that appeared in the Baltic countries, he GRASPED the Teachings. Later he came and wrote other articles for he was deeply interested. He had never heard of the Cause until he called at the hotel that day.[4]

When Martha arrived in Reval, the minister of foreign affairs sent his motorcar and a secretary to show Martha around just as the ministers of Latvia and even militarily controlled Lithuania had done. They, in turn, received gifts of the words of Bahá'u'lláh, gathered between the covers of a book. She bestowed similar gifts on the American consuls in these countries.

A large public lecture in Reval was again arranged by the Esperantists, who, as her extended family, did for Martha what the Bahá'ís would do if they existed in these lands. When the time came for Martha to continue her journey to Finland, across the Baltic Sea, remarkably, at a temperate time of year, it was the Esperantists who brought gifts of flowers and books and saw her off.

It had now been a little over four years since Martha had sailed out of Seattle for Yokohama in March 1923. Her next stops would be Finland, Sweden, and Norway, before attending the Esperanto congress in Danzig, Poland, at the end of July. Gifts from Ella Cooper, Lena Lee, and Rouhanieh Latimer had refurbished Martha's wardrobe in preparation for the busy months ahead. They had sent lingerie, night clothes, and slips, along with warm clothes for cooler climates. Some had come to her in Geneva, some in London, more in Berlin. Martha felt outfitted for a long time to come and was delighted to know that she would not have to buy clothes; her money could instead be spent for visas, boats, trains, and shelter.

Martha found that the Finnish people in Helsinki, the southern-most city in Finland, were open, cordial, lacking in prejudice, and eager to investigate the truth. After arriving during the second week of May 1927 and spending the first two weeks writing, she notified the Esperantists of her presence, and talks were arranged immediately. The first was given in a park to four hundred listeners, whom Martha described as "a thoughtful, quiet, orderly crowd."[5] Among the other, by now usual, recipients of visits and literature were editors, libraries, peace societies, some ministers of the government, and the president of Finland.

Before leaving this Scandinavian country, Martha went up to Turku, the second largest city and a university and scholastic center. With only six hours on this stopover, there was no time for a lecture; but she was met at the train by two professors, both Esperantists, who introduced her to people at the university and helped her to put books in the library.

The enduring aspect of the printed word, even in the brief existence of a newspaper, was made especially clear to Martha in Finland. An article that she had given to a Vienna paper more than a year ago had been reprinted and circulated in Finland and in many of the places that Martha had visited over the past year. Neither of her escorts in Turku had heard of the Bahá'í Faith until they read one of her articles in a Finnish newspaper. With Martha as a visible connection, both were now eager to learn more about the Faith and were interested in following its news and progress.

From Turku Martha sailed across the Baltic Sea and into Stockholm, on the east coast of Sweden. At the first lecture, given in a private school the crown prince and his son had both attended, the vitality of the printed word was again evident. One member of the audience was a professor who had read an article by Martha reprinted in a Göteborg newspaper. The professor, she learned, had sent for literature and had put *Bahá'u'lláh and the New Era* on his list of university lectures.

Soon after her arrival in Sweden Martha sent books to the royal household—Queen Victoria and Crown Prince Gustav Adolph. The gifts were acknowledged by a lady-in-waiting for the queen, and a baron for the prince. Both attendants would read the books, acting somewhat like literary tasters, before passing them to their royal superiors. But there was not the public stir in royal circles to these spiritual ideas that had occurred in Bucharest.

The details of travel and intercity decisions were all solved by the Esperantists, who met Martha at the train and took her everywhere, including the University Club in Uppsala. One resident of Uppsala, the Archbishop of Sweden, also received a visit from Martha.* After a long talk, she left him two key books on the Bahá'í Faith, *The Kitáb-i-Íqán* (the Book of Certitude) from the pen of Bahá'u'lláh, and Dr. Esslemont's *Bahá'u'lláh and the New Era.*[6]

Among the organizations who made forums available for her lectures in these Nordic cities were the Theosophists and the ever-growing peace societies. In Stockholm the presidents of every peace society came together to call on Martha at her hotel, where they spent a long and fruitful evening discussing the Bahá'í principles for world peace. After giving her letters

---

*Nathan (Lars Olof Jonathon) Söderblom, Archbishop of Uppsala 1914–31, was a pioneer in the ecumenical movement. He was a professor of theology at the University of Uppsala and at Leipzig and wrote several important theological works. He was awarded the Nobel Peace Prize in 1930.

of introduction to peace societies in the other Nordic countries, these disciples of peace brought Martha to call on the mayor of Stockholm, Mr. Lindhagen. He became a real friend, would attend Bahá'í sessions at the Danzig Esperanto congress, and later would be a connecting link to the Swedish mayor of Jamestown, New York. The threads of contacts wove in and out of the cities of the world and even stretched over mountains and oceans, helping Martha to weave the message of unity.

The Swedish National Esperanto Congress was a focal point for Martha's travel plans in this Scandinavian country. When she spoke on "The Bahá'í Movement And Esperanto" in a huge theater and before a vast audience, the talk was simultaneously broadcast over the radio.[7] It was her first experience with broadcasting while addressing a visible audience. Other times she had broadcast from a studio, but she took her new experience in stride. Six newspapers published résumés of the lecture, which she had prepared for the press. In all, that address reached thousands through the audience, the airwaves, and newsprint.

Martha's Esperanto skills had gained greatly through her regular use of the language. In Geneva in 1925 she had taken the lower examination for Esperanto; now she felt prepared to take the higher examination, which was given once a year at the Swedish congress. Four Swedish men and Martha Root took the exam, for which she received a diploma on 6 June 1927, identifying her skills in essay writing, defense of her work, and translation. In addition, there was an oral exam where skills in pronunciation and grammar were tested. Martha passed each category with the Swedish word *berömlig,* meaning worthy of praise, cum laude.

It was in Stockholm that Martha visited a man of unusual skill and capacity, Mr. H. Thilander, who was blind and deaf, and badly crippled, but had mental and physical energy that was hardly diminished by his handicaps. He printed five of the world's most important magazines for the blind. One of Martha's articles had been given to him, and he was eager to learn more about the Bahá'í Faith. Soon after meeting Martha, he translated Big Ben into braille and sent out more than seven hundred copies as a supplement to one of his monthly magazines. His efforts increased, and he made enormous contributions to Bahá'í literature for the blind, with the costs of his work defrayed in part by Martha's American friends.

Martha traveled across Sweden during the last week of June 1927 and headed for Oslo, Norway. Here one of her most important teaching experiences took place:

> from there a talk on Esperanto and Bahá'u'lláh's Peace Plans was broadcast all over Europe. Advance letters had been sent to fifty cities including all the Capitals asking the Esperantists to announce this talk in their newspapers. The Esperantists of Oslo were most cordial and remarkably efficient. (Also among the Esperantists in Stockholm were some of the educationists and editors and members of Parliament.) They all helped me beyond all words to express it. We can never thank them enough.[8]

Despite a very tight schedule Martha still took time to look up a Norwegian relative of Mr. and Mrs. Adolph Dahl, who were earnest Bahá'í workers in Pittsburgh.

From Oslo Martha traveled by train and an additional three hours by car to Uddevalla, in southwest Sweden. It was to this border town that two Swedish Bahá'ís, who had been unable to meet Martha in Sweden and who could not get passports into Norway, brought a Bahá'í from Brooklyn, New York, who was also living in Sweden. It was the time of the eclipse of the moon. The atmosphere was gloomy, and the countryside was pelted with torrential rains, as had been the case for every day Martha was in Norway. Yet she remembered the day's being

> so HAPPY for us four Bahá'is that it stands as one of the great days of our lives. . . . How we wish you could all have been with us in that house on the border in the little upper room, which Mrs. Erickson took for the five hour conference. We brought our lunch, and it was a feast of Heaven![9]

A highlight of the meeting for the Swedish Bahá'ís was the translation of portions of *Bahá'u'lláh and the New Era* by Mrs. Rudd, a Bahá'í from Boviken, Sweden.

After a lecture at a famous ski resort, Martha participated in the annual Peace Congress of Norway in Voss, in the southwest part of the country. There she lectured on 3 July, gave out Bahá'í literature, and made friends among peace advocates and editors, who would publish articles about the Bahá'í plans for peace in their journals. Though her trip to Voss was out of her way and expensive, the positive response made the cost and effort worthwhile.

Bergen, the largest Norwegian port, would be Martha's last stop in the Nordic countries. She devoted the entire two days to the media, meeting with newspaper reporters and speaking "through the Bergen radio," with gratifying results.[10]

On 8 July 1927 Martha sailed out of Bergen and down the North Sea toward Rotterdam in The Netherlands. From there she would make her way via rail to Brussels, Belgium, to attend the VII Congres Mondial Des Associations, which would start on 17 July. Martha's choice of an economical third-class passage to Rotterdam would have put her in dormitory-like accommodations, twenty-four to a room, uncomfortable, lacking in privacy. However, other forces were at work:

> The Director of the Steamship Company who heard the Radio talk and was interested in peace, met me in the Steamship Office. He changed my place and himself chose the finest room on the ship and told the Captain to give me that room alone. I wrote him a letter of thanks and sent him "Promulgation of Universal Peace". It was a wonderful confirmation, because I had economized so much to go back to one more International Congress. I had not been first class in a ship since I left the United States nearly five years ago.[11]

Such kindnesses continued to shower Martha in response to her selfless efforts to teach the message of Bahá'u'lláh. Her travels through the northern countries in the spring and early summer of 1927 had again led her to many new friends in strange lands. In addition to the Bahá'ís, she had discovered her association with Esperantists to be a valuable asset when seeking forums for her talks. And there would be many more talks, both in Brussels and beyond.

32   The Summer of 1927

Expenses had been high, especially in Norway and Sweden. The Peace Conference of Norway, although a rewarding event, was an added expense; the border conference in Uddevalla, Sweden, yet another unexpected expenditure. Martha had requested that an additional seventy-five dollars be sent from her funds. That was almost gone, and she had written for more. Roy Wilhelm's check had not come, and the expenses of the Danzig congress had to be paid. Martha turned to Julia Culver, who came to the rescue, providing roughly half the amount necessary for mounting the two Bahá'í sessions at the congress.

Before traveling to Danzig, Martha stopped in Brussels to attend the Congres Mondial Des Associations. The intense mid-July heat of the Belgian city was an uncomfortable contrast to the cool of the Nordic countries, and with the effects of the intensive work in Norway and Sweden Martha became ill and was forced to rest for a few days. It meant canceling an anticipated trip to Antwerp, but it gave her time to get letters written and refine the arrangements for Danzig.

At the Palais Mondial in Brussels, where the Congres Mondial Des Associations was held, Martha gave the greeting from Shoghi Effendi and spoke on the principles of the Bahá'í Faith. It was translated into eloquent French by the director, Dr. Paul Otlet, who spoke on what it would mean to civilization if those principles were actually put into effect, were truly lived. From this congress was issued an invitation for a permanent Bahá'í exhibition in the Palais Mondial. "Who will arise to do it?" Martha asked. "If some one starts, I feel sure all countries would send something, their books, magazines and pictures."[1]

It was now time to move on to Danzig, to the Nineteenth Universal Esperanto Congress, 28 July–3 August 1927, that had occupied so much of Martha's time in planning and arranging. When she learned that a Jubilee Tree was to be planted to commemorate the twenty-fifth year since the first worldwide Esperanto gathering, Martha wrote to Haifa, asking for little packages of soil from the Tombs of Bahá'u'lláh, the Báb, and 'Abdu'l-Bahá, and to Roy Wilhelm for soil from West Englewood, New Jersey, where 'Abdu'l-Bahá had spoken in 1912.

There were more and more attendants at these congresses as the awareness of Esperanto spread. This would be Martha's third Universal Esperanto Congress and the third time the Faith was officially represented. At the opening session Martha read words of greeting from Shoghi Effendi. Again there were two Bahá'í sessions, the first being a featured event of the congress at which Dr. Ernst Kliemke, president of the Esperanto Society of Germany, was the speaker. Martha chaired this session with a special feeling of pleasure because Dr.

NINETEENTH UNIVERSAL ESPERANTO CONGRESS
Danzig (now Gdańsk), Poland, 31 July 1927. Martha Root
(standing, in white) represented the Bahá'í Faith at the planting
of an oak tree to mark the twenty-fifth anniversary
of the holding of universal Esperanto congresses.

Kliemke had recently become a Bahá'í. At the second Bahá'í session Martha gave the main talk, speaking on "'The Bahai Scientific Proofs of Life After Death.'"[2]

At the planting ceremony for the Jubilee Tree, held on the day between the two Bahá'í sessions, Martha presented the soil from Haifa, Palestine, and West Englewood, New Jersey; it was an additional opportunity to speak about the Faith before hundreds. The oak tree was planted in a new square named Esperanto Ground; it would be nurtured by soil from all over the world, signifying the universal spirit that created and would nourish it.

One of the joys of a congress such as this was the meeting of people from all over the world and the renewal of friendships from the cities and provinces that Martha had visited in her ceaseless travels. She had more and more respect for the value of regional and international gatherings, whether for peace, or Esperanto, or education, or religion. Many participants seemed drawn to the Bahá'í teachings, especially the younger generation, after hearing of them through these gatherings.

As there was much writing to be done after the congress, Martha accepted an invitation from Julia Culver to visit her in Geneva. It was a very small apartment, but with Julia's involvement at the Bahá'í Bureau, Martha was counting on a period of quiet in which to write.

She left Danzig immediately after the congress and was accompanied on the train by Lucy Marshall of San Francisco, who would remain a close friend, and John Cooper from Seattle. Along the route to Geneva they stopped in Berlin for a day to attend a meeting and to visit with the Bahá'ís. Among those whom Martha met was Badí'u'lláh Maḥmúdzádih, a deeply spiritual Persian living in Russia. He tried, along with other friends, to get Martha a visa for Russia, which she hoped to visit after Danzig. The visa, however, was unattainable. The publicity that Martha generated about the Faith, while a positive element in most cases, would act only as a deterrent in Russia, where the strictures were being increased, and where the climate for spiritual exploration was approaching its nadir. Persecutions against the Bahá'ís were beginning, and the first Bahá'í House of Worship, built in Ashkhabad, Turkistan, would soon be taken over by the Soviets.

In Geneva, the global center for more than three hundred international associations, Martha saw wonderful opportunities for alerting world visitors to the Bahá'í Faith. She also relished meeting many Bahá'ís from the United States. But August was to be primarily a time for writing, and she wanted to be assured the privacy for her work. She had written to Julia from Brussels:

> If I should come right after the Congress would there be just you & me in the apartment? Do you think I could get a lot of this writing done there? Could I just shut myself up and write some days each week? I could see about my own little meals, I don't want you to have any cares. I *must* get the writing done in August. But we could have some meetings too, and see people certain days.[3]

September, Martha felt, could be a time of concentration on presenting the Faith. She hoped that Mountfort Mills, the Dreyfus-Barneys, and others could be invited to speak during the month when the League of Nations, as well as other international groups, would be in session.

During her stay with Julia, Martha was not limiting her writing to articles or a printed record of current activities. She was paving the way for a visit to Iceland at some future time, and she started sowing the seeds. She sent literature to nineteen places in Iceland, names and addresses all secure in one of her address books.

A large part of Martha's luggage was given over to literature on the Bahá'í Faith. She gave away hundreds of books in the course of her stay in different countries. Unable to count on new supplies being in a place when she arrived, and not stopping in many cities long enough to have packages catch up with her, she carried vast supplies of books with her. The inventory would eventually be restocked when Martha reached a spot where she would settle in for longer periods.

Shoghi Effendi, recognizing Martha's contributions, wrote of these in a letter to the Bahá'ís that would be printed in the

April 1929 issue of *Baha'i News Letter.* The closing paragraph said:

> I appeal to individual believers and Bahá'i Assemblies alike to reinforce by every possible means the earnest strivings of such a precious soul, to respond speedily and entirely to every request that from time to time she feels moved to address to her fellow-workers in every land, to strive to attain the high standard of stewardship that she has set, and to pray from the very depths of their hearts for the uninterrupted continuance of her noble endeavors.[4]

In response to this appeal, boxes of books would be sent to Martha, without charge, to whatever spot on the planet they were requested.

Martha stayed in Geneva through mid-September and the gathering of the League of Nations. After finishing her writing, she arranged some talks and lectures, both for herself and for visiting Bahá'ís. With Julia she entertained modestly, and she also assisted with receiving visitors and giving out information about the Bahá'í Faith at the International Bahá'í Bureau.

But the world was waiting for the message of Bahá'u'lláh. It was time to move on.

33   Return to the Balkans

On 19 September 1927 Martha left Geneva, crossed Switzerland and Italy, and headed for the Balkans, where she would spend the next few months. She stopped at Trieste on the Adriatic Sea, then went on to Belgrade, deep in Yugoslavia, before going to Rumania. There in Bucharest she would spend two weeks and have her second meeting with Queen Marie. She described the atmosphere of the "Paris of the Balkans" as being

> so fascinating to tourists, so different from any other city. . . . Calea Victoria, Bucharest's fashionable thoroughfare, that is always so thronged one wonders how the many motor cars and bevies of horse-drawn carriages ever "arrive" through such a narrow, picturesque moving picture of aristocratic Rumanian life. . . . She liked riding through it all again, coming up from the train to her small hotel.[1]

While in Bucharest, Martha would give lectures and write newspaper articles, but her primary purpose was to visit Queen Marie. On 9 October Martha was again to be received at a time when the queen was seeing no one but members of the royal family. She was in a period of mourning for her husband, King Ferdinand, who had passed away on 20 July 1927.

The queen was staying at her summer palace, Peleshor, in Sinaia, high in the Carpathian Mountains. Martha would need to make a four-hour trip on a rapid express train in order to reach it. Carrying only two pieces of luggage, one containing gifts for the queen and a white dress for the special visit, and the other full of personal items and a change of clothes, Martha reached the station in a pouring rain. Suddenly, a thief ran by and snatched the less valuable valise right out of Martha's hands. "If I ran after him," she decided, "I could never get him

& would miss my train & miss my visit to the Queen—so I let the suitcase go!"[2]

After making the trip to Sinaia in the midst of the torrential rainstorm, Martha was happy that the next morning arrived clear and crisp. It was a sparkling October day in this beautiful little resort town where the "villas grace the mountain slopes as jewels in a tiara of autumnal glory."[3]

Despite fashionable custom, Martha decided to walk to the palace "to enjoy the thrill of passing through those enchanting roadways leading gracefully up and up, and to see at close range the splendid little seventeenth-century church and monastery, shining like a pearl . . . in this diadem of mountain splendor." But Martha had another reason for walking. Referring to herself in the third person, she revealed that

> Deep in her heart, too, was the longing to go on foot and humbly to the first Queen of the whole world who had publicly written of Bahá'u'lláh's great Principles for this universal cycle. . . . In the centuries ahead when Bahá'u'lláh's Teachings are lived and fully understood, the name of Her Majesty Queen Marie of Rumania will stand as the first Queen who wrote and explained the power of these universal principles to bring the permanent peace.[4]

The draught of mountain air and the clear October day stirred Martha's poetic powers as she described the hills, the monastery, the church where the royal family attended services. She passed through the white courtyard and mused that it was probably to this very spot that the disciple Andrew brought the "Glad-tidings of the Christ." Past the church and up through the great park she walked, under the ancient, tended trees. The estate contained two palaces, the larger Palace Pelesh, and Peleshor, especially known as the queen's home, built by the late King Carol for King Ferdinand and Queen Marie and their children. Martha "walked on past the magnificent immense Palace Pelesh, where King Ferdinand, with his Queen-wife's arms about him lifting him higher, had courageously passed from this home into the House of Many Mansions promised by His Lord. . . ."[5]

The smaller palace sat in the midst of terraced gardens, which Martha thought in her experience were unsurpassed. On entering the palace

> Ladies in Waiting stood in the great hall to receive the visitor. They were the same fine women who had greeted her two years before in Controceni Palace, but now they were dressed in black. . . . One explained that Her Royal Highness Princess Ileana was still at the church, but had left word she would receive the guest when she returned. . . . The other Lady in Waiting took the writer up the broad, circular open stairway to the Queen's drawing-room on the next floor.[6]

Arriving in the presence of the queen, Martha was again struck by the originality of her garments and by her beauty. "But," Martha observed, "it is the radiance in her eyes and the tender smile one loved most and will remember longest."[7]

Queen Marie conversed with Martha about the queen's much publicized journey in October 1926 to the United States, where she had been received with enthusiasm and ceremony. The Bahá'ís, having read Her Majesty's several syndicated articles concerning the Faith, stayed in the background but acknowledged her presence. The queen, through Martha Root, wanted to thank

> "all those Bahá'í friends in America who sent me the lovely bouquets in all the cities through which I passed. How it touched my heart! Wherever I came, those nosegays always on my table, nothing personal, never saying who had brought them, never able to thank anyone, just sent with the love of the Bahá'ís of those cities, went straight to my heart! No one ever understood how much those bouquets meant to me!"

Referring to her role in spreading the message of the Bahá'í Faith through her articles, she told Martha, "'With bowed head I recognize that I, too, am but a channel and I rejoice in the knowledge.'"[8]

Martha had saved the gift from the Bahá'ís of Mashhad,

Persia, for several months in order to present it to the queen at this second meeting. In an article for the *Bahá'í Magazine: Star of the West* Martha described the gift as "an illumined sheet, on which was inscribed a Prayer of Bahá'u'lláh. It was adorned and blessed in the center with a lock of Bahá'u'lláh's own shining hair. She . . . will have a frame specially designed for it, and in the oval she will place a small photograph of 'Abdu'l-Bahá. . . ."[9]

This treasure was deeply appreciated by the queen, whose sense of the artistic was both innate and cultivated. When referring to the polished gold letters on the illumined work, she remarked that " 'It is in the most perfect taste of all the Orient! I know how rare and beautiful it is!' "[10]

Princess Ileana had been studying Bahá'í books since Martha's first visit. On returning from church, she invited Martha to her room on the third floor of the palace, where she asked, "How does one become a Bahá'i?"[11] Martha found the princess to be very beautiful, serious, and sweet. Like the queen, Ileana loved having flowers around, and there were over one hundred pink roses in bowls and vases in the apartment. There were also pictures of a spiritual nature, including one of 'Abdu'l-Bahá and numerous books, among them nearly all of the writings of Bahá'u'lláh and 'Abdu'l-Bahá published in English. She told Martha that she passed many of the Bahá'í books on to her friends. Sincerely touched by the beauty of the Bahá'í revelation, Ileana offered to translate the tiny blue booklet into Rumanian.*

Political forces were already at work that would, twenty years later, replace the monarchy with the People's Republic of Rumania. Such forces were eating away at the fabric of the royal family, whose image of morality was of tremendous importance to a Catholic and Rumanian Orthodox society. False stories and rumors were fed to newspapers, one reporting that Princess Ileana had run away with a naval officer; the date of this fabricated escapade was the same day she had spent with Martha Root. "Poor Rumania is so upset," Martha wrote to

---

*Princess Ileana did translate both the blue booklet and the booklet "What is the Bahá'í Movement?" into Rumanian.

PRINCESS ILEANA OF RUMANIA
the daughter of Queen Marie. She translated some
of the Bahá'í writings into Rumanian.

Ella Cooper, "the Queen does not have an easy life—but [she?] did not say anything about the politics."[12]

Despite the theft that had marred the beginning of Martha's trip to Sinaia, her visits with Queen Marie and her daughter were totally satisfying. Martha's love and admiration for the queen grew during this meeting, and the queen was equally responsive to her visitor. "She was so lovely to me," Martha added appreciatively, "she kissed me twice and put her arm about me. It was a heavenly visit to Sinaia."[13]

When Martha was back in Bucharest, she had two thousand blue booklets printed in French, most of which were given out at lectures. She made plans to have them also printed in other languages of the Balkans—Bulgarian, Serbian, and Greek—as the palpable unrest stirring among the Balkan people greatly concerned her: "The times are so bad here, the unrest so great, certainly the Balkans are an arsenal[;] one match would set Europe aflame." It was only a matter of time before these forces would change the face of government in this pocket of Europe. Martha felt that the teachings might be "the only hope of these dear Balkan peoples."[14]

But it was not only the Balkans that were affected. The fingers of war were reaching out to touch all the countries of Europe. She felt the seething unrest in Germany and in the Baltic countries as well and feared being trapped in the middle of an active war. She communicated her forebodings to the Guardian. Shoghi Effendi knew that the guns and afflictions of war would eventually fill Europe and Asia, but the time was not yet ripe for conflict. There were still a few years of respite; the immediate future would be spared. He sent words to comfort her:

> As to the matter of an eventual war that may break out suddenly in Europe, do not feel in the least concerned or worried, Dearest Martha. . . .
>
> The prospect is very remote, the danger for the near future is non-existent. Should complications arise, and travelling become perilous in Europe, you must rest assured that the Beloved Family will receive you in their midst with open arms, and the haven of Mount Carmel will be your Shelter and refuge in case a storm breaks out in Europe. Do not feel disturbed at present, however, and with an assured heart and mind, concentrate all your powers and splendid gifts upon the pursuit of your noble and arduous task. Bahá'u'lláh watches over you and the Supreme Concourse overshadows you, as their heroic and exemplary herald on this earthly plane.[15]

Martha was relieved and reassured, as she believed implicitly in Shoghi Effendi's words. She was also touched by the concern of those in Haifa for her safety and felt secure with Mount Carmel as a promised haven. Now she saw before her a longer period of work than she had anticipated, a gift of time to gather her strength and carry on her work. She would be returning to Bulgaria, a prospect that pleased her. The ground there was fertile, and Martha was eager to move forward.

34 Bulgaria and Constantinople

En route to Sofia, Bulgaria, where she would spend three weeks, Martha stopped on 17 October 1927 for two days at the border city of Ruse, on the Danube River. The Esperantists in this, the fourth largest city in Bulgaria, had arranged a lecture in a theater, and five hundred came to hear Martha Root of America. In addition to her usual forms of communication she concentrated her efforts on the educational institutions and met with their directors.

As often happened, there was that one young man among all who heard Martha speak who became fired with the Bahá'í Faith, wanted to work for it, and asked to be kept informed of news of the Faith. He could not have chosen a better person to feed a spiritual appetite or nurture a new garden. Martha was the champion cross-pollinator. "I try as much as possible," she reported to friends and family members, "to link the youth of one country with those of another—my visit to a country I hope, is only the beginning of spiritual events, the youth themselves are the ones who will carry it far, far!"[1]

Arriving in Sofia on 19 October, Martha found an openness, a responsiveness, that captivated her. The National Convention of Women's Clubs was meeting for three days, and Martha arranged to address them in Esperanto. It was the key that opened the doors in Sofia. Invitations to speak filled every day and evening, interviews were given, and the people offered friendship and assistance. She told Ella Cooper that "The love of these people & their help astonishes me." And they were helping in most remarkable ways:

One paper is using as supplement "What Is the Bahai Movement?" in Bulgarian language[.] I got out 10,000 for $20. (couldn't afford the booklet so just put it all on one page[)].

They did the printing & sent out 3500 for me gratis, and next week they will at their own expense get out a *Bahai Number.* [2]

That quality of Martha's that prompted others to assist her had not diminished with the years. If anything, it had increased the ardor of her acquaintances, who wanted to alleviate any difficulties she might encounter, to smooth the way, and in many cases to participate in the work at hand. She allowed them the privilege.

After leaving articles with the newspaper editors, Martha had them reading about the Faith and was anticipating several appearances in print after she left. She was especially happy when editors had broader interests, which seemed to happen frequently in the Nordic, Baltic, and Balkan countries. The editor of the best daily Bulgarian paper had twice been minister of education of the country. He had used one of Martha's articles and promised more.

When speaking opportunities appeared, Martha ventured out of the city. One such opportunity came at the American School in Samokov, where the president's wife gave a dinner for her, and four hundred attended the lecture.

In Vratza (Vrattsa), four hours from Sofia by train, there was an astonishing response to the widely publicized lecture arranged by the Esperantists. It is difficult in our time, with our sophisticated means of communication and transportation, to understand the eagerness of the Bulgarian people to hear a lecturer from another land and to appreciate the extent of inconvenience many experienced in order to learn about the Bahá'í Faith. "It was the first time," Martha wrote, "a public lecture had ever been given in that city by an American (or English) individual, and the first public Esperanto lecture ever given there by an Esperantist from another country." [3] Over five hundred attended the lecture, including the mayor and city officials. What was extraordinary was that Esperantists from neighboring villages walked twenty-five miles each way in a heavy rainstorm to hear Martha Root.

There were only two universities in Bulgaria, the Free University and Sofia University, and Martha spoke at both. In Sofia there was an interesting variety of other forums for her lectures—the Red Cross Training School for Nurses, the Tourist Club, and the Vegetarian Restaurant. Martha often had her lunch in this restaurant in order to share time with friends, by-passing her habit of eating in her room. The restaurant became a meeting place for people interested in learning more about the Bahá'í Faith, and it was Martha's hope that study classes would follow.

King Boris II and his sister Princess Eudoxie again received books, by messenger, from Martha. As king, he belonged to the Orthodox Church; his sister was a Catholic, creating a division of religious loyalties between royal duty and inherited belief. Martha was disappointed but not surprised that no dramatic response came from the ruling family to the revelation of Bahá'u'lláh.

Bulgaria, Martha felt, could be a pivotal country in the sense that the people were open-minded and responsive; with concentrated teaching the Faith could sweep the country. She left no avenue unexplored in introducing the Bahá'í teachings to these Balkan people. "All is well," she noted, "but it takes every bit of strength to do the daily work & it has seemed impossible to write even postcards."[4]

One of her goals was to have Bahá'í material printed in Albanian, Greek, and Serbian, as these were countries targeted for the future. "Then," she explained, "I shall feel I have done the very utmost to help the Balkans." She thought that the Faith would be the only source of guidance and comfort they could turn to "in the terrible World-Flare that may come in the future or . . . in the next five years."[5] When writing to Agnes Parsons about the critical political situation, Martha revealed her determination to foster the growth of the Faith in Bulgaria:

I look at dear suffering Sofia and pray Baha'u'lláh that in 25 years Sofia will have a grasp of the Teachings like unto New York.

I see the souls awakening, I see the ways of Baha'u'lláh opening out[.] We cannot be discouraged. We can not [*sic*] refuse to take our share of the physical pain that comes to all for the body does & always will fail us, but Baha'u'lláh said: "Blessed is the soul that brings another to the Law of God and has guided him to Eternal Life. This is one of the greatest actions in the sight of God. The Spirit of Bahá be upon you!"[6]

On 19 November, with the temperatures beginning to drop, Martha arrived at the second largest city in Bulgaria, Plovdiv, which was situated on the Maritsa River. Having advance notice of her itinerary, the Esperantists, with the Arts and Press Club, jointly sponsored a lecture soon after her arrival. To her delight, she met friends from London who were lecturing in the Balkans on behalf of Esperanto. Nearly every night they invited Martha to their room to share a hot supper, and they were helpful in many ways during her visit.

In Stanimaka (now Asenovgrad), twenty miles outside Plovdiv, the Esperanto Society arranged a public lecture, to be preceded by a conference with the Esperantists. Martha, with her London friends and three other Esperantists, made the trip by horse and carriage, a rather festive day's outing that was almost frivolous in Martha's schedule.

Although the constant lectures and difficult travel were hard work and tiring, Martha liked what she was doing. When she left Bulgaria and decided to include Constantinople (now Istanbul), that fabled Turkish city, in her travel plans, she felt a measure of excitement. She took a visa for only one week, as she predicted that a lecture would not be possible during the visit, but she still wanted very much to stop there. "Constantinople," she wrote, "is not much out of my way en route to Greece. Also I shall pass through Adrianople. It gives me a thrill to think of going to the cities where Baha'u'llah was exiled and I long to meet the friends in Constantinople."[7]

Her nearness to the cities that had housed Bahá'u'lláh during a portion of His exile, and places where many of His writings had originated, caused a spiritual and philosophical spring to well up in Martha. In a letter to friends she poured out her thoughts:

How much Baha'u'llah endured to give us these Teachings! And I see the New Day breaking! I see that the new divine civilization will again bring a great progress to all mankind. It is very blessed for us all to live in this Day, to know, and to serve—and courageously to go forward amid difficulties and illness, for life is not easy for anyone. It was not easy for Baha'u'llah and His family, nor for those early believers, nor is it easy for you. "All suffer and yet no less, bear up", and they are the radiant ones with shining eyes, and when they speak one sees the Truth in their lives and actions! "And when they have passed it seemed like the passing of exquisite music". That is the way you live, each one of you to whom I send this letter of love.[8]

Surely, those chosen friends who received this letter felt Martha's nobility radiating through her words and into their beings. Perhaps they would value more their unique place on the roster of the early Bahá'ís in the West. She would help them upward on the rungs of the spiritual ladder.

Martha would close out the year 1927 in Constantinople. The last twelve months had been good ones, with a minimum of difficult days because of illness, and a maximum use of time and opportunities for spreading the Bahá'í message. Yet she felt nothing unusual about her stalwart achievements; she was simply carrying on as usual, a matchless accomplishment.

There were no opportunities for public lectures in Constantinople, as Martha surmised, but she visited Robert College and also arranged for a translation into Armenian of a Bahá'í book. She put this Turkish city down for a return visit and, in the last week of December, sailed out through the Aegean Sea. Her destination to the southwest was Athens, home of Greek mythology and cradle of the unmatched art and architecture of a bygone Golden Age.

35   Greece, Yugoslavia, and Czechoslovakia

New Year's Day 1928 saw Martha lecturing to six hundred persons in Athens. The newspaper publicity throughout her stay was choice, imbued with vitality. One paper published a series of three articles, exploring in depth the principles and history of the Bahá'í Faith and the relation of the Faith to Christianity. The articles were so well done that Martha bought great numbers of these issues and gave them out instead of Bahá'í booklets, saving her literature for leaner times.

During her stay in Athens Martha took time to further her studies in Esperanto by attending the Helena Esperanto Institute. At the conclusion of the course she took an exam and received a diploma qualifying her to teach the language, which she now used with proficiency and beauty.

Traveling to northern Greece, Martha stopped on 10 January in Salonika, where she spoke at the university, a perfect setting for her topic "'Bahá'u'lláh's Principles for Universal Education.'"[1] Within a few days she was again in third-class accommodations venturing northward on the train to Belgrade, Yugoslavia—a trip that would hold prospects for accomplishment in both social and scholarly circles.

The queen of Yugoslavia, Marie Mignon, would soon present her mother, Marie of Rumania, with an infant grandson (19 January 1928). The Rumanian queen, with Princess Ileana, planned to join the royal family in Belgrade in January and was pleased to learn that Martha's schedule would bring her to the capital city during this stay. On 18 January Martha arrived in Belgrade and was invited to tea at the royal palace on the twenty-first. It was a captivating visit with Queen Marie and Princess Ileana. Martha was especially pleased with the queen's remark: "'The ultimate dream which we shall realize is that the Bahá'í channel of thought has such strength, it will serve little by little to become a light to all those searching for the real expression of Truth.' "[2]

A piquant touch was added to the afternoon tea when they were joined by Yugoslavia's four-year-old Crown Prince Peter, who had his own little cups and saucers.

There were subsequent visits with the royal family—occasions that were enchanting and full of warmth and charm. One was a special afternoon tea with the little children of the family and the princesses, who wanted Martha to tell them more about the Faith and Bahá'u'lláh's descendants in Palestine. Her ease with youngsters—never playing down to them, communicating with them in a way they understood and trusted—was remarkable.

During a visit with Their Royal Highnesses Prince Paul and Princess Olga on 1 February 1928 the princess noted that Princess Ileana had translated some of the Bahá'í writings into Rumanian. She suggested to her husband that they might help Miss Root by translating some of the writings into Serbian. Since Prince Paul had been educated mostly abroad, he felt that Professor Bogdan Popovitch of Belgrade University, a former teacher of the prince, would be the perfect choice for such a task. He went to his desk and wrote Martha a letter of introduction. According to Prince Paul, the professor was the greatest scholar in Serbia and the greatest master of the Serbian language.

Martha visited the professor a few days later in his study at the university and found him to be enthusiastic about the task: "'I shall be very glad to translate this booklet, (1) because the Principles are so excellent, I do this for Baha [Bahá'í]; (2) I do it for Prince Paul whom I love so much, and (3) I do it for you, an American who has come to us so graciously and sincerely!'" Others in Belgrade were surprised at the professor's generosity of time and scholarship and the beauty of the work. They commented, "'He never does anything like that, he is so busy!'"[3]

Like many others, Professor Popovitch was susceptible to the purity of Martha's spirit and motives. The day before she left Belgrade, he came to her hotel, although he had been ill for two weeks, and brought "long-stemmed fragrant lovely red roses and a box of candy." He had charged nothing for the superb translation, moving Martha to remark, "How kind he was!"[4]

Another Belgrade scholar of note, Professor Staitch, made a beautiful translation into the Croatian language. He was a friend of Professor Popovitch, and both professors were friends of Dr. Auguste Forel. The thread of friendship and admiration wove in and out of Martha's life.

The Croatian translations were immediately useful to Martha when she traveled to Zagreb, in the Croatian region of Yugoslavia. There she gave five public lectures that were enthusiastically received by the people in this northwestern part of the country. Especially well received was the talk given to the two-thousand-member Croatian Women's Club. She also had a meeting with the leader of the Peasant Party, Stephen Radich, a few weeks before he was assassinated in the Parliament. Her fears for the Balkans were not quieted.

When Martha arrived in Prague in the middle of March, she sensed a difference from either of her former visits. This time President Thomas Garrique Masaryk was not abroad, and that was a good omen. Almost before Martha put down her luggage, she arranged a meeting for 20 March 1928.

As the first president of the republic, Thomas Masaryk was often called the George Washington of Czechoslovakia. A visionary, yet a practical man, he was involved with government, but he eschewed politics. In one of his books he had written:

> "Who redeemed mankind? Neither a politician, nor an economist, nor a socialist, nor a demagogue. It is really sublime how in the political and social unrest of his time Christ keeps aloof from all politics; how easy it would have been for Him to win over through political and socialistic agitation. He, however, demands the perfection of character, requires the deepening of feeling; He wishes people to become good because He knows that only thus will they find contentment for their souls."[5]

A leader with such a philosophy could not help but appeal to Martha. On her previous visits to Czechoslovakia, President Masaryk, through his secretary, had extended official courtesies to Martha Root, and Edvard Beneš, his minister of foreign affairs, had entertained her at the castle. Now at last, in this colorful Balkan city, Martha would meet the president himself at the great castle, the "White House" of Czechoslovakia.

Accompanied by the secretary, Mr. Vasil K. Skrach, Martha was brought to the president's library, where a tall, impressive Thomas Masaryk welcomed Martha Root. They spoke of peace and the roads to peace. When referring to the League of Nations, he told Martha that it "must be backed by the peoples of all countries. The diplomats alone cannot make the peace." In answer to Martha's question about the best way to promote universal peace, he replied: " 'Do what you are doing. Spread this teaching of humanity and not wait for the diplomats. . . . Take them to the diplomats, the Peace Societies, the universities, the schools, the churches, and also write about them. It is the people who will bring the universal peace.' " [6]

The visit was all she had hoped for. In a letter to Shoghi Effendi and Roy Wilhelm, written on 13 April, she wrote:

President Masaryk . . . was so lovely to me and since then everything has been done to help me with the work. This visit with him was announced in all papers and from the Castle was sent out a story about the Cause and they sent out Abdu'l Baha's picture, so the newspapers had good articles.

The President's Club is the Spolecensky Klub, it is the most famous club here and often welcomes the foreign guests in the name of the President. This Club gave a dinner for me, gave a membership card to the club during my stay, invite[d] me to the opera, and Monday take me for a . . . [day-long] automobile excursion—and I tell them about the Cause and put two books in their library. . . . [7]

After his meeting with Martha, President Masaryk sent her an invitation to visit the Parliament, where he would open the peace ceremonies. Martha managed to get another invitation for Louise Gregory, who would leave for Sofia soon thereafter. Louise had been introduced over the past few days to Martha's friends and contacts in Prague, and the way would be smooth if Louise ever wanted to return to do more teaching.

Martha was certain that President Masaryk "does love our

LOUISA MATHEW GREGORY
the wife of the Hand of the Cause of God Louis G. Gregory,
in Sofia, Bulgaria, 1929. Mrs. Gregory, Louise to her friends,
spent many years teaching the Bahá'í Faith in Europe and was
one of a number who watered the seeds planted by Martha Root.

Cause." It was her only explanation for "all this kindness" and "these silent courtesies, one by one pouring in."[8]

Another invitation to the castle came from the president's daughter, Dr. Alice Masaryk, a woman involved in social and humanistic groups. She sent a car for Martha, and the visit turned out to be warm and fruitful. Martha's hope was that, like her father, his daughter would read the Bahá'í literature that Martha had given the president.

The impression that Martha Root made on President Masaryk and his associates was certainly favorable. Their response was a cornucopia of goodwill, generous acts, and tangible offerings. Martha was elated,

but this next is also really wonderful! The Ministry of Foreign Affairs and this Club have given me a pass to go about

12 cities in Czechoslovakia, the mountain resorts, the famous bath resorts, the industrial centres etc and I am to write an article about it. I start April 15, and the pass is good for two weeks. They have made out the schedule.

It was a wonderful opportunity for Martha; the doors had opened, and she was passing through. Her only complaint was that "I shall feel like a tourist!" But she added, "You will see what a marvelous opportunity it will be to meet people and blaze our Cause over Czechoslovakia! Baha'u'llah has done this!"[9]

The costs of such an extensive side trip were an important consideration, but Martha was certain that "I can manage it financially to pay my room in the different hotels (it will be a different hotel every night almost) and it is too great an opportunity to miss. Also, it will show President M and Mr. Benes . . . that I am doing my best to get the Cause to their country—and it looks as if they are doing their best to help me."[10]

Another consideration was her weariness from her teaching work, which had taxed her strength daily. "Do not feel a very good Bahai," she confessed, "get so tired, tonight can hardly write this letter, but perhaps this journey around Czechoslovakia will be a little rest. The conflicting forces, the suffering, the unrest in Europe weight the soul."[11]

Before leaving on her tour, Martha found time to send out more than one hundred letters in preparation for three upcoming Esperanto congresses; she was aided by an Esperantist secretary, provided through the financial generosity of Julia Culver. While in Prague, Martha interceded on a human level for a man who had been sentenced to prison for speaking out against military service. She spoke about him to President Masaryk, and apparently her intercession met with some success. She noted that "His sentence is postponed indefinitely, so perhaps he will not need to go. I do not know whether my speaking to Pres. M did any good, but the fact stands that the youth did not go to prison."[12]

Prague would always hold a special place in Martha's heart. In a letter to Roy Wilhelm she told him that "It has been a great event to come to Praha, and a confirmation Baha'u'lláh has showered His Favors. Everybody has helped here & am very happy over the work. Gives me new courage. . . . Everything has gone just like a miracle." Such a positive atmosphere in Czechoslovakia, all the kindnesses, had left Martha's heart full of happiness and gratitude. At the end of the letter to Roy, she especially mentioned Harry Randall, who had suffered severe financial reverses, and sent her love and approbation— "He is one of our greatest." She closed, writing all around the margin, over the top, and down the other side, with these words: "Roy, you have been so good to me. I can never thank you for all you are to me, but Baha'u'lláh knows how deeply I appreciate you! May Baha'u'lláh bless you always."[13]

Martha gave her last lecture in Prague on 13 April and prepared for her twelve-day journey through western Czechoslovakia. But first she had to make a trip to Brno, southeast of Prague, in the center of the country. Four societies in this Moravian industrial city had invited her down for a public lecture. She was pleased to go since the city of Brno had a special status among Bahá'ís: it was the home of the first Bahá'í in Czechoslovakia—Milosh Wurm, who had died in the First World War. Mr. Wurm had published the first Bahá'í book in the Czech language, and it was fitting that Martha was able to distribute her own Czech booklets, which had recently been printed in Prague. She made a special effort while there to visit Mr. Wurm's mother, who had become one of the great peace workers, often lecturing throughout Europe.

Following the stop in Brno, Martha began her twelve-day tour through Czechoslovakia, beginning on 15 April. Although it was informative, stimulating, interesting, it was hardly a rest. Every night Martha, with all of her luggage in tow, stopped at a different hotel. Nevertheless, the itinerary took her through mountains and valleys with spectacular scenery, and to health spas and resorts and places with such quixotic names as the High Tatras, Franzensbad, Pieštany, Marienbad, and Karlsbad. Martha somehow managed to arrange two lectures during this Balkan adventure amidst the rainbow hunters.

The heart and spirit of Czechoslovakia, Martha felt, were close to the Bahá'í teachings. As she turned her attention toward other parts of Europe, she took comfort in being the instrument for aligning this heart and spirit with the message of Bahá'u'lláh.

36   The Summer of 1928

Martha's tour ticket brought her close to Dresden, Germany, where she resumed her Bahá'í regime at the end of April. She found a place to stay and wrote her articles and letters perched in a tiny room in a " 'non-alcohol' little house," which was "all right and very cheap."[1] Without a lapse, Martha lectured every night in Dresden, and later in Leipzig and Gera, before moving on to Berlin, where she lectured through May.

Summer 1928 was a time of international, national, and regional conferences, and Shoghi Effendi asked Martha to concentrate her efforts on them, realizing that there would be large numbers of participants from all over the world. Starting in May and going through September, Martha was at one gathering or another, beginning with the Esperanto Congress of Germany at Frankfurt am Main. Special Bahá'í sessions were arranged, and one of her talks was broadcast. A few days later she left for Brussels to attend several conferences. From her little room at the Hotel Termines Nord she arranged the voluminous details of programs, printing, and lodging for friends. Later, between 30 July and 2 August, she assisted with Bahá'í arrangements at the Inter-religious Congress at The Hague, where she stayed four days at the Hotel Pomona. Throughout her travels she made a special effort to meet friends of Roy Wilhelm's and others who put her in touch with summer travelers or residents in the various cities. It was a packed schedule.

After several trips to Antwerp to work with printers on materials for the various congresses, Martha settled there for a brief stay on 3 August to participate in the Twentieth Universal Esperanto Congress. Since 1925, when the Bahá'ís had first participated in the annual Universal Esperanto Congress, it was the focal point around which Martha arranged her travels;

as soon as one terminated, plans were under way for the following year. In 1928 the usual anticipation was tempered by a feeling of injustice that troubled Martha, who rarely allowed herself to be offended by persons or by events with negative overtones. But this was different. To Lucy Marshall, who had attended the congress in Danzig, she wrote, "Six months after the Danzig Congress the Esperanto Bureau in Geneva sent me a bill for $15 for our hall for Bahaij Fakaj Kunvenoj [special meeting]. It hurt me—for I had done so much to help that Danzig Congress. Had written about it and announced it in every radio talk." Despite her dismay, her pragmatic side took over: "But life is short, and I paid it without making a fuss for we need the Esperanto organizations for our Bahai Cause and the Esperanto organizations need our Bahai Cause."[2]

Although Martha realized that the Esperanto Bureau was hard pressed for money, she still did not think it fair for them to

One of two Bahá'í Esperanto sessions held as a part of
the Twentieth Universal Esperanto Congress, Antwerp, Belgium,
August 1928. Martha Root (standing, second row, center) spoke
at one session, and Lydia Zamenhof (front row, seated, in white),
who also served as honorary president, spoke at the other session.

have charged her. She told the congress organizers in Antwerp that she would not pay for a room there, as *fakaj asocioj* (specialized associations) such as the Bahá'í Faith were supposed to receive a room at no charge. Sensing discrimination against the Faith, she made it clear that she expected the Bahá'ís to have the "same privileges and opportunities as other fakaj asocioj."[3] The bill for fifteen dollars had cost the Esperantists dearly, as it had alienated, or at least dampened the enthusiasm of, Esperanto's most vocal and peripatetic champion. While Martha normally arrived early for the annual congress in order to assist with the arrangements, this year she did not.

The Antwerp congress also provided other tests for growth. The woman in charge of preparations, who was not friendly to the Bahá'í Faith, agreed to allow Bahá'í literature to be placed on the tables but cautioned Martha that she "must not make any propaganda."[4]

Although Martha was asked to speak at the opening of the congress on behalf of the Bahá'ís, after prayerful consideration, she decided to turn the presentation over to Mr. H. S. Muḥammad Rawḥání, of Resht, Iran. Martha wrote to the congress director to explain the arrangement and enclosed a donation of five dollars to help the congress. Her response to the unfriendly attitude was not to show resentment but love. She wrote to Roy Wilhelm, "There must be love & more love."[5]

Despite her difficulties at the congress, Martha was successful in arranging two Bahá'í sessions, which were well attended and excellently programmed. Lydia Zamenhof spoke at one session, Martha at the other, and Lydia was the honorary president at both.

After returning briefly to Brussels for an Esperanto meeting, Martha spent the next three months, mid-August through October, in Switzerland. There she spoke at the Inter-religious Congress in Le Locle and at the Esperanto Congress of Switzerland, 23–24 September, in Bern. She also attended the preliminary sessions of the Universal Religious Peace Conference and was present for the gathering of the League of Nations. In October she lectured in Lausanne, Le Locle, La Chaux-de-Fonds, Neuchâtel, and Morges, took time to go to Amriswil to meet the only Bahá'í in the area, and stopped in Zurich to visit some professors at the university and the theological school, where she arranged lectures for the future.

Apart from the joy Martha felt at these numerous conferences, where she could see the rising interest in the Bahá'í Faith and the increase of serious investigation of the teachings by so many probing minds, the high point of Martha's summer was her visit in Yvorne, Switzerland, with Dr. Auguste Forel. She had written earlier of his enormous influence on scientific thought in Europe and on other continents, and of the great esteem in which he and his opinions were held. To Roy Wilhelm she described her impressions of the meeting:

> Dr. August[e] Forel does not speak English, but his daughter from Canada & her children are spending two years with him, so she translates everything . . . I *love him* . . . and it was a peak event in my life to meet him. I hope you can meet him, for you would love him too. (And you would weep a little to see how much he has suffered & how brave and fine & strong he is.)[6]

Another bright spot in Martha's summer was meeting old friends from America, who traveled to Europe for one conference or another. "It is so *good* to see the friends from home," she told Roy. "It seems almost like a dream—to[o] good not to be true! Am very thankful."[7]

Martha had another reason to be thankful: her health was better. Although there were some bad days, some times of exhaustion, and the unbearable summer heat in Antwerp, her physical condition was basically stable. She wrote to Roy in September that she was "feeling worlds better."[8] Her good health, she thought, must be the result of a fruit diet recommended by Julia Culver, who had been doing her part to monitor Martha's health and keep it on an even keel. It was possible to stay on the diet only when Martha's area of activities was relatively circumscribed. Soon she would be back in the hospices and economy hotels, taking food in snatches or preparing it on her little collapsible stove.

37 The Universities of Germany

For the next seven months, November 1928 to June 1929, Martha carried out a two-fold plan that would keep her in Germany, with one or two excursions out of the country. On one level she would again visit all the Bahá'í centers and would visit twice every university in the country except two. She would inform professors about the Bahá'í Faith and prepare the ground, then return later to lecture. On another level the Esperantists would set up a lecture schedule, and Martha would speak to their followers in forty cities.

This undertaking took Martha to virtually every major city in Germany, where she was assisted by contacts made at conferences throughout Europe and by others she had met through letters of introduction. Her vast coverage of Germany, where Shoghi Effendi urged her to concentrate her efforts, can be appreciated by recounting the places visited in the last six weeks of the year 1928: Stuttgart, Esslingen, Heilbronn, Karlsruhe, Zuffenhausen, Göppingen, Geisinglinger [probably Geislingen], Tübingen, Munich, and twelve cities in Saxony, where talks were arranged by the Esperanto League of that region.

Along the way there were individuals whose friendship enriched these journeys. Almost always the librarians of the state or city libraries graciously went out of their way to facilitate Martha's work. In Munich the wife of the American consul general invited Martha to their home to discuss the Bahá'í teachings. Even the rector of the Episcopal church, who had heard 'Abdu'l-Bahá speak in Boston, helped Martha to arrange a lecture. "He sees only good in this Movement," she remarked, "and he has arranged for me to speak at a tea in the American Library, which is really like an American Club in Munich. . . . He will announce the Lecture from his pulpit Sunday."[1]

Despite the kindnesses, the travails of being constantly on the move were great. In each new place Martha had to find an inexpensive, but decent, place to stay; shop for food to prepare in her room; locate buildings, residences, or individuals she planned to visit; and work out travel within the city, usually on trolley cars or trains. There were early morning trains to catch, and overnight travel often meant sitting up in a coach. Such difficulties Martha rarely mentioned, even to her closest friends.

When she went to the universities, she looked up the professors of comparative religion and those who taught Persian or Arabic, the Orientalists. Most of them had been to Iran, knew of the Faith, and were eager to know more. Many had visited Palestine and the Bahá'í shrines and gardens. They admired the teachings and the central figures of the Faith. Although they had some of the literature, Martha gave them additional books, which they were eager to study and put in their libraries. They also arranged to have more books sent to them in a variety of languages, making the teachings available to students from many cultures.

By the end of November Martha was in Munich, where she celebrated Thanksgiving. This American holiday had always had special meaning for her. She wrote in a letter to her friends that she was "going to a Thanksgiving Dinner for 100 guests in one of the large hotels here. . . . It was on Thanksgiving Day that my beloved Mother went into the Kingdom of God. I have thought of her so much this morning and prayed for her happiness in that beautiful Realm where we too shall join her." She added, "At Christmas and New Year I shall rise very early and pray for you each one. . . . My health is ever so much better this year, so I have new courage. Please think of me as always happy in my work." [2]

In Berlin the Oriental section of the university library, part of the great state library building, was a place of fascination and friendship for Martha. The director, Professor Weil, had spent time in 'Abdu'l-Bahá's garden in Haifa. Another new friend, Professor Mittwoch, the head of the Oriental section, and a professor of Arabic, was eager to arrange a lecture on the Bahá'í Faith.

While Martha was looking through the card catalogue in a small room of the main library, another friendship developed. "Suddenly," she wrote to friends, "Prof. Franz Babinger, Prof. of Islamic Literature, came along and the Librarian introduced me—think of it, in a city of more than four million people, I meet the one man who has written about the Bahá'í Cause and is INTERESTED!"[3]

Professor Babinger had written fifteen pages about the Bahá'í Faith in the second edition of *Lectures on Islam*, volume 2, and he was in the process of preparing volume 3. As he had not seen *The Bahá'í World* or *Bahá'u'lláh and the New Era* before, Martha gave him copies of these publications. Reflecting on such a high point in her stay in Berlin, she wrote:

> To me it was a wonderful Confirmation meeting Dr. Babinger. That day I went to the University, I felt so ill with grippe that I had to lie down after I dressed to go. Then I decided to TRY and I used my Christmas money to take a taxi (it did not cost much). The weather was way below zero and I had to be there by eight o'clock in the morning, and it had been one o'clock the night before when I had come back from a [lecture] in North Berlin, and had had to sit up in bed to breathe.

For Martha physical discomfort was always secondary to the joy of success: "When I came back from the University . . . I prepared my dinner, and after all I went to bed without eating it, I was so tired—but I had MET Prof. Babinger! I had MET Dr. Mittwoch and several others!"[4]

Both Dr. Babinger and Martha were delighted to have discovered compatible interests, and they pursued the friendship:

> I invited Prof. B. to tea—he could not come, he had a class. He invited me to tea the next day, I could not go, I had a lecture. I invited him to tea the next day and invited three Bahá'ís to meet him. I made sandwiches and prepared a lovely tea, wore my best white dress—and he did not come! I telephoned later to say good-bye and to ask why he did not appear, and HE SAID: "Why did you not come to tea with

me today? we waited the tea until six o'clock!" So you see we
had misunderstood each other. . . .[5]

Martha would soon be leaving for Poland, but there was still
time for a visit with the professor. She wrote of it as if it were a
romantic encounter:

> Then he came, and we did not have any tea at all! I was
> dressed ready to go to the train, but nothing mattered. We
> said what we had to say to each other—I ran upstairs, undid
> the bags and took out the Bahá'i books to show him. . . .
> Then I gave him my own copies of "Baha'ullah and The
> New Era" and a few others. He is a great man and young, I
> would think he is still in the thirties. . . . I had had a box of
> candy given to me and I put that into the package of books
> which I did up for him.[6]

Among the items she gave the professor were Bahá'í pamphlets
translated into the Albanian language. They were a product of
her earlier efforts, and she was pleased that he would take them
to Albania when he traveled there the following March.

After this meeting Martha decided to postpone her trip for
three or four days. Looking at the irony of the situation, she
thought that "it seemed pathetic and comic" to have "toiled
the night to get everything packed and strapped," only to un-
pack everything to stay a few more days. She had realized,
however, that it was a perfect arrangement for privacy and
accomplishment. After going to the train station to get a re-
fund for her ticket, she returned to her room and began her
writing—unanswered mail, arrangements for future congresses—saving only one-half hour per day for visitors. "The work
is piled so high," she exclaimed, "it will harm the Cause if I do
not get some writing done."[7]

Before she left in February to lecture in Breslau (now Wro-
claw), the sought-after lecture at Berlin University was granted
and scheduled for 28 February 1929, with invitations extended
to the Oriental Societies of Berlin. Martha traveled to Breslau
in the bitter-cold winter weather, more suited to arctic regions.
Her economical room had little or no heat; she wore layers of

clothes, including leggings, and kept her arctics, or snow boots, on indoors. Hot tea helped to keep her warm day and night.

Martha went second class on a train from Breslau to Warsaw. There was a coal shortage, it was forty-seven degrees below zero, and third class was a guarantee of no heat. "I opened my valises," Martha wrote to Julia Culver, "& took out about everything I possessed & put it on! My train was 6 hours late & the train became so cold we had to go to a station where there was a little wood fire. . . ."[8]

Martha spent two weeks during February in Warsaw; apart from a recurrent case of hives, her visit was a total success. She worked with Lydia Zamenhof on an Esperanto translation of *Bahá'u'lláh and the New Era*. Martha intended to submit the translation to Pastro Andreo Che, one of the world's finest Esperantists, and Dr. Privat, head of the Universal Esperanto Society, for their comments to make certain that it would be the most perfect translation possible. There was heat—wonderful heat—in the hotel room where Lydia came mornings and afternoons to work on the translation. Each evening she would return home to spend most of the night preparing for the next day. Lydia, who had become a confirmed Bahá'í, had a law degree and expertise as a linguist and was eager to use her skills for the promotion of the Bahá'í Faith.

Back in Berlin, after a brief stop in Breslau for a second lecture at the university, Martha began preparing for her 28 February talk at Berlin University. She felt the talk to be a pivotal one, as the university's prestige would help her to gain entrée to university circles that might otherwise be unresponsive. But problems appeared. Dr. Ernst Kliemke, the Bahá'í who was president of the Esperanto Society of Germany, was to have given a résumé in German of Martha's lecture. He was suddenly taken ill and died within twenty-four hours. It was a shock and a loss to Martha. With permission from his wife, Martha arranged to speak at the funeral. Although she prepared a talk, Dr. Kliemke's family refused to let her speak because of traditional religious beliefs. Her sense of loss was made more poignant by this refusal.

On the way to the funeral Martha stopped at the American

consulate to pick up her mail. Among the letters was one from America, bringing news that shook her and darkened the world of reality: Harry Randall was dead, a victim of arteriosclerosis. Martha's world stopped. She was stunned, dazed; her heart stopped, then pounded.

Feeling bereft, and surrounded by a negative atmosphere for her talk at the university, she wrote to Julia, "The lecture in Berlin University was so important—and you see how everything had fallen through & my heart was not functioning right. I just cried to Baha'u'lláh to *help me*, and He did!"[9]

Shaken to the core, Martha felt that she had no will of her own, that everything was in spiritual hands, and she proceeded with the lecture plans. On 28 February, just before she was to speak, Martha had a vision:

> Harry was standing beside Bahá'u'lláh; he was silent, he looked so noble and his face had that sweet smile. He did not speak to me, but Baha'u'lláh spoke and told me that Harry was with Him, that He, Baha'u'lláh, would help me, that Harry would help, that every Angel in the Supreme Concourse was in his place *to do his part*, and that Martha would be in her place *to do her part*. That gave me the courage and the physical strength and the assurance to arise and do it. I was ill, my heart, but the Spiritual strength came.[10]

Martha gave the lecture as planned and was astonished that "Everything went so well. . . . it was the greatest of anything in Europe that I have done—in results!" Of those results she elaborated:

> A man came from the leading newspaper & wrote about the lecture. The Prof. of Arabic came forward & voluntarily offered to give the resumé in German & then he spoke beautifully. Later invited me to his home—and he will use [one] of Baha'u'llah's books as a text book next year. The Head of the State Library (second only to the British Museum . . .) asked to take the collection of my books to their Library for two days to study them & now they will order a copy of each kind of Bahai book in each lang. in the world. . . .
> Many other things happened.[11]

The success became an effective balance to the deep sense of loss Martha felt at Harry Randall's passing.

Martha's campaign did not slacken. She moved on to Frankfurt am Main and then to the universities at Heidelberg, Darmstadt, Freiburg, Marburg, Kreuznach, Würzburg, Bonn, Göttingen, Giessen, and Münster. To her schedule was added Halle, then Kiel, Rostock, Greifswald, and the Oriental School in Hamburg. At every stop Martha put books in the libraries and met with professors, often going to their homes. She also found time to prepare for the German Esperanto Congress, which would open in Frankfurt am Main on 31 March.

In most of these places she arranged an exhibition of Bahá'í books, rather like a traveling librarian that also lectured. Her topic at every university was "The Bahá'i Movement." To protect an interested English professor at a Catholic university from criticism, Martha changed the title to "The New Internationalism," but it was the same talk.[12] She always spoke of Esperanto, Dr. Zamenhof, and the Esperanto Bahá'í literature as well.

The university campaign involved an enormous amount of work—hundreds of letters and miles and miles of travel on trains and trolley cars. When traveling, Martha often had to stand, and she carried her bundles of books relentlessly through the cold and wet of the German winter and spring. It was a rarity for her to refer to the laborious aspects of her work, but she wrote to Julia, "Oh, it is so difficult, no one knows until they try it, and even with the two trips—each university has had at least ten letters from me to get things arranged. It is just a miracle from Baha'u'lláh that these university doors opened."[13]

Martha's heart was warmed by the results of her work, but the rest of her was very cold. Her room provided little comfort or respite from the bitter weather, causing her to "just shiver all the time. . . ." "I had such a chill," she told Julia, "my teeth just chattered & I had to go to bed. I drank very hot water & puffed the feathers thick in the bedcovering & rolled myself into a ball to keep under this 'square' of warmth. . . ." Thinking ahead to July in Geneva, she envisioned that "my room in Geneva will have a gas stove, O bliss!"[14]

It was a time of hard work and debilitating journeys, of physical and mental discomfort. Travel expenses were high, money was low, expected support preparing for the congresses was not forthcoming, and Martha, paying for everything, was scraping the bottom of the barrel. "I just keep praying the Ahmad Tablet and 'keeping on,'" she said. "I think of Marshal Foch, he said 'My centre is destroyed. My right has fallen back. Situation excellent. I attack!'" She added that he had also said, "'Only that one is vanquished who thinks that he is vanquished.'"[15]

Returning from one university trip, Martha found her cash down to ten dollars. She was trying to sell something to solve the immediate financial pinch, while waiting for her funds from home, when she found, stuck to the lining of her wallet, a twenty-dollar traveler's check, tucked away years ago for an emergency. "It was one of the greatest confirmations," she thought.[16] Shortly after, a draft of one hundred dollars arrived from Roy Wilhelm just in time. Somehow, Martha always got through—not easily, but surely.

The university lecture schedule ended in June. After over seven months in Germany her task was completed. She had a strong sense of accomplishment and was happy to think that Bahá'í ideas were germinating in the halls of learning. After such a prodigious achievement, she was now ready to carry on in a new arena.

38 An Unfamiliar Face of the Balkans

It was summer 1929. Martha's route from Berlin would initially take her to familiar cities and familiar scenes, including
Geneva, where she had spent much of the last four summers,
and Budapest, where she would attend yet another Esperanto
congress. Coming down from Germany, Martha stopped at the
University of Zurich to lecture before going on to Geneva. She
spent the month of July in this city on the lake and attended the
Universal Congress of Education.

On 1 August Martha left Geneva to be present at the opening
of the Esperanto Museum in Vienna, part of the great National
Bibliothek. Here she saw an exhibition of Bahá'í Esperanto
material. Among the literature on view was one piece that especially intrigued her: "the first Esperanto booklet 'What Is the
Bahai Movement?'" Martha had translated it in 1925 with the
help of Dr. Esslemont, holding the press until she "had a telegram from Dr. Esslemont that they were perfect and until the
International Esperanto Committee in Geneva said the
same."[1] While in Vienna she met the president of the Austrian
Republic and arranged for Bahá'í books to be sent to him. Later, at a reception celebrating the museum's opening, she spoke
on the same program with him.

Summers meant congresses to Martha. This time she traveled to Budapest during the first week in August to participate
in the Esperanto congress being held there. The Bahá'í session,
so thorny in its planning, and so uncertain in its early stages,
was a triumph. Things got done, expenses were paid for, and a
new roster of participants became involved, replacing those
who had passed on or dropped out. The Hungarian Press Club
entertained foreign journalists, to whom Martha had the
"great privilege" to give a talk about the Faith; later the president of the club called on Martha at her hotel.[2] Another new

acquaintance, the secretary of the Writers' Club, became a friend.

The last few weeks had been a period of relative ease for Martha, who, following customary ways, shared her experiences with friends and acquaintances. But they would all be left behind as she picked up her itinerary to travel on, alone, into the unfamiliar. At the behest of Shoghi Effendi, she had been preparing for several months for a "long[,] long journey towards the East again," which would take her to Albania, Turkey, Egypt, Palestine, Iraq, Iran, India, Burma, China, and Japan. The arrangements had been made in Berlin for the Eastern journey months before and had been a source of consternation for her, as "some of the visas like Albania etc I could only get in Berlin. I have to get 15 visas. Oh, how I wish they would abandon visas!"[3]

With all the traveling of the past years, and the journey in the immediate future stretching out before her, Martha wrote to Julia Culver with a touch of wistfulness, "If I should come back to Europe, perhaps I could find some work & settle down for a year in each place & thus be able to help a little," adding, "I leave it all in His Hands."[4] But Martha's destiny was not to be the easy chair in front of the fire, nor resting on a quiet beach with the water lapping against the shore. Not even the relative calm of settling down in one place for a year would be in her future. She was destined to roam, to teach, to love, to endure.

During the third week in August Martha headed for Albania, but with her it was never a portal-to-portal trip. As she sailed down the Adriatic Sea, she came upon the city of Dubrovnik, Yugoslavia, sparkling and irresistible. Spending five wonderfully productive days there, she sent out the Bahá'í message via newspapers to distant points of the country.

Martha left behind the ordinary traveler as she entered Albania. Because this country had no railroads, she went by auto from Durazzo (now Durrës) to Tiranë, the capital situated in the mountains. Although six passengers could be accommodated, the autos would leave whenever there were three or four passengers, who would then have to pay for all six seats.

In order to learn about this little country, Martha arose at

*Passport photographs used
by Martha Root (clockwise, starting
on left) in 1915, 1922, 1928 and 1932,
and 1937.*

4:00 or 4:30 every morning to absorb its history, government, and personality. She studied its place in the Balkans, its language, religion, and the king's education and outlook.

Spurred on by the American ambassador's assurance that it was impossible to see the king, Martha wrote the king a letter, which included the Bahá'í greetings of Shoghi Effendi. She enclosed an article about the Bahá'í Faith printed in German, as her study revealed that the king spoke this language.

Martha twice called on the French-speaking prime minister, whom she found to be charming and kind; her articles appeared in the newspaper, with favorable editorial comment. She also visited the library several times and presented Bahá'í books. By the time all of this was accomplished, she felt confident that "Everybody in Tirana knew I was a Baha'i."[5]

Faith and persistence had once again succeeded, as Martha discovered that she would be able to meet the king. Her subsequent royal audience became a vignette in Martha's life that had a folkloric quality about it, with the flavor of a Tolkien tale:

> The Prime Minister invited me to an audience with His Majesty Zog, King of the Albanians, Sunday, September first, in the Royal Palace in Tirana. It was very formal, in honor of the second anniversary of his being king. This invitation meant friendliness to our Cause,—you can hardly imagine how much it meant. The invitations were very few. No foreigners were invited except the Ambassadors from the different Legations. The Prime Minister told me to come to the Chancery at ten o'clock. In the Chancery were nineteen ladies, relatives of the King. . . .When I came into the room, the acting President, announced me as a Baha'i. Well, I made a little speech to these ladies and it was interpreted to them. We had a very lovely hour and then we went in big motor cars (a walk of about four minutes) to the Royal Palace. I had no motor car and did not need one, for they invited me to go with them.[6]

Of meeting King Zog she recalled:

> Never shall I forget those moments. He stood in the drawing room in his army dress uniform and his Ministers stood

about him in semi-circle. They were in black, full evening dress. When I shook hands with him I said in Albanian language their pledge, "Besa-besen." That means "I pledge you my loyalty."[7]

There was about Martha an earnest, little-girl quality that took seriously the pledging of truth and loyalty, harking back to the "cross-my-heart-and-hope-to-die" stage of childhood. When Martha was told "besa-besen," she believed it: "If any Albanian tells you that it means he will stand the truest kind of a friend, no matter what happens. They extended 'besa-besen' to me in inviting me. . . ."[8]

After Martha's visit with the king she was escorted to the royal palace of the king's mother. There she was presented to the king's five sisters, then taken to meet the queen mother in another drawing room. "Attended by two boys, her grandsons, in full military dress," Martha remembered that the queen mother "was all in black. She looked so kind and good, like a madon[n]a mother of the world."[9]

Despite the intense heat and dry weather, making frequent changes of clothing necessary due to the clouds of white dust over everything, it turned out to be a wonderful visit. Traveling to Albania had been a frightening idea for Martha, and she had gone with apprehension; now she wanted someday to return in order to visit the dervishes and tell the Albanian people about the Bahá'í revelation.

But she had deep concern for these new Balkan friends, feeling that "Albania is the most dangerous point in the Balkans. A match set to Albania would blow up Europe." Its crucial geographical location, she realized, would make it a source of commercial and political dispute. She confided to Roy Wilhelm that "the situation is very grave politically in Albania. Between you & me the King never walks out, his life is most carefully guarded. . . ."[10] Martha invoked the help of Constantine and St. Jerome, two Albanians in the world beyond, and she urged friends to pray for this beleaguered country. She hoped for a rapid response from the Bahá'ís if she should ask for books to be mailed there, which she did request within a few days of leaving.

For four years Martha had traversed the European continent, where she had made good use of her Esperanto and had
attracted at least one royal personage to the Faith of Bahá'u'-
lláh. Whether in Geneva, Prague, or Bucharest, she had witnessed the unific power of her message in the face of growing
political tension. But the Bahá'í message was meant for Oriental as well as Occidental. Carrying her visa-packed passport,
she would leave the largely Christian culture behind and move
into lands of Eastern thought. It remained to be seen what response she would get among the Muslims.

39   Turkey and Balcic, Rumania

It was the first week in September 1929 when Martha sailed from Albania to Brindisi, Italy, en route to Turkey. Late summer was a delightful season to sail to Constantinople, a voyage that would take her through the Adriatic and Ionian seas, skirting the Greek islands in the Aegean, and into the Sea of Marmara. When Martha learned that her ship would be three hours late sailing from Brindisi, she unstrapped her bags, got out her typewriter and paper, and wrote to friends an account of her Albanian adventure. Time was priceless.

By mid-September Martha was back in Constantinople, known as the "Sublime Porte."[1] Constantinople was the former capital, the center of power, of the Ottoman Empire, which had reached into Europe, Asia, and Africa at its height, and had included Turkey, Syria, Mesopotamia (Iraq), Palestine, Arabia, Egypt, the Barbary States (Morocco, Algiers, Tunis, Tripoli), the Balkan States, and parts of Russia and Hungary. As prophesied by Bahá'u'lláh, the tides of war and history had diminished the empire to a fraction of its earlier range.

This ancient city of mosques and minarets evoked memories of Bahá'u'lláh's exile and imprisonment. When Roy Wilhelm sent packets of tea to Martha, she responded, "I think of Baha'u'lláh a prisoner with His family in this city and how hard it must have been for him to eat. I wish He could have had Roy's tea!" There were other reasons to be grateful for the tea. She found it indispensable to the modicum of comfort that she allowed herself. It had sustained her in the subzero weather of Breslau and Frankfurt and in the heat of Albania and Constantinople. And shopping was not exactly a pleasure. She confided to Roy, "I truly do not know how I could travel without it [the tea]. I do not complain, I wish to be a good soldier, but sometimes I see so much that is so dirty and revolting in shops & everywhere that I just try to buy something that is covered up, an egg, or an apple or a melon & eat that with a good cup of tea."[2]

Public lectures were not possible in Turkey, although it had officially become a republic in 1924. On a visit to Ankara, the new capital, Martha met with the minister of foreign affairs, Teufik Rushdí Bey, whom she considered a great man, and she also talked with the leaders in education and the press. With all of them she discussed religion, despite the fact that severe restrictions had been placed on Bahá'í activities, and one had to be very careful. They evidently did not feel threatened by Martha Root, as they invited her to be a special guest at the festivities on 29 October that celebrated the founding of the republic. It was unfortunate that her schedule made a return visit impossible.

As she was leaving Ankara, "a young man in the American Embassy" offered to accompany her to the train. He was the same gentleman who had taken her out to lunch during her first day at the hotel in Ankara. She was reluctant to accept his offer on the day of her departure because she was traveling in third-class accommodations. "I went alone," she remembered, "but those three fine young men from the American Embassy[,] two Turks and one American[,] came down to the train, looked me up in the third class and 'saw me off' waving me out of sight!"[3]

Martha interrupted her itinerary to visit Queen Marie and Princess Ileana. It was an eighteen-hour boat trip up the Black Sea from Constantinople to Costanza, Rumania, from where Martha was escorted to the queen's palace in Balcic. Built on the edge of a cliff, with terraced gardens going down to the shore of the Black Sea, the palace was known in Turkish as *Tenha-Yuva*, "a solitary nest."[4] The announcement of Martha's arrival at this secluded palace was not ordinary. Referring to herself in the third person, she drew a word picture of the event:

> She sat alone in the motor car halted at the royal entrance gate while her card was being sent on to the palace in the distance.

Suddenly a bugler comes out on the cliffs far above and to the right and began to play a welcome. Yodlers on still higher rocks echoed the sweet sounds.[5]

There were several other guests at the palace; but when the meal was over, all the guests but one retired to the guest palace. It was Martha Root who was invited back to the queen's apartment to share a quiet time with the dowager queen and Princess Ileana. During their visit, the queen extolled the abilities of her daughter, who sat next to her on the divan. "'Whenever I have a difficult mission which requires amiability and diplomacy,'" the queen said, "'I send Ileana. I can always count upon her to do it as I would do it myself, and she has youth and strength, which are added assets.'"[6]

Queen Marie gave Martha some autographed pictures and assured Martha of her love for the Faith and its ambassador. Martha also carried away the memory of spiritual and physical beauty, which the queen created wherever she dwelt.

Because Martha's journey would take her away from the better traveled routes of most Westerners, and because she wished to cover any eventualities, she wrote to Roy Wilhelm from Constantinople in September:

I hope I shall never need to cable for money, but if I should, I would cable you and ask my cousin (by letter) to send it to you. My cousin does not have a cable address & it isn't easy to send it from a little town (everybody over here knows your National City Bank.). I know you would do this for me if any unfor[e]seen emergency came up, illness or anything. . . . (I would not try to explain everything by cable—only just cable the sum & trust you to understand. But I hope I shall never need to do this.[7]

Within a month Roy received a cable from Beyoğlu, Turkey, which read: "Hundred Love Martha." Roy obliged. A week later, on 15 October, he received a second cable reading: "Please wire hundred dollars here Martha." Because Martha's plans had changed, putting her two weeks behind schedule, Roy did not realize that she was in a region of Turkey that was

TENHA-YUVA
("a solitary nest"), the secluded palace of the royal family in
Balcic, Rumania, on the Black Sea, where Martha Root
visited Queen Marie in autumn 1929

not on most maps, where she was waiting for funds before moving on. He had wired the first sum to Haifa, thinking she would pick up the money there. Realizing his mistake, he then wired $150 to Beyoğlu. One month later Martha was still trying to locate the funds and cabled again: "Cabled twice from Constantinople, received nothing, never heard name Beyoğlu, please wire hundred Root American Consul Port Said."[8]

Expenses were very much higher than expected, and emergencies surfaced. Martha's glasses had been stolen in Brindisi, whisked out from under her as she set them down. She saw the thieves, but she was about to board the ship. They were her "eyes" and had to be replaced. In Constantinople she needed a dentist for a badly aching tooth. And throughout her extensive travels, even at third-class rates, her funds were constantly being dissipated.

She was also a victim of visas, which were necessary even between cities in Turkey. "One has to have a special visa and
stamp to go to Angora [Ankara]," she noted. "I got that but no
one told me I had to get one to leave Angora. No one told me at
the little Turkish hotel or at the Embassy or at the Press or at
the station."[9]

When she returned to Constantinople, she reported her arrival to the police, who were difficult. "They made me pay a fine
of five dollars because I had not gone to the police in Angora
and reported that I was *leaving!*" There was a young Turkish
Bahá'í in Constantinople who had lost his position because of
his religion. He tried to make communications a little easier,
but he could not change the decision. "Every breath in Turkey
has been a prayer," Martha admitted, "one has to be so very
careful."[10]

It was mid-November before the Beyoğlu funds reached her.
Although Roy wanted to make this sum a contribution to Martha's travel expenses, she insisted that the money be returned to
him through her cousin Sidney Hart, including the cost of
Roy's cables and six percent interest on his money. She urged
each of them not to scold her, but to follow instructions. It was
done her way. "This is life," she wrote to both of them, "and I
must see this through and do my work. . . . [and] when I pass
out I shall not have been a burden to anybody. . . . [I] pray
God to shower His Blessings upon you. . . ."[11]

Martha was particularly firm at this time about maintaining
her financial independence and integrity, as she had recently
received from a friend a letter that irritated her. The friend,
who had limitless funds, was the same woman who had offered
Martha financial assistance during the first visit with Queen
Marie in Rumania. In a letter to Roy, Martha noted the great
good done by her friend and praised her fine qualities; but she
added:

[She] wrote me she heard that some one was paying all my
expenses now so that I am O.K. She sent me $40. as a love
token & gave me a little reproach that I travel so economical-
ly. . . . You know Roy that no one pays all my expenses.

You have helped me & Julia helped me with all that Esperanto work & Julia has been good to me, but no one has paid as much as I have paid. Sometimes I have rec[eive]d a gift from two or three friends then sometimes for a very long time I have not had any gift except your dear gifts.[12]

In response to the letter Martha began to tally the gifts she had received from this friend, recording the use to which each was put. Martha recalled that she had allowed the friend to pay for her passage when they were traveling to Portugal on the same ship. But Martha had insisted on traveling third class, while her friend went first class. In Geneva her twenty-dollar gift had gone to pay Martha's office rent at the International Bahá'í Bureau. "Any gift that has ever been given me," Martha noted, "has been used towards the travelling or for the Cause. No one has ever paid for my food *nor* have I *ever* used a penny for clothes or anything personal."[13]

Traveling seemed to absorb more and more of Martha's funds, even when going third class. "For ex[ample]," she told Roy, "the ticket from Cairo to Jerusalem is . . . first $25 and nearly . . . $10 third class. I take the third but stopping over these places & changing the trains with all my bags will cost $2. taxi to train & to hotel in Jerusalem $1 each [way] . . . Hotel room Jerusalem $1.50 or perhaps $2. and that is the way it is all the time." Economy would be especially important with the long journey ahead through new paths. But she felt the journey was absolutely essential: "it is truly a matter of life and death this Bahá'í work. . . . We give our all & are trying to give it wisely."[14]

On 31 October Martha left Constantinople, taking the train through Turkey as far as Adana. It was a five-day trip, and Martha traveled third class, riding in a special section for women. From Adana she went by boat to Rhodes, Cyprus, Alexandretta, and Beirut, docking in Port Said, Egypt, during the second week in November.

It was Martha's third visit to this Mediterranean country. Her three weeks there were spent doing Bahá'í work as diligently as if she were in some place other than in the shadow of the Holy Land. She had written ahead for some appointments, made her usual contacts, organized an Esperanto club, and was entertained by intellectuals, businessmen, and the media. A lengthy article by Martha, with photographs of 'Abdu'l-Bahá and of the Rumanian royalty, would appear when Martha reached Haifa.

One of her most striking experiences in Cairo was an audience on 14 November with the nephew of King Fuad, His Royal Highness Muḥammad 'Alí Páshá, in his home at the Manial Palace. Martha found this writer and philosopher, whom she called "one of the greatest Princes of this wonderful land of the Pharaohs and the Khedives," to be a man of grace and accomplishment.[15] One of his most appealing traits was that he had known and loved 'Abdu'l-Bahá. Another notable event was meeting Madame Hoda Charaouwi, a person who had done tremendous work and had dedicated her immense wealth to help raise the station of women.

In Cairo at that time was a young woman, Bahia Faraj'u'-lláh (later Mrs. Robert Gulick), who remembered both meetings. Martha Root had received permission from the parents and from the principal of the school to take Bahia to act as Martha's interpreter. Bahia, who had seen Miss Root at several Bahá'í events, was astonished, thinking herself not expert enough in English. She marveled at the honor and privilege that such a task bestowed upon her.

They went first to the palace and then to Martha's appointment with Madame Charaouwi. Bahia observed that Martha was a humble lady who wore simple clothing. Although she did not think Martha was beautiful in a physical way, she found that Martha attracted people wherever they went. She was impressed that Miss Root carried her food with her in a little basket and that she would not go to restaurants, in order to save every penny for her work.[16]

Another memory of Martha's visit to Egypt comes from 'Azíz Yazdí, a Bahá'í now working at the Bahá'í World Center in Haifa:

I was a young man when I met her in Port Said, Egypt on her way to the Holy Land. She introduced me to Esperanto.

Gave me my first lesson and helped me organize the first
Esperanto Group of Egypt. During this trip she went to . . .
[Cairo] to an appointment she had with Prince Mohamed
Ali, uncle [nephew] to King Fuad of Egypt. . . . she
went . . . 3rd class (i.e. sitting on wooden benches. . . .)

When she reached [Cairo] a delegation from Prince Mohamed Ali were waiting at the railway station to welcome
her. They first looked at the compartments of the first class.
She wasn't there. They then tried the second class, in vain.
Then on their way out they spotted an old woman coming
from the direction of the 3rd class carrying her own luggage.
This was Martha Root. Notwithstanding this, the Prince
paid her homage and tremendous respect.[17]

Martha left Cairo at the end of November and, en route to
Jerusalem, stopped in Ismailia to speak in the afternoon. She
went on to Qantara to speak with the Bahá'ís from 10:00 P.M.
until midnight, when her train left. No time lay idle; every minute was embroidered with teaching.

Martha had written to the high commissioner of Palestine,
requesting an interview during her brief stay, and telling him
she was a Bahá'í. After arriving in Jerusalem, she was received
by that city's governor. Later she had an interview with the
grand muftí of the city and with the directors of the great
mosques. As she had done throughout her travels, Martha's
activities in Palestine were reaping the rewards of a goodwill
ambassador for the Faith. It was a positive excursion in a mul-
tifaith land. Now her course was set once again toward Haifa
and the World Center of the Bahá'í Faith.

40   Haifa Revisited—Damascus Discovered

At 8:00 P.M. on 25 November 1929 Martha Root arrived for her second visit to Haifa and the Bahá'í holy shrines. She would approach the close of the decade on Mount Carmel, finding spiritual renewal in a place close to those spirits whom she loved. It was the closest Martha would come, ever, to relaxation.

Shortly after her arrival Martha was invited to a meeting attended by 'Abdu'l-Bahá's wife, Munírih Khánum, and several other women. One fourteen-year-old girl read a welcome message in English, a language that many Persian Bahá'ís were striving to learn, and Martha responded that she hoped someday to feel worthy of such a welcome. Any further words failed her because of her weariness after her journey, and her heart "was just too full to speak."[1]

Shoghi Effendi had returned to Haifa the morning of Martha's arrival. He sent for her and, after greeting her, said, " 'Martha, always remember what I have told you, I wish you to take very good care of your health.' "[2] Martha recalled that "We had such a happy little talk just about 'news' . . . he chanted so marvelously, it was heavenly at the Shrines. . . ." "He is my great ideal of a Guardian," she wrote to Roy Wilhelm. "Oh, I see his great reality,—I just cannot describe how beautiful it was to meet him."[3]

A few days after Martha arrived, Shoghi Effendi became ill and ran a high temperature caused by a serious infection of the throat, which eventually had to be lanced. Martha did not see him for another three weeks. Her plan had been to stay nine days, but the Guardian sent messages to her, urging, " 'Do not hurry on, stay a little with us.' "[4]

Martha was staying at the Western Pilgrim House, a newly erected building that accommodated Bahá'í visitors to Haifa.

330

The building, given by Harry Randall, was not quite ready for use during Martha's first visit in 1925. Memories of loved ones flooded her thoughts, as she wrote to Roy Wilhelm about people and mementos of the past:

> I thought of 'Abdu'l Baha, His passing, of father & mother & your father [Mr. Wilhelm] & here I am in Harry's house, this Pilgrim House and imagine my thankfulness to see my mother's table-cover on the table, our butter knife on the butter plate, a tray cloth embroidered by my dear Mother on the tea tray & our silver ware. . . .[5]

Also here on God's holy mountain were gifts from another Bahá'í living in the West. "I came to this *home,*" Martha's letter to Roy continued, "for if our Master's Home is not ours, where is our home! and I saw how everything is linked together & your lights & the picture of the 'Door' you took was enlarged & framed in this same room."[6]

As in the past, her visits with the Greatest Holy Leaf, Bahíyyih Khánum, etched beauty, and purity, and strength upon Martha's consciousness. At eighty-two, even though Bahíyyih Khánum was ill with pneumonia and had not walked for two months, she retained spiritual qualities that continued to shine forth. "She received us sitting up in bed," Martha remembered. "Dressed so lovely . . . she is perfectly beautiful and very exquisite." When the Greatest Holy Leaf told Martha that she would pray for her success in service, Martha asked her "please to pray for me selflessness, evanescence and a love that would radiate to every soul I ever meet."[7]

Before leaving the Greatest Holy Leaf, Martha received from her a "beautiful little red ringstone" as a token of her love and admiration. One of the Bahá'ís present, who looked askance at Martha's habit of giving away her precious gifts, asked Bahíyyih Khánum, "'Should not Martha always keep the ring[?] . . .'" Bahíyyih Khánum replied, "'I could not say that. I know if she gives it away it will be a great sacrifice for it is very dear to her. But if she feels it would do a great service to the Cause somewhere and she gave it, it would do good.'"[8]

Very much aware of the volume of work that faced Shoghi

Effendi, Martha wanted to help with the writing, but he was too ill to work. He sent word that he wanted her to rest; to the others he said, "'Do not give her anything to do, she must rest'."[9]

Nevertheless, Martha was anxious to serve the Bahá'í friends that had made her stay in Haifa "a great holy experience."[10] She decided to give a tea party using one of the packets of tea sent by Roy Wilhelm to give her sustenance as she traveled through less accessible countries. She arranged a festive affair. The four gardeners at the holy shrines on Mount Carmel were the guests of honor; twenty guests from the Eastern Pilgrim House were also invited. Later Martha gave a second tea for the Bahá'ís living near Bahá'u'lláh's resting place at Bahjí, with some guests coming from Akka and two nearby villages. She assured Roy that the tea was deeply appreciated.

Although Shoghi Effendi's illness had prevented Martha from seeing him, she decided to go ahead with her plans to leave Haifa and travel to Syria, Iraq, and Iran. The journey was to be an experiment; if it proved safe for Martha Root, Shoghi Effendi would send a commission through. He was aware of the dangers inherent in such a trip, and he would pray for Martha's safety.

It was not until three days before Martha was to leave that Shoghi Effendi was able to see her again. Although he urged her to stay, she was already much behind schedule and knew that the weather could be a problem if she delayed her journey any longer. On Christmas Day 1929 Martha left the Holy Land, left the spiritual atmosphere that had enveloped and nurtured her, and set out for the East.

Her immediate destination was Damascus, Syria. Even in this stronghold of Muslim culture, Martha went to the newspapers and left articles about the Bahá'í Faith, held a press conference in her hotel, and gave the reporters literature and a picture of 'Abdu'l-Bahá. Her articles were printed in the newspapers, and copies of them would be waiting for her when she reached Tehran.

Mr. Y. A. Rafaat, whom Martha had met in Haifa, accompanied her around Damascus and acted as her interpreter.

Along with a Persian lady from Shiraz, he would be Martha's traveling companion as they began their trip across the vast desert to Baghdad. In Damascus they arranged with a travel company to join a caravan of many cars for the desert trip. Of the subsequent journey Mr. Rafaat recalled:

> We were three passengers in a big seven passenger's car, two drivers were in the front seat. . . . There were no[t] any paved road[s] or signs indicating the road, the drivers were driving over the existing wheel prints. They drove from early morning until midnight without stopping. We reached a place where the British people had dug a well for water and had built a small hotel and station for cars. The caravan stopped there for some rest. We were able to eat and take a few hours rest. They started at 5 AM with high speed and at 2 PM we reached the border of Mesopotamia [Iraq].[11]

Martha thought it was "the easiest trip I ever took," despite the fact that many people found the trip to be difficult.[12] But then, most people do not travel for days, third class, sitting on plank-board seats, and eating whatever food might have been packed.

The month on Mount Carmel, the visits to the holy shrines, the spiritual animation all gave Martha a reservoir from which she could draw sustenance in the weeks to come. She was not a stranger to unusual environments and alien cultures, but the next four months would unfold new wonders and experiences. Martha was eager to embrace them all.

41 Iraq and Iran

At the border of Syria and Iraq there were two cars waiting for Martha, both containing members of the Bahá'í Spiritual Assembly of Baghdad. They escorted her into Baghdad, whose ancient name means "'City of Peace,'" on or near New Year's Day 1930, and took her to a hotel, where they saw to her comforts.[1] Although the city was still antagonistic to the Bahá'í Faith, Martha went with Mr. Rafaat to the newspapers and gave them prepared articles about the Faith, which were printed along with news of her arrival.

Several years before, the government had taken the houses in Baghdad where Bahá'u'lláh had lived in exile between 1853 and 1863. Although Bahá'ís consider these houses to be holy places, they were open at that time only to Muslims. The clergy and religious teachers of Iraq were still a dominant force, and their prejudices against a new voice were deep, their vision narrow.

On 2 January 1930 Martha was granted an audience with King Faisal of Iraq. She dressed as one would to be received by a king—in a "very simple and elegant white robe with white gloves and shoes and head dress." She met the king at the garden encircling the secretariat, on the bank of the Tigris River. This handsome, scholarly monarch, who had met 'Abdu'l-Bahá in Palestine ten years earlier and had admired His humanitarian efforts, impressed Martha as being himself a great humanitarian. Referring to the thorny problem with Bahá'u'-lláh's houses, the king said, "'I assure you that absolute justice will be done. We have formed a committee to look into those houses. As it is now, it is a great mistake.'"[2] Martha had faith, perhaps naively, in his efforts; but not one to leave an opportunity untouched, she also met with the high commissioner of the British Empire in Iraq and with the governor of Baghdad. Although the League of Nations in late 1929 had upheld the Bahá'í claims to Bahá'u'lláh's houses, the directives were not followed, and the property remained in the hands of the Muslims. Many years before the seizure Bahá'u'lláh wrote:

> Grieve not, O House of God, if the veil of thy sanctity be rent asunder by the infidels. God hath, in the world of creation, adorned thee with the jewel of His remembrance. Such an ornament no man can, at any time, profane. Towards thee the eyes of thy Lord shall, under all conditions, remain directed.[3]

> In the fullness of time, the Lord shall, by the power of truth, exalt it in the eyes of all men. He shall cause it to become the Standard of His Kingdom, the Shrine round which will circle the concourse of the faithful.[4]

Martha could not go to any of Bahá'u'lláh's homes, but she could visit the Garden of Riḍván, where, shortly before His exile to Constantinople, He had declared that He was a messenger from God. In this city on the banks of the Tigris River, many of Bahá'u'lláh's writings had been revealed, including the Hidden Words, the Tablet of the Holy Mariner, and the Kitáb-i-Íqán (or Book of Certitude), which revealed the mysteries of past revelations and explained the progressive unfolding of spiritual truth.[5] Martha immersed herself in the spiritual splendor of her surroundings and absorbed the lingering grandeur of Bahá'u'lláh's presence.

From Baghdad, Martha traveled south to Basra, at the mouth of the Tigris, which was close to Abadan, Iran, the site of the Anglo-Persian Oil Company. Long before oil had become the crown jewel of modern living, the oil companies employed tutors and interpreters. The education director of the Anglo-Persian Oil Company during Martha's visit to Basra was a Bahá'í, Dhikru'lláh Khádem. Mr. Khádem recalled that everyone was aware of Martha's presence, but one who was particularly touched was

> a very old man, eighty to eighty-five, who would never come out. People rarely saw him; they called him a "bird." He

lived in Basra on the banks of the Tigris. One day he did appear and said that a lady called "Martha" was staying at the hotel and was talking about Bahá'í.

The people were so attracted to her that they would wait for her to come out of the hotel and then followed her, as many as one hundred, walking after her in the street.

The bird, who would never come out, came out for Martha—he said something happened when she was there. He loved her.[6]

This incident had made such an impression on those in the area that it appeared in the bulletin of the Anglo-Persian Oil Company.

A new car was hired on 9 January by the Baghdad Spiritual Assembly to take Martha from Baghdad to the border of Iran. Although the customs officials treated Martha with courtesy and invited her in for tea while the officials went through all her boxes and belongings, they told her that she would have to burn any Bahá'í books. Martha replied, "'I know, and I did not bring any.'" Later, pouring oil on troubled waters, Martha wrote a letter thanking them for their courtesy, but she added:

"The teachings of Baha'u'llah are not against Islam. If you will read the books you will see where he speaks about the station of Muhammad, and people know about the station of Muhammad through Baha'u'llah. . . . The Christians do not believe in Muhammad, and you allow their books to come across the border . . . the Cause of Baha'u'llah acknowledges the station of Muhammad, . . . yet you will not allow the Baha'i books to pass the border."[7]

Devoted as she was, Martha had no longing to be a martyr. She wanted to use her life to serve the Faith and spread the message, not to die for it and leave work undone. Yet she was in the land where Bahá'ís by the tens of thousands had been tortured and massacred for scores of years by the fanatical elements. The possibility of martyrdom was real. She wrote:

we came to another place where I learned a lesson which I had to learn. Shoghi Effendi had told me not to be alone anywhere. But it just happened that everybody had left the

automobile and I was alone, and a great number—nearly
100 young men—came up to the automobile and said, "You
must get out". I said I did not wish to get out, but they said,
"You must, we are soldiers." And in the meantime they had
called one by one to ask about me, and everybody in that
place knew I was a Baha'i teacher, and I said: "Baha'u'llah,
one has to learn to be a martyr". One cannot, as one would
who expects to be shot in the next minute, say honestly "I
wish to be a martyr." and when I got out I got out very slowly, and they looked everything over for opium.[8]

A subsequent episode just beyond the border contained elements of an Arabian-nights story. Martha was told to go see a
doctor down by a rushing river. As she walked toward the river,
she was followed by soldiers, who turned her over to a little boy
and then gave him a vial of white powder. Martha wondered
whether her fate was to be drowned, poisoned, or shot. After
being taken to several places and questioned, with everything
she said being written down, she was told by the police to
"'wait for a few hours.'" Martha demurred, "'I do not want
to wait,'" adding, "'I shall go back to the border and wait until
everything is right for me to enter Persia.' And I ordered the
automobile to go back, and the Chief of Police said 'Everything was all right,['] that we could go forward. . . ."[9]
Martha was on Persian soil. It was January 1930.
She felt deeply about the land her feet had touched, felt its
sanctity. Recording her impressions for the readers of *Bahá'í
Magazine: Star of the West*, she wrote:

Persia, the land of Bahá'u'lláh, the scene of the life and
martyrdom of the Báb, the childhood home of 'Abdu'l-
Bahá, the long caravan routes over which passed Qurratu'l-
'Ayn [Ṭáhirih] and the other eighteen "Letters of the Living" [the Báb's first followers], the soil made fragrant by the
pure blood of countless thousands of devoted [followers]—
O reader! let us approach with reverence our pilgrimage to
this sacred birthplace of the Bahá'i Faith![10]

Shoghi Effendi wanted Martha to be met only by the Spiritual Assembly in whatever part of Iran she appeared. By way

of credentials she carried with her a letter from the Guardian, written in Persian, that announced to the Bahá'ís the visit of

> the Leader of the men and women teachers, Her holiness Miss Martha Root. . . . It is incumbent and obligatory upon all the beloved of God and hand maidens of the Merciful One in that sacred land to receive that noble soul with their hearts and souls, and to perform the ceremonies of hospitality towards her with all respect and the utmost affection. . . . [He urged them to] spread banquets and adorn gatherings and assemblages . . . [for] that chosen one of His Holiness the Almighty and the bearer of the fame of the cause of Baha, both in words and in deeds. For this unique believer with an astonishing power and matchless courage and constancy has raised the cry of Ya Baha'u'alláh [sic] in the loftiest places and brought the sacred name of our blessed Faith to the hearing of mighty personages including Princes, Ministers, erudites and royalty. She has thus represented before the eye of the great men of the world the wronged ones and workers of that land as a people of eminence and excellence. She deserves every kind of love and affection and is worthy of infinite honor and glorification.[11]

The Persia that Martha Root entered was not far different from the Persia during the time of the birth of the Bahá'í Faith in 1844. The winds of change had not yet touched this ancient culture; agriculture was still primitive, and education was limited to a very small percentage of the population. Religion was rigid, ritualistic, and fanatic, requiring women to wear the chador, or veil, when in the presence of people other than family members. As a result the Guardian urged Martha to use discretion in her activities and to be aware of the "requirements and exigencies of time and place." He did not want her to create situations that caused "tumult and outcry," arousing the hostile feelings of the enemies of the Faith.[12]

Word of her coming spread like a brush fire, and her route and schedule seemed mysteriously known. Despite Shoghi Effendi's wishes Martha was met by hundreds of people, including Bahá'ís, who lined the way for miles and often waited all night to catch a glimpse of her. In some places it was highly dangerous for people to be identified as Bahá'ís, but Martha recognized their presence through their signals. In other places the Bahá'ís' welcome could be more open. Along one route they wore ancient pastel costumes and signaled the car to stop while they played an ancient Persian instrument, danced, and sang a song of spring. It was a royal welcome indeed.

Martha's route from Baghdad to Tehran spanned five hundred miles, most of which were over difficult mountain roads. Crossing the Zagros Mountains during cold and snowy weather, the caravan found that the mountain roads were often blocked, and they would have to wait for hours until a passage was cleared. At least twice Martha's party had to stop overnight in a "coffee shop"—a crude building with a dirt floor that turned to oozing mud, several inches deep, when the donkey drivers piled in and deposited their melting snow.[13] A storeroom was cleared, a quilt was hung at the opening for privacy, and Martha slept on a table, with coats piled on for warmth.

In one of these places a fire was made during the night in the brazier. The windows had been hermetically sealed, which almost caused the guests to be asphyxiated. Only Martha's weak voice, calling in the night, roused a companion who broke open a window.

After stopping at Ghassrih-Shirine and Kermanshah, Martha and her companions traveled through the snowy mountain passes into Hamadan. Twenty cars, filled with Bahá'ís, ushered her into the city. One who had come with her from Kermanshah remarked, "'Not even emperors and kings have twenty motor cars awaiting their approach.'"[14] She spent three days in Hamadan giving public lectures and meeting the Bahá'ís, of which there were a great many. Everywhere she went, she was protected by the authorities, although the religious climate in Hamadan was freer than in other places.

When she arrived in Qazvin, she was escorted by a procession of about forty-five cars, some having traveled ninety miles over the treacherous, snow-drifted roads to meet her. Qazvin was the home of Ṭáhirih, one of the initial eighteen followers of the Báb. She was the first Persian woman to lay aside the veil and the first Bahá'í woman to champion the equality of the sexes. She was martyred in Tehran in 1852—strangled with a

*Martha Root with members of the Spiritual Assembly of the Bahá'ís
of Hamadan and a few other friends during her historic
1930 trip to Iran*

white silk scarf that she herself had given to her captors. Ṭáhirih's final words were " 'You can kill me as soon as you like but
you cannot stop the emancipation of women.' " [15]

No Westerner had ever been to Ṭáhirih's home, but Martha
managed to arrange a visit through the hotel owner, who knew
a nephew of Ṭáhirih's. The Bahá'ís, aware of the intense hostility in Qazvin, said, " 'But you can't do that. . . . You would
never dare to go to the house of Qurratu'l-'ayn'.' "

Martha realized the risk involved, especially since her presence in Qazvin was not exactly unnoticed. Across the hall from
her hotel room were five soldiers watching her door, day and
night. She asked a Bahá'í, " 'Why are those men always watching me?' " " 'Everyone in Persia is watching you' " was the reply. [16]

Nevertheless, Martha went to the beautiful old palace—
now less well cared for—that had been Ṭáhirih's home while
growing up. When Martha reached the little room where Ṭá-

hirih had studied, she knelt, bowed her head to the floor, and prayed. Although she did not realize it, many relatives of Ṭá-hirih's came in and viewed this phenomenon—a Western woman from the other side of the world paying spiritual homage to one who was martyred, and justifiably so, they felt.

One relative came forth and told Martha that he was not against Ṭáhirih; it was an honor, he felt, to belong to her family. He invited Martha to the hotel, where he wept and admitted, "'I have known for 20 years that I should be a Baha'i, but I have never had the courage to do it.'" That, he promised, would change, and he would go to Haifa and speak to the Guardian. He gave Martha much information about the early Bahá'í heroine, which Martha would later include in her book *Táhirih the Pure, Irán's Greatest Woman.*[17]

As Martha left Qazvin for Tehran, this relative of Ṭáhirih's stood up with his arms linked with Bahá'ís. A brilliant rainbow appeared that enveloped them in a pastel arc, a cosmic and spiritual unification. However, the joy in her heart was somewhat tempered when she discovered that the same five soldiers from her hotel were following her out of town. "It was not funny to have those men watching me all the time," she admitted later.[18] But now Tehran lay on the horizon, darkened for decades by its rejection of the Bahá'í message that Martha Root sought valiantly to share.

42 The Heart of Persia

Shoghi Effendi had cautioned Martha to be especially careful in Tehran, where prejudice was high and restraint not always practiced. Martha was greatly relieved when only five members of the Spiritual Assembly came to Qazvin to escort her to the capital. Before long, however, it was evident that the Bahá'ís were out in legion to meet her.

As they started into the city on a cold day in the middle of February, the Bahá'í owner of the hotel where Martha would stay asked her to get into his automobile. "When we got to the gate," Martha reported, "it was so unusual—such an immense crowd of people—so many automobiles and if they knew it was a Baha'i coming, no one knew what would happen; but we had to wait to get a ticket to get into Tihran. . . ."[1] The Bahá'ís had taken many precautions, among them asking four policemen, who were Bahá'ís, to guard Martha's car as they entered the city.

This was Tehran, the birthplace of Bahá'u'lláh, the city where He had been reared, and where His father had been a minister of the royal court. Bahá'u'lláh's first imprisonment had taken place here in the Síyáh-Chál, the Black Pit, where He was put in irons and bastinadoed. It was in that gruesome spot that He had received the announcement of His mission on earth. Martha was touched with awe by the nearness of these sacred places.

At the hotel Martha's room was elegant, with French doors opening into a courtyard. She realized the danger of such visibility and accessibility and asked to be changed to a less grand but safer place. The Bahá'ís graciously responded, " 'Tell her this hotel is just like her coat—it belongs to her.' "[2] For her added safety no one came to see Martha without having first been received by one of three brothers who owned the hotel.

A street scene in Tehran, Iran.
Little had changed since the beginning of the Bahá'í Faith
in 1844 and Martha Root's visit in 1930.

Even the barber who tended Martha's hair had to be a trusted individual.

Rumors were rampant, and the bazaars were fertile ground for spreading them. Even before Martha arrived, a newspaper article reported that a woman would soon come to Iran who was "'the daughter of Abdu'l Baha, but she wears American clothes and speaks English to deceive the people.'" The article added suspiciously, "'She is a fisher of Kings.'"[3]

After being entertained at the hotel with a dinner, attended by two hundred guests, Martha settled down to her public lecturing and journalistic work. She interviewed the heads of government and governmental departments, including the minister of finance for war, and sent the resulting articles to Washington and Cairo. The articles, which were also sent to many newspapers in America, gave a positive impression of the Persian government, as Martha hoped to build good relations between these two countries. In response to her questions of what America could do to help, there was an eager request for American educators and lecturers to send their ideas or, better still, to personally come to Iran and teach.

Her trip through Iran, Martha explained to government officials, was an experiment. If it were safe for her, others would come, and ideas and tourism would flourish. Subtly, she ensured her protection in this hospitable, yet prejudiced and hostile country.

While in Tehran Martha hoped to arrange for an audience with the sháh, Riza Khán Pahlavi. She had met and interviewed his minister of the court, Mr. Teymúrtásh, and she hoped that the minister would arrange an interview. The request was followed with a letter in which Martha described the peaceful and unifying elements of the Faith and reaffirmed Bahá'í recognition of the Prophethood of Muḥammad. If the sháh wished, Martha would send him some books to read that she hoped would lay his fears to rest. But the audience with the sháh did not eventuate.

Even though this monarch proved to be inaccessible, Martha's kindness would still reach him. "In a separate envelope but without any written word," she wrote to Mr. Teymúrtásh, "I am sending to Him, through you, my dearest treasure, a little locket which has been my joy and protection. Also . . . I enclose a little Esperanto-Persian dictionary. . . ." Included along with these gifts was "the Star, a little Esperanto pin for His Most Royal Highness the little Crown Prince."[4] In view of the history of the Bahá'í Faith in Iran, and of the ruthless tyrannical actions of those in power toward its followers, one can only be amazed at the courage and child-like trust that guided Martha's efforts.

Remembering Shoghi Effendi's admonitions, Martha never went out except to give talks and lectures. When she did go out, she was never alone and always rode in a closed automobile. Threatening letters came, and Martha acknowledged that "There are enemies, but Bahá'u'lláh has protected me, [and] I did not reply to their letters."[5]

During her visits with the Bahá'ís in Tehran and elsewhere, Martha realized that they were very much aware of the House of Worship being built near Chicago. They also knew about

Martha Root (front row, center) with a group of Bahá'í women in Tehran, Iran, 1930. Most of the women have abandoned the veil.

the need for funds to continue the work. One woman remembers the day Martha Root came to her home. Even though she was just a toddler who sat in Martha's lap, she was so inspired by Martha's presence that she took off her little earrings made of gold coins and gave them to Martha for the Temple Fund.[6]

During her several weeks in Tehran, Martha regularly visited Dr. Susan B. Moody, a physician and teacher from the United States who had been working in Iran for several years. She was seriously ill during Martha's stay, recuperating from pneumonia, and Martha saw to her comforts. Always concerned with giving that extra measure of happiness, Martha had a blue silk robe made for the patient, certain that the color would cheer her.

North of Tehran was the city of Tabriz, the site of the martyrdom of the Báb. In the first week in April Martha made a pilgrimage to the spot, where she viewed the prison where the Báb had been incarcerated. Her mind envisioned the day of His execution on 9 July 1850, and she relived that drama of eighty years before. It was in this prison that the Báb was advising His amanuensis when the guard interrupted to take Him to His execution. It was not yet time, the Báb told him. " 'Not until I have said to him all those things that I wish to say can any earthly power silence Me. Though all the world be armed against Me, yet shall it be powerless to deter Me from fulfilling, to the last word, My intention.' "[7] The guard, armed with earthly power, would not listen. The Báb was brought out to the city square with the disciple who wished to die with Him, and both were strung up and suspended from a spike hammered into the building.

Sám Khán, colonel of the regiment ordered to carry out the execution, had begged to be released from this loathsome duty. The Báb said, " 'Follow your instructions, and if your intention be sincere, the Almighty is surely able to relieve you of your perplexity.' "[8]

Three files, each of 250 men, discharged, in turn, their bullets. The area was black with the smoke of 750 fired rifles; and when the smoke cleared, the disciple was standing untouched, with ropes severed. The Báb had disappeared. There was astonishment and confusion. A thorough search was conducted, and eventually the Báb was discovered back in His cell, where He was finishing the conversation that had been interrupted. Ten thousand spectators, including European news reporters, standing in the barracks and on the housetops, witnessed this strange event.

The Báb then told the guards, " 'I have finished My conversation with Siyyid Husayn. . . . Now you may proceed to fulfill your intention.' "[9] Sám Khán refused to have his men carry out the execution, and another regiment was found. The Báb and His disciple were once again suspended, the order given, and the bodies fused together by the volleys of bullets from 750 rifles. Only the Báb's face was untouched—no bullet had marred that Beauty.

Storms and earthquakes shook the land; famine and pestilence broke out. The entire regiment that performed the execution met with violent deaths within three years.

Now Martha Root, a Bahá'í from the West, had come to this city of Tabríz, so precious to Bahá'ís. She was treated with every courtesy. The chief of police invited her to a garden party with the commander in chief of the army. As they sat beneath the window of the cell that had been occupied by the Báb, Martha marveled at the strange march of history and the spiritual power of unity. Both of these men wanted to read the Bahá'í writings, and Martha sent a list of books that she wished the National Spiritual Assembly of the United States and Canada to mail to them. The writings of Bahá'u'lláh's revelation, which was born in their land, would reach them from America.

Martha had barely arrived in Tabríz when a message came from the Bahá'ís in the village of Sísán, asking her to come for a visit. This was impossible, they were told, because blizzards had closed the road. Undaunted, hundreds of men from the village went out and cleared the way for miles. Martha went. Even she, the recipient of so much affection by the Persian Bahá'ís, was overwhelmed by the love of these simple farming people.

Exceptional compassion and response also poured forth from the Persian Bahá'ís as Martha journeyed south to Qum,

Kashan, Isfahan, and Yezd. In Kashan she was presented with a prayer rug; woven into its center was a Bahá'í symbol, the Greatest Name, surrounded by a poem of Bahá'u'lláh. There a young man came to her who "had a terrible affliction in his eyes caused by Influenza, and he had heard that she had been . . . successful in healing through prayer, and he . . . asked her to pray for him." Martha did pray for him, using her new prayer rug, "and the next morning something broke in his nose, and his eyes cleared up immediately."[10] The rug was later presented, through an official, to the emperor of Japan and was housed in the Imperial Palace.

Toward the end of April, Martha arrived in Shiraz, the birthplace of the Báb. On 4 May 1930 she was taken to the house in which the Báb had first declared His mission, in a second floor room, to Mullá Ḥusayn. One who accompanied Martha reported that "At her first sight of the House, she fell on her knees and wept and wept. 'To think,' she sobbed, 'that such a great message should have come from such a small House!'"[11]

In this city of nightingales and roses Martha was treated like visiting royalty by the officials, who held a public reception for her. She spoke later in the exquisite public gardens, where the residents thronged to meet her.

Only the mullás, or religious teachers, were not pleased. They still harbored as much prejudice toward the Bahá'ís as they did during the lifetimes of the Báb and Bahá'u'lláh. In Shiraz the most important mullá twice preached about Martha in the mosque, but Martha wrote:

> in Shiraz I did not feel afraid at all, for I had a vision in the House of [the] Báb[,] and Bahá'u'lláh told me He would protect me . . . I went in the streets[,] walked to [the] House of [the] Báb and [of the] grandparents of Shoghi Effendi[,] and lectured each day and in Shiraz I spoke before many Moslems at each lecture. There were 1100 men present at the meeting in one Garden in Shiraz.[12]

Martha's faith in Bahá'u'lláh's protection was constantly affirmed. While visiting Persepolis, the ruins of the ancient

Martha Root at the House of the Báb
Shiraz, Iran, 4 May 1930

capital of Iran lying thirty miles northeast of Shiraz, she was startled by the sight of nomads on horseback galloping furiously toward her. It seemed as if she was about to be deliberately run down when she discovered that they were young Bahá'ís. They had come to welcome her with a flourish, reaching down to gather pebbles as they galloped by. One can imagine her pleasure—and relief.

Bushire would be the last city on her tour. After four months in Iran, spring had come. It was May, and the roads to Bushire were muddy and practically impassable. A Persian friend, who had gone on ahead, wrote back to caution her about the water, which would have to be boiled, and about the flies and mosquitoes, which she could keep away if she brought netting. But he especially warned her of two dangers—the roads and the mullás. He advised Martha to go in by airplane.

Surmounting her doubts, Martha arranged a flight. It was her first airplane trip, and it delighted her. "In Bushire there was great excitement among the Mullahs about my coming," Martha wrote the Wilhelms, "—but I fooled them. They had looked for me twice by motor car & then I suddenly came by air (there was great wisdom in that)." [13]

She was taken directly to the home of the only Bahá'í woman in Bushire. In order to ensure Martha's protection, a "'cook'" and a "'butler'" were sent to assist. [14] There was much activity in that home—dinners, luncheons, teas—and Martha spoke at all of them, not only to Bahá'ís, but also to friends of the Faith and those investigating its teachings.

A major in the military invited Martha to visit the Bushire hospitals, staffed, to his surprise, primarily by Bahá'ís. Later they went to dinner with the governor. Recalling this visit a few weeks later, Martha expressed her joy: "Oh, it was so good to go to Bushire and see those patient fine Bahá'ís and tell them about the Cause in the West and to explain the Cause to their friends. So few ever go to Bushire, for the climate & fevers are so bad." [15]

As Martha prepared to go to India, she reflected on her meetings with the families of historic martyrs; she had seen entire villages spiritually renewed because of a recent Bahá'í martyrdom. She now understood somewhat better the dangers that had beset Bahá'u'lláh, the Báb, 'Abdu'l-Bahá, and the followers of the Faith. She realized the ever-present danger and knew that she, too, had lived in the midst of it. To avoid detection and possible difficulty Martha went to the harbor and boarded her ship at 3:00 A.M. Although the heat was extreme, she spent the entire night with the windows and doors tightly secured. She left the birthplace of the Bahá'í Faith the next day and sailed down the Persian Gulf toward Bombay.

Her long-held dream of visiting Iran had been realized. When she left this land of contrasts—of spirituality and brutality, of backward living and exquisite art, of primitive ways and magnificent structures—she looked back on her experiences with gratitude:

> Persia, blessed Land of Bahá'u'lláh, I lived a lifetime in those four months. . . . Many times each day now, I stop and thank Bahá'u'lláh for the journey through Persia, and . . . I thank Him that through His Bounty and Favor this servant came safely. Step by step was the inner drama, I do not like to say I was sometimes afraid. [16]

Martha Root (standing, back row, center) was the honored guest at a celebration for the Twelfth Day of Riḍván, Shiraz, Iran, 1930.

Y. A. Rafaat, her traveling companion, observed that "She showed astonishing kindness to the Iranians. . . . meeting families who had martyrs or were persecuted, she was moved and showed deep sympathy. . . . she was kind, soft and calm." "I had a special reverence toward her," he added. "She was considered a Saint. . . ."[17]

The effect that Martha Root had on the Persian believers can be gauged by a letter to America from the Spiritual Assembly of Tehran:

> "The arrival in Persia of our beloved spiritual sister Miss Martha Root once more unfolded to the public eye the grandeur of the Cause and the Power of the Divine Word. People who, as proved by history, looked upon foreigners with enmity and bitterness, and considered association with them as contrary to religion, now, thanks to Bahá'u'lláh's Teachings, shed tears of joy at the sight of their American sister.
>
> ". . . How we wished our American brothers and sisters were here to perceive the spirit of love which pervaded the meetings held for Miss Root; the eagerness with which friends rushed to meet her; and the devotion and enthusiasm with which every one listened to her sweet glad tidings. . . . [We] perceived the fervor and the intensity of the feelings of the audiences, and the profound effect which Miss Martha Root's words, emanating from a divinely confirmed source, produced upon those hearing her, who could scarcely repress the flow of tears of exultation, and who rejoiced in the realization of true love and oneness taught by Bahá'u'lláh.
>
> "The Bahá'ís of Tihran regard Miss Martha Root as an angel of purity, and as a true Bahá'í, that is 'the possessor of all human virtues.' She has attracted the hearts of all the friends. . . ."[18]

43   India and Burma, 1930

May to August was not India's most attractive season. It was the hottest time of the year when Martha arrived in Bombay during the third week in May, and the monsoons would be sweeping the subcontinent by the time she left. Furthermore, the political scene was as hot as the weather. It was the time of Mahatma Gandhi's civil disobedience, and the country was in turmoil. Martha wisely informed everyone that she was not there to speak about politics, only about the Bahá'í Faith.

On 6 April 1930 Gandhi had completed his three-week-long march to the Arabian Sea, where he picked up a handful of salt, thus breaking British law and giving the signal for civil disobedience. At his side was Sarojini Naidu, a poet and one of the great women of India, appointed by Gandhi as his next in command. Mahatma Gandhi was imprisoned, but the campaign had been launched.

As agreed, Mrs. Naidu, on 15 May, led twenty-five hundred volunteers in a march on the Dharasana Salt Works, 150 miles north of Bombay. It was to be a peaceful protest, but it became a bloody page in history. Mrs. Naidu was arrested the next day, but the volunteers, unresisting because of Gandhi's wishes, were mercilessly beaten by the authorities. The death toll soared, but the incident changed the attitude of the Indian people from one of subservience to one of self-determination.

Martha arrived in Bombay within days of the Dharasana encounter. Despite temperatures well over one hundred degrees she caught up with her writing and gave lectures and interviews. At the beginning of June she went to Poona to renew her acquaintance with the Khosrove family, who had been helpful to her during her first visit to India fifteen years earlier. They owned the National Hotel where Martha stayed, and there was

353

a quality about them that touched her deeply. She gave them a set of Bahá'í books that had just arrived for her, and she immediately sent off for another set.

Three miles north of Poona, Yeravda Prison, formerly the palace of the Aqa <u>Kh</u>án, stretched out in the Indian summer. Here Mahatma Gandhi, spiritual leader and heart of the Indian people, and Sarojini Naidu were confined. Martha visited the prison and brought Bahá'í books with her, but she was not allowed to see Gandhi. However, the inspector general of the prison accepted a book to give to him, as well as one for the prison library.

Later, accompanied by Mrs. Naidu's husband, Dr. Naidu, and their daughter, a magazine editor, Martha was permitted to visit Sarojini Naidu. Learning that she was an avid reader, Martha brought her nine Bahá'í books, together with a few of Ṭáhirih's poems and some special gifts. The visit was warmly received, and Mrs. Naidu later became a strong proponent of the Bahá'í Faith.

Although the Indian people were generally peaceful, there was a seething atmosphere beneath their demonstrations. Martha feared that their nonviolent methods would spill over into violence; her feelings proved to be accurate. In June she, too, experienced the unrest in Lahore. As she was leaving the YMCA, a wild mob was passing by. A companion urged her to return to the building until the crowd had moved on. "They are so against English," Martha reported to friends, "they would think I was English & perhaps turn on me. . . . I think I must do what I do quickly, for things may get so bad any day, that I could not give any public lectures."[1] Officials had already banned lectures in Delhi in June, and Martha rearranged her travel plans in anticipation of speaking there later. But the situation continued to be threatening.

Martha left Bombay for Hyderabad, Deccan, in south central India. Here she was a guest of the state and had lavish accommodations during her stay. From Hyderabad she went to Surat, where she had a full schedule of breakfast meetings, teas, dinners, small gatherings, and public lectures. All of her activities were carried on in an average 109 degree heat. It was

IṢFÁNDIAR BAKHTIARI
a devoted Bahá'í who accompanied Martha Root on her travels in
India and Burma in 1930 and again in 1937-38. He presented
this photograph to Miss Martha Root, "my spiritual mother."

difficult for her system to adjust to such unrelieved hot weather, and she was ill for a few days. Dr. Naidu, who was visiting the area, gave her some medicine to dispel the constant nausea. Eventually, she picked up her schedule and made the two-day train trip across the Sind Desert, where in places the temperature rose to 125 degrees. She raised her travel class a notch, going second class rather than third on this trip to offset the danger to her health.

The Bahá'ís saw to it that Martha did not travel alone. Mr. Iṣfándiar Bakhtiari, of Karachi, accompanied her on the long route from Karachi to Lahore, a city where the political unrest was clearly evident. Nevertheless, Martha found people in Lahore with great spiritual capacities. One of her lectures was introduced by the judge of the High Court, one of the most prominent persons in the city.

With the intense June heat in Lahore, it was all Martha

could do to carry on, but carry on she did. Among others, she met with the atheists, who wanted to ask questions about religion, and with the Theosophists. One of the religious groups Martha admired most was the Brahmo Samaj Society, which she found to be open and spiritually motivated. The society made arrangements for Martha's lectures and entertainment as she moved through India, much as the Esperantists had done in other countries.

Pritam Singh, a magazine editor in Lahore, and a Bahá'í, had arranged most of Martha's lectures and interviews in his city. Along with Mr. Bakhtiari, he accompanied her to Simla, the summer seat of the government and a celebrated resort. Whether it was the height, the fog, or the rain, some aspect of the place did not agree with Martha, and it was very hard on her health. She used a ricksha to get to her appointments, most of them three to five miles away.

One of the high points of Martha's visit in India was the invitation by the maharaja of Patiala, chancellor of the Chamber of Princes (similar to the British House of Lords) to be his guest at The Chail, Simla Hill, in late June. The fifty-mile motor trip in the Himalayan Mountains took six hours over steep and dangerous roads. Martha was given a four-room suite in a palatial guest house, set in vast lands. The maharaja was an avid sportsman, and Martha, with other guests, attended a cricket match on the grounds before she was able to meet with him. To Martha he combined all princely qualities, and he showed interest in her work. When leaving, she gave him a silk handkerchief from the "Land of Bahá'u'lláh." "It was a chapter in Bahá'í history," she reported, pleased at the opportunity.[2]

From Simla Hill Martha went on to Delhi, Lucknow, Benares, Patna, Bolpur, and Calcutta. Constant travel and lectures were fitted into a nineteen-day period between 3 and 22 July. The Brahmo Samaj Society and the Theosophists arranged lectures—and even managed one in Delhi. The publicity was good, especially in Calcutta.

Martha spent a few days each in Delhi and Lucknow, and by the second week in July had reached Benares (now Varansi). This ancient city on the sacred Ganges River was the seat of

Hinduism, where pilgrims came from all over to bathe on the steps of the Ganges, the symbol of purity and salvation. Benares, with fifteen hundred temples, combined sanctity with learning, as scholars flocked to the Hindu university. Like most of the universities it was picketed—that is, the men and youth would lie down, forming a carpet of bodies over which one must walk to enter. They hoped to compel professors and students to abandon their scholarly pursuits and work for the freedom of India. Martha's scheduled lecture was canceled, but she spoke to the chancellor and the professors.

Benares was also the All India Headquarters for the Theosophical Society. Here Martha was able to speak to the four hundred students at their school, and the Theosophists offered to publish an article on the Faith in the *Theosophical Review.*

As was her custom, Martha had written ahead for an appointment with the lofty maharaja of Benares. She had little hope for a meeting since he was steeped in orthodoxy, and she was a Westerner. She was astonished when she learned that he would receive her. On the appointed day the maharaja sent his car for her; but because of illness—perhaps fear-induced—his son, the younger maharaja, graciously welcomed her. Martha felt that it was a triumph of sorts.

After a brief stop at Patna, Martha traveled to a spot that had a magnetic pull for her, Santiniketan, site of Rabindranath Tagore's Visva-Bharati (International) University. Tagore— poet, musician, artist, educator, historian, lecturer—was in Europe, but Martha was welcomed and gave two lectures. She was impressed by the school and put books in the library. She hoped a philanthropic Bahá'í would set up a chair for Bahá'í studies, which would add one more to five existing chairs for other religions.

Calcutta would be Martha's last stop in India. There were lectures, and she was widely entertained. On 2 July she had an audience with His Highness the Maharaja of Mayurbani, a man of universal outlook. So important did she consider this meeting that she postponed her sailing to meet with him.

Martha's last lecture in India in 1930 was held on the evening of 21 July in a Buddhist temple in Calcutta. The publicity that the Brahmo Samaj Society and the Theosophists had arranged was especially good here, but the temple's location "in the center of the university picketing square" threatened attendance. However, 150 persons braved the scene. "Perhaps Baha'u'llah wished the lecture in that storm-tossed center," Martha wrote. "Police with mounted guns on motor cars and many hundreds of picketers were in the square outside, while inside the hall we spoke of Baha'u'llah's Solution for these very problems."[3]

By the time Martha's day of departure arrived, the monsoon season had begun. Although the rain had cooled the air somewhat, it was still hot. But Martha admitted that she could "always stand heat better than cold."[4] There were recent memories of subzero temperatures that made the temperatures in India seem tolerable.

Leaving Calcutta on 22 July, Martha retraced steps she had taken years earlier. It was a time of return. She went to Burma and spent a short time in Mandalay, Kunjangoon (the all-Bahá'í village), and Rangoon. In each of these Burmese centers she was received like a visiting dignitary. She lectured, often sponsored by the Theosophists and other leading groups. In Rangoon she spoke four times at the university, where she was interviewed and where articles were published. The Burmese possessed a sublimity of spirit that endeared them to Martha.

On 7 August 1930 Martha sailed out of Rangoon through the Bay of Bengal to Singapore, at the tip of Malaysia. She spent five days there before sailing up the South China Sea to Hong Kong, where she arrived on 22 August. Martha was back in the land she loved.

44   Return to the Far East and Hawaii

The sights and sounds of Hong Kong captivated Martha as much in August 1930 as they had six years earlier; but the special attraction, as always, was the Chinese people. This second visit to China would have an entirely different flavor from her 1923–24 sojourn, and it would last for two months, not twelve. Although she gave several lectures, Martha concentrated her energies on writing articles, each one different, for the newspapers. Her always healthy respect for the power of the printed word had increased as she saw articles spread through regions and countries long after their initial appearance, and far from their place of origin.

With the determination of a zealot Martha managed to have thirty articles published within a relatively short time in Hong Kong, so hospitable and responsive to her efforts in 1924. The record was equally impressive in Canton, where all the papers carried her stories on the Bahá'í Faith. One of her most satisfying accomplishments was a two-page spread in a special supplement of the *Canton Municipal Daily News* on 23 September 1930. The article featured a photograph of 'Abdu'l-Bahá and included the texts of three broadcasts that Martha had made over the Canton radio: "'New Universal Education,'" "'Esperanto As a Universal Auxiliary Language,'" and "'What Is the Bahá'í Movement?'"[1] It was almost twenty-one years to the day since Martha's first double-page story on the Faith had appeared on 26 September 1909 in the *Pittsburgh Post*.

One of the most rewarding aspects of Martha's return to China was seeing tangible results, the blossoming of seeds she had sown during her first China venture. In the cities that she had previously visited, many Chinese scholars had embraced the Faith. Some of the Cantonese Bahá'ís made translations of

Martha Root's Corona typewriter, her constant traveling companion on her worldwide trips and the only item, other than one suitcase, she was permitted to take when she was forced to flee Shanghai in 1937. With it she typed countless releases that resulted in newspaper coverage in many languages, in many countries.

her lectures, which were printed and handed out to the news media. These new Bahá'ís were fulfilling 'Abdu'l-Bahá's prediction that a few knowledgeable Chinese Bahá'ís would take the Faith to their people. In Shanghai it was the scholarly Dr. Y. S. Tsao, former president of Tsing Hua University, who thrilled Martha by offering to translate *Bahá'u'lláh and the New Era* into Chinese.

Agnes Alexander, who at the behest of Shoghi Effendi had reluctantly returned to Japan after four years at home in Hawaii, met Martha in Shanghai, along with Mr. Ouskouli, his two daughters, Mr. Sulaymání, Mr. Touty, and Dr. and Mrs. Tsao. It was a spiritually invigorating time, "ten heavenly days working together for Bahá'u'lláh."[2] Philosophical and humanistic groups sought out the speakers, lectures were given, and homes were made available for smaller discussion groups. It was Martha Root's favorite activity—spiritual skylarking with help from Persian and Chinese friends. A barrage of articles appeared in Shanghai, where the newspapers cooperated fully. Nowhere had Martha found the coverage of the Faith so generous as in China.

During a brief visit to Nanking on 6 October, Martha gave a lecture to her largest Chinese audience, with two thousand present, at the National Central University. Her topic to the largely male audience was "'International Education For the New Age.'"[3] The few females present must have rejoiced in learning of the lofty position in which the Bahá'í Faith places women—not only in education but in all aspects of life.

The political situation in China in some cases limited teaching opportunities. In Shanghai and Nanking the broadcasting studios were closed because of the turbulent times. The year 1930 saw the beginning of the war between the entrenched government and the Communists, a war that would eventually change the face of China. It was Martha's hope to avert disaster by spreading the Bahá'í Faith or at least giving the Chinese people a window of hope for the future. She did her best.

On 22 October Martha sailed for Japan, where she would spend the next two months and would be one country nearer home. Tokyo seemed to be Martha's *bête noir:* On her first vis-

AGNES ALEXANDER (left) and MARTHA ROOT
in Japan, probably in 1930. Martha felt the crowning
achievement of the trip was her delivering a message
from Shoghi Effendi to the emperor of Japan.

it she had lost all her luggage; on her second stay she was trailed as a "Red"; the third visit would again present difficulties.

After joining Agnes Alexander in Tokyo, Martha lost no time in arranging talks at universities, high schools, and other places where young, searching minds could be reached. More newspaper articles appeared, and there were lectures to clubs and religious groups. One of Martha's most successful encounters in Japan was with Mr. Noma, the "Magazine King of Japan" and publisher of the *Hochi Shimbun,* one of Japan's great newspapers.[4] The paper arranged a conference on the Bahá'í Faith, held on 20 December, with three distinguished speakers in addition to Martha Root. Over two thousand attended. It was a complete success, with waves of response coming long after the event.

To Agnes Alexander, the crowning event of Martha's trip to

Japan was the broadcast of a widely publicized talk over the Tokyo Central Broadcasting Station.[5] The presentation was heard all over Japan, and the text was published on the front page of the *Japan Times*. Fifteen other newspapers printed reports of the talk. Because Martha would accept no remuneration when speaking about the Bahá'í Faith, the radio station presented her with a bolt of exquisite rainbow-colored silk as an expression of appreciation.

Looking beyond her lectures and broadcasts, Martha had as her ultimate goal in Japan contacting the Imperial Household; and much to Agnes Alexander's distress and embarrassment, Martha could not be stopped in setting about to achieve her purpose. On 9 November she received a cablegram from Shoghi Effendi, probably prompted by Martha, that communicated his good wishes to the emperor of the ancient regime.

However, gaining admittance to those close to His Imperial Majesty, Hirohito, was not easy. Japan did not bend as gently to Martha's will as did China or the other countries visited. She was severely rebuffed on several levels. The American ambassador refused to give her a letter of introduction, which she wanted as a Bahá'í, not as a journalist. Such a letter, they said, would have to be obtained through the Foreign Office. But the Foreign Office refused to comply in no uncertain terms. The firm, unyielding resistance deeply troubled Martha. She turned for help to a powerful, well-placed friend, Baron Sakatani, the vice-president of the League of Nations Society of Japan, a former minister of finance, and a member of the House of Peers. He wrote letters of introduction to the private secretary of the minister of the Imperial Household and to the private secretary of the minister of foreign affairs. Still nothing happened.

Like a modern-day John Paul Jones, Martha had just begun to fight. She was convinced of the importance and urgency of her mission. She turned to one of her most trusted friends, Dr. R. Masujima, an important lawyer who had helped Martha earlier to send seven Bahá'í books to the emperor of Japan through the minister of the Imperial Household. Magically, resistance disappeared:

Dr. Masujima, and his secretary Mr. Y. Soma arranged to bring me informally to have a talk with this Minister of the Imperial Household. . . . So the three of us went together at 11 oclock on December 9, 1930[,] to the Offices of the Imperial Household in the Imperial Garden, inside the moat, and the walls. It was telephoned when we were coming through the gates.

We gave two sets of cards, one at the gates, one at the Imperial Offices. The telegram [from Shoghi Effendi] that I had received on November 9, I gave over to the Minister of the Imperial Household on December 9. It had taken all that time to do it.[6]

Martha brought precious gifts for His Imperial Majesty. Among them were the Bahá'í writings, with notations of the special references to Japan, accompanied by the exquisite prayer rug she had received in Kashan, Iran. She also gave him a brilliant red ringstone that 'Abdu'l-Bahá had given Siyyid Muṣṭafá Rúmí of Burma; on Muṣṭafá's wedding day he in turn had given it to his wife, and she thought it should grace the finger of Martha Root. An irreplaceable gift was a painting of a phoenix clutching a tablet of Bahá'u'lláh in its claw; the entire painting, full of color, was a message written in Persian script and was the work of 'Alí-Muḥammad Varqá, the Bahá'í martyr. Martha had learned that the phoenix was a favorite symbol of the emperor's. All the gifts were wrapped in white Fuji silk.

Martha was rewarded with approval from the minister. She explained in her notes:

I am so happy and encouraged, for I feel it may be epoch-making for the Cause, that His Excellency, the Minister of the Imperial Household, unexpectedly turned to me and said, "In the future you need not reach me through an intermediary, you may write to me directly, and send me what you wish. I will read it, and then use my judgement [sic] in directing it to the Imperial Family."[7]

The prize in Japan had been won. To Martha this was her crowning achievement.

As Martha was waiting to sail from Yokohama on 30 December 1930, a sightless Bahá'í, Mr. Tokujiro Torii, arrived. Traveling alone from Kyoto, he wished to meet Martha Root before she sailed. He later wrote to Agnes Alexander:

"Songs of waves at the near seashore remind me of Miss Root on the ocean, whom I met for the first and last, but I felt the fragrance of Abha and found love and peace which shines through her. It is my great regret that I could not have much time to be with her, but praise God, He gave me that unforgettable hour. Everything was made clear in my way that day and 'Abdu'l-Baha guided me to the ship without uneasiness in my heart. I could really understand the words, 'Trust in Him and He will guide you.' "[8]

Mr. Torii and Martha Root would meet again.

On 8 January 1931 the *Taiyo Maru* nosed its way into the iridescent spot in the Pacific, Honolulu. Martha would spend nine days as the guest of Katherine Baldwin, a gracious Bahá'í and relative, by marriage, of Agnes Alexander.

But it would not be a time of rest. Martha delivered at least one major lecture every day in addition to talks at various clubs, luncheons, teas, dinners, and schools of all levels. The publicity was constant and well done; for those who could not come to hear her, she made four radio broadcasts. And she found time to renew a friendship with Mr. Coll, editor of the *Honolulu Advertiser,* who had been associated with her on one of the Pittsburgh papers.

The stimulation of Martha's presence in Honolulu was like a shot of adrenalin to the Bahá'í community there. Many interested persons were drawn to the Bahá'í Faith because of Martha; she brought the Faith into the limelight and made it a vibrant experience.

Hawaii was her last stop after eight years away from her native land. She had been a worker on all the world's continents. There had been little rest in all that time; every second was devoted to spreading Bahá'u'lláh's message of peace. In the intervening years there had been hundreds of talks to thousands of listeners—rulers and peasants, educated and simple folk—in climates hot and cold, in conditions primitive and luxurious. All were woven into the tapestry through Martha's love. She boarded the ship, luggage stowed, and sailed out of Honolulu Harbor. Hawaii moved back in time as San Francisco loomed ahead.

45 On Native Soil

En route to San Francisco, the *Tatsuta Maru* pitched and rolled as Martha tried to get off a letter to the National Spiritual Assembly of the United States and Canada and the National Teaching Committee. Typing was not easy, as Martha's letter revealed: "Please let me explain," she wrote, "that this ship is doing far more than its 'daily dozen' exercises. The tywrter lurches from side to side and I am obliged to stop and hold the machine and hold on to my chair and I do this typing when I can hit the keys."[1] Her humor was intact.

Until she was able to confer with the National Teaching Committee and assess the situation in America, she felt it would be difficult to complete a working schedule. Shoghi Effendi wanted her to devote her attention to the university circles in America, but she would also plan for any other activities suggested by the committee. It was clear that Martha Root was not home for a rest. America was simply another field for activity, albeit an especially dear one because it was where her old friends and family lived. Her return was an opportunity to renew old ties, but it was not a retreat.

Martha arrived in San Francisco on Thursday, 22 January 1931. The next day she gave her first talk to the Berkeley Commonwealth Club. It had been eight years since Martha had seen her native land; yet not a day was taken for rest or time out to reminisce. The pace was set, with broadcasts, lectures, and meetings in San Francisco, Geyserville, Los Angeles, Pasadena, Fresno. Along the way she spoke at colleges and universities, including a lecture at Stanford University, about which she was especially pleased. At Stanford she also interviewed the president emeritus, David Starr Jordan, who had been deeply impressed with 'Abdu'l-Bahá when He spoke there in 1912.

Valera Allen, a Bahá'í teacher in Swaziland for almost thirty years, was in the audience when Martha spoke to the Bahá'ís in San Francisco. She vividly remembers that evening:

> As you know Miss Root has always been described as rather plain in appearance. One got that impression until she began to speak and then she lighted up and became a flame of inspiration. Personally, I sat glued to my chair, fascinated by her voice and words. . . . she spoke of her travels and the beautiful receptivity of those to whom she spoke . . . people of all walks of life—presidents, royalty, humble villagers, large gatherings in India, Burma and South America. She was absolutely dynamic. . . . as a new Baha'i it was even more thrilling because even then I wanted to pioneer.
>
> She seemed to be very perceptive. After the meeting everyone crowded around her asking questions and hearing her comments. I felt too new to push my way in to her so stood rather to the back. She caught my eye, stepped down from the platform, pushed her way through the crowd, came to me and without a word she gave me a big hug, kissed me, turned around and went back to her place on the platform. You can imagine my feelings of joy, which . . . remained with me always.[2]

Three weeks among friends in California moved into the recent past, and another pattern in the kaleidoscope appeared as the train took her up the Pacific coast into the northwest. Martha arrived in Eugene, Oregon, on 13 February for a family visit. Claude, the younger of Martha's brothers, had moved from Cambridge Springs to Michigan with his family in 1925 and had later brought them farther west to Oregon. Real estate was Claude's business, but he did not seem to hold the key to success; deals that appeared firm somehow melted away. From her limited funds Martha occasionally sent him a small sum. He had no real knowledge of the sacrifice involved, but he was one family member who was kind and loving to his sister. Claude's twenty-four-year-old daughter, Anna, an intelligent, perceptive, and gentle person, was another who seemed to appreciate the unique work of her Aunt Martha.

The visit to Eugene was a time for renewing the family ties that Martha kept alive from whatever continent she happened to be inhabiting. She sent cards and gifts throughout the year, especially on birthdays and holidays. Yet sweet as reunion in Oregon was, it could not totally usurp her work. The ten days at Claude's home were interspersed with Bahá'í activities, including a lecture at the University of Oregon in Eugene, a school that, although small, had an impressive cosmopolitan outlook.

On 23 February Martha made her way north to Portland, Oregon. There she spent two weeks with Bahá'í friends and maintained a full schedule of lectures, including one at the university. Ten more days of lectures were delivered between 11 and 23 March in Denver and other Colorado points, where hundreds of listeners at colleges, universities, and clubs heard the message of Bahá'u'lláh.

Martha could not move toward a destination without stopping to speak at places along the way. She was like the hands of a clock, moving to an ultimate point, ticking off places en route, and, when the ultimate point was reached, moving on again. The time had come, Martha's clock told her, to move east toward home. On 26 March 1931, eight years after she had sailed out of Seattle for Japan, Martha Root was back in Cambridge Springs for a ten-day visit.

She was the guest of her brother Clarence, executor of her father's estate, and his wife, Donna. Their visit together was a time to strengthen the cords of conciliation and love that bound Martha to the world and those around her. Although homeless, as though she were a wandering troubadour trumpeting the Bahá'í Faith throughout the world, Martha nourished a deep love and concern for her family that was legendary. She prayed for them, wept over them, and tried to have them understand what she and her life were about. Her love touched their lives, but her purpose never reached them.

Of all the members of Clarence's family, his daughter was the closest to Martha. Ruth was a sweet and simple soul, who returned her aunt's deep love but could not grasp her mission, although Martha blindly believed that Ruth was on the threshold of embracing the Faith. Ruth had married Roy Canfield, who had worked in her father's store but had later started a trucking business. He was embarrassed by this Bahá'í woman, despite her international reputation, and was hostile to the ideas she represented. Many of Martha's letters and gifts to Ruth had to go first to Lucy Wilson, who acted as an emissary. Lucy, who loved and understood her old friend, claimed a portion of Martha's time to gather the golden threads of her journeys and to enrich Martha's days in Cambridge Springs.

The town had been anticipating the return of its famous daughter. They greeted her, fussed over her, and noted the striking changes after almost a decade's absence. A public dinner was held, with Dr. Logan, an old family friend, presiding and introducing the town's most famous individual. People crowded the rooms to hear Martha speak. The headline in the local paper read: "Martha Root Visibly Affected by the Welcome of Childhood Associates: Quiet, Unassuming, Cultured World Traveler Speaks with Great Power as She Pleads for World Peace at Rotary Club."[3] There were other talks and social gatherings during her brief stay. Her humility and self-effacement were astonishing to her friends and acquaintances as they grasped, however minutely, the breadth of her experiences.

The mood was positive, but there was a dark side to Martha's visit. Here in Cambridge Springs the grim, searing pain took hold and stayed with her until mid-April. It affected the back of her neck and penetrated her head. Not since Australia in 1924 had this bedeviling antagonist attacked her with such intensity. Along with prayers, she turned for hope to a statement 'Abdu'l-Bahá had written to Agnes Parsons ten years earlier: "'I hope through the Power of the Holy Spirit Martha Root will be cured.'"[4]

Despite the pain, Martha did not linger in Cambridge Springs. She left for Champaign-Urbana, Illinois, where she spoke four times in four days, 9–12 April, at the University of Illinois and addressed many groups and secondary schools.

From 13 April through 4 May, Martha spoke several times every day in Chicago, where she broadcast even during the week of the Bahá'í national convention. At the Fellowship of Faiths, in the Uptown Temple, two thousand persons were present, with twenty-five hundred more turned away, for a program Martha shared with four proponents of other religious and political views. She spoke at Northwestern University many times and at a variety of churches, schools, and clubs. It was a stiff pace, and Martha confessed in a letter to Mrs. Parsons, "I came into Chicago at noon yesterday and at one o'clock left the hotel to speak in a large church. I leave the hotel 6:45 A.M. tomor. morning and speak three times in Northwestern University before noon. My bags are not even unpacked. . . ."[5]

As the Bahá'ís gathered from all over the United States and Canada for the national convention, Martha once again was in the bosom of her Bahá'í family. Very few could envision the totality of her work and the daily sacrifices she had made, with limited strength and physical discomfort; yet all knew of her vast contributions and sensed her special place among them. Louis G. Gregory, reporting on the convention, tried to keep the record impersonal, eliminating names and personal statements.

> But in the case of Martha, the outstanding personality of the convention, an exception must be made. Our great international teacher, whose simplicity, severance, devotion, self-sacrifice and ceaseless activity render her a magnet of attraction to numberless souls, was voted the freedom of the floor, a privilege which she did not use unless called. Each time she spoke eager ears and hearts devoured her words. Her clear grasp of the teachings, prayerfulness, humility, unfailing kindness, fearlessness and love truly make her a sign of God. "Like unto a bird she has flown around the world." Always on the wing, ever singing the songs of Abhá, how wonderful is she![6]

For Martha the convention was a feast of love and friendship, a gathering of souls devoted to Bahá'u'lláh and His principles for peace on the planet.

But beyond the convention there was work to do. After interviewing the mayor of Chicago, Martha left for Madison, Wisconsin, for six days of lectures, 5–11 May. She returned to Pennsylvania to speak at Alliance and Allegheny colleges and then focused her attention on the New York area. Columbia University was a world in itself. Here Martha exchanged ideas with President Nicholas Murray Butler; with Professor Arthur Hummel, lecturer in Chinese history and chief of the Division of Chinese Literature in the Library of Congress; and with Dr. Robert Hume, professor of the Institute of Religions. She also spoke to their classes and was cheered by the interest and response of the students.

Martha left the halls of academia behind as she traveled to Geneva in upstate New York to meet with the National Teaching Committee. Together they would work out the best use of her time for visiting university areas in the eastern part of the country. Shortly after arriving in Geneva, surrounded by lakes and vineyards, Martha was again struck down by an illness that incapacitated her for four days. Under the compassionate care of Mary Collison, a Bahá'í friend living in Geneva, Martha's health improved, and ever Martha, she resumed her schedule.

The National Teaching Committee, appointed by the National Spiritual Assembly, was aware of the needs of Bahá'í teaching efforts throughout the country. This knowledge formed the basis for the committee's directives. With Martha Root, however, the committee felt no need to formulate a set program. Her presence was welcomed, and her schedule was aided in those areas where Spiritual Assemblies existed. The National Teaching Committee approved totally her commitment to speak at universities and wherever else talks could be arranged.

On her calendar Martha saved at least two weeks for one of her most important visits—a reunion in West Englewood with Roy Wilhelm and Mrs. Wilhelm, who were like a loving brother and mother to Martha. From various global points she had sent tender messages back to these two, giving insight into events in her life that few knew about, and offering her prayers for their well-being, for Mrs. Wilhelm's health, and for the Lord to make Roy rich because he generously bestowed his funds wherever they were needed and useful. Martha had often yearned for their presence and had written many times into the wee hours of the morning to visit with them by letter. She missed Roy's smile and laconic humor, and Mrs. Wilhelm's wisdom.

Despite the burdens of travel, Martha collected stones from all over the world and periodically mailed them back for Roy to use in walks and walls at Evergreen Cabin in West Englewood and at his summer camp in Maine. There were even stones from the Wailing Wall in Jerusalem and the Imperial Gardens in Tokyo. By the time Martha had safely got through Iraq and Iran, there were stones from all the Bahá'í shrines and holy places. She had sent both Roy and his mother many gifts received in the course of world travels, and had brought back to America those she could not trust to the mails, such as engraved silver cuff links for Roy.

Now after almost nine years Martha could again hold Mrs. Wilhelm's hand, share her past years with this second mother, and comfort Mrs. Wilhelm in her illness. Martha met with the National Spiritual Assembly at Evergreen Cabin on 12 June and stayed on to speak at the Souvenir Feast of 27 June, an annual event commemorating 'Abdu'l-Bahá's visit in 1912. James Morton, who saw Martha at that Souvenir Feast in 1931, wrote of his impressions: "Those June gatherings at West Englewood are becoming more and more inspiring. Something in them takes hold of us with irresistible power. What a marvelous radiance emanates from our Martha after her wonderful worldwide experience! I have rarely known anything like it."[7]

Martha received many invitations for brief or lengthy visits with friends, but rarely would she accept and then only if the spot lay in the path of a teaching schedule. One such bidding came from Agnes Parsons, who hoped to lure Martha to her summer home in Dublin, New Hampshire, and thus interrupt Martha's vigorous pace. The possibility of success lay in the fact that Dublin was not too far from Eliot, Maine, where Martha planned to be at Green Acre, the Bahá'í summer school, by 5 July. Mrs. Parsons urged:

come to Dublin for a thorough rest, not to see people, but to drive and be quiet. I shall make my plans to be at Green Acre during part of the time you will lecture. I am confident

*Martha Root (seated, center) with six members
of the National Spiritual Assembly of the Bahá'ís
of the United States and Canada, Mrs. Wilhelm, and Bertha
Herklotz at the Evergreen Cabin, West Englewood, New Jersey,
12 June 1931. Clockwise, from bottom center: Roy Wilhelm,
Mrs. J. O. Wilhelm, Martha Root, Bertha Herklotz, Alfred
Lunt, Siegfried Schopflocher, Carl Scheffler, Louis G.
Gregory, and Horace Holley*

Shoghi Effendi would wish you to come to Dublin, even if
only for a few days. It is only 90 miles from Green Acre. It
will be a place of pilgrimage you know. And you should have
a rest, if only a tiny one. *When* you come to Dublin, we shall
have a few hours of real, true, vital quiet![8]

Dublin had been a source of beauty and wonder to 'Abdu'l-
Bahá in 1912 as he viewed the unending green of the mountains, the spacious lawns, the fields and meadows that were a
contrast to the stark, parched landscape of the Middle East.
When Martha visited the spots edified by His presence, her
sense of mission was reinforced. She arranged a broadcast
from the radio station in nearby Keene and gave a major talk in
Dublin, publicized with invitations sent out by Mrs. Parsons.

A bit of heaven for Martha was her return to Green Acre, of which she had written:

The souls who come are charmed with the spirit of the place. Then longing to be one with it, they realize their lack of capacity—in humiliation and sorrow they lift their eyes to Abdul Baha begging to be strengthened, to clothe themselves with His Garment of servitude and sever themselves. Many of the travelers drifting to these doors are irresistibly attracted by the Torch of sacrifice. All light their candles at the Flame of God.[9]

For two weeks Martha lectured and basked in the spiritual vitality of Green Acre. She visited schools and universities in the area before going with several friends to the Wilhelms' summer camp in Lovell, Maine. It was a brief period of relaxation, but Martha did not let it become a habit. Her fall schedule was already mapped out, and by the last week in September it was in full swing.

Martha moved between New York, New Jersey, and Pennsylvania with the ease of one moving from room to room. The details of her lectures and broadcasts in the New York City area were arranged in part by Marion Little, a close Bahá'í friend living in New York, who was assisted by the New York Spiritual Assembly. But Martha still preferred to make her own contacts, and she brought along her letters of introduction, credentials, and experience. She had printed a complicated, many-sided, multifold document that conveyed letters of thanks and commendation from persons of rank the world over. It was impressive and eloquent.

By 1931 Evergreen Cabin in West Englewood had become a Bahá'í center, where meetings, receptions, and talks by distinguished visitors were held. When Martha learned that Dr. Masujima—the gallant friend who had made possible her visit to Japan's Imperial Household—was in the New York area, she arranged for him to lecture at the cabin on 2 October. The event was one of many in Martha's ongoing effort to bring the Orient and the Occident a few steps closer together.

In October she gave several broadcasts in New York, spoke several times at Columbia University, and appeared twice at Hunter College. She also addressed the Esperantists and the Real Estate Society, and lectured on international economics in White Plains, New York. From her room at the Allerton Hotel she used her spare moments to arrange speaking engagements in Washington, D.C., and to plan a reunion in a more familiar landscape, Pittsburgh.

Martha returned to her adopted city, where she made broadcasts, was feted, and gave talks to small audiences and big ones. Doris and Willard McKay, friends of Martha's, were living in Pittsburgh at the time, and Mrs. McKay vividly remembers the penetrating effect on those lives Martha touched during her stay:

Another Baha'i friend and I met the train. . . . [Martha] ran to meet us with outstretched arms and—fell headlong into a wet place on the concrete platform! Her coat was soaked and had to be sent to the cleaner's before Martha could venture out. But it was all made to seem like a "lark."

The next afternoon the Pittsburgh friends gathered to meet Martha at Alice Parker's apartment. There was the hush in the room that was to become familiar before Martha began to speak.

She spoke drolly about her experiences and about the power of prayer upon which she relied to open doors of opportunity. She said[,] "Whenever I enter a new city for the purpose of teaching the Faith, first, I say the Tablet of Ahmad, ten times." We felt free and at home with Martha, laughed many times, prayed more deeply than we had done before, planned out a full schedule for the week to come.

Because of her travels Martha had become a sort of personage . . . so we had no difficulty in arrangements for meetings and publicity. We all stayed with her as much as we could. I was fortunate; I think I went to everything. I remember going with her to a luncheon held by a few of her old press associates in a press club dining room. . . . [They were] witty, sophisticated, fashionable! Our little Martha was like a queen among these people: a personage.

There were two meetings with the Negro population, one

at the Ebenezer Baptist Church. I sat in the rear as Martha spoke from the pulpit with a sea of dark heads between us and I wanted to go, if necessary, *crawl*, up the long aisle to her side, such was the magnetic pull of her presence there.

The only meeting that could have been called "formal" was in the lecture hall of the Carnegie Library to which university people had been invited. On this occasion Martha wore a long dress, had had her hair coiffured and carried a bouquet of long-stemmed roses. She truly personified an ambassador from a King as she gave the proclamation of Baha'u'llah's Message with dignity, poise and pride!

. . . The rather spare body, the plain unpowdered face, the close-cut hair, the neat, but not spectacular dress and plain low-heeled shoes; the quiet never assertive voice, were so strangely potent and attractive that government heads, royalty, colledge [*sic*] presidents in eastern and western countries listened to her and made opportunities for her to address large gatherings. Part of her lure was the question why this little lady had such charm. Who was she? from what level of spirit had their defenses been conquered?

Reflecting on Martha's talks, Mrs. McKay felt that "Most unusual in her varied set of Pittsburgh meetings had been her extremely simple subject matter. . . . Whatever she said seemed chiefly a means to convey a Universal Love and its Source. I seem to be making the point over and over that Martha's was a communication of Spirit."[10]

At the end of October Martha spent time in the Philadelphia area before going to Washington, D.C. She broadcast on universal peace and lectured at Swarthmore and Haverford colleges and Temple University, among other schools. She was pleased. "Everything here is going like a series of miracles. The Power of the Holy Spirit is here! *I am with the precious Revell family & we are all working very hard.*"[11]

Although Martha was eager to secure speaking engagements during her stay with Agnes Parsons in Washington, she was also trying to ensure a quiet time for writing articles and a record of her work for Shoghi Effendi. She wrote to Mrs. Parsons, "I feel that in Washington sometimes I can shut myself

up in my room and write & that you will see that I get this done,
you are so sweet and fine. . . . You rest my spirit and make it
happy." Martha anticipated unusual opportunities for teaching in the nation's capital. She felt that "great doors could
open in Washington—I mean in those diplomatic circles if we
could *call* and speak with some of those Ambassadors it might
help the countries. I feel such an urge to try." [12]

And try she did. Martha arrived in Washington on 2 November 1931, and before she left five weeks later, the world of international representatives had been opened, responding to
the combination of Martha Root's credentials, Agnes Parsons'
diplomatic ties, and the spirit of both. Among Martha's papers
was a cable to her from Shoghi Effendi that read:

Kindly convey President Hoover on behalf followers Bahá'-
u'lláh, world over, expression their fervent prayers for success of his unsparing efforts in promoting cause of international brotherhood and peace, a cause for which they have
steadfastly laboured well nigh a century.

Haifa [13]

Whenever an important event, such as meeting an American
president, was a possibility, Martha would often suggest to
Shoghi Effendi that he send a cablegram of greetings. The cable would then provide a reason to seek a meeting. A subsequent letter intimates that Martha Root and Agnes Parsons actually did speak to President and Mrs. Hoover about the
Bahá'í Faith. [14]

In 1931 the country was slipping deeper into an economic
depression. The stock market had collapsed two years earlier,
in October 1929, and the outlook for prosperity was growing
dimmer. Martha gave many talks on Bahá'u'lláh's solution to
the economic problems, and some listened. But tradition, especially in government, was strong; old ways prevailed, and
the people suffered.

Washington and Baltimore were college and university centers, and Martha, ever mindful of her charge from Shoghi Effendi, spoke at many of them, including Howard University.

She had hoped to do a tour of the colleges with Louis Gregory, but her schedule was full, and she asked Willard McKay to go in her place. Mr. McKay and Mr. Gregory, the first man tall and fair, the second, tall and dark, together embarked on a sort of freedom walk in December 1931 and spent eighteen days touring Alabama, Tennessee, and Ohio. At every stop they demonstrated the power of Bahá'u'lláh's teachings to bring racial unity to America.[15]

As a testament to the esteem felt for Martha Root, almost one hundred persons attended a banquet held in Martha's honor by the Bahá'ís of Washington, D.C. Martha carried with her the precious memory of this event when she turned northward toward Cambridge Springs to spend Christmas with her relatives. Along the way she stopped in Pittsburgh for several lectures and broadcasts. Doris McKay, who attended all of Martha's talks in this cultural and industrial city, admitted later to a friend, " 'I have looked more than I have listened. There is a light burning in that fragile porcelain.' " " 'She has no personality. She can't be found, but HE can be found. The people follow again lost music. . . . She is the one apostle of the Western world.' "[16]

During Christmas week Cambridge Springs again feted its global traveler. Crowds spilled over into the lobby of the Bartlett Hotel to hear Martha praised and to listen to her experiences from around the world.

There would be no tapering off of activity during the cold winter weeks ahead. Martha's typically packed schedule included attendance at a national student meeting in Toledo, Ohio, and lectures at Boston and Harvard universities during the first week of January 1932. Lorna Tasker, a close friend of Doris McKay's who heard Martha speak that week in Boston, recalled:

"I sat there in the audience and looked at Martha, saw the Light in her being burning so clear and unwavering and something melted in me . . . I looked at the people around me. Their faces shone. Then I let myself slip into the prevailing spirit of the hour. It was soft, joyous, fluid, suffused with light. It seemed to me that the Master stood there among us and that from Him we all took life. I wept, feeling that I had come home."[17]

After a visit to Worcester, Massachusetts, Martha went on to Montreal. There she was a guest of Sutherland and May Maxwell, in whose home 'Abdu'l-Bahá had stayed in 1912. There are some vibrant memories of her visit. Martha wanted very much to broadcast a talk about the Bahá'í Faith while she was in Montreal. She was told that it would be impossible in a French Catholic city to speak about another creed over the airwaves. Martha was determined, and negative feelings simply revitalized her. After a phone call there was a vague hope that someone *might* talk to her. Bahiyyih Randall Winckler, who spent much time with Martha in Montreal, related:

> As we were going out the door there was a vase of flowers in a little recess in the hallway, and she reached into the vase and pulled out two tulips. . . . I said, "Martha, what do you want those for?" She said, "Oh, I don't know, but I'm taking [them]. Off we went in the car to the broadcasting station and up in the elevator, Martha still carrying these two tulips. . . . When we got out of the elevator we stood in a sort of anteroom and said what we wanted, and the door of the manager's office was open, and he looked out and saw Martha, and he said, "Come in, come in." And she came and handed him these two tulips. And he said, "How did you know? Today is a special holiday in Holland and nothing could have been more beautiful to me today than to receive these two tulips!"

The station manager was from Holland. After he had the tulips put in a vase on his desk, he asked, "'Now what can I do for you?'" Bahiyyih observed that Martha "had penetrated directly into that man's heart. . . . when she got there she knew why she had the tulips. . . ."[18]

Martha gave the broadcast, using statements about the Bahá'í Faith from renowned individuals that had been painstakingly gathered over the years. Her sonorous voice, so suitable to broadcasting, was complimented. Martha had filled the airwaves of this French city with an inkling of the Bahá'í Faith, and she was pleased.

It was in the Maxwell home that Martha gave Bahiyyih Winckler a gift wrapped in white tissue paper. Bahiyyih was shocked when she discovered that it was a cord worn by Bahá'u'lláh. She strenuously protested having it, feeling it was much too precious for an ordinary mortal to possess. But Martha was equally adamant. She wished to honor Harry Randall's family. The hallowed article lay unopened for many months, almost too precious to handle. But, as predicted by Martha, it did inspire many persons to live through some difficult times. In 1952 Bahiyyih told Shoghi Effendi about her possession, and he, too, was stunned. She brought the cord, wrapped in a beautiful silk scarf, to Haifa, where it rests in the International Archives.

Martha's last four days in the United States were spent in and around New York City. After a talk there on 19 January, she traveled north to speak at Vassar College in Poughkeepsie. On 21 January she returned to West Englewood, New Jersey, for one last lecture before boarding the ship in New York City the next evening. Amid these lectures and broadcasts Martha had to pack, wind up loose ends, and prepare for another sojourn on another continent.

At dawn, 23 January 1932, twelve months after Martha had reached San Francisco, the S.S. *Europa* set out into the Atlantic toward Cherbourg, France. Martha Root had done what Shoghi Effendi had asked, and more. As she left America, she received from Roy Wilhelm a reassuring note sprinkled with wisdom and humor:

> Well, dear Martha, away you go . . . we'd like to keep you here with us—but you well know that the bee which hugs the hive doesn't gather the honey—so we're glad to speed you towards your work—in God's care.
> . . . don't run yourself too close nor too fast. Unduly squeezing may retard the highest efficiency which, in view of so very few workers, is of *first* import. "*Wilhelmite*" is thus far a spring in which Baha'u'lláh deposits as fast—even

faster—than the Water is withdrawn. . . . Keep me informed at all times as to your financial outlook say for sixty
to ninety days ahead of you.

Roy was well aware of Martha's difficulty with staying healthy
on a rough ocean. He wryly advised, "The old Spanish remedy
is best—to lie down, head northward, under the shade of a pine
tree." [19] It was just the light touch Martha needed to send her on
her way. She would not necessarily follow his advice, either in
terms of her itinerary or the alleviation of financial stress. But
she felt blessed in having such friends.

46 A Change of Pace

The S.S. *Europa* docked in France during the last week of January 1932, and Martha immediately made her way to Geneva for the historic disarmament conference. Convened in February 1932 and destined to run until June 1934, the conference was the first such gathering of representatives from many countries that attempted to halt the ever-advancing production of arms. Martha, with Mountfort Mills, attended most of the early sessions.

Geneva became Martha's field of activity for the next three months, during which time much of her energy was directed toward renewing or cultivating friendships among the representatives of countries throughout the world. With Mountfort Mills accompanying her in order to share these contacts, Martha gave each of them Bahá'í literature, including Shoghi Effendi's newly published *The Goal of a New World Order.*[1]

During the first week in May, Martha left her work in Geneva to the care of others and went to Czechoslovakia to arrange for a translation into Czech of *Bahá'u'lláh and the New Era*. Prague would be her base for the next eighteen months, as Shoghi Effendi wished her to settle in this pocket of Europe in order to continue her work from previous years and help form a Spiritual Assembly. For Martha it was an experiment; while she would comply exactly with Shoghi Effendi's wishes, she was not sure how it would work out. It became a "we'll see" situation.

After initiating the translation work in Prague, Martha left for Poland on 14 May to work with Lydia Zamenhof. En route to Warsaw, Martha stopped in Olomouc, Moravia, for the National Czech Esperanto Conference. It was a special event for the Czechs because they were unveiling a monument to Dr. Zamenhof. Standing just beyond the entrance to a large park, the statue had been engraved with the names of organizations devoted to universal peace. When Martha noticed that the engravers had left a space in the middle, "just this one line in the center left," she convinced the authorities to add one more name to the list. With only hours to spare before the opening of the conference, the engravers went to work and filled the blank space with "LA BAHAA MOVADO——HAIFA, PALESTINO." Martha was thrilled. "Can you think what this will mean!" she wrote to Shoghi Effendi. "That monument may stand for hundreds of years and every one who goes to the park will ask and perhaps search what is the Bahá'i Movement."[2]

After a teaching stop in Jägerndorf (now Krnov), arranged by Esperantists, Martha arrived in Warsaw on 18 May. Because Lydia Zamenhof was thinking of leaving Poland, Martha wanted to work with her before she left. Her admiration for Lydia's brilliant mind and spiritual depth had increased over the years; she felt that Lydia was a born translator and one of the great souls of Europe.

The Zamenhof family was well known in medical and intellectual circles. Lydia's brother and sister, and many aunts and uncles, were doctors. The family, as well as many friends, had begun to express their resistance to Lydia's Bahá'i connections. There was distinct pressure for Lydia to involve herself in other pursuits. She translated *Quo Vadis* into Esperanto, which pleased her family, but she continued with her Bahá'í work and with translations of the Bahá'í writings, much to their displeasure.

During Martha's stay in Warsaw, she and Lydia visited libraries and universities around the city. Martha gave a tea for Lydia's friends—"and [I] made the tea myself"—but felt a lack of interest among them in spiritual matters, which seemed true throughout Poland.[3] Although traditional forms of worship were strong, any new faith, even Protestantism, was suspect.

One of Martha's most rewarding days was spent in southeastern Poland with the rector of Lublin University. Skilled in ancient and modern languages, he was a priest who had met

'Abdu'l-Bahá in 1914. When an hour's appointment stretched into the evening, the priest sent Martha back to the train in his private carriage, "drawn by two prancing horses."[4]

By early June Martha was back in Prague, where she secured the services of Pavla Moudra, one of the country's finest translators and a friend of the Bahá'ís. President Masaryk's secretary, who had become a close friend and adviser to Martha in her work, had approved of her choice of translator; and President Masaryk himself agreed to allow his statement about the value of the Bahá'í principles to precede the foreword of Dr. Esslemont's *Bahá'u'lláh and the New Era*. Martha was elated. She felt the president's contribution to be a triumph for the Bahá'í Faith, for the Czech people, who loved and were proud of their president, would feel that his words had put the stamp of approval on an unknown element.

Although Martha no longer involved herself in the planning of the Esperanto congresses, her interest remained high. In late July 1932 she traveled across Europe to Paris for the annual Universal Esperanto Congress, 30 July–8 August. On her way back to Prague she stopped just outside of Vienna to visit Queen Marie and Princess Ileana, now the Archduchess Anton of Austria, in Mödling, Ileana's home. Both Marie and Ileana had continued to correspond with Martha, keeping her abreast of their activities. With them was Queen Marie of Yugoslavia, another daughter of Rumania's Queen Marie. Wearing clothes that Ella Cooper had given her, Martha felt well turned out, fit for the royal visit. When she was leaving, Ileana, carrying Martha's coat, walked her to the gate; Martha wanted Ella to know that Ileana had admired the coat, a gift from Ella.

Summer 1932 had brought a blue note with the passing in July of the Greatest Holy Leaf, Bahíyyih Khánum. There was sadness at no longer having that exalted presence near; but there was joy that, at eighty-five, she had been released from a world that had been a source of torment for most of her life. She had lived long enough to see Bahá'u'lláh's teachings begin to take root in the world; to see Shoghi Effendi emerge as a strong, compassionate, and inspired Guardian of the Faith; and to see Martha Root carry the message to almost every country on the globe.

Shoghi Effendi was crushed by Bahíyyih Khánum's passing. To him she had been a spiritual mentor, a living reference to the times of Bahá'u'lláh and the birth of the Faith, to the early days of suffering and persecution. A sagacious and perceptive being, Bahíyyih Khánum had embodied the traits of a perfect Bahá'í, combining kindness and forgiveness with strength and dignity. Her passing was a cruel blow to Shoghi Effendi, who eulogized her and called on the Bahá'í world to commemorate fittingly the life of this spiritual woman who had graced the planet for a large part of a century.

Martha continued to send Shoghi Effendi detailed reports of her work, along with newspaper clippings and magazine articles that were generated wherever she was teaching. Her communications were acknowledged by letters from the Guardian's secretary, with personal remarks attached by Shoghi Effendi. The reports, received in the midst of work or sorrow, refreshed him; here was evidence that every day the Faith was being spread. After the passing of Bahíyyih Khánum, he wrote to Martha:

I hasten to express in person my keen & abiding sense of appreciation of your stupendous efforts for the spread of our beloved Cause. I have been too overwhelmed with grief to write during the weeks following so terrific a blow. Your words of cheer & sympathy I immeasurably value as they come from one whose share in bringing genuine satisfaction to the heart of the Greatest Holy Leaf stands unrivalled. My heart overflows with love & gratitude for the imperishable example you are setting to the followers of God throughout the world.[5]

The pace had slackened during the summer, and August in Prague was relatively quiet. But Martha's tormenting pain was back and continued to be assertive. "I get a pain that doesn't seem to want to go away," she confided to Ella Cooper. "I massage it, bath[e] it, give it gymnastics! And now I have come out to the little park beside the railway station to write this letter. . . ."[6] Martha did not consult a doctor but bowed to the pain in her own way and prepared for a busy fall and winter. The new translations formed the basis of a study class, her

Esperanto work was ongoing, and there were teaching opportunities among members of the diplomatic corps and several clubs.

Her first major lecture of the fall was held in the new Charlotte Masaryk Hall, in the old section of the city. To save the expense of a taxi Martha decided to walk to the building. It was not a wise decision:

> The street was narrow and very uneven, and cobble stones and the darkness, anyway I had a terrible fall. I threw out my arm to protect my face, fell on my side, but I did strike my head too. It just seemed as if I looked into eternity! I felt so hurt, I said: "O GOD, how can I speak! You MUST help me, for I have done my utmost!"

Martha picked herself up and walked the rest of the way to the hall. She had only a few minutes to rest, wash off the blood, and arrange her hair before going on stage. Despite the injury she was pleased with the evening: "I believe I spoke better than if it had not happened," she noted, "for I had seen how short our days can be, and I had seen that GOD came to help me. . . . It hurt my side and cut my head and I felt bruised all over, but today I feel better and know 'this too, will pass away!'"[7]

Martha's pace was stepped up as she increased the lectures and broadcasts and continued to write articles for newspapers and periodicals. She was living at the Zensky Klub, which housed seventy girls and women who spoke a variety of languages and pursued varied careers. One resident, a Canadian opera singer, became a close friend of Martha's. There was not much heat at the club, but considering the world economic climate, Martha was thankful to have a roof over her head.

For warmth in her room she wore a coat given to her by Mrs. Parsons; Martha wrapped a leather belt around it and felt quite stylish. She continued to be spared the expense of buying clothes, except for "a little two dollar summer straw hat" worn long after the heat of summer.[8] Experimentation with her wardrobe still took imaginative flights—she informed Ella Cooper that she had dyed the white and blue flowered dress brown. The tops of worn dresses could, with a little cutting and stitching, be turned upside down and used as waists. They worked beautifully, Martha discovered. After years of being constantly on the move, Martha had a feeling of confinement by being relegated to one spot. She communicated her uneasiness to Shoghi Effendi, whose secretary responded, "Shoghi Effendi does not wish to restrict your movements unnecessarily, especially for a person like you who for so many years had the surface of the whole globe upon which to roam[.]"⁹

By the end of January 1933 Martha was ready to move on from Prague. The need for good translations of Bahá'í literature loomed larger in importance, and Martha could further this work while still staying in central and southeastern Europe, as Shoghi Effendi had wished. Mrs. Pavla Moudra had already completed the Czech translation of *Bahá'u'lláh and the New Era* and had begun a translation of the Kitáb-i-Íqán; Dr. Sommer-Batek, another friend, had voluntarily translated the Hidden Words. Before leaving Prague, Martha arranged for the forewords to be written for these translations. She realized that the translations could not be published immediately because of the world economic situation, reflected in Martha's funds and those available from Haifa. But she was at least heartened by the knowledge that the translations "will be ready . . . when people come after me who can publish them!"¹⁰

On her way to Hungary Martha stopped for a week in Vienna, where she was delighted to find Dr. Howard and Marzieh Carpenter from California. There was also Franz Pöllinger, Martha's deeply spiritual, selfless friend of four years earlier. So devoted was he to the new revelation that he had tacked the Bahá'í principles on the door of his humble dwelling. Soon the Carpenters, Martha, and Franz were all working together. It became a typical Martha Root week, with lectures at the university and before the Theosophists, the Women's League for Peace and Freedom, the Quaker Society, and the Student Forum. Broadcasts, luncheons, and teas rounded out the week's activities. For Martha the schedule was typical. For the others it was exhausting.

The Carpenters accompanied Martha to Hungary and Yugoslavia. In Györ, Hungary, they stopped to visit George Steiner, a scholarly Bahá'í who was gravely ill. His translation into Hungarian of *Bahá'u'lláh and the New Era*, which would be his last work, was near completion. Martha and the Carpenters arrived in Budapest during the second week of February. It was here that Martha rendered a unique service: she met a man at her hotel who *had* to have his trousers pressed for an important engagement; nowhere could he find anyone to perform the service in time. Martha found an iron and pressed the gentleman's trousers, probably finishing her task just before one of her own engagements.

One of Martha's attributes was the ability to give others confidence, particularly when called upon to speak. Marzieh Carpenter, young and inexperienced as a speaker, found herself sharing the platform with Martha Root, whose public talks seemed beyond count. Together they addressed numerous clubs in Hungary and Yugoslavia and received superb publicity, with stories and pictures of these events.

In the third week of February they went to Belgrade, Yugoslavia, where Martha arranged for Professor Bogdan Popovitch, whom she had met in 1928, to write the introduction to the Serbian translation of *Bahá'u'lláh and the New Era*. The translation was being done by a Bahá'í, Draga Ilich, a woman who was partially paralyzed. Although Mrs. Ilich's mobility was limited, she wanted very much to have a picture of herself standing with Martha Root. Moments before the picture was snapped, Mrs. Ilich had difficulty keeping her balance; she held on to Martha, and they both tumbled over backwards. But "thanks to Baha'u'llah's bounty" they were not hurt. Composure restored, and looking calm and serene, they posed for the picture.[11]

Before leaving Belgrade, Martha was invited to tea once again with Prince Paul and Princess Olga. It had been five years since Martha had seen this royal couple, but, like the other meetings, this one was stimulating and satisfying.

After a very full seven-day stay, she traveled out of Yugoslavia to spend the next three months, March through May, in Bu-

MARTHA ROOT (left) and DRAGA ILICH
of Belgrade, Yugoslavia, 1933. Mrs. Ilich translated
Bahá'u'lláh and the New Era *into Serbian.*

dapest. There she broadened her lecture circuit and oversaw
the publication of George Steiner's translation of *Bahá'u'lláh*
and the New Era, with an introduction by Hungarian scholar
Rustum Vambéry. As summer approached, she returned to Yugoslavia for an Esperanto congress and was invited for another
visit with Princess Olga, who was also entertaining her two sisters, Princess Elizabeth and Princess Marina of Greece. Martha was always asked back.

Martha was doing the kind of traveling that she liked. While
waiting for books to be translated and published, she moved
from one country to another, speaking, interviewing, and
everywhere leaving literature. She stopped for five days in Albania, where she had visited in 1929, and was delighted to find
a Bahá'í residing there—Mr. Refo Chapary, who had left New
York to work and teach in his native country.

There was even a spot of relaxation during the summer when
Martha attended the National Esperanto Congress in Bulgaria, 14–18 July 1933, and along with the Esperantists, went
into Rumania and took a trip down the Danube. Before return-

MARTHA ROOT
Belgrade, Yugoslavia, 12 July 1933

ing to Belgrade early in August, she went on to Greece to arrange for a translation into Greek of Dr. Esslemont's book.

Translations were now in progress in all of the Balkan countries, due primarily to Martha Root's foresight and persistence. Now was the time, she decided, to fulfill another goal close to her heart.

47   Adrianople—Land of Mystery

Martha long had a burning desire to visit Adrianople (now Edirne), the site of Bahá'u'lláh's exile between 1863 and 1868. It was in this city that He had openly proclaimed His mission to many leaders of the world and had admonished them to rule with justice and equity. Adrianople, once the flourishing capital of the Ottoman Empire, from which the light of Islam had radiated to the West, had already felt the effects of Bahá'u'lláh's warning:

> "The day is approaching . . . when the Land of Mystery [Adrianople], and what is beside it shall be changed, and shall pass out of the hands of the king, and commotions shall appear, and the voice of lamentation shall be raised, and the evidences of mischief shall be revealed on all sides, and confusion shall spread by reason of that which hath befallen these captives at the hands of the hosts of oppression. The course of things shall be altered, and conditions shall wax so grievous, that the very sands on the desolate hills will moan, and the trees on the mountain will weep, and blood will flow out of all things. Then wilt thou behold the people in sore distress."[1]

In the years since Bahá'u'lláh's residence in Adrianople the city had become the victim of three Balkan wars and the First World War. Its population had been decimated from a once vibrant city of two hundred thousand to a shrunken city of forty thousand.

Martha turned her sights in the direction of this ancient capital. The journey would not take her out of southeastern Europe, where she was concentrating her efforts, and Shoghi Effendi viewed the trip as an opportunity to uncover Bahá'í

MARION JACK
a pioneer for the Bahá'í Faith for many years in Sofia,
Bulgaria, here photographed at the Bahá'í summer school,
Esslingen, Germany, 1933. She accompanied Martha Root
to Adrianople in October 1933.

history. No Bahá'í had been to Adrianople to identify the places where Bahá'u'lláh had lived during His exile. Martha would be accompanied by Marion Jack, a Canadian living in Sofia, Bulgaria, who was continuing the work started there by Martha. Marion, who had first heard about the Bahá'í Faith while studying art in Paris, would use her craft to sketch and photograph the houses in Adrianople. Martha would write of them.

They arrived in Adrianople near midnight on 17 October 1933 and checked into the Hotel de l'Europe, the only hotel in the city. Transportation was by horse and carriage over cobbled streets. Unlike Constantinople, which had become quite westernized, the flavor of this diminished city remained distinctly Turkish.

Martha first, but carefully, set about making friends, the initial step toward acceptance. After arranging for an interpreter, she pursued the fragile clues pointing the way to Bahá'u'lláh's former residences. By the end of three weeks she had succeeded in locating all of the houses where He had lived. Still alive were a few persons who remembered meeting both Bahá'u'lláh and 'Abdu'l-Bahá, remembered their deep kindness and generosity. Martha was brought to meet them. "'Oh,'" one said, "'how many grapes did we receive from the hand of Bahá'í Big! He gave us so many grapes always!'"[2]

When Bahá'u'lláh was living in Adrianople, He would often go to the Murádiyyih Mosque to pray, and Martha wanted very much to go there. Muṣṭafá, a Turkish driver, took them in his horse and carriage over the cobbled streets, clean and white after a drenching rain, to the mosque. Martha recorded, in an article in *The Bahá'í World:*

> Leaving Mustafa and the carriage at the foot of the hill, we walked up the steep, needle-eye road lined on each side with little shops and a mill where a horse goes round and round turning wheels to grind the olive into oil. The Murádiyyih Mosque crowns the slope and, just as we were coming, the muezzim came out on a parapet of the slender, graceful minaret and . . . chanted the call to prayer.[3]

Martha entered the hushed building, empty but for the caretaker. She marveled at the exquisite Persian tile work, done long ago, a source of fascination and study to artists the world over. In this beautiful little mosque Martha became lost in meditation:

> the outer things were almost as if I did not see them, so absorbed was I in the consciousness that this was a place where He had prayed and where God had spoken to Him as of old He had spoken to Moses in the Burning Bush! I was impressed how in all His exiles, Bahá'u'lláh seemed always to live close to the mosques—the symbols of the divine in the earth-plane. In His hours of prayer in these terrestrial edifices God certainly revealed to Him how the dead world was to be revivified. . . .
> Kneeling with forehead to the rugs in this memorable mosque, the writer felt with a throb of wonder how far Bahá'u'lláh had come to meet our Western world! Adrianople

was His closest approach—in the outer plane—to our Occident: but all these thoughts dropped into subconsciousness as one bowed in silent love in His Living presence. He was there in that mosque! And the one listening heard anew that His Teachings, the Logos, carry in Themselves the Power that will make of this world of earth a high paradise. The moments there were sublime, not to be described but experienced![4]

Almost twenty years later, in 1952, Bahiyyih Winckler went to Adrianople at Shoghi Effendi's request and became the first Western Bahá'í woman to visit the city since Martha's visit. At the Murádiyyih Mosque she met the same caretaker who had tended the building during Martha's visit. He remembered Martha and recalled:

"'She's the woman who came here and threw herself down and prayed all day long, and when it came night time and I had to close the mosque, I had to tell her to leave. I have never seen such devotion, such adoration, such a profound sense of dedication. . . . I shall never forget her, this wonderful woman. . . . She seemed to be absolutely lost in prayer . . . hour by hour went by and she hardly moved, she was as if she had been transformed outside of her body.'"[5]

There were others in Adrianople who remembered Martha with equal clarity—the hotel people, the interpreter, the mayor. They came to meet Bahiyyih Winckler, to pay their respects, because they had never forgotten Martha Root. They loved her and spoke with glowing enthusiasm and warmth about this woman who, although among them for only a short time, had left an indelible memory.

It took two weeks for Martha to locate two of the residences of Bahá'u'lláh; within a few days two more were discovered—all in ruins. She also located the caravansary, which was Bahá'u'lláh's first shelter in the city. One home was near the Sultán Salím Mosque, a magnificent edifice where Bahá'u'lláh had sometimes prayed. He was probably living in this house when His food was poisoned by His half-brother. Until Ba-

Governor and mayor of Adrianople, Turkey,
with Martha Root (front row, third from left)
and Marion Jack (front row, far right)

há'u'lláh's death, His trembling hand was a reminder of that
act. All of the houses were photographed and sketched by
Marion Jack while the Turkish people gathered round and exclaimed, " 'Áferin! Áferin!' (Bravo! Bravo!)" as they saw the
lines take shape on paper.[6]

Although the search for the houses was her first priority,
Martha did not neglect her role of goodwill ambassador for the
Bahá'í Faith. She contacted the governor, the mayor, and the
prefect of police, and sent articles to the newspaper. One issue
had a front-page story, "Adrianople Through New York
Eyes," by Martha L. Root. The officials had become interested in Martha's pursuit. They promised to follow up on the history of the days when Bahá'u'lláh, His family, and His followers lived in Adrianople. They would send their findings to
Martha.

Bahá'u'lláh had once said that under every stone in Adrianople He had planted a seed.[7] Martha was the first Bahá'í visi-

tor to this city, the first to move the stones and give the seeds light, to uncover them and stimulate their growth.

The visit to Adrianople, from where Bahá'u'lláh was banished to Akka, was a pinnacle in Martha's life. She had now touched the soil in each country of Bahá'u'lláh's nearly forty-year exile. Being near Bahá'u'lláh's houses, the caravansary, the mosques—walking where He had walked, praying where He had prayed—renewed her spiritual vigor. She was now ready to pick up the threads of her work. On 6 November 1933 she left Adrianople to return to Europe, where she would continue to weave the message of peace.

48   New Struggles and Victories in Europe

Shoghi Effendi was delighted with the results of Martha's journey to Adrianople in 1933, as history was being uncovered—and made. After leaving Adrianople, Martha returned to Sofia, Bulgaria, early in November to spend a month working with Marion Jack. They each had a room in the same house and every evening invited friends into Marion's room, the larger of the two. Martha brought in her table, chairs, and two cups, and they served tea and cakes and spoke about the Bahá'í Faith. During the day Martha carried on her writing and arranged public lectures, which could bring more publicity than the small gatherings in Marion's room. She was working every minute and was very tired. But she and Marion were able to form the nucleus of a group, and within a year Marion helped to form the Bahá'í Spiritual Assembly of Sofia, the first one in the Balkans. Their efforts had not been unrewarded.

There was much praying for assistance during the worsening economic depression throughout Europe. Because the dollar had been devalued, it went less far, and there were fewer of them. Agnes Parsons sent Martha a gift of money, which she hoped would be used for something personal. It could not have come at a more opportune time. In a letter expressing her warm thanks, Martha admitted, "You can not [sic] know what this wonderful help means to me, for this has been my hardest year. . . . I go forward resolutely just as long as I possibly can. I can't economize any more than at present and keep living."[1]

It was a beautiful letter to Agnes Parsons, in which Martha relived the rich and busy days in Washington, which seemed like paradise, and praised the glorious race amity work that Mrs. Parsons had pursued. "When I feel how short is the time for all of us," Martha confessed, "I would like to write often to you all & tell you how much I love you . . . and all our friends. . . . [We must] do our very utmost now in these few days we are still on the Earth-plane."² It would be Martha's last letter to Agnes Parsons. On 19 January 1934 Mrs. Parsons was hit by a car while crossing a Washington street. She died four days later.

Lucy Wilson had been with Mrs. Parsons during those last weeks and had been helping her with Bahá'í work. Martha was grateful for Lucy's calm, compassionate presence there. Nevertheless, the loss stunned Martha: "It was a great shock, it gave me the same kind of heart attack that I had when Harry went—but then in those first moments I thought: 'Oh Nur is with 'Abdu'l Bahá!' "³ Still, she lamented the loss of a beautiful soul, a gracious companion, a devoted worker for the Bahá'í Faith, and Martha wondered who could ever take her place.

In mid-December 1933 Martha went to Rumania to see about the translation and publication of *Bahá'u'lláh and the New Era*, a project which took several weeks. Shortly before Martha had planned to leave, Queen Marie returned from Austria and again invited Martha to Controceni Palace on 16 February 1934. The queen was delighted to learn about the publication of Dr. Esslemont's book in Bucharest and to know that the book would be available in the language of the Rumanian people.

It was at this audience that Queen Marie granted Martha permission to tell about a gift she had given to Martha in 1928, six years before. " ' "Always you are giving gifts to others," ' " the queen said, " ' "and I am going to give you a gift from me." ' " Upon Martha's simple dress the queen pinned an exquisite brooch of " 'two little wings of wrought gold and silver, set with tiny diamond chips, and joined together with one large pearl.' "⁴ Queen Marie was parting with an historic ornament, given to her by her royal relatives many years before.

Martha could not keep such grandeur for herself. This lovely jewel was sold to a devoted Bahá'í as a means of raising funds for the House of Worship in Wilmette. Later the jewel came to rest in the archives at the Bahá'í World Center in Haifa. It was the archives' first royal gift, via Martha Root.

With the publication of the Rumanian edition of *Bahá'u'-lláh and the New Era* completed and lectures and writing behind her, Martha journeyed to Belgrade to see how the translations were progressing there. On alternate days she visited Draga Ilich, who had done the Serbian translation of *Bahá'u'lláh and the New Era,* and together they worked on a translation of the Hidden Words of Bahá'u'lláh.

Although Martha's health had been relatively good, her sojourn in Belgrade was marred by physical distress. The pain in her head and back of the neck was a source of continual aggravation, and there were also times of stomach discomfort. This Martha attributed to the lingering effects of ptomaine poisoning in Adrianople, but it was actually another symptom of her advancing cancer. In Belgrade there was no balm to soothe the distress. Martha described her discomfort to Lucy Wilson:

> I arose at 5 A.M. I was going to type letter with carbons about my visit to Queen Marie of Rumania. . . . It is very cold here & no heat in my room for nearly a week now, & I had such a headache (took cold from the cold weather) I went to bed after a cup of vegetable tea. At 8 A.M. I tried again to work & took a cup of black coffee, but the pain in my head I couldn't work. [5]

Still, there was no slackening of pace. With the Greek translation of *Bahá'u'lláh and the New Era* already in progress, Martha arrived in Athens the third week of March to oversee the work and the book's publication. The translator, Dionysios Devaris, a brilliant editor of an Athens newspaper, was beguiled by the Bahá'í teachings and had written a series of articles about them during Martha's earlier visit to Greece. Together Dionysios and Martha visited the Areopagus (Mars' Hill), where a passing photographer took a picture of them with the ancient Acropolis in the background. Martha had a strong feeling that history was repeating itself; for it was on the Areopagus that Saint Paul had delivered his message to the Athenians. As a result, one person, Dionysius the Areopagite, had become a Christian. Centuries later all of Greece was following the teachings of Christ. The miracle of Saint Paul could occur again, Martha felt.

With the translation arrangements completed and a few lectures given on the Faith, Martha left Greece six weeks later and

MARTHA ROOT and DIONYSIOS DEVARIS
the Athenian editor who translated Bahá'u'lláh and
the New Era *into Greek. At the Acropolis in*
Athens on 15 April 1934

made her way northward to Austria and then to Kaunas, Lithuania, to take part in the National Esperanto Congress. She also looked up old contacts that she had made seven years ago, established new ones, and continued to publish articles.

To Martha the Esperantists were as mentally stimulating as ever, and she reveled in the exchange of ideas that was a part of their gatherings. Both she and Lydia Zamenhof traveled to Stockholm in late July to give major lectures at the Twenty-sixth Universal Esperanto Congress. Martha was moved by Lydia's inspiring presentation, which she praised for its depth and brilliance.

During Martha's unscheduled moments in Stockholm she fitted in letter writing to close friends, keeping them current with her schedule, responding to news from home, and thanking them for clothing, which spared her funds. She was especially pleased, overjoyed, to learn that Lucy Burt Steeves, of Martha's Union City, Pennsylvania, days, had become a Bahá'í. To Lucy Wilson, burdened with the pain of arthritis,

MARTHA ROOT
in Stockholm, Sweden, 24 August 1934,
following the Twenty-sixth Universal Esperanto
Congress in late July. She is wearing a
sweater Lucy Wilson knit for her.

Martha sent reasurring words about handling physical distress:

> Sometimes when we feel it's the last straw, Baha'u'llah blesses some effort which proves glorious beyond anything we could dream. The blowing of the Breaths of the Holy Spirit do not depend upon our poor physical bodies, thank God, but on Baha'u'lláh's Bounty. . . .
>
> I came through the gates of this station in Stockholm, so tired, so ill, so almost discouraged not knowing where I was going to stay, but Baha'u'lláh helped me and I did get settled . . . & He has helped me to get started.[6]

Martha's activities of the past few months were not going unnoticed by Shoghi Effendi in Haifa. On 9 September 1934 his secretary sent a letter acknowledging several of Martha's own letters, and Shoghi Effendi penned a grateful postscript:

How deeply I appreciate, nay prize, your stupendous efforts in the service of the Cause while in Lithuania, & in the course of your visit to the Balkans, in Central Europe & now in Scandinavia. You are carrying aloft with inspiring courage & exemplary zeal & constancy the standard of Bahá'u'lláh. You are shedding imperishable lustre on His Faith. You are setting an immortal example to His followers. You are rearing for yourself a goodly mansion in His Kingdom. My heart overflows with gratitude for the work you are achieving with such an indomitable faith & in such hard circumstances. . . . I feel you should concentrate on Scandinavia which stands in such dire need of Bahá'í apostles such as you.

Your true & grateful brother,
Shoghi

Along with his letter Shoghi Effendi returned three pounds sterling to Martha that she had sent him as proceeds from the sale of some of the *Bahá'u'lláh and the New Era* translations. In the appended note of explanation he said, "[I] wish you henceforth to expend whatever you may obtain from the sale of the 'New Era' in different languages on your own dear self & for the purpose of promoting the work in which you are so devotedly engaged."[7] The evidences of Shoghi Effendi's deep affection and appreciation were a balm to Martha's soul and a spur to her plans.

In October violence struck the royal family of Yugoslavia with the assassination of King Alexander, married to the daughter of Queen Marie of Rumania. Prince Paul, who had been so helpful to Martha, would act as regent for the little Crown Prince Peter, with whom Martha had had tea. It brought the unsettled world conditions into her immediate circle. But she was grateful for having had the opportunity to bring the teachings to the Balkans.

Martha stayed in Stockholm until mid-December 1934, working, writing, making friends. She spent much time study-

A postscript appended by Shoghi Effendi to a
letter written on his behalf on 9 September 1934 to
Martha Root, commending her for the "imperishable
lustre" she had shed on the Bahá'í Faith through her
work in the Balkans, Central Europe, and Scandinavia

ing the school system and writing about education in Sweden. The royal family was away, but there was a promise for a future audience.

Difficulties lay ahead. On 6 December Martha had a bad fall in the Grand Hotel and was taken to the hospital—a chamber of horrors for her regardless of the doctors' skill and kindness. She would not spend a night and was released after treatment, but she needed to see a doctor and therapist almost every day during the remainder of her stay in Stockholm. It marked the onset of a series of physical problems.

On 19 December she left Stockholm for Oslo, Norway, with a full schedule mapped out. Martha would share her goals with Johanna Schubarth, who had been working alone in Oslo and who was slated to do the translation of *Bahá'u'lláh and the New Era* into Norwegian. Within a week Martha became seriously ill with influenza, which progressed into less easily treated ailments.

Johanna, who was a trained nurse, took a room adjoining Martha's in the Hospz Hotel. When Martha was well enough, she was moved to a larger and warmer room, where Johanna installed a cot and stayed with her. Despite the more hospitable surroundings, Martha greeted in the new year, 1935, still seriously ill in a Scandinavian city.

Shoghi Effendi was notified of Martha's postponed plans because of her infirmity and became deeply concerned. "Distressed your illness," he cabled to her. "Urge absolute rest. Praying fervently. . . . Shoghi."[8] When the influenza began to improve, Martha started having fainting attacks. The doctor, brought in by an insistent Johanna, stated that the heart was not at fault; but weakness was undoubtedly caused by a lack of food. Martha's poor nutrition was partly due to a more stringent economy and partly due to a system that was becoming less receptive to food.

"Never but once before in my life have I been so ill," Martha wrote to Ella Cooper, "and that was in an accident when I was 24 yrs. old [the bicycle accident in 1896]. . . ." But she felt fortunate to have a nurse there in her need. "Only her wonderful care has saved my life. . . . How many times she has prayed the Healing Tablet 9 times holding my head, held my hand at night and prayed Allah-u-Abhá! How many times rubbed me and pulled me back to consciousness." This heaven-sent nurse also had an attractive attribute, "a keen sense of fun," and Martha was pleased that "she makes me laugh, she is gentle like mother."[9]

During the weeks of her ungracious malady, she learned that Richard St. Barbe Baker, an Englishman deeply interested in the Bahá'í Faith, was in Oslo giving a lecture to the Royal Norwegian Geographical Society. He knew of her work and, when she sent for him, he came at once.

> The first impression she gave was that of being terribly frail and perhaps nearing her end. Her eyes belied the first impression. They shone as if she was having a foretaste of Glory—a glimpse into Heavenly Places. As I bent over her bed to hear what she was saying she confided to me that she had been sent by the beloved Guardian to take the Baha'i message and Proclamation of Baha'u'llah to the two Kings of Scandinavia. . . .
> Her voice died away in a whisper. She closed her eyes and her lips moved as in prayer. I stood in silence earnestly praying for her that her passing into the Abha Kingdom might be painless. . . . Her tired body lay there now reposing peacefully. . . . Would that my life be taken in her place. Would that I could give her my perennial vitality. My deep Baha'i love surrounded this frail servant of the Cause.
> Time ticked tensely. . . . I watched for returning life. Perhaps only seconds later she sighed and then began breathing. Her eyes opened. At first they had a distant look, as if she had forgotten my presence. . . .

Martha then recited a prayer and, speaking "without difficulty," asked Mr. St. Barbe Baker to go immediately to Stockholm as an emissary of Shoghi Effendi and present the king of Sweden with a Swedish translation of *Bahá'u'lláh and the New Era.*[10]

Without a moment's hesitation Mr. St. Barbe Baker went to Stockholm and called at the office of the prime minister. There he introduced himself as an English conservator of forests who had served in Kenya and in Nigeria's mahogany forests, and who was lecturing in Norway by invitation of the Royal Norwegian Geographical Society and the British Council.

> I asked if it would be possible to meet His Majesty . . . as I had been asked by a dying woman in Oslow to deliver to His Majesty a message from the Guardian of the Baha'i Cause, Shoghi Effendi. The Prime Minister said that would be an easy matter, as he was expecting His Majesty in seven minutes' time.
>
> "You may walk towards the Palace and you will meet His Majesty and the Royal Family walking in this direction. Introduce yourself and walk back with them here." [11]

Everything went according to plan. Mr. St. Barbe Baker explained the circumstances that brought him there and presented the king of Sweden with the book.

> His Majesty gave me a message for Martha Root and a gracious message for Shoghi Effendi, and assured me that he would read the book with interest. His Majesty was gravely concerned at the threat of further wars and agreed that it was as one family we must go forward into the future. [12]

Mr. St. Barbe Baker took the next train back to Oslo and found Martha sitting up in bed, the crisis having passed. "It was not necessary for me to report what had happened," he noted. "She knew and had followed me on my journey and knew that I had been helped by the Prime Minister, and that we had been permitted to fulfil the work with which we had been entrusted." [13]

This incident was the deciding factor in Richard St. Barbe Baker's life. After nine years of studying the Faith, he became a Bahá'í in London during the first week in February 1935. When he passed on his good news to Martha, he wrote, "Do you know you are a wonderful inspiration, especially to a very young believer like myself." He charted the persons who, over the years, had influenced his decision, and he concluded, "Last but not least my friendship with you, in Oslo . . . strengthened my convictions. . . ."[14]

It was a fairly long recuperative period, but by April Martha was feeling healthy enough to give an occasional lecture and an important broadcast that was beamed throughout Europe. "My soul had to learn new lessons," she said of her illness, "perhaps we have to go through all these experiences, for they are a part of life."[15] *Bahá'u'lláh and the New Era* was published in Norwegian and was on display in several shop windows. The publishers sent a copy to every newspaper in Norway, and the reviews were very good. Martha and Johanna Schubarth also sent a copy of the book to each of the thirty Norwegian newspapers in America. It was a time for rejoicing.

But there was a sadness along with the good news: the first of T. T. Root's children had passed away. From Cambridge Springs Martha learned that her brother Clarence had succumbed to asthma and pneumonia on 17 April. She asked Shoghi Effendi for special prayers at the shrines in Haifa and sent money home for flowers. A cable to her family read, "Weeping with you all. Prayers, love, courage. Dear Clarence with Christ, father, mother. He will welcome us heaven. Martha."[16]

Life went on, and Martha resumed her work. On 9 May 1935 she was granted an audience with His Majesty King Haakon of Norway. She was deeply impressed by the humanistic responses and observations of this king, and by the spiritual promptings that were the key to his world vision. Like all monarchs, he represented a state religion and, therefore, exercised caution when discussing the Bahá'í Faith; but he was favorably inclined toward all he had learned and was drawn to the social principles of the Faith. Martha's audience with this unusual monarch was like reaching a mountaintop in Oslo after a winter in the valley: the sun was beginning to shine through.

49 The Rhythm Quickens

Although Martha was more careful about her health, teaching remained uppermost in her mind. She outlined a reduced schedule, but it was not exactly sedentary living. By June 1935 she was in Copenhagen, Denmark. Johanna Schubarth accompanied her and stayed for nine days before leaving Martha in the hands of her old friend Johanna Sorensen. Together Martha and Johanna, two who had worked in tandem before, were involved in Bahá'í activities for a month in Denmark before sailing on 7 July across the Norwegian Sea to Reykjavik, on the west coast of Iceland.

Years before, Martha had started planting the seeds in Iceland by sending Bahá'í literature and had recently sent the Norwegian translation of *Bahá'u'lláh and the New Era*. Martha had deep admiration for Iceland, one country in the world that had declared its neutrality. It stood for peace as a way of life, and it was the only country where there was no poverty, and where education reached all.

Martha felt better there than she had for a long time. The work went well, and newspaper publicity was superb. There were numerous articles, interviews, and pictures; and there was the miracle communicator, radio, on which Martha spoke twice. She brought books to the leper colony and spent hours in the libraries and museums, where she was deeply moved by the spirituality emanating from the works of Iceland's greatest sculptor, Einar Jónsson. Everywhere Martha found affability, hospitality, intelligent awareness of issues and the need for education, and great activity among the Theosophists. The first mention of the Bahá'í Faith in an Icelandic newspaper appeared on 14 July 1935. It was a month of beneficence.

Martha sailed back to Norway in August. During her few days in Bergen she met a person who had heard her radio talk in

MARTHA ROOT (left) and JOHANNA SCHUBARTH
a Bahá'í who nursed Martha through a serious illness,
Oslo, Norway, 1935

1927, investigated the Faith, and become a Bahá'í. It spurred
Martha on to give another talk on 13 August before leaving for
Stockholm and sailing for Finland.

In all the Scandinavian and Baltic countries Martha sensed
the vitality and integrity of the northern people. "I tell you,"
she wrote a few months later, "that the Bahá'í culture of the
North may be a rose that blooms later, but when it does bloom
it will be fresh, fragrant, exquisite! The flowers of the North
pos[s]ess a freshness all their own!"[1] If Bahá'u'lláh's teachings
for world peace could be established in Scandinavia, Martha
felt, this region would lead the way to the formation of a Universal League of Nations that would unite the nations of the
world. Martha was years ahead of her time, as that institution
would come into being in 1945 as the United Nations, with its
first secretary general, Trygve Lie, of Oslo, Norway.

From Helsinki Martha wrote a letter to Shoghi Effendi and to Roy Wilhelm outlining her work in Europe for the next year. It was a formidable program. Then, acceding to the wishes of Shoghi Effendi, she would return to the United States and accept an invitation to rest at the Maine retreat of the Wilhelms. "Then perhaps I could go through our country," Martha suggested, "crossing the continent working together with the different Assemblies, and after that go to Japan and China. I wish to die 'with my boots on', trying to serve Bahá'u'lláh."[2]

One reason Martha felt she could not stop traveling was that her articles on various lands encouraged other Bahá'ís to "do something to further the work in those places." Also, her serious illness in Oslo had made her more conscious of her limitations of time and strength:

> I know the steed (the body) is slipping down as the years go by, but the rider (the spirit) is upheld by the Supreme Concourse those Chosen and Favored Angels. I will not do less than my very best, and I beg you dearest Guardian and you dearest friend Roy, to pray for my Guidance and to advise me.[3]

Martha followed her proposed plan, with one or two substitutions, and for the next ten months zigzagged her way from northern to southern Europe. After two months in Finland she left late in October to follow a reverse version of her 1927 itinerary through the Baltic countries and visited Tallin, Estonia; Riga, Latvia; and then Kaunas, Lithuania, for the third time. Publicity in each of the cities was more than she could have hoped for, and her contacts with writers and educators were exceptionally fruitful. As news of the Bahá'í Faith reached scholars, it found its way into their books and lectures. She felt certain that interest would continue after her visit. But she wrote, "If Buddha had one hundred hands, the Bahá'i teacher needs just as many, and also needs one hundred hearts—by that I mean, the Bahá'i teacher must get one hundred others inspired to wish to help the souls they hear about."[4]

Martha made her way by train down through central Europe and the Balkans to consolidate earlier work. By late November

1935 she was back in Prague. Each time she came to this city, Martha paid homage to President Masaryk, whose eighty-five years had lessened neither his leadership nor his keen intellectual interests. He had recently written a book on religion; and because his interest in the Bahá'í Faith remained high, he wanted to read every Bahá'í book. Along with the books Martha sent him roses, his favorite flower—nine yellow roses accompanied a volume of *The Bahá'í World;* a bouquet of red and white roses went along with a copy of *Gleanings from the Writings of Bahá'u'lláh* to mark his deceased wife's birthday.[5] This was Martha's extravagance of a dollar or two.

The president of the Writers' Club of Praha (Prague) had translated the Kitáb-i-Íqán. Money was in short supply, but Martha was a resourceful being. She paid for his work with a beautiful fur coat, a gift to her and worn only once. The translator sold it to a publisher, who bought it for his twenty-year-old daughter; Martha assured her it would bring her blessings.

At Christmastime 1935 Martha was again in Belgrade, Yugoslavia, where she would stay for three weeks. She spent the holidays with Draga Ilich and visited with Princess Olga, whose husband, Prince Paul, was now regent. After traveling down to Sofia, Bulgaria, to work for two weeks with Marion Jack, Martha boarded a train to Bucharest, where she had her eighth audience with Queen Marie.

By the time Martha reached Athens in February 1936, her strength was waning. She spent much time in bed, where she wrote, rested, and tried unsuccessfully to arrange an audience with King George II of Greece. Here she read *Gleanings from the Writings of Bahá'u'lláh,* Shoghi Effendi's recently completed translation of choice selections from Bahá'u'lláh's writings. Among its pages are explained spiritual history, past and present, mankind's destiny, and guidelines for living on earth. "Those words are such a joy, such a comfort," Martha wrote to friends, "they help to understand life and death and the Great Beyond."[6]

The readings were especially comforting at this time, as she was deeply saddened by the death of Howard Carpenter, at age twenty-nine, in California. She had loved working with Marzieh and Howard in Vienna and the Balkans in 1933 and had been stimulated by their mental and spiritual sparkle. She sent money for a remembrance to a California friend, Ella Bailey, who in turn bought a yellow rose tree that was planted at Howard's grave.

Although her stay in Greece was brief, Martha did manage to meet the mayor of Athens and members of the diplomatic corps. At the end of February she received a cable from Shoghi Effendi that read, "Advise visit states August. If convenient visit northern Europe before August. . . ."[7]

Martha, ever responsive to Shoghi Effendi, fitted Scandinavia into her plans. She picked up her trail, which wove in and out of the countries in this eastern pocket of Europe, and returned to Belgrade and then Vienna. Here she spent Naw-Rúz, the Bahá'í new year on 21 March, with Franz Pöllinger and other Austrian Bahá'ís and was received by Ileana, now Archduchess Anton. Martha then made her way back to Prague.

Since her last stay in Czechoslovakia, Edvard Beneš had succeeded Thomas Masaryk as president of the country. Martha had been his guest at the palace in 1926, had participated with him in an education-for-peace program in 1927, and, at the disarmament conference in Geneva in 1932, had had a lengthy two-hour tea with him. At that time they had discussed the Bahá'í Faith and its implications for the world. Now, on 22 April 1936, Martha met again with this educator, peace worker, and new president of Czechoslovakia. It was a wonderful interview, confirming for Martha the extraordinary thinking of Masaryk's disciple, whose ways could bring prosperity and tranquillity to the world. Dr. Beneš had been an admirer of the Bahá'í Faith since first encountering it at the First Races Congress in London in July 1911. "Peace is the work of men," he once said, "exactly as war is the work of men. I am of the opinion that governing people are always responsible for the wars. The responsible people in certain numbers can make the wars, or they can establish the peace."[8]

Such an admonition was timely in 1936. The world was changing, growing ugly. It was not the spiritual nature of man that was gaining ascendancy but dark forces that were surfacing. The fingers of war, which Martha had felt moving in Germany and reaching into the Balkans, were becoming an arm of aggression, threatening, victimizing, and would grow into a body of destruction as the Second World War enveloped Europe and absorbed the world.

In the next decade the Bahá'ís in Europe would experience increasing opposition to their beliefs. A Bahá'í in Budapest, J. Ruh-Angiz Bolles, would write to Martha about the harassment of the Bahá'ís by the Catholic press and the police and their denunciation of them as Communists. The secretary of the Budapest Spiritual Assembly, Mrs. Bolles told Martha, withstood four mornings of questioning by the authorities, who unsuccessfully tried to use a translation of *Bahá'u'lláh and the New Era* as their evidence.[9] Elsewhere in Europe the Nazis had taken power in 1933. In 1936 they would close the first European Bahá'í summer school, in Esslingen, Germany. By 1937 the National Spiritual Assembly of Germany would be dissolved and all Bahá'í activities forbidden. In March 1938 the ban would be extended to Austria.

When Hitler's troops marched into Czechoslovakia in 1938, President Beneš resigned and headed the exiled Czech regime in London until 1945. He returned to Prague after the Second World War and resumed his presidency. The intervening war years throughout the world were a time of devastation of places and people and the human spirit.

As the summer of 1936 approached, Martha's relentless effort to infuse Europe with the teachings of Bahá'u'lláh was directed northward. As though gathering round her brood of children, she packed her seventeen pieces of luggage, picked up her cane, which now was among her necessaries, and headed for Scandinavia, as Shoghi Effendi had advised several months earlier. By the first week in June she was back in Helsinki, where she stayed until 12 July. After brief stops in Stockholm and Oslo, Martha Root sailed from Bergen on 18 July 1936 aboard the *Bergensfiord*, bound for New York.

She had been gone from her native land a little over four years. In that time she had struggled to overcome the vagaries of life and had continued to spread the Bahá'í Faith. Although the work went forward, the body was failing, and Martha knew that time was on the wing.

50   The Skylark at Home

"'Beloved indefatigable Martha sailing New York Bergens-fiord,'" cabled Shoghi Effendi to the National Spiritual Assembly of the Bahá'ís of the United States and Canada in July 1936. "'Feel certain believers will accord befitting welcome well beloved star servant of Bahá'u'lláh.'"[1] Martha's friends needed no nudging to be at the pier on 27 July to greet her. She was met by Roy Wilhelm, Mountfort Mills, Marion Little, and Mildred and Rafi Mottahedeh, among others. Only two of her seventeen suitcases had personal belongings, but all went with her to the Prince George Hotel on East Twenty-eighth Street, near the Mottahedeh's offices and showrooms for their exquisite china.

Martha stayed on in New York, resting, writing, and arranging her affairs before returning home. Each day a secretary from the Mottahedeh firm went to the hotel and took dictation for Martha's letters of thanks and information to friends sprinkled around the globe.

Cambridge Springs was awaiting Martha's return, the townspeople having been alerted by the newspaper to her arrival in the United States and having been promised public talks about her latest adventures. There would be none this trip. When Martha arrived during the second week in August, she rested and shared time with her family, Lucy Wilson, and Doris McKay, who came from nearby Jamestown, New York, to visit.

Martha and Doris went with the family on Sunday morning to a service at the Baptist church, where Martha had been denounced twenty years before. In the evening friends and neighbors were invited to share a social and informative evening, but Martha became ill and asked Doris to take over for her.

The crisis passed, and the next morning Martha took Doris on a tour of childhood scenes and introduced her to old friends and familiar places. "On the way to her brother's grocery store," Doris recalled, "she again became ill and had to lean up against a tree for a few minutes until her strength came back. Then we walked on; the same cheerful, enthusiastic, determined Martha!"[2]

The malady was not discussed; it simply was. Her friends had known of her long illness in Oslo and realized that this visit home must be a time of rest. Responding to the wishes of Shoghi Effendi, three members of the National Spiritual Assembly—Roy Wilhelm, Mountfort Mills, and Horace Holley—were to monitor Martha's health and activity, to see that there were no teaching trips until recuperation was well under way.

MARTHA ROOT and HESHMAT ALAI
at Green Acre Bahá'í School, Eliot, Maine, August 1936. After
Martha's death, Mr. Alai, who lived in Tehran, accepted
with reverence a spoon that had belonged to Martha.

The Bahá'í summer school at Green Acre was not to be missed, and for three days, 15–18 August, Martha breathed in the spiritual fragrances of that matchless spot. She met old friends and new and gave a talk before traveling north to the Wilhelms' summer camp in Lovell, Maine.

Roy Wilhelm liked to feel close to the rustic life. He called his West Englewood, New Jersey, property "Evergreen Cabin" and his summer quarters in Maine "Evergreen Camp." The latter was a beautiful retreat in the Maine hills, rather like a Swiss villa, which Roy thought would be a perfect place for Shoghi Effendi to stay if ever he could come to the United States. It was not just a reclusive home but was a limited working farm, with five hundred maple trees that were tapped for maple syrup, and nineteen goats that produced milk year round and kids in the spring. Roy took great pride in the working of the camp and was a staunch believer in the health-producing advantages of goats' milk.

Martha arrived on 18 August and stayed for two months at this halcyon spot. Here, in the crisp New England summer air, she was nursed back to comparatively good health by the loving ministrations of the Wilhelms and the tenders of the kitchen and the goats. It was a time of seclusion—seclusion from newspapers and conferences, from appointments and interviews. This was the rest so long promised but never taken. It was now enforced by those who cared about Martha and took her welfare into their own hands.

Visitors were discouraged; only one or two of Martha's most intimate friends that she insisted on seeing were allowed. Among them were Bahiyyih Winckler (then Lindstrom) and her husband, who were told that Martha was exhausted and ill and should be visited only briefly. They went upstairs and found Martha sitting up in a mammoth bed, the diminutive body almost lost in the vast space.

Bahiyyih was deeply concerned about Martha's obviously diminishing health. She asked Martha why she would not see a doctor. "'Bahiyyih, I can't,'" she replied. "'If I went . . . they would tell me what to do, that I could never travel any more [sic], that I could never do all the things that I want to do,

BAHIYYIH RANDALL WINCKLER
daughter of Harry Randall and, like her father,
a close friend of Martha's

and I shan't be told that, and I shall just go on until I can go on no more.' "³ Martha knew that she was working against time.

When asked why she had never married, she did not mention her accident during the prime of young womanhood but rather focused on the later years: she could never have done her work—her speaking, writing, and traveling—had she been married. Marriage would have divided her attention.

By mid-October Martha was stronger and, having passed a doctor's examination—a prerequisite of the national committee—was ready to tackle a limited speaking schedule. With the help of the Regional Teaching Committee, an itinerary in New England was worked out. However, considering her fragile health and the travel involved, it was still a challenge. A sample week from an engagement book reflects the pace:

October 25: "Spoke at Mrs. Nancy Bowditch [home, Brookline, Mass.]"
October 27: "Spoke in Boston"
October 29: "two meetings at the home of Mr. & Mrs. Harold Bowman[,] Salmon Falls, N[ew] H[ampshire]"
October 30: "Spoke at Green Acre, at Mrs. Greenleaf's home"
October 31: "Spoke in Worcester[,] Mass[.]"
November 2: "Came to N.Y."
November 3: "Came to Roy's home[.] Conference with Horace & Mountfort"
November 4: "Went to Feast & spoke [West Englewood, N.J.]"[4]

On 10 November Martha was back in New York to lecture to Professor Robert Hume's students at Columbia University. Four days later she was in Atlantic City, New Jersey, where at least one day was devoted to reading and walking.

Under the guidance of her three mentors, another limited program of lectures was arranged, this time for New York, Philadelphia, Washington, Baltimore, Pittsburgh, and Union City, Pennsylvania. In the last city she renewed old friendships and especially enjoyed spending time with Lucy Burt Steeves, who marveled at Martha's spiritual depth and humility.

Returning to New York, which had become an anchor point for her activities in America, Martha spoke in early December at a meeting on East Twenty-second Street. One woman who attended that meeting was inspired by Martha's presence: "She was plain looking, yes, but was immaculately neat and, I felt, smartly dressed in tailored clothes, with her short hair smooth, straight and well groomed. She spoke with a combination of self-assurance and real humility, which made her a strong speaker."[5]

At that time Martha's wardrobe was being attended to by Marion Little and Loulie Mathews, two women who had good taste and were able to afford fine clothes. But expensive or not,

Martha's clothes were always spotlessly clean, neat, and well pressed, which she managed despite living in transit out of luggage.

During the second week in December, Loulie Mathews drove into New York to see Martha. Mrs. Matthews and her husband were planning a teaching trip to South America, and she "felt the value of the voyage depended upon having her [Martha Root's] advice."

The moment I arrived in New York I drove . . . to the Martha Washington Hotel where I found her in a cubicle—it couldn't be termed a room. Martha was surrounded by small bags and bundles in preparation for her coming trip to Europe.* How calm she was! I felt like a small tug beside an ocean liner—would I ever attain such magnificent poise!

Martha was delighted to learn of their impending South American trip, and after relating some of her own experiences, gave some addresses and a gift, a letter from 'Abdu'l-Bahá. "Taking my arm," Mrs. Mathews remembered, "she walked with me to the elevator reminding me that *every* minute belongs to God, not every other minute."[6]

In addressing the Bahá'ís at the Bahá'í center of New York on 12 December 1936, Martha expressed her joy at being among them. "I thought of how the lark goes up into the sky and sings his song again and again. It is wonderful to work with the friends, the spiritual skylarks. . . . [If] we are a very polished surface, we are receptive to the light like a mirror. If we work together we can make the world like a rose-garden."[7]

Christmas was spent with relatives in Cambridge Springs, but Martha sorely missed Lucy Wilson, who was in California. For the week at home Martha gave no public talks, did no writing, and saved the time to concentrate on heart-to-heart talks with her family. She yearned for them to understand what she was doing and why, and hoped to instill in them an appreciation for the greatness of the Bahá'í revelation.

---

*Martha Root was always in transit, but she would not sail from America for another six months.

Early in January 1937 Martha took the short train ride from Cambridge Springs to Jamestown, New York. She needed time alone to work. After checking into the least expensive room at the YWCA without announcing her presence to the McKays or other friends, she settled in to rest and write and make a dent in the more than one hundred waiting letters, almost all asking questions that needed answers. She also hoped to write a radio talk about her broadcasting experience on five continents.

Amidst her hours of concentrated effort she took time to see a chiropractor, who gave her temporary relief from the ever-persistent pain in the head and back of the neck. After several days, when she could point to some accomplishments, Martha telephoned the McKays. Doris arrived in record time with a basket of fruit, a welcome change from Martha's diet of buns and tea. Over the days Doris helped with the letters, took dictation, and got Martha out of her room. They took brief walks around town and shared dinner at the McKay home.

On 17 January Martha broadcast a talk from the Jamestown radio station on the universal rewards of Esperanto. Martha also paid a long overdue visit to Mayor Carlson. This Swedish socialist had been mayor of Jamestown for many years. He was an old friend of Mayor Lindhagen of Stockholm, an ardent Esperantist, whom Martha had first met in 1927. Martha had a book from his friend; she arranged an appointment, and, with Doris McKay, called on the mayor. Doris witnessed the grace and skill with which Martha conducted the event:

Martha talked about the beauty of Stockholm, her pleasure at meeting the friendly mayor [who had sent a message with a book]. Then came the expected question: Why was she in Stockholm? She told him of her travels for the Bahá'í Faith, mentioned the scope of her travels, some of the people met. It was fascinating. The mayor asked her about the Faith but by now we had taken enough of his time. Instead she left him some carefully selected literature. We left him *beaming*. Martha instinctively knew that she could not make the old gentleman a Bahai, but she had made him a friend.[8]

A high point of Martha's Jamestown visit was the arrival in town of Dorothy Beecher Baker, a wonderfully energetic, perceptive woman who would become a well-known, well-traveled Bahá'í teacher, and a member of the National Spiritual Assembly of the Bahá'ís of the United States and Canada. She was introduced to Martha by Doris McKay during lunch at the YWCA. "Dorothy deferred to Martha . . . completely," Doris noted, "as if bowing to her station. . . ."[9] Martha left Jamestown for Buffalo on 19 January 1937. In this wintry city on the Canadian border, Martha had planned to stay a day or two with a Bahá'í friend, Frances Esty, give some talks, and later go to Rochester and Syracuse. When she arrived in Buffalo, she had a temperature of 102 degrees and was put to bed. It was influenza. She could scarcely breathe; and without the immediate and expert care summoned by Mrs. Esty, Martha might not have survived. She had the finest doctor and an attentive nurse, whom she called "Peri," which meant "angel" in Persian. Although terribly ill, Martha was surrounded by loving care and was bedded down in a spacious, well-run home, in a guest room that faced the park. To Lucy Wilson, also a close friend of Mrs. Esty's, Martha wrote, "There is so much of sweetness in this experience that I feel I have been ill in heaven. . . ."[10]

By the first week in February Martha was out of bed, although she was still attended by a nurse. Mountfort Mills spent two days in Buffalo during Martha's recuperation and, after speaking at a luncheon, gave her some advice: " 'Now put that New England conscience of yours away, Martha, and don't think you must work, and *don't* change your mind and stay in this winter weather but *go* to Calif[ornia]!' "[11] Martha had her own timetable, and California was a few weeks away.

While she struggled to regain her health, Roy Wilhelm's mother had a stroke and four days later passed away. Just before the stroke, as Martha lay in bed, she had a vision: Mrs. Wilhelm, for whom she had such deep attachment, came to her to say good-bye. She was prepared for the news when it arrived, but her heart ached for Roy, who was, she felt, the most loved Bahá'í in the country.

In addition to her grief over Mrs. Wilhelm's passing, Martha was disappointed that the talks in Syracuse and Rochester had to be canceled. From Buffalo she wrote to Minnie Setz, who had arranged the Syracuse visit: "Still, dear sister, hard as illness is, mine has taught me a lot and one lesson is patience and not to complain but to see that even illness, if God sends it, can be a means of coming nearer to Him, it can have an inner bounty, an inner service to His Faith." "I have another side to me that isn't ill," she remarked, "please forgive the illness & soon I shall be *well.*"[12]

By the third week in February Martha felt strong enough to return to Jamestown. She took a room at the Jamestown Hotel, as there was no elevator in the YWCA, and she tired easily. She prayed fervently for official word from her Committee of Three—Roy, Mountfort, and Horace—to let her continue her travels. The waiting, for her, was a time of trial. Fortunately, Doris McKay was there to offer comfort: "One day," she wrote, "I found Martha shedding bitter tears. The hoped for letter from the NSA had still not arrived with its permission for her to be on her way. When, at last, it did come she flew like a bird out of its cage."[13]

That letter gave Martha permission to travel to the West Coast. Without losing a minute, she left Jamestown on 24 February 1937. Weeping on Martha's shoulder, Doris McKay saw her off on the train. She sensed a long separation. "'I wonder,'" she wrote in her journal, "'if we will ever see each other again here on earth.'"[14] Martha returned home to bid her relatives and friends good-bye. It would be her last visit to Cambridge Springs.

Although the committee allowed Martha to make the cross-country trip, they curtailed all but the most benign work. She stopped for a few days at Dorothy and Frank Baker's home in Lima, Ohio. While there she gave a talk only to Bahá'ís; they flocked in from all the surrounding regions—Cleveland, Toledo, Cincinnati, Columbus. On the day of the talk Martha stayed in bed until 2:00 P.M. and went back upstairs after the gathering was over four hours later, but she said it was a celestial meeting. While in Lima a broadcast was arranged but canceled after Martha received a message from the committee that

DOROTHY BEECHER BAKER
a member of the National Spiritual Assembly of the
Bahá'ís of the United States and Canada. She was
named a Hand of the Cause of God in December 1951.
Mrs. Baker, when she first met Martha in 1937, "'deferred
to Martha . . . completely as if bowing to her station.'"

said she was to give no public talks. She was afraid the broadcast would be considered a public presentation, and she
wanted to follow absolutely the instructions of the committee.

On 9 March 1937 Dorothy Baker put Martha on the train to
Chicago. Dorothy—statuesque, handsome, assured—had
been deeply touched by Martha's purity, radiating love, and
humility. Dorothy wrote to her:

I have just come from putting you on the train, and I want
to put my arms around you just once more. It seems as if it
could not be true that I will go into the front room and not
find you there looking so sweet and smiling encouragement
at me. You must go now and smile encouragement at the
whole world, and I very much want you to. Only it is Dorothy feeling a little homesick now, not Dorothy who loves the

Cause of Baha'u'llah better than life itself, who is speaking. . . . I was even cross to the poor little porter, wasn't I? I wish that he could know that it was only homesickness speaking. I will pray for Baha'u'llah to give him a special blessing, and to let me give someone else a greater measure of service in his place. Dear porter; dear world, how much more I must learn to love you all—as Martha does.

Saying goodbye to the world's greatest Baha'i teacher should not be as hard as this was. Great people usually are not so hard to part with; their greatness adds a certain strain. With you, it is that you are Martha; dear, selfless, angel Martha; so humble before the children of the Beloved that it might fool the undiscerning and make proud the simple.[15]

One of Martha's special friends, John Mirt, met her at the station in Chicago. She had put him through college and, in Pittsburgh, had trained him to become a journalist; now he was an editor on the *Chicago Daily News*. Martha viewed him almost as a son, or little brother—she called him her darling Johnny—and he treated her as though she were his mother and mentor. In Chicago he arranged for her hotel room, taxi, luggage, and invited her for lunch and dinner with him on every day that it was possible.

Knowing Martha's tendency for being excessive about her scheduled activities, the committee wanted her to go straight through to the West Coast; but a stop in Chicago was necessary to complete her travel plans west. Shoghi Effendi had urged complete rest during her stay in the east in preparation for her historic trip across the continent, and her expectation was to visit numerous cities en route. But the instructions from Roy, Horace, and Mountfort were clear: such a plan was ruled out; it was to be rest all the way. Even in California no public meetings were to be allowed. After Martha's lifetime of nonstop service, only a committee of the National Spiritual Assembly could slow her pace. She ached to teach but was quiescent. To the committee she wrote:

I may go many times around the world, I may be in Chicago again, on the other hand I may never be in this city again. . . .

. . . It breaks my heart if you think I do not obey, I am trying to. And I want you to know I appreciate your love and consideration for my health—I know my health better than any one [sic], and that is why I am so eager to do what I can, when I can—for perhaps I can not [sic] go across our loved continent again for a long time.[16]

Although Martha felt like a bird with its wings clipped, she was uncomplaining. She was delighted to find that Angela Morgan, a poet, was in the same Chicago hotel. Years before, when Martha was in London, Angela's mother became ill and died. Martha's busy schedule was put aside as she sat for hours on end, and into days, with the patient and then with Angela. She comforted her and brought peace and reassurance into her life. It was an experience Angela Morgan never forgot, and she was eternally grateful to Martha.

Angela, with Monroe Ioas and Sarah Walrath, had the priceless experience of taking Martha Root to the House of Worship in Wilmette. It was still under construction, but great strides had been made since Martha's visit in 1931. The dome was in place and the ornamentation under way. Martha's visit evoked memories of the Ideas Committee of 1920 and became a thrilling and moving experience for her:

It is the most spiritually beautiful building I have ever seen. I shall remember it here and in all the worlds of God. I had not dreamed it could be so celestial, so beautiful. How thrilling to have had a part, even a small part, in its being "brought into reality." First we drove past and then came back so we had the great view of it twice. Mr. Ed Struven explained it all so wonderfully to us when we went inside—and my inner eye saw so much. . . . At the last as I knelt and prayed upstairs under the dome, it was in the peace and the holy [?] of 'Akká that this servant knelt & rec'd the benediction. I am so satisfied that I could come and see this holy place & see its glory, *learn* its lessons and feel Bahá'u'lláh's Presence there. So much I learned—one thing I mention: the drawing for the bronze door so *lovely*, the *roses*, all, all, so lingeringly lovely. I thought of dear Mr. Bourgeois working years ago in West Englewood, his wife selling ice-cream cones to make the living while he worked; and like a flash came the thought

BAHÁ'Í HOUSE OF WORSHIP
Wilmette, Illinois, with ornamentation under way, much as it
would have looked when Martha Root first saw it in 1937.

that as now we work sometimes under the greatest difficulties and hardships, someday those coming after, perhaps,
will see "roses" and "loveliness" and exclaim with joy and
be uplifted by the human "doors" (the souls) to whom we
humbly tried to tell of the Baha'i Faith. [17]

For years Martha had carried pictures of the House of Worship
model with her all over the world; now she absorbed the con-
summation of that idea. The erection of the House of Worship
had become both a triumph of spirit over economic hardship
and strife, and a visible symbol of the growth of the Bahá'í
Faith.

There was another memorable experience for Martha in
Chicago—a reception given for her by the Bahá'ís that brought

together old and new friends, some from her earliest years of inquiry and commitment. The hall was filled—"truly it was an 'event'." Martha was deeply moved, "so satisfied to see them once more," for, she wrote, "I do not expect to return to Chicago again."[18]

After writing an article, by invitation, for the *Chicago Daily News* and looking up some Esperantists who might be helpful during Lydia Zamenhof's proposed visit to the United States, Martha left Chicago before the annual convention because of her physical restrictions. She boarded the tourist train for California with a basket of fruit from Monroe Ioas and an elegant hamper of lunch from Sarah Walrath; both friends were familiar with Martha's habit of nonattention to self. Predictably, there was a young woman on the train who was ill—a consumptive heading for the dry climate of Arizona—and Martha took care of her, sharing material and spiritual bounty.

By 17 March 1937 Martha was settled in room 15 at the YWCA in Pasadena. It was a peaceful atmosphere in which to gather strength after the long trip before calling Lucy Wilson and another old Bahá'í friend, Amelia Collins.[19]

Sailing dates were explored and plans mapped out for living in the Orient. She shared the possibilities with her committee:

In Japan I may only stay two or three weeks. (Japan is very expensive, I can't stay there very long.) I expect to make my long stay in China and I must earn a little by teaching English lessons. I plan to get to China before the cold weather comes, and shall get my ticket from San Francisco to Hong Kong, with stopovers (any length of time) in Yokohama (one hour by electric train from Tokyo) and stopover at Shanghai.[20]

Friends begged Martha not to start out again on a distant voyage with her health in such a precarious state. Her sense of mission urged her forward, but doubt slipped in, confusing what had been a clear-cut decision. Roy had written to her:

There is one remark in your letter that deserve[s] a challenge. You say "Well anyway Baha'u'lláh will go with me." No, Martha Bahá'u'lláh goes with us just to the extent that we use cautiousness & wisdom. We can[']t blame things on Bahá-u-lláh if we strain that law in any degree. I know too well that a good many of my troubles this past two years . . . [were] avoidable. "I am going to be wiser now."[21]

From "Milly" Collins, who knew Martha's temperament and dedication, she drew strength and wisdom as Milly encouraged Martha to go forward with her plans. Martha, in turn, gave strength and courage to Milly as she waited through the days and nights of her husband's terminal heart ailment.

News arrived that delighted Martha: Lydia Zamenhof was, indeed, coming to the United States. Martha compensated for not being able to greet Lydia and share her days in America by writing to Bahá'ís and Esperantists of influence and urging them to do their utmost to extend their love and kindness to her. Another stunning piece of news was the announcement of the marriage of Shoghi Effendi to Mary Maxwell, daughter of May and Sutherland Maxwell of Montreal, who had such strong ties with Martha from the time she entered the Bahá'í Faith. Mary Maxwell would henceforth be known formally as Rúḥíyyih Rabbaní but would be called Rúḥíyyih Khánum by the Bahá'ís. Martha wrote, "I think of our Guardian and Mary and pledge my devotion to them forever."[22]

When news of Martha Root's presence in the area reached the Bahá'ís, she was invited to speak to them, which she was eager to do as long as the audience was limited to Bahá'ís in order to conform to the directives of the committee. The Bahá'ís gathered from miles around to hear her. One person who was there recalled the evening:

I remember seeing this mousey-looking small grey woman come in and be presented. I thought: How is it possible that such a looking person could be the great Martha Root! Then she began to talk—and she was ablaze and ignited all the Bahá'ís present. A never-to-be forgotten experience. She was presented with a huge bunch of red roses, and the dear guest really left the hall with none of them, as everyone rushed to her to touch her and thank her and to take one of the roses as a souvenir (almost a holy relic!) I among them.

Then I was received by her in her tiny hotel room. She had a sort of wardrobe trunk . . . and half of it or over was filled with Bahá'í books and literature.[23]

In mid-April Martha boarded a train to San Francisco. She wrote to Lucy Marshall, who had invited Martha to stay with her, "I better go to a Y.W.C.A.—for I do not like to be in any one's [sic] home and not do as others do. I get tired when I talk too much & sometimes I lie down three or four times in the day. I do not relax easily."[24]

Claude Root's daughter, Anna, having left seven years of teaching and an unfaithful husband behind, was at the San José School for Teachers. Martha made a point of being in San José on 17 April to share Anna's birthday. From this visit on, Anna gained a broader comprehension of the meaning of her Aunt Martha's life and a greater understanding of the Bahá'í Faith. This interest would increase in the months after Martha's departure.

In some ways the California experience, as in Chicago, was frustrating. Martha confided to Ella Cooper:

I hope to have one meeting with just the Bahá'ís before I sail. . . . I can not [sic] do much—I must take the rest as my Committee wished. O Ella, dearest only you can understand how hard it is, not to meet all the friends and work together. Sometimes I think it would be better never to go to a city than to go & not visit with all the friends.[25]

One way Martha nipped the frustration was to travel north to Portland, Oregon, where she spent five days with the Latimers, and then to Eugene, where she spent five additional days with Claude and his wife. The visits were a radical change from those of the past, when Martha would arrive, put down her bags, and soon be off giving lectures. However, she did talk to the Bahá'ís in the Portland area, and again they came from great distances to hear her. Any other lecturing was out of the question. It was enforced conservation of strength; and although disappointed, Martha was obedient.

With Martha's sailing set for 20 May, she made her way back to San Francisco to prepare for the trip. Of those last days in the United States there are reminiscences by a few Bahá'ís who had spent time with Martha. Among them are the recollections of Joyce Dahl:

> I was invited along with two other young women [Myrtle Dodge and Edith Clark]. . . . The spiritual food she gave us had a purpose. She wished us to be a group of young ladies. . . . She used the example of a tree putting forth blossoms, and we were to be blossoms. We would correspond with each other and create bonds of unity that would help us spread the Word.[26]

Martha also asked these "blossoms" to pray for the success of an upcoming meeting in a Bahá'í home in San José. They were to say the Tablet of Aḥmad nine times per day for a week before the meeting. The subsequent gathering, Joyce Dahl noted, was a success.

Marion Holley (Hofman), whose mother was a Bahá'í, had first met Martha in 1931. Marion had just finished four years at Stanford University, where she was greatly influenced by the agnosticism of her university instructors. Martha stayed at the Holley home in Visalia for a few days, and Marion acted as chauffeur. She observed that Martha "was very timid of fast driving; in fact, I drove very carefully and slowly, with Martha in the front seat, but even so she was afraid. . . . when I read about Martha's trip over the Andes by mule . . . I felt that it must have taken great courage to do this."[27] When Martha addressed the student body at Fresno State College, her simple approach, Marion thought at the time, failed to hold the attention of the audience, which was used to more intellectual fare.

By the time of the second meeting with Martha in 1937, Marion was an active Bahá'í. Martha spoke at a large gathering on 17 May, and Marion recalled

> walking down the street with her after her meeting, and realizing something of the quality which she so manifestly possessed—her absolute faith in Bahá'u'lláh—as well as a great sweetness of character. These spiritual qualities had escaped

me completely on our first meeting, because I saw her then only through the eye of intellect. I have always been grateful for this last brief meeting.[28]

As Martha's departure time neared, she gathered together all the earthly possessions that would accompany her to the Orient and beyond, just as they had when she sailed from Seattle fourteen years earlier. Those years had taken their toll, and illness had left visible signs that were evident even to the most casual observer.

Martha was now three months short of her sixty-fifth birthday. Her hair was already white; the luminous blue-green eyes, which still startled people with their depth and brilliance, were framed with glasses; the five-foot–three-inch form had shrunk; the face was etched with lines of pain. But the spirit of her inner being had moved closer to the surface and had added an ethereal softness to her expression; the still firm step was less swift, but the inner fire and sense of purpose burned as keenly as ever.

Lucy Marshall helped Martha pack her things, and then it was time to go. Lucy viewed the scene:

Martha has in her purse a second-cabin ticket around the world, via Japan, China, Manila, Singapore, Calcutta, Colombo, Port Said, Italy, France and London to New York with stop over privileges. . . . The seventeen pieces of baggage are re-packed, containing for the most part books, pamphlets, loose manuscripts kept seperate [sic] by lots folded in thin cotton cloths, radio talks, photographs of all the rulers who received Tablets from Baha'u'llah, and clothes necessary for the voyage. About a small leather suitcase Martha said: "This is the kitchen for I usually prepare my own food. It was given to me by Lady Blomfield." About a spacious carry-all, she remarked: "Roy Wilhelm had this made for me and it is most useful for it holds a lot." Each has an interesting history. . . . Managing this baggage is a sufficiently difficult task.[29]

In addition, there were six large packages of books and pamphlets. All were sent to the dock, and Martha was ready. Her friends flocked to the ship to wish her bon voyage and spend a few last precious minutes with her. Lucy Marshall described those last moments:

> May 20 is here, the TATSUTA MARU ready and Martha a true queen greets each friend with a certain ceremony. Martha is photographed and interviewed by a reporter from a leading newspaper to whom she gives the Baha'i Message and a red rose bud. People watch Martha moving about the ship with her retinue wondering who she is for they feel the spiritual vibrations. Time is up; Martha gives each a rose, anoints each forehead with perfume, breath[e]s a gentle Alla-o-Abha and bestows a farewell kiss. We gather at the dock, about fifty of us waving roses while Martha elevates her bouquet and trails over the ship's side a turquoise scarf[,] her lips saying again and again, "Alla-o[-]Abha."
>
> So blessed Martha, her period of ill-health past, dons her armour of service and with shining eyes and heart overflowing with love, valiantly sets forth, not alone, but companied by a host of chosen angels, the prayers of the Guardian and of the friends. She hears the cry of the orient in its hour of dire distress and hastens there to offer the supreme remedy.[30]

Joyce Dahl has written that the parting was an event of great poignancy. Many of the Bahá'ís "had a foreboding" that Martha "was leaving the United States for the last time." But Martha's departure was not an occasion for sadness. Rather, "it was truly the departure of a 'queen'. . . . She made it a spiritual occasion of lasting effect. Her consecration to the Faith was the power which melted the barriers on her way."[31] Another person who saw Martha off recalled, with a touch of humor, "We saw her almost immediately after coming to the rail, speaking with a Japanese lady at her side, and everyone was saying, there, she's telling her about the Faith."[32]

With anchor weighed, the *Tatsuta Maru* pulled away from the pier, the sonorous whistles triumphantly announcing the ship's freedom from confinement as it faced the open seas and carried its precious cargo. Martha waved her turquoise scarf at the fading forms in San Francisco, then turned her eyes toward the East and the mystery of the Orient. For Martha, a leave taking was always coupled with a returning. It was a circular motion.

Part 4 / *The Warp and the Weft*

51 Cataclysmic Moods of Man and Nature

It was a summer ocean over which the *Tatsuta Maru* sailed. When the ship stopped in Hawaii for several hours on 25 May 1937, Martha was met at the pier by friends, who greeted her with traditional Hawaiian floral leis. She was also interviewed at the pier, as she had been, almost routinely, in other parts of the world. Without losing any time, she visited a Chinese professor at the university and then spent the day with Bahá'ís as the guest of Katherine Baldwin. With the Committee of Three left behind on another shore, Martha felt freer to resume what was for her a regular schedule; but while she still felt the echoes of the committee's concern, she would be judicious about her activities in order to conserve her strength.

The beauty of the islands penetrated her being, and she felt a power in them. In a letter to her friends she observed that

> The Hawaiian Islands have a unique role in the drama of a New World Order. Situated between the Orient and the Occident, with a population representing both the West and the East, the Bahá'ís there can be a potent force for international understanding and peace in the Pacific.[1]

Back on board the ship, and sailing for Yokohama, Martha obtained permission to give her lecture "What is the Bahá'í Movement?" The talk drew strong criticism from three American missionaries who asserted that only Christians could be saved. However, their comments only strengthened the Bahá'í message for most of the passengers, who had been reared in Eastern religions. At the request of the captain, who had introduced her talk, she wrote an article about the lecture and the Bahá'í Faith, which she had mimeographed. Even before Martha set foot on Japanese soil, journalists on board were eager to know more about the Faith, and the duplicated articles were ready to give to the waiting press corps.

Martha's arrival in Yokohama marked the beginning of her fourth visit to Japan. But this time there was no Agnes Alexander waiting for her at the pier. Agnes had gone on pilgrimage to Haifa and from there would return to Hawaii. With Shoghi Effendi's perception of the dangerous world condition, Agnes' return to Japan would be postponed indefinitely. Martha would be doing no spiritual skylarking with her old friend.

During her three weeks in Japan Martha accomplished a remarkable amount of work. There were many meetings, lectures, and interviews, all of which generated publicity that warmed her heart. People sought her out, and Martha's connections from past visits were invaluable. Arthur Garrels, the American consul general, whose friendship dated back to her 1915 efforts in Egypt to get funds to 'Abdu'l-Bahá, gave a dinner for her in his home and invited her to speak about the Bahá'í Faith. Martha traveled from Tokyo to Kyoto, Osaka, Nara, and Kobe. She spoke along the way to Esperantists and managed to visit almost every Bahá'í in Japan.

One of the qualities that drew those in other lands to Martha was her open-mindedness. Wherever she traveled, she strove to meet the leaders of other religions and movements rather than to avoid them because of their different beliefs. As she listened to their philosophies, she shared her own ideas and exchanged literature. In Japan there were several such movements, and Martha urged their leaders to consider using Esperanto as a means of broader communication. They, in turn, did not feel threatened and would remember her with fondness.

Mr. Torii, the blind Bahá'í who had met Martha in 1930, which he thought would be for the last time, did have another opportunity to meet her. With his wife, he entertained Martha and spent as much time as possible with her, sharing the Bahá'í teachings and absorbing her love. When it was time for Martha to leave, he and his wife went to the pier and waited devotedly until the ship sailed, unperturbed by journalists and photographers who gathered for final interviews and pictures. Martha had her last glimpse of this troubled, beautiful country on 26 June, when her ship headed toward China. She would be

*Martha Root (front row, left) on her last visit
to Japan, June 1937. With her are Mr. Tokujiro Torii, a
blind Bahá'í whom she had met in 1930, and (standing, right
to left) Mrs. Tokujiro Torii, Mrs. Torii's sister, and Mr. Kikutaro.
Martha is holding a picture of Mr. Torii's son.*

the last Bahá'í to visit Japan until after the Second World War.

The city of Shanghai loomed ahead. It was for Martha another homecoming, and she anticipated months of fruitful work among the Oriental people. After finding quarters in the Shanghai International Settlement, she started distributing a number of Bahá'í books. She met with the Bahá'ís and set up speaking and broadcasting dates. But she could feel the disquiet that permeated the air.

The tension between China and Japan was extreme. The waters had been churning since 1915, when Japan had set out twenty-one demands to China. The leaders of tiny waterbound Japan looked with envy toward the vast lands of China, with its resources of manpower and material. Their choice of action was clear—they would provoke war, bring China under Japanese suzerainty, and then turn their sights toward the world. Martha had stepped into an inferno.

The Shanghai International Settlement was deemed to be

MARTHA ROOT
in Shanghai, 1 July 1937, before the
bombings forced her to leave in late August

safe from attack as the cauldron boiled at the hottest time of
year. Martha continued her work. To libraries she sent Bahá'í
books in Chinese and English, with letters of explanation. She
had already lectured at Nankai University, where she knew the
president, and was in the process of mailing them books when
she learned that the university had just been destroyed by
bombs. The uneasy peace had been shattered:

> August 8—I had a large number of books with explanatory
> letters ready to mail—my inner vision warned me to get
> them out to the people. I found my street so blocked with fif-
> ty thousand Chinese people fleeing into the Shanghai Inter-
> national Settlement area carrying their household belong-
> ings in their arms . . . [or] in rickshas that I was afraid to
> step outside the door into that mob.[2]

With the help of Persian friends and "No. 1 boy," a young
man from the settlement, Martha succeeded in getting books
to the post office for mailing. The next day, when traffic was a
little lighter, a Persian driver in a loaned car took her to set up
talks in the various YMCAs, as well as other places. Most of
those she contacted could think of nothing but protection for
their people and were not scheduling events.

Martha always brought a gift, however humble, when meeting others; it was a token of love, a bridge between individuals or cultures, and it made an occasion of the visit. To the Chinese women who were rolling bandages to bind the wounds of those soldiers ravaged by war, Martha brought, among other gifts, "a hand-embroidered towel mother had made for me years ago; . . . I wanted her to have a part in serving China and I felt that up there in the Heavenly Realm she was praying for us all."[3] Somehow it did not seem to be the perfect gift for the occasion.

On 10 August Martha met with the Bahá'ís, and together they read from Bahá'u'lláh's writings and said a prayer for protection. She likened that meeting to the Last Supper. The next day the attacks began:

> August 14—The air . . . [raids] came over the Shanghai International Settlement! The whirring, the stacatto [sic] louder and louder . . . over our heads, then a . . . [silence] then the horror, the shock, the shaking house and the awful explosions of bursting bombs, it was HELL upon earth! . . . I was on the fifth floor, the top floor and I thought our house was falling. I was living one-half block from the place they were aiming to bomb and less than two blocks from Palace Hotel and Cathay . . . [Hotel] where the bombs crashed . . . [through] thundering death. I prayed Ya Alláh-El-Mostaghas!* and bowed my head thinking the next one might fall on me. It was doomsday! The mind lives a lifetime in a moment! But the planes soared farther away and the bombing stopped for that time.[4]

Martha called the American consulate, but their building was no safer than hers, and she realized that it would be difficult to fit four thousand nationals into one consulate. More important, she knew she did not have the strength to go, to battle the crowds and the debris. Such a climate of unrest would limit any further Bahá'í work, and she prepared for flight. Much of her luggage had not yet been unpacked, and she gathered the rest of her articles together:

---

*O God, the Refuge.

444 THE WARP AND THE WEFT

twelve . . . [suitcases] were in perfect order with everything
in each one tabulated, but I called No. 1 boy and Coolie boy
and feverishly piled on top of each bag the . . . [contents]
of the table, the bureau drawers, the clothes press, locked
and strapped every bag and had them put in a pile in the hall.
The books had already been pa[ck]ed and strapped—it was
a relief to work and try to forget.

Martha had just finished packing when the planes came again:

We ran out into the hall in the middle of the house, the
twenty of us and hurried down the narrow stairway to the
elevator—the elevator only came to the fourth floor. We
stayed down there till dark. I sat with bowed head and
prayed, but with each explosion it seemed as if I never could
survive another. Never in my life have I seen such nervous
people, it does something to the human system, it shocks
and strains and undoes the physical organism. . . . That
evening the air raids ceased about seven o'clock and machine gun war continued outside the settlem[e]nt. Sunday
August 15—I had . . . [slept] with my clothes on, with my
coat and handbag on the chair beside the bed. The airplane
raiding began at six o'clock. The morning paper stated that
more than . . . [twelve] hundred had been killed by the
bombs the day before in our settlement.[5]

All meetings were canceled. The British Steamship Company promised Martha a ticket to Hong Kong for 25 August,
and the American consulate urged her to take it. Among the
Bahá'ís who were still able to contact her was Mr. Ouskouli,
who was staying in his office in the capitol building a short distance from Martha's lodging. When he came to see her, she had
him pack up forty parcels of six small books each, which she
would take to Hong Kong. But by the time they were ready to
go, the phones had stopped working, and the devastation from
the sky had recommenced. Martha repeated over and over
again some words from the Bahá'í writings, " 'By Myself, We
have accepted from you that which you desired and We will be
with you in all times.' " Although she had doubts about the
propriety of praying for her life, she supplicated, " ' Thy Will,

Thy Will! Give me the courage! But O God, please make it as easy for us as You can!' "[6]

On 16 August, early in the morning, the bombs once again pelted Shanghai. Although she felt ill, she made her way to a telephone on the lower floor of the house and tried for hours to reach the British Steamship Company in order to confirm her trip to Hong Kong. All the lines were busy. When her call did go through, the response was not reassuring. " 'The government has commandeer[e]d the ship for British subjects, we could not give you the passage.' "[7]

Undaunted, she telephoned an American steamship company, the Dollar Line, and was offered a passage on the *President Jefferson* the next day. The ship was, unfortunately, bound for Manila instead of Hong Kong, but Martha had no choice other than to accept the passage. She promised to get to the ticket office as soon as possible, and then she returned to her room. But there was no comfort; the bombings increased, and she was nauseated. A tenant in the house recommended that she go to a hospital where she would be safe. But Martha replied, "No, . . . this place is like my home, if I pass, I will pass here."[8]

Once the phones were again working, Martha called the American consulate and asked them to notify the Dollar Line that she was too ill to get there with the money. But she begged them to keep her name on the list. When the final arrangements were made, Martha was told that she would be allowed to take only one suitcase. Mr. Ouskouli offered to take the rest of Martha's luggage but gave her no guarantee that it would be safe. Fortunately, she was permitted to take her typewriter when they learned she was a journalist.

During the night before Martha's departure, the airplanes continued to drop their bombs until midnight. Martha huddled downstairs with the other people in the house, who were singing popular songs. "The more deadly and deafening the explosions, the louder they sang," Martha recounted. " 'Be a good sport!' was their motto. One could not say much about prayer to them, but they were brave and kind. One cannot face death over and over in this bomb explosions [sic] and not be completely unnerved."[9]

Fraught with fear, Martha was startled the next morning when she opened her bag and saw a tiny package fall into her hand. Upon it was written, "'Alláh-u-Abhá!* A Hair from the Head of Bahá'u'lláh.'" A passage from the Kitáb-i-Íqán flashed through her mind: "'one Hair of Whose Head is worth more than all in the heavens and the earth'." For Martha the package was a "Promise of safety" from Bahá'u'lláh.[10] Perhaps she would not die in Shanghai after all.

Martha was ready to go, but before she left, she called for "No. 1 boy and Coolie boy," the two teenagers who had helped her during her stay in Shanghai. "Their service and nobility," Martha said, "would be fine in any race, in any country." She put her arms around them, handed each a small sum of money, a gift to her when she left San Francisco, and admonished them to save it to buy rice when they ran out of food. It was difficult for Martha to leave them behind, for she had tried to be "true to them as a mother would be."[11] She hoped that they would not starve or fall victim to the bombings. That was their farewell.

Martha made one last phone call to the steamship company to confirm her ticket and was told that she could not go unless she had purchased her ticket the day before. With a touch of panic she replied, "'I must go, I'm coming with my bag. My name is in your book!'" Mr. Ouskouli was waiting, and they quickly climbed in a ricksha and raced to the steamship office. All that Martha carried with her were a few Bahá'í books, the manuscript of her book on Ṭáhirih, and a few changes of clothing. "As I ride down the street . . . with my bag and typewriter on my lap," she recorded, "my mind says: 'Now I too, am a refugee, . . . fleeing through the streets to find safety!'"[12]

When she arrived at the ship's office, there were five hundred Americans trying to get tickets. As she handed the agent her passport and the money for her own ticket, she wondered if he would still honor her reservation. He smiled and, to Martha's relief, said, "'I'll give you a ticket'." After saying their

---

*A greeting among Bahá'ís meaning "God is All-Glorious."

good-byes, Mr. Ouskouli helped Martha into the tender that would take her to the anchored ship. She wrote:

> The tender was packed! No flowers, no songs. Husbands with lifted hats tried to smile bravely to wives and children as we were hurried down stairs [*sic*] out of sight. . . . In our tender were one hundred and fifty children, seventy five [*sic*] of them less than six years old. Suddenly . . . we hear the airplanes go up. (A promise had been given there would be no fighting in the air when the women and children were evacuated.) We tried to crouch to the floor, there was wild excitement, two explosions came, but we moved forward. Twice snipers shot over the tender, but we were unhurt.
>
> Then another danger came. We had come up from downstairs to the deck . . . ready to go on board the President Jefferson, after a two hour ride out to sea. The waves were so high, the tender pitched[;] we were falling one over another. The Navy men called out to go back down stairs [*sic*]. It seemed impossible, but men helped us and we went down. Water was pouring into one porthole. A strong American sailor pushed that porthole shut, but as he could not fasten it, he braced his whole strength against it and held it. . . . The tender almost turned somersaults. Children shrieked with terror, women fainted and many people became fearfully seasick. But the tender reached the President Jefferson and was anchored against her. [13]

When Martha boarded the ship and sat down in what was the music room, there was a group of Chinese waiting to take the tender back to Shanghai. She spoke about the Bahá'í Faith to a man sitting next to her and discovered that he was a journalist returning from Columbia University. " ' I know the Bahá'í Faith very well,' " he said, to Martha's surprise. " 'I know you, you are Miss Martha Root and you gave us a lecture about the Bahá'í principles in the University of Michigan at Ann Arbor in 1931.' " [14] The strands stretched far.

When it was Martha's time to hand in her ticket, the purser discovered that she was on the wrong ship. The passage had been reserved for the *President McKinley;* Martha was on board the *President Jefferson.* The ship's crew certainly would not deposit her into the ocean, and the purser assured her that he and the crew were happy for her presence.

The ship, normally accommodating seventy-five passengers, now had seven hundred. Cots were placed in every available space. Martha gave it a worldly glance: "The place looked like what might be a beautiful American harem! So many pretty girls and young women in every modish type of shorts and slacks and negliges [sic], with . . . [fingernails] and toe nails [sic] delicately tinted." One woman on shipboard remembered Martha from her visit to Singapore in 1930. "'We always remember you,'" she said, "'for when you left you shook hands with every one of . . . [the] servants. . . . You were a Bahá'í.'"[15]

A telegram of welcome to the refugees reached the ship from Manila, where there were no air raids, no machine guns. Forgoing dinner, Martha was one of the first to disembark, as she wanted to mail her account of the Shanghai adventure as soon as possible. The place was packed with servicemen and boy scouts, and a band played a rousing welcome. Also, there was a refugee committee to assist the travelers to find lodging. Martha was interviewed by a newspaper reporter, and the next day a headline read, "A Bahá'i lecturer says war is hell."[16]

A gentleman named Mr. Gourlie waited on shore to assist her. As they were going down the long central aisle at customs to get Martha's suitcase, she was startled:

Suddenly in this immense and very high structure of cement and steel the ground began to shake violently and to move up towards our faces! The noise above of steel and rattling iron made me think that airplanes were raiding Manila and the explosions were tearing up the earth under our feet!
. . . We tried to run forward, but we were very far from the exit. People were stampeding, rushing, crushing! Then the lights all went out. Officials cried: "Stand still! Don't crowd!" Mr. Gourlie said to me: "Be calm! Don't be afraid! Don't be afr[a]id!" I replied: "Yes, I am calm, I am not afr[a]id!" But all the time I thought: "the crowds are crushing us, the earth will swallow us, the whole building is crashing down on us!" I thought it was death! Then all at once the floors stopped moving up and down, then the . . . [lights]

came on and there stood the officers, clubs upraised commanding the people not to crowd.[17]

Martha survived it all. After escaping from the bombing in Shanghai, she was greeted in Manila with one of the worst earthquakes in The Philippines in a century. She was grateful to have come through both tragedies unscathed. But she was concerned about the loss in Shanghai of her papers, the work of a lifetime, which included the irreplaceable, information-filled address books from all over the world. Thus far, it had not exactly been an idyllic, restful journey for a convalescent. But Martha was happy; she had received a telegram from Shoghi Effendi: "'Praying fervently yourself Shanghai friends. Love. Shoghi.'"[18] The message seemed too precious to keep to herself. She would try to have it sent through amateur radio to the Bahá'ís in Shanghai.

Although there were finer accommodations in the Manila suburbs, Martha chose a little hotel in town run by Cantonese; she had not had the opportunity to teach them while in China, but she would manage it in Manila. It was noisy and hard to write at the hotel, but she loved it and the Chinese who ran it. She told American travelers about the hotel, and it was filled almost to capacity before she left. The restaurant was crowded every day. "I helped to 'Americanize' it," she said. "We are great pals."[19] It was an exchange of courtesies; the Cantonese owners were soon inviting Chinese journalists and friends to learn about the Bahá'í Faith.

Despite the comparative peace of Manila after Shanghai, Mother Nature was not quiescent. As often happens, lesser earthquakes occurred after the major upheaval, and a typhoon followed. When Martha explored the possibilities of getting to Singapore and Hong Kong, she learned that Singapore had an outbreak of cholera and Hong Kong was about to receive hundreds of refugees from the blighted city. After searching among twenty steamship lines, she booked passage to Bombay. But she postponed being vaccinated for smallpox and cholera so that she could work in Manila without being interrupted by a reaction from the serum.

Travel costs continued to be of concern to Martha, especially after her decision to be less Spartan about her living accommodations. From Manila she wrote to the National Spiritual Assembly of the Bahá'ís of the United States and Canada and wondered if they might possibly advance her some money on her Keystone Company stocks. The firm was a sound and secure stereopticon company owned by her cousin Sidney Hart, but one slow to yield financial bonuses. "I would use it," she explained, "to travel II Class and in British or comfortable Indian hotels through India for then my health would be better and I could do better work for Bahá'u'lláh. I'm so eager to do my best for the time is very short." She went on to say, "I believe the great world war will soon be upon us. Also my years are few." Having made the suggestion, Martha, who had always maintained her financial independence even at the risk of health and basic comfort, was anxious lest the National Spiritual Assembly feel she might need support. She withdrew the proposed idea and went on to emphasize that "this letter isn't asking you to do anything about that Keystone [stock]. Everything is Bahá'u'lláh's and I know each soul must solve his own financial problem—Bahá'u'lláh tells us so, and *I will*. I'm trying. I'll be independent of everything save Him." [20]

Martha also expressed to the National Spiritual Assembly her regret at having had to leave many Bahá'í books in Shanghai that had been supplied by the Assembly. "I hope you won't be sorry you gave me so many books for Japan & China," she wrote with a touch of remorse. "I had mailed some of them to Chan S. Liu, and if Shanghai isn't burned entirely (and it *may* be) the books will be found and treasured by the Chinese." [21] The idea of being the cause of loss, waste, expense, or inconvenience to anyone made Martha distinctly uncomfortable. This feeling was especially acute when she was communicating with a loving and cooperative National Spiritual Assembly. However, the National Assembly, more concerned for her safety than for the books, was thankful that Martha Root, who had practically become a national institution, was alive.

On 31 August 1937 Martha went aboard the *President Pierce* and sailed out of Manila at dawn the next day. She was headed for Bombay to open another chapter in her life's work, sow more seeds, and weave more strands of unity and peace.

52 India—Beyond the Possible

As the *President Pierce* skimmed through the South China Sea and around the Malaysian Peninsula, Martha renewed her spiritual resources and prepared for the work ahead. After a brief stop at Penang, the ship sailed into Colombo, Ceylon (now Sri Lanka), in mid-September 1937. When Martha stepped onto the pier, she began one of the most ambitious and intensive teaching trips of her lifetime—a fifteen-and-a-half-month journey through India, Ceylon, and Burma during which she would reach millions of people with the message of Bahá'u'lláh.

In Colombo Martha spent a month teaching and resting before going on to Bombay, India, where she arrived on 15 October. She was met by hundreds of Bahá'ís, including the National Spiritual Assembly of India and Burma, which had especially arranged a semiannual meeting to be held there during Martha's stay.

Mystic India, with its population of 350 million in 1937, was quieter than it had been during Martha's 1930 visit, when mobs roamed the streets and machine guns were mounted on police cars outside the Buddhist temple in Calcutta where Martha gave her last talk. Now India was like a somnolent tiger, watching, waiting, before springing to action. Mahatma Gandhi used the years between 1934 and 1939 for negotiation, searching out ways for India's independence; meanwhile, he was carrying on countless activities of planting, educating, spinning. Unfortunately, Gandhi was ill when Martha was in his vicinity; hence these two great peace workers never met.

In anticipation of Martha's arrival, the National Assembly had arranged a lecture tour for her and had mobilized the Bahá'ís throughout the subcontinent to assist her in every way possible. They would defray a substantial portion of her expenses, which Martha did not consider a compromise of her integrity, as she was responding to specific teaching directives of the National Assembly. Martha undoubtedly added considerably to the skeleton arrangements that were set up.

A fair-sized book could be written on Martha's incredible teaching trip through India. Her travels were vast, her lectures and meetings seemingly beyond human scope. Each day was filled. She would travel first with one person, whose schedule would give way to another, and to yet another, as Martha intrepidly went forward. She made a point of meeting and interviewing scholars of the East, getting their philosophical views and seemingly always favorable comments about the Bahá'í Faith.

Martha started her teaching program in Bombay, where lectures were introduced by government officials. Press representatives were in attendance, and she generated the sort of publicity for the Faith that any public figure would envy. Martha went on to Surat and Poona, after which she made the two-day trip across the continent to Calcutta on the west coast. From there she sailed across the Bay of Bengal into Rangoon, Burma.

Martha was back in stride, perhaps a shade less vigorous, but still taking on an enormously difficult schedule. In Burma she lectured daily in Rangoon, Mandalay, Toungoo, Daidanaw, and Kunjangoon, all involving arduous traveling from one place to another. Everywhere she was introduced by persons of note. Bands played, and choirs chanted. The gargantuan spirit in the fragile frame was eloquently received. It was noted that " 'Miss Martha Root created a stir in the religious circles of that great city [Rangoon] of 500,000 souls comprised of almost all civilized nations of the world.' "[1]

With fifteen youngsters Martha started a children's class and had them all memorize passages from the writings of Bahá'u'lláh. She was beguiling with children and was tolerant where others scolded. It was as if she saw beyond the occasionally annoying habits of the child to a full-blown, loving human being, encased within the miniature body.

In Mandalay, Martha was cheered by meeting an old friend, Siyyid Muṣṭafá Rúmí, who had been " 'efficiently and faithfully promoting the Bahá'í Faith in Burma for sixty years!'"[2] It was his ringstone that she had given to the emperor of Japan in 1930. Martha was more impressed than ever with Siyyid Muṣṭafá's keen intellect and the sweep of his accomplishments, including his fine translations. She noted that, even at the age of ninety-four, he led an active life. "From 5 a.m. till nearly midnight he is busy. . . . [He] walks or goes by . . . [street]car all over Mandalay. . . ." When he took Martha to the train station, his eyes filled with "tears of love" as he arranged her bags and saw to her comfort. Incredibly, Martha wrote, "With bowed head . . . I could only pray O Baha'u'- llah make me a Bahai teacher!" And she thanked Bahá'u'lláh for the beauty of the days in Burma and for "the immeasurable bounty for meeting the friends" there.[3]

On 23 November Martha began the two-day boat trip back to Calcutta, where she participated in the Second Indian Cultural Conference during the first week in December, followed by the First Convention of Religions, 8–11 December. Rabindranath Tagore, poet and scholar, was to have presided at the cultural conference where Martha was scheduled to speak. When he became ill, Sarojini Naidu, Mahatma Gandhi's helper, was asked to officiate. Mrs. Naidu spotted Martha Root sitting in the front row and had her escorted to the platform to sit beside her. Such were the honors and attention given to Martha Root.

It seemed to be the season for conferences. Martha tried to attend as many as possible of those with a universal focus. She was at the Ninth All-India Oriental Conference, 20–22 December, in Trivandrum, Travancore, and the International Theosophical Convention in Adyar, Madras, between Christmas Day 1937 and 3 January 1938. Accompanying her was Iṣfándiar Bakhtiari, a member of the National Spiritual Assembly of the Bahá'ís of India and Burma, and her traveling companion in India in 1930. Martha predicted that great opportunities for teaching the Faith would result from speaking at such conferences, for "the Call is raised to thousands, the newspapers carry the resumés [sic] of the lectures and there are innumerable opportunities to speak individually with people of capacity, the thinkers of India; for it is usually the progressive, liberal souls, those determined to help make a better world, who go to such congresses." Later she remarked, "The great scholars of this and the coming generation will be quickened or left unawakened perhaps by the way we present the Cause to them."[4]

In these cities Martha did not limit herself to the conferences. She covered a broad range of clubs, schools, and special groups where she spoke and also maintained contacts with the press, scholars, and librarians.

Following the conferences Martha was joined by two new traveling companions from Ajmer, Dr. K. M. Fozdar and his wife, Shirin, who had also spoken at the First Convention of Religions in December. Together they sailed to Colombo, Ceylon, on 5 January to spend ten days on this island off the southeast tip of India. It was Martha's second visit there in four months. They lectured at Colombo University, the Ramakrishna School, and the Women's International, Parsi, and

MARTHA ROOT with DR. K. M. and SHIRIN FOZDAR
who traveled with her in India and Ceylon in 1938,
Shirin for several weeks

Rotary clubs. The latter lecture was broadcast over the radio from the luncheon table and was subsequently printed in the Colombo newspapers. Another broadcast was made by Shirin Fozdar, who spoke about the Persian poet Ṭáhirih and sang one of her poems.

Dr. Fozdar returned to his hospital work at Ajmer, but Shirin traveled back to Madras with Martha via Bangalore and Mysore. Along the way they spoke at universities and made broadcasts. Shirin "is not only a very fluent speaker," Martha noted, "but they called her the Bahá'í nightingale of India when she sang the Qurratu'l-'Ayn [Ṭáhirih] songs!"[5] On 31 January both of them were honored as guests of the state in Hyderbad, Deccan, where Martha broadcast a talk within one-and-a-half hours of arriving.

There were five packed days in Hyderabad before Martha and Shirin boarded an early train for Poona, a city that Martha called a "Bahá'í paradise" and "one of the high spiritual lights in India." There she found that the Bahá'ís had made expert arrangements that were better than any she had encountered in all her travels. "The entire stay was so WELL arranged," Martha remembered, "that even New York and Tihrán would say 'Bravo!'"[6] Separate teas were given in Martha's honor for lawyers, for educators, and for journalists, who received copies of Martha's talk on journalism. She gave several lectures, one to an audience of one thousand in a theater. And she paid visits to the Bahá'í school in Poona. "The children gathered round her," one Bahá'í remembered. "They were not afraid of her as they were of other older persons who came, but the way she spoke made them feel one with her. . . . she had a deep, rich voice, like a caress. . . . they felt the love offering from her. . . ."[7]

Two sisters, Monira and Gol Yaganegi (later Monira Sohaili and Gol Aidun), vividly remember Martha's visit to the school on 7 February 1938. "Her face stayed with me throughout childhood," Monira, then six or seven, recalled. "I could never forget the vision of this wonderful person, her face was so radiant. . . ."[8]

Martha sat at one end of the hall facing the twenty to thirty students. She had brought gifts for the youngsters: she called each one's name and gave each a prayer book with the name written in—for example, "Very dear Monira"—together with a spiritual message and encouragement to teach the Faith. When Gol, the older sister, was to receive her book, they were all gone, a miscalculation of one. But Martha said, " 'You can have my own little moneybag.' " And she took out a little purse and gave it to Gol. An older girl, about twelve, who sensed Martha's station, burst into tears at this prize, Martha Root's own little purse, given to some other child. She went into a room and would not come out. When Gol was asked to give up her gift to soothe ruffled feelings, she turned it over, reluctantly; years later she still regretted the necessity. Martha, ever resourceful, gave her a picture of 'Abdu'l-Bahá and wrote on the back words attributed to Bahá'u'lláh: " 'If one speck of a jewel be hid in a stone and that stone be beyond the seven seas, until I have sought and found that jewel, my hand from its search will not stay.' "⁹ Martha added warm, personal words, the date, and place—February 7, 1938, Poona, India.

Mr. Yaganegi, who later owned the National Hotel where Martha was staying, kept her room, number 9, for special Bahá'í guests. In his will he instructed that half the earnings of the hotel be used as scholarships for poor and deprived children to attend the New Era High School in Panchgani, near Poona, in the name of Martha Root.¹⁰

Early on the morning of 9 February, Martha and Shirin took a train back to Bombay. There Martha discovered, to her delight, that her luggage had been rescued from the Shanghai bombings and had been sent to Bombay by Mr. Ouskouli with a traveler from Peking. It was a welcome reunion with old companions—her various suitcases containing massive amounts of literature and the indispensable address books. Martha was happy.

Martha was also happy about the unusual newspaper and magazine coverage that she was able to achieve. Over two hundred articles about the Faith had appeared in Ceylon and India since her arrival in September. She urged "all Bahá'í teachers when possible, to carry a typewriter and make out good resumés [sic] of all lectures and give out to newspapers. When one speaks, one may speak to hundreds, but through the press one can reach tens of thousands and sometimes hundreds of thousands."[11] Martha, with typewriter and luggage, was ready to set out once more from Bombay on her tour.

In cities and towns, in theaters and universities, in schools and auditoriums where lectures were given, the audience was generally receptive and enthusiastic, though not always. In one city a woman who was opposed to the Faith protested loudly that Martha's speech was not the subject advertised and that it was irrelevant. Martha stepped down from the platform, walked to the woman, warmly embraced her, and returned to her place. The disrupter was nonplussed; it was not the expected answer to an argument. Martha continued her talk unruffled, not at all disturbed by the outburst.

On 13–14 February 1938, again traveling with Işfándiar Bakhtiari, Martha made her second trip to the Visva-Bharati University of Rabindranath Tagore. She felt deeply privileged to meet, finally, this world figure, this Nobel-prize-winning poet. His humanistic ideas radiated beyond the borders of India, and his views often determined Mahatma Gandhi's actions. In 1912 he had met 'Abdu'l-Bahá in Chicago and had ever after been impressed with the ideals of the Bahá'í Faith. Someday he hoped that a "Bahá'í Chair of Religion" could be established at his university.[12]

In the environment of tolerant thought and artistic pursuits, practiced in an atmosphere of goodwill and spiritual integrity, Martha lectured to the student body and the professors. Many of them practiced Brahmo Samaj, founded by Tagore's grandfather, who designed the movement especially to combine Hinduism and Christianity. The school was made up of Hindus, Muslims, Sikhs, Christians, Buddhists, and followers of other Eastern religions. A professor, Alex Aronson, a refugee from Nazi Germany, had been welcomed in India after completing his studies at Cambridge and was teaching at Tagore's university. "I was for many years the only 'white' man (i.e. European) teaching at the university," he later wrote, "and succeeded in adjusting myself completely to their way of life. . . ." When he listened to Martha speak, he was disturbed:

I experienced a strong feeling of protest—not against Baha'i about which I knew next to nothing then—but against the intrusion of "white" cultural values which I thought had no place in India. Indians, I felt, could very well take care of themselves, especially in matters of the spirit. To me at that time the West (which of course included America as well) was all potentially Nazi, anti-spiritual, anti-intellectual, anti-moral.

During Martha's lecture Mr. Aronson stood up before the assemblage and spoke against what he thought to be "unwarranted interference in matters of which the West was not qualified to speak." He later realized that he had spoken against the Bahá'í Faith out of ignorance of its teachings; but he remembered that "Martha Root took my protest-speech with much equanimity."[13]

It was not Martha's way to be contentious. When there were hostile remarks, she let them stand and continued in her unique way to demonstrate love. As a result, the unattractive qualities of the adversary stood out by contrast. This is not to say that Martha refused to deal with differing ideas when there was honest intent; they were encouraged. But when Martha was confronted with blind antagonism and hostility, there was no refutation, and no discussion followed.

In early March Martha went on alone to Surat to finish some writing. She stayed at the home of N. R. Vakil, the first Hindu to become a Bahá'í. Martha would walk out and sit by the waterfront; it was there that she put the finishing touches on her book, *Táhirih the Pure*, the story of one of the earliest followers of the Báb, and the first woman to recognize Him. Years later Monira Sohaili went with Dorothy Baker to this home, overlooking the water. "Dorothy Baker stopped at the very threshold of the room," Monira recalled, "she didn't go further. All standing there wondered why she suddenly stopped; she was in deep thought with a far distant look, and then she came in and sat down and said, 'You know that Miss Martha Root was here.'"[14]

Martha returned to Bombay on 15 March to pick up an undeviatingly heavy schedule of lectures and broadcasts. One who was asked to assist Martha during her stay in Bombay was thirteen-year-old Meherangiz (now Munsiff), a child from a deeply spiritual Bahá'í family. Her life was forever enriched by her days with Martha Root, whom she described as a "diminutive, fragile looking figure with blue sparkling eyes and short-cut white hair." Meherangiz recalled that Martha was given a large, comfortable room in "one of the leading western-style hotels overlooking the Arabian Sea," where Meherangiz spent many hours alone with Martha. She observed Martha immersed in prayer,

> in the typical eastern fashion over a small mat spread on the floor. She recited many prayers some from the prayer-book and many by heart, in her impressive soft voice. The sincerity exuding from her prayers and that sincere face with closed eyes when in the seclusion of her own chamber was so pronounced that it made me feel that she had some sort of direct connection with . . . [Bahá'u'lláh] and the Almighty.

Meherangiz became aware that Martha suffered from a painful back ailment that she kept a secret from others lest they become "unduly concerned" for her health. Although she alleviated her distress with a hot-water bottle, she "showed little concern for her health or regard for personal comforts" but "on all occasions . . . showed unwavering determination to serve the Faith. . . ."[15]

An amusing incident observed by Meherangiz reinforced her feeling that Martha might have a direct line to Powers beyond:

> a leading citizen of Bombay . . . had presided over a public meeting addressed by M.R. He hurried away after the meeting, giving the excuse that he was much worried about his mother, who was suffering from cancer and was on the verge of death. M.R. consoled him . . . and assured him that she would pray for his mother's health, that night. Next day this gentleman contacted a local Baha'i and conveyed that his mother's health had miraculously taken a turn for the better. However he was not particularly pleased . . . because the

woman was his step-mother, who was wealthy and he would stand to inherit a small fortune in the event of her death. He respectfully indicated that M.R. need not trouble herself with more prayers for his step-mother. I recollect beloved M.R.'s reaction of "Oh dear!" when this incident was reported to her. A charming chuckle crept over that sweet face which showed her age and toll taken by many years of weary travels.

At another time Martha was advised not to travel north to a particular town because the weather during that time of the year was "fierc[e]ly hot." But she was determined to make the trip, and she brought Meherangiz with her. After a "long exhausting journey by train," they arrived at their destination, which was, as predicted, "intensely hot" and "uncomfortably dry." The next morning, however, the villagers were amazed to find that

> there had been unexpected drizzles during the night, the morning was filled with cool breeze, and some jasmine flowers exuding their light scent. Such a change in the weather, the local inhabitants had not known in their life time. We Baha'is know that the weather had acknowledged the presence of a special person in that region![16]

Martha later told her young companion that she would pray for her to become a Bahá'í teacher and travel all over the world. Meherangiz knew that her limited circumstances would not permit trips outside of India. But events were shaped differently: "During the last three decades . . . ," Meherangiz wrote in 1980, "I have had the bounty of visiting and travel-teaching in 110 countries and main islands of the world. . . ."[17] She felt that Martha had not only set the tone and the example, but had somehow managed to arrange the rest of the details.

Martha stayed in Bombay for nearly three weeks, 15 March to 5 April 1938, after which she spent a week with Shirin Fozdar at her home in Ajmer. Part of Martha's time at the Fozdars' was used to prepare a talk, "What the Baha'i Faith Can

MARTHA ROOT
21 March 1938, Bombay, India, was welcomed by children
who garlanded her with flowers and presented a pageant
in her honor. Martha, knowing her tenuous hold on life,
was uneasy when she saw herself flanked by angels.

Do For Poverty," for the upcoming All Faiths' League Convention, opening on 18 April in Indore.[18] The talk commanded broad attention. Martha had seven thousand copies printed for widespread distribution, and the United Press sent out two hundred copies to newspapers throughout India. The article was still appearing as late as July, when it was published as a four-column story in the *Rangoon Times*. Martha estimated that the talk appeared in three hundred thousand newspapers.

Among the fifteen hundred scholars and religious leaders present at the All Faiths' League Convention was one participant who read a paper expressing the need for a "great universal religion." After he explained what it should inculcate, a well-known Hindu professor stood up and said, " 'The Baha'i

Faith we have been hearing so much about in this Convention is a universal religion and it inculcates all your suggestions and more. The Baha'i Faith is READY, why not accept it for a universal religion?' " [19] Such was the result of Martha's work.

On 25 April Martha Root and Shirin Fozdar arrived in Karachi for the annual Bahá'í convention of India and Burma. According to Martha, the convention and public meetings created a stir throughout the city; she noted that "every one was talking about the Baha'i Faith." [20] It was a week of meeting friends, teaching, and festivities.

Martha stayed on in Karachi to devote the next three months to a personal goal—the publication of her book on Ṭáhirih, on which she had been working whenever possible since 1930. She had been fascinated by the story of this early follower of the Báb, a first-rank poet who had achieved a spiritual stature and a place in history as a woman and a martyr, and whose work went beyond Iran and into Europe. Her uniqueness, the mystery of her, prodded Martha to write, "My soul thrilled to understand her!" [21]

The history gathered in Qazvin, Iran, from relatives and townspeople, the visit to Ṭáhirih's home, the mood of the place and the times, made it an irresistible topic for a writer. It was especially so for Martha Root, whose life had strong similarities to Ṭáhirih's, notably the sense of purpose. "No thinking man or woman wishes to die," Martha wrote, "without having done something for humanity and for the future generations." As she probed into Ṭáhirih's life, Martha's sense of her own limitations appeared: "Sometimes I have asked myself: 'Was Ṭáhirih great enough instantly to say, "O God, I give my life to establish this Faith among mankind," or did she too, need to be trained by the Infinite God to long to give her life as a martyr to serve this new universal Revelation?' " [22]

Three thousand copies of *Táhirih the Pure, Irán's Greatest Woman*, by Martha L. Root, rolled off the presses in Karachi in 1938. Immediately, the exodus of the work through the mails began, as one thousand copies were mailed out all over the world. Martha felt the power of the printed word: "A preacher preaches to a few hundreds or thousands or tens of thousands,

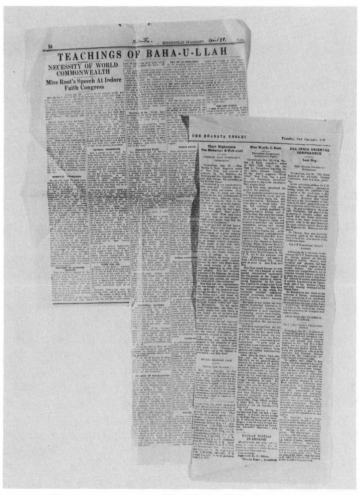

*Newspaper accounts of the Ninth All-India Oriental
Conference in Trivandrum, Travancore, December 1937, and
the All Faith's League Convention in Indore, April 1938. The
two events afforded Martha Root opportunities to reach hundreds
of thousands of people through her oral and written presentations.*

but a book can be a preacher for centuries and to millions yet to be born."[23]

Within a short time translations in Japanese, Czech, Urdu, and Persian were already under way, and fan letters from around the globe were reaching Martha in India. Her vision was being realized "to have the Báb, Baha'u'llah, 'Abdu'l Baha, Shoghi Effendi and Tahirih go together, in this book, on a teaching tour around the whole world!" Martha urged the cooperation of friends everywhere in speaking about Ṭáhirih "in women's clubs, in universities and high schools, over the radio. . . ."[24] Not for many years had this Persian poet received such widespread attention.

Although publishing matters occupied most of Martha's time in Karachi, she did not abandon teaching; she gave talks and lectures several times each week. She again met Sadhu T. L. Vaswani, whom she had first met in 1930. This sage, seer, and educator had met 'Abdu'l-Bahá and was considered one of the four great men of India. He arranged for Martha to go to Hyderabad, Sind, to give a series of twelve lectures, and he personally presided at most of them.

While Martha recognized the importance of meeting scholars, nobility, and leaders of thought, she did not overlook those of the lower social or intellectual strata. There was no stratification in Martha's eyes; all were the handiwork of God. The men of the untouchable caste were astonished, and sometimes embarrassed, when Martha Root offered her hand to them. But it was, nevertheless, a shaft of light in a dark world of rejection. One man in Karachi who desperately wanted to hear her speak was suddenly taken ill with a high temperature and was unable to go to the lecture. When Martha learned of the situation, she left the postlecture gathering and made her way to the place where he lived. It was more a hovel than a room, tucked away at the back of the restaurant where he worked. In this hot, airless space, large enough to hold a cot, and filled with the noise and sounds of people in the streets, Martha sat down by him, took his hand, and said a healing prayer. He never forgot her kindness, nor did he overcome the wonder that she, with half of India at her feet, would come to him, especially in such mean surroundings.

With the publication of her book behind her, Martha left Karachi on 4 August 1938 and started on a long trip to north India, accompanied by Iṣfándiar Ba<u>kh</u>tiari. An enormous amount of literature had been used in the ten months since Martha arrived; now she carried ten thousand pamphlets entitled "The Universal Religion," which were printed in English.[25] Along with many others, these would be given out within the next few weeks.

At Lahore, a center of heat and culture, the colleges were not in session. Since there was little opportunity for public talks, Martha and Mr. Ba<u>kh</u>tiari started on 8 August for Kashmir and the ranges of the Himalayas. They traveled by bus-lorry, the epitome of discomfort under the best of conditions, but frightful with the monsoon season upon them:

> The storms had washed out the mountain road and the thirty motor lorries including ours, had to halt by the mountain road for the afternoon and the night. Next day we walked over the landslide and finally got started in the rain for Srinagar, the summer capital of Kashmir, called "The Jewel of the North". The altitude was very hard for my heart, but Bahá'u'lláh helped me. Wonderful opportunities came in this state, the largest in area in India "blooming on the tops of the mighty Himalayas".[26]

One of those opportunities was an invitation to speak at Krishna's birthday celebration on 19 August, an official function attended by four thousand persons. On her last day in Srinagar, Martha addressed an equally large group, with the aid of loudspeakers, at the Kashmir Exhibition Grounds. Despite these sparkling opportunities, the trip was arduous and a challenge to the physically fit. For Martha, who was ill and in intense pain, it meant surmounting the insurmountable.

Joined by a Bahá'í editor from Lahore, Pritam Singh, on 29 August in Rawalpindi, Martha and Iṣfándiar Ba<u>kh</u>tiari toured the northwest frontier provinces of India, where the Bahá'í Faith had not been known. After a stop in Peshawar, almost sixteen hundred miles from Bombay, they arrived in Gujrat, where they found arrangements primitive, but effective: "Handbills were printed six hours before the lecture," Martha

noted. "Then quickly, men beating drums preceded the hand-
bill distributers [sic] through the streets. The lecture took place
in the Town Hall, the Mayor presided and five hundred people
attended. Always booklets were given out and books put into
the public libraries." A poignant incident that touched Martha's heart occurred as she was about to leave the town: "One
old man at the lecture, was so touched that Bahá'u'lláh had
suffered so much to give His Message to the world, that he
came to the railway station with a bed for one of us to rest on
till the train would start at 4 a.m."[27]

With Martha giving lectures in each place, the trio stopped
at Jammu, Sialkot, Gujranwala, and Lahore. Martha went on
to Simla, where the first Bahá'í summer school of India was
held between 19 and 30 September 1938. A telegram from
Shoghi Effendi assured the Bahá'ís that the school would be
successful, for Martha Root was in attendance. As in 1930, the
altitude in Simla was very hard on Martha's heart. To make it
easier for her, the entire summer school was held at the small
Imperial Hotel where she was staying. Meetings for the first
three days were held in her room, which was larger than the
closet-sized hospice rooms of yore. To Martha it was a

happy, vivid and thrilling spiritual experience for the Bahá'is themselves, for never before have so many of them,
particularly the youth, come together at one time and they
were heard to say that they would attend all future Bahá'i
Summer Schools in India no matter where they are held. The
Bahá'i Summer School has also awakened the Baha'i youth
to their own selves; it has answered many baffling questions
in their young hearts and given them the vision of what Bahá'i youth ought and can do in this critical cataclysm of the
modern world.[28]

Attending the summer school was a quiet time for Martha, a
time of respite, a time to gather strength for the months ahead.
Starting on 5 October, she began, in Lahore, a grueling several-
week tour of the universities of northern India. It was a spectacular feat of endurance, a tour de force, incredibly demanding of the most stalwart travelers and speakers. It was
accomplished by Martha without complaint or reference to

The first Bahá'í summer school in India, 19–30 September 1938. Held in Simla, it was attended by Martha Root (seated, center) from the United States, and by Bahá'ís from Iran, Burma, and all the Spiritual Assemblies in India.

*Martha Root, in the center, wearing a hat, with
a group of Bahá'ís in Calcutta, India, 1938, during her
last monumental trip to the subcontinent*

health, although she was beset by increasing pain, her resistance waning.

After several lectures at universities in Lahore, Martha spoke almost daily—morning, noon, afternoon, and evening—in Amritsar, Jullundur, Ludhiana, Patiala, Delhi, Aligarh, Agra, Rampur, Lucknow, Cawnpore, Allahabad, Benares, Patna, and Calcutta. She covered the territory from the northwest to the southeast of India. Most of the lectures were attended by several hundred persons. She also met with dignitaries and professors, had audiences with Indian princes, and sandwiched in time for visitors during unscheduled hours. It was a virtuoso performance; but in a letter Martha wrote to Lucy Wilson in December 1938, a new note entered: "I am just the same Martha[,] only life gets too much for me."[29]

Martha again crossed the continent from Calcutta to Bombay, where she arrived on 16 December. Here she would spend her last two weeks in India lecturing and putting the finishing touches on a brilliant performance for the Bahá'í Faith. It was

The Bahá'ís of Bombay gathered on 27 December 1938 to bid farewell to their beloved Martha Root (seated, second row, center) after her historic fifteen-month trip to the subcontinent.

time to say good-bye to her Indian friends, among them the members of the National Spiritual Assembly, who had come to Bombay on 26 December to hold a meeting and bid a special farewell to their stalwart teacher. At the annual Bahá'í convention the following April their admiration became clearly evident in their report: "'The most outstanding feature in the year . . . has been the teaching activities of our beloved sister, Miss Martha L. Root. This star servant of Bahá'u'lláh toured from Bombay to Mandalay, and from Srinagar to Colombo. . . . Miss Martha Root has opened the whole of India for us. . . .'"[30]

Shoghi Effendi continued to be amazed at the scope of her work and expressed his gratitude: "India is astir with praise & admiration for you. What you have achieved in that land is truly historic & marvellous."[31]

Martha attended a farewell gathering in her honor on 27 December and addressed those friends she would leave behind:

> We have had the God-given privilege to work together for fifteen and one-half months; we have been so happy because we were in perfect unity and because we found souls interested in these great new Teachings of Bahá'u'lláh. . . .
>
> I know of no country where I would have wished so much to work during these months to promote these blessed Teachings as here in India, mystic India, trained for so many centuries in high cultural religions. India has been preparing for six thousand years to understand well this Message of Bahá'u'lláh in this day, for a new World State, for universal religion, for cosmic consciousness and for the oneness of mankind. India is sensitive to the call of the spirit. She has the habit to put eternal . . . values high. . . .

Martha closed her address with these words: "if I should go to the Heavenly Kingdom before you do, I will ask Bahá'u'lláh There, please to let me pray for you and help you. And when you come into the Abhá Port, may I be there to welcome you as you welcomed me when I came into your beautiful harbour in Bombay!"[32]

Fifteen months after her arrival in India, Martha sailed out of Bombay Harbor on 29 December 1938 and headed for Australia, Tasmania, and New Zealand. From there she planned to sail to Hawaii and on to San Francisco. Martha had commemorated her sixty-sixth birthday during the monsoons in north India. Her previous birthday was celebrated in Shanghai, shortly before the bombing. It had not been an uneventful interval.

Now Martha Root was aboard yet another ocean liner starting on the long journey home.

53 Australasia—Finishing the Work

On board the S.S. *Strathaird,* Martha Root rested and reflected. She thought of how much had happened since she had left San Francisco in May 1937, less than two years before. It was not the bombing, the earthquake, the typhoon, or the landslide and monsoons that occupied her mind; nor was it images of the numerous ships, trains, trolley cars, and lorries that had taken her over the miles and miles of India. To Martha the miracle was how much teaching had been done—the conferences and meetings, the university lectures, and the extraordinary publicity generated in India and Burma. She felt it was the best work she had ever done.

She thought about Queen Marie's passing in July 1938, and she smiled at the vision of the queen's reception in the next world. She thought also about Lydia Zamenhof's visit to the United States and the influence of her gentle, brilliant presence among the Bahá'ís and the Esperantists.* These reflections kept Martha's mind off the severe deterioration of her health. She was in extreme and constant pain, a fact known only to those attendants of her stateroom. The condition of her back, which she euphemistically called lumbago, had worsened to the point where she could not reach down to open her suitcase. When the ship stopped at Ceylon on 1 January 1939, Martha uncharacteristically did not go ashore; instead, she met reporters and gave interviews on shipboard.

Despite her worsening physical state and the ugly face of war leering at the world, Martha was looking forward to a full

---

*Lydia Zamenhof returned to Warsaw on 28 November 1938 to be with her family as the situation worsened in Poland. The Zamenhof family members were all taken to concentration camps. Her brother Adam was shot in 1942. Her sister Sophia was shot in 1944, and a few days later Lydia was put to death in a gas chamber at Treblinka Concentration Camp.

program of visits to Perth, Adelaide, Melbourne, and Sydney,
Australia; Hobart and Launceston, Tasmania; and Auckland,
New Zealand. She hoped the National Spiritual Assembly of
Australia and New Zealand would approve her plans and
would arrange a comprehensive schedule similar to that of India's well-organized teaching effort. She urged that accommodations be made for her in YWCAs or small hotels, rather than
in private homes, for "It helps me to concentrate more on my
lectures. . . ." "You know I love to be with friends," Martha
explained, "but several times I have become very ill because I
did too much and I did not rest in between the busy contacts
and lectures."[1]

When Martha landed at Perth on the west coast of Australia, where it was summer in January, she was given a tumultu-
ous welcome, swelled by letters and telegrams from all over the
country. The first of her lectures was given on 10 January 1939,
followed by daily presentations for two weeks; she also made
two broadcasts. Martha initiated a pattern of giving teas for
the press and broadcast directors, which she would do, with
the help of friends, in each city subsequently visited. Her fading physical strength, evident to all who met her, was offset by
the strong, radiating spirit that Martha brought to the area.

The S.S. *Stratheden* carried Martha on the four-day voyage
from Perth to Adelaide. She did not luxuriate in fine quarters
because of her condition. But, happily, her humor had not
succumbed to pain, for she quipped, "This is a very nice
ship . . . the topcabins are Deck A and my deck is Deck G, so
you see I 'go deep' in whatever I do! The air is poured down to
us generously, so it is very good."[2]

Because she was traveling tourist class, Martha shared her
room with several others. Her back was slightly better than
when she left Bombay; but it was still a searing affliction, and
the suitcase remained inaccessible. In order to type the necessary letters, Martha stood up in the cabin, with her typewriter
on the dresser, and tapped out arrangements for teaching and
outlined future plans while she subdued thoughts of pain. "My
back would not be WELL even if I did not do one thing but
think about it," she wrote to her friends, "and I thank God I
can work a little longer—I am so HAPPY in the work, because

I see how it helps many souls. By being very careful to protect my time and my strength, we get a great deal done."³

When Martha arrived in Adelaide on 28 January, it was clear that her health was in a precarious state. After one or two lectures, all engagements were canceled, and she was forced to rest. Dr. Stanley Bolton, a Bahá'í chiropractor in Sydney, was contacted, and he willingly rearranged his schedule. Surprisingly, Martha consented to treatment. To friends she confessed, "I am terribly afraid of Doctors, truly I am, terribly afraid, they almost always stop all my work." But at this stage Martha realized that medical help was imperative. Of Dr. Bolton she wrote, "I musn't be afraid . . . of him, a beloved brother, who comes 1,200 miles at his own expense to help a Baha'i whom he has never even seen!"⁴

Martha Root, Adelaide, Australia, February 1939, with members of the National Spiritual Assembly of Australia and New Zealand. Dr. Stanley Bolton, the chiropractor who gave Martha temporary relief from her increasing pain, is on her right.

Dr. Bolton arrived with his professional table, X-ray machines, and his considerable skill, to try to bring relief to Martha. And he had some success. "It helped me very, very much," she admitted, "it gave me relief and I could breathe so much easier. . . . [Do] you not think it is a miracle of Baha'u'llah that Dr. has helped me so that I can complete the important tour through Australia, Tasmania and New Zealand?"[5]

Dr. Bolton must have been astonished by the attitude of his patient, so badly in need of his ministrations. She reported, "And spiritually it has all been good. As soon as he arrived we prepared interviews and he wrote them out and I telephoned the reporters. . . ."[6] The result was immediate publicity in newspapers reaching over five hundred thousand subscribers. Later Martha prepared agendas for the twenty-six lectures already scheduled for Sydney in order that Dr. Bolton could take the information back with him. Both were delighted to learn that they would be sailing from Australia to America in May on the same ship; Martha felt, as she so often did, protective wings about her.

The Bahá'ís were all praying for the return of Martha's health and strength. As soon as she was able to walk, she resumed her schedule and broadcast a talk, " 'Tahirih, Iran's Greatest Woman,' " on Adelaide's largest radio station. There was a vast listening audience. The station director was more than pleased with the result and told Martha, " 'It is a perfect broadcast!' " Martha, too, had a special feeling about the talk. "Perhaps I could write a better one, but this is thrilling, gripping it moves me until it seems to be Tahirih speaking her own self to the modern world."[7]

In Hobart and Launceston, Tasmania, Martha continued her pace and gave more than sixteen lectures during her week there, with every engagement met. After a similarly demanding week in Melbourne, she traveled to Sydney early in March. Martha's work in this shimmering harbor city was a prodigal use of energy, a labor of love. She gave forty lectures in the next four weeks, along with several broadcasts. Although Sydney was the home of Dr. Bolton, neither he nor anyone else could deter Martha from her course as long as she felt that even one more soul might be touched by the message of peace. However, even Martha recognized the fact that she "overdid in Sydney." "It was wonderful," she remarked, "but I cannot do so much any more [*sic*]. . . ."[8]

While there, Martha had a mild heart attack, which forced her to rest in her berth during the four days on shipboard between Sydney and New Zealand; she went out of her room only for lunch. Charlotte Moffitt sailed from Sydney with Martha and stayed with her for two weeks. She was an especially comforting presence under the circumstances.

The warm hospitality in Australia extended to New Zealand; the Bahá'ís' joy at having Martha Root among them was evident wherever she went in this idyllic land. In Auckland she was met at the pier on 26 April by friends and journalists, for whom she had prepared notes, and was taken to the Stonehurst Hotel. Installed in a charming room on the ground floor with a fireplace, Martha immediately went to bed and spent the first day greeting callers as she rested. She felt enriched by renewing friendships of years past; among her visitors were friends who had joined her in Haifa in 1925 and for whom she had the deepest affection.

Although the cool weather necessitated having a fire going both day and night, sunshine poured in and provided warmth while Martha sat in the garden just outside her window. Recalling Martha's stay there, one of her friends wrote:

> The Management & staff soon fell in love with our Martha. They waited on her with evident pleasure. The manageress . . . gave an afternoon tea at her own expense, [one] that Martha had ordered, saying "This is my share"! and when we went to settle up when Martha left, we were told no extras were charged for meals & service in Room because she was ill & needed it & was so sweet.[9]

The Bahá'ís in New Zealand had arranged a full schedule for Martha's month-long visit. Beginning on 27 April, she was to give two lectures each day to clubs, churches, societies, and the People's University. After praying for divine assistance, Martha regained her courage and worked incredibly hard,

Martha Root (front row, second from left) with
Bahá'ís in Auckland, New Zealand, spring 1939, in one
of the last pictures taken of her

spurred on by her increasing recognition of weakness. "Only
the strong faith of her soul & spirit . . . kept . . . [the body]
going," observed one friend. "The . . . [veil] of her body had
worn so thin, she appeared all spirit. . . ."[10]

One of her last public lectures, "Bahá'í Scientific Proofs of
Life After Death," was given to an overflow audience in Bahá'í Hall. Many had come, Martha noted, because they had
lost beloved relatives or friends and wished to " 'find truth and
comfort.' " The talk seemed to Martha inspired. She confessed, " 'Perhaps I could never give it like that again, but it
thrilled me. The Teachings, the proofs, are such a spiritual se-
curity; I think I love that lecture most of all.' "[11]

On the day before she was scheduled to leave Auckland, she
spoke at the Chinese church. She was overjoyed to be among
the Orientals who had come to hear her speak. After the meeting she shook hands with each one, answered their questions,
and spoke some Chinese to them, giving as much of herself as
though she were as healthy as ever.

The next morning, 29 May 1939, the *Mariposa* entered
Auckland Harbor en route from Sydney to San Francisco. On
board were Drs. Stanley and Mariette Bolton, both chiroprac-

tors, who would accompany Martha back to her native land. Martha joined them at the pier, and after meeting with the press, spent the day at Bahá'í Hall, where she greeted and bid adieu to all her Auckland friends. A phonograph record made during those last hours reproduced Martha's voice saying a prayer and the Tablet of Aḥmad. She finished the recording with a farewell, "Alláh-u-Abhá, always Alláh-u-Abhá." Her pace is measured, her tones are rich. The farewell was captured for generations to come.

With the Boltons and several close friends still surrounding her, Martha boarded the *Mariposa*. The ship, scheduled to sail at 5:00 P.M., did not leave until five hours later, and Martha and her friends were delighted to share a little more time together. The Boltons were sailing first class, and Martha was traveling cabin class; they would be several decks apart, with accommodations and amenities a world apart. Martha would be sharing her room with four other passengers. A friend who was a nurse later went with Martha to her cabin and helped her undress. The nurse reported, "'I had to lift her into her berth she was so exhausted!'"[12]

The *Mariposa* slipped out of Auckland Harbor at 10:00 P.M. and sailed into the night, headed for San Francisco. It would stop en route at Suva, on the Fiji Islands; Samoa; and Honolulu. Martha was looking forward to disembarking for a few hours at each place. But her health was growing worse, the physical pain increasing in her leg and back and neck.

When the ship reached Suva, Martha was not going to miss an opportunity for teaching. She dressed for the occasion. She wrote, "I put on the red dress & coat & hat & had the steward help me upstairs. . . ." There she spoke with a customs official and gave him some Bahá'í literature. She had not expected to go ashore, but relatives of friends were there at nine o'clock with a car. Habits died hard for Martha Root; she accepted the invitation and went into Suva to visit a newspaper editor, a library, and a school. "It was so lovely," Martha wrote back to New Zealand, "but oh, I had to hold my neck with both hands & twice I got out of [the] car my leg hurt so. . . ."[13]

Neither food nor rest would relieve the travail of Martha's

body. The daily ministrations of Stanley and Mariette Bolton could no longer allay the pain. It surrounded, encompassed her, as she fervently prayed for time to work a little longer for Bahá'u'lláh.

54   The Skylark Soareth

Following Martha's suggestions, the Spiritual Assembly of the Bahá'ís of Honolulu arranged a full program for the hours when her ship was in port. The plans had been completed via cable between land and ocean: Martha would meet the press and give interviews soon after arrival; at 10:30 A.M. she would broadcast; there would be a luncheon with twenty guests at the Baldwin home at noon, and a public meeting at two o'clock.

Many friends were at the pier to meet Martha on the morning of 7 June 1939. As time ticked away, and Martha did not appear, the Bahá'ís became concerned. It was not until an hour and a half after the ship had arrived that Martha came into view. Scarcely able to move by herself, she was walking with the help of two friends. Henriette From, who had lived at the Baldwin home for twenty years as a governess, had come to the pier on behalf of Katherine Baldwin with car and driver to escort Martha. Henriette had received a message from her only two days before and "never suspected anything of a serious nature. . . ."[1] Thus it was a shock for Henriette to see the state to which Martha's health had deteriorated.

Martha, who was still in a nightgown when her friends arrived, at first refused to leave the ship, but she was persuaded that it would be better to spend the day in a cool, comfortable room on shore than in a stuffy stateroom shared with four others. When Martha finally agreed, her friends helped her to dress, and she was taken to the waiting car. Henriette From wrote to Martha's relatives:

We drove home as carefully as possible. I tried to support her shoulders to minimize any jar for the least move, especially of her head and neck, caused great agony. We got her to bed as quickly as possible and tried to make her comfortable, but she was in such agony and so helpless that she could not even hold a glass of water.[2]

All plans were rearranged, and Mariette Bolton made the broadcast in Martha's place. Henriette felt that Martha was in no condition to continue her voyage; but because Mr. and Mrs. Baldwin were in Washington, D.C., making decisions was difficult, and Henriette did not wish to make any plans until she had first consulted a doctor. To her relief, the situation was simplified when Martha made the decision not to go back to the ship and asked that her baggage be brought ashore. Some of it was removed from the ship, but the rest sailed on to San Francisco, where it was later picked up by Lucy Marshall.

When the luncheon guests left, Martha was moved from the cottage to the main house. Here Henriette and Elizabeth (Utie) Muther, an elderly, loving friend, could care for the patient during the night. Martha was running a temperature and reluctantly consented to have a doctor. "He found the patient very ill," Henriette reported, "too ill to make a satisfactory examination and advised that she be moved to the hospital. . . . perhaps you know Martha's aversion to Doctors and hospitals, and ill and suffering as she was I did not have the heart to go against her wishes."[3]

Martha felt that the ailment was sciatica or possibly arthritis, certainly nothing more serious. Although she refused to see another doctor, she gratefully accepted the constant treatment of Henriette and Utie, who relieved the pain with "baking lights and electric pads, Epsom salt baths and Analgesic-Balm rubs, & absolute rest and quiet." Two days after her arrival Martha felt well enough to dictate a letter, which revealed the torment of her condition to Roy Wilhelm and other friends:

Was so very ill on ship, [e]specially last day . . . I screamed with the pain in my neck, terribly inflamed muscles. I thought I would pass. I came to these friends and everything is being done for me. . . . the first night they sent for their doctor. I was in such pain, it was hard to swallow. I could not lift my head. . . . I have *suffered*, but I am quite a little better. I can swallow, the nausea is gone, my leg that had hurt me every day, sciatica or something, is better. My neck is a little better but oh, it hurts me so! Utie prays for me (all the believers do) and Utie says *she knows* Bahá has heard their prayers. . . . I am better, I can even lift my head alone but it is quite difficult. . . . It is so heavenly here with them.[4]

Martha continued to make plans, but now they were conditional. She was still planning on a trip to San Francisco, Oregon, New Orleans, and then South America, in fulfillment of Shoghi Effendi's wishes. However, she realized that she would not be able to attend the Bahá'í summer school in Geyserville, California, and was certain Shoghi Effendi would understand. She did not want him to know of her illness; she would wait and write him when she was better. For the moment, however, she felt that she should recuperate for a few days before booking another passage to San Francisco.

As the days with Martha progressed, Henriette became more aware of the gravity of the situation and felt the need for professional guidance. Although the Baldwins' physician, Dr. Nils Larsen, director of the Queen's Hospital, was away, Henriette suggested that his associate, Dr. Molyneux, be consulted. Martha again consented, reluctantly, but refused to discuss her condition directly with the doctor. Ailments and treatments had to be transmitted between doctor and patient through Henriette or Katherine Baldwin. It was as if a dreaded name or verdict might somehow terminate hope. Weeks later Henriette wrote, "During all this time Martha has never once referred to the real nature of her illness. It is as if she could not bear to mention it, but from veiled remarks I feel that subconsciously, . . . she has feared and dreaded this since 1912." Eventually, Dr. Molyneux completely won Martha's confidence, "with great tact and patience," and convinced her after several days to have some X rays taken.[5] They disclosed the merciless rampage of cancer, existent since 1912, stemming from two lumps in her breast. Dr. Larsen's report noted:

> Miss Root has a history of a breast tumor of some twenty years duration. During the past six months she has been having increased bone pains, particularly in the back, with

transmission down the legs. She is gradually becoming more and more incapacitated from walking or moving. The pains have become so intense that the only thing that will give her any relief is morphine.

Examination of the breast reveals a typical carcinoma. Xrays [*sic*] of the bones show many areas of rarefaction [thinning] in both the vertebrae of the spine and in the pelvic bones, which are typical of metastatic [spreading] car[c]inomas.

Diagnosis: Hopeless car[c]inoma of the breast with metastasis to the bones.

Treatment: . . . a matter of keeping the patient as comfortable as possible.[6]

The enigmatic nature of Martha's illness through the years had finally been clarified by the medical report. Her decreased mobility was the result of the spreading cancer, which had caused her bones to become paper thin; the lesions on the bones, also caused by the cancer, were the source of Martha's excruciating pain.

When the cause and the advanced stage of the illness were known, Dr. Larsen prescribed morphia hypodermics, starting with very small doses, to alleviate the pain. Again, Martha initially resisted; but the doctor "led her on with great patience step by step until he won her complete confidence. . . ."[7] Two or three days later she agreed to take the medication. Both her doctors seemed to Martha to be archangels; she responded to their gentleness, their compassion. Two full-time nurses were also called to duty, and these, too, she considered to be heaven sent.

The Baldwins were at their summer home on Maui, and Katherine Baldwin was torn between mothering her family and wanting to be with Martha. Traveling back and forth, she managed both and stayed in close touch by telephone when not able to be present.

Martha's surroundings were like a prelude to elysian fields. The climate was perfect. Her room overlooked green lawns dotted with flowering shrubs and avocado and mango trees, a sight she loved, all within view of her bed. As the weeks progressed, her condition grew considerably worse. Another

nurse was added to give her twenty-four-hour care; the doses
of morphine were increased as the pain took over.

Although Martha was delirious and often lost consciousness, she never lost her sense of responsibility. She insisted on
paying all her medical expenses from money on hand and from
five hundred dollars worth of uncashed checks from many
countries. To Sidney Hart she dictated a letter that instructed
him to send more funds in stipulated amounts; to Bahá'í
friends she sent messages of teaching possibilities; she dictated
her will, primarily the disbursement of her belongings—her
books, her clothes, her mementos.

On 10 August 1939 Martha marked her sixty-seventh birthday. Letters, cables, flowers, and gifts arrived from many parts
of the world. The messages were read to her a few at a time over
the following days. She was also presented with a birthday
cake, which she could not eat; but she enjoyed blowing out the
nine lighted candles. In honor of the occasion the Spiritual Assembly of Honolulu—who regularly kept fresh flowers in her
room—gave Bahá'í books in Martha's name to the local libraries.

Her periods of consciousness grew fewer, but her dedication
had not changed. "In her waking hours as well as in her
dreams," Henriette observed, "Martha continues her teaching
mission. Sometimes it is an individual she is addressing and
again it is an audience. . . ."[8] Martha was often in the world of
the spirit and was always quite surprised when she moved back
into the world of reality. The name of Shoghi Effendi, whispered over and over again as in a litany, was often on her lips.
There seemed to hover about her being a spiritual energy; her
presence was felt outside the rooms, and an aura of love
seemed to spread far beyond her physical confines.

Katherine Baldwin was deeply moved by Martha's presence
and felt the privilege of having her in her home:

. . . I have felt a great responsibility because she does belong to the Baha'i world, in addition to my own personal
love for her. . . . everything we can possibly think of will be
done for this glorious Soul, whose name will pass down in

history from age to age as the outstanding teacher of this present age. Often I find myself wondering why we in Hawaii have been so outstandingly blessed as to be given the tremendous privelege [*sic*] to care for our beloved Martha during her last illness. The thought is almost more than I can stand at times![9]

Martha prayed to Bahá'u'lláh to hold her hand, to give her strength, to help her endure. One prayer in particular was filled with meaning for Martha, and Henriette, with her hand on Martha's forehead, read it to her more and more frequently: "From the sweet-scented streams of Thine eternity give me to drink, O my God. . . . To the heaven of Thy loving-kindness lift me up, O my Quickener. . . ."[10] The beauty of the words spilled over her, penetrating her consciousness to bring peace and comfort.

With life ebbing away, it was difficult for Martha to communicate; she had wanted to ask Shoghi Effendi's advice about some practical matters, but now it was too late. She said, "My severe illness caught me three months before I was prepared for it. . . . Of course, dear ones, I might surprise you all and get well, for everything is in the hand of God. . . ." With the assistance of Henriette, however, she was able to send one last letter to relatives and friends, her limitless love emanating from every word:

I am so near the shores of Eternity. . . .
I thank you each and every one for all that you will do to help me, and I thank you for your love. I do not speak, so late tonight, of the glorious side of life after death. We shall all walk together arm in arm you and I, and in the mystery of God the Baha'is will confere [*sic*] together, understand each other, and I say to you, beloved of my heart, I am glad to go through this terrible agony, for if it came it must have come for a purpose to each one of us. If our love for each other has been deepened, if this servant has been able to witness for her Lord, if the ties between India, Australia, New Zealand and the Hawaiian Islands . . . [are] strengthened, then I have not come in vain. Everything has been successful.[11]

Surrounded by cheerfulness and love, with Katherine Baldwin and Henriette From at her bedside, Martha closed her eyes, a beatific smile on her face. In the quiet of the afternoon of 28 September 1939 she slipped into unconsciousness and moved from this world. It was a gentle, peaceful leave-taking.

Martha was on another journey; the course was uncharted but was one she had often explored in spirit. There would be no need for her twenty-three pieces of luggage. Neither would she need her score of address books, her portable kitchen, her books, her manuscripts. No need for a visa; not even the earthly shell was necessary. Martha embarked on this trip unencumbered. Only her loving, shimmering spirit was moving out on this, the most exciting of all her journeys.

MARTHA LOUISE ROOT

'Abdu'l-Bahá advised Martha Root "to travel . . . to the
different parts of the globe, and roar like unto a lion
the Kingdom of God," adding that she would witness "wide-
reaching consequences" and "extraordinary confirmations."
At the end of Martha's life Shoghi Effendi cabled: "Present
generation her fellow believers recognize her first, finest
fruit Formative Age Faith Bahá'u'lláh has as yet produced."

55 Epilogue

Hawaii, scintillating jewel of the Pacific poised between East and West, offered its beauty to Martha Root for her last home. Her gravesite was nestled beneath a pink-shower tree in a quiet corner of Nuuanu Cemetery, a resting place simple and beautiful.

Martha felt there was a reason for her being halted in Hawaii, a reason, not yet understood, that would be revealed in the future. Her last statement on Hawaii seems, in retrospect, greatly significant, as she referred to the islands' "unique role in the drama of a New World Order" and noted that "the Bahá'ís there can be a potent force for international understanding and peace in the Pacific."[1]

Years before, one of Martha's relatives, amazed by her Odyssean journeys, had asked where she expected to be laid to rest. Of all the places she knew, Martha said that she would prefer Honolulu. Was it her iron will guiding her earthly journey even to its final moments, or was it divine reward for unequaled services? Certainly, her dying in Hawaii seemed a kind of affirmation of her whole life: Ever moving between East and West, North and South, the new and the familiar, Martha made the world her home. Its residents were a reflection of the diversity and beauty with which God has endowed His creatures. Nordic types and those with darker skins—they were all Martha's family, and she wanted to serve them with her love and with the message of Bahá'u'lláh. Her life was truly a symbol of world unity.

Although Shoghi Effendi was aware of Martha's fragile health, he was unprepared for the finality of her death. So recently she had been sending back reports from India that testified to incredible feats of stamina as she braved the heat and the cold, the monsoons and the landslides. And shortly before

India she had survived the Shanghai bombings and the Manila earthquake. Not only did these calamities fail to stop Martha; there was not even a perceptible lagging. She carried on, although her nerves were taut, and she was at times overwhelmed with pain. It seemed that Martha was eternal. Only she knew how rapidly her physical impairment progressed. Therefore, when the end came, Shoghi Effendi was stunned.

To the Bahá'ís of Iran, whose love for Martha was fathomless, the Guardian cabled, in Persian:

> "The Pure Leaf, the illustrious teacher, the sign of detachment, the torch of love and affection, the example of courage and faithfulness, the consolation of the people of Bahá, Martha Root has ascended to the summit of eternal habitation. The Concourse on High received her with the shouts: 'Welcome O Glory of Teachers (men and women)! Well done, well done, O Thou who hast sacrificed thine all in thine attraction to the Kingdom of the Lord of manifest signs. Blessed art thou a thousand fold for this shining, exalted, lofty, inaccessible station!' Inform the entire friends of the necessity of holding special gatherings throughout the provinces for two full weeks in honor of her noble station."[2]

To Roy Wilhelm, who had first introduced Martha Root to the Bahá'í Faith, Shoghi Effendi's secretary wrote on his behalf that her death "constitutes the heaviest blow which the teaching force not only in America but throughout the entire Bahá'í world has sustained since the passing" of 'Abdu'l-Bahá. It was "distressing news" and "a great shock," but the Guardian hoped that Martha's uninterrupted efforts over the years would "serve as a source of continued inspiration to the present-day & future generations of Bahá'í teachers, to whom she will indeed ever be the very embodiment of those teaching qualities which only a few Bahá'í teachers, whether in the East or the West, can claim to have attained."[3]

Such moving tributes reveal the extent to which Shoghi Effendi would miss his world ambassador, his incessant worker and publicist for world understanding and peace. Martha was one of the very few Bahá'ís who toiled perpetually for the Faith, unswerved by personal needs or comfort, one of the few whose every waking and sleeping thought was the Cause of God on Earth. Who would now give the countless talks and broadcasts in India and America? Who would write the hundreds of articles for newspapers in China, or South America, or Australia? Who would correspond with Dr. Tsao, or Edvard Beneš, or Princess Ileana? Who would ask Shoghi Effendi to send a message to Emperor Hirohito or King Haakon or the Esperanto congresses? Who would find people such as Dionysios Devaris and Draga Ilich to do the translations? Who would go to Estonia, Brazil, South Africa, and Iceland?

Within a week of Martha's passing, Shoghi Effendi sent a formal acknowledgment of her death to the American Bahá'í community. The text of the cable read:

> Martha's unnumbered admirers throughout Bahá'í world lament with me earthly extinction her heroic life. Concourse on High acclaim her elevation rightful position galaxy Bahá'í immortals. Posterity will establish her as foremost Hand which 'Abdu'l-Bahá's will has raised up first Bahá'í century. Present generation her fellow believers recognize her first, finest fruit Formative Age Faith Bahá'u'lláh has as yet produced. Advise hold befitting memorial gathering Temple . . . [honor] one whose acts shed imperishable lustre American Bahá'í community. Impelled share with National Assembly expenses erection monument symbolic spot, meeting place East West, to both which she unsparingly dedicated full force mighty energies.[4]

In the cable Shoghi Effendi not only expressed his abundant praise for Martha's work but also conferred upon her a rare honor—the title "Hand of the Cause of God." This lofty station, bestowed only by Bahá'u'lláh, 'Abdu'l-Bahá, and, lastly, Shoghi Effendi, posthumously placed Martha Root in the company of some of the most learned Bahá'ís in history, among whose obligations are to protect the Bahá'í Faith and to inspire and encourage the Bahá'ís in their teaching work. Yet Martha's appointment was a double honor, for Shoghi Effendi also stated that posterity would establish her as the "foremost Hand" that 'Abdu'l-Bahá's will has raised in the first Bahá'í century. The few who had achieved the station of Hand of the

Cause of God when Martha died were pure and spiritually motivated individuals, detached from earthly comforts and demands, and dedicated to disseminating the Bahá'í teachings. Surely, this was Martha—and more.

The honor was Shoghi Effendi's final expression of admiration for this indefatigable Bahá'í teacher. Two years earlier he is reported to have talked about Martha's rare qualities to a group of pilgrims in Haifa: Some individuals may have faith and be willing to give their lives for the Cause yet may have moral weakness. Of the dawn-breakers, those earliest defenders of the Faith, "'They were heroes,'" he said, "'but not saints. Martha Root is a hero and a saint.'"[5]

As the news of Martha's final days became known and awareness circulated of the burning discomfort she had so long endured, praise for her years of endeavor mounted. An old friend wrote to Katherine Baldwin:

> now you know what a miracle she has been all these years traveling and accomplishing for the Cause of God. . . . If anyone lived and moved by the Power of the Holy Spirit it has been Martha. . . . Martha accomplished by the confirmations of Baha'u'llah, and we need hardly refer to this for everyone must know it *as a fact of history*.
> . . . think of the record she leaves—the greatest of all miracles of our time,—it seems to me,—for to accomplish what she has as sick as she has been all these years, is something which generations and generations after us will marvel about.[6]

Years later another old friend, Roy Wilhelm, penned his own tribute to his life-long co-worker and devoted friend: "'Martha was a unique,'" he wrote. "'She seemed to have been born for her special work. I doubt if there is another who has brought attention to the Faith to so many tens of thousands over so many corners of the earth. I sometimes think my chief reason for being born was to get Martha started.'"[7]

Once started, Martha never stopped. As a young woman she relished adventure for its own sake. But once she became a Bahá'í, she faced adventure with a purpose. 'Abdu'l-Bahá's injunction in the Tablets of the Divine Plan—to "travel, even though on foot and in the utmost poverty," to raise "the call of 'Yá Bahá'u'l-Abhá' in cities, villages, mountains, deserts and oceans," to "promote the Divine teachings"—was the impetus for her life's work.[8] With these words her constant companion, she found the strength to endure difficulty after difficulty.

The physical arrangements for living were in themselves a travail: Every few days Martha had to wash her clothes in whatever little sink was available, dry them somehow, mend and press them, usually late at night. She made all her own travel and lodging arrangements, wrote countless notes to secure her endless appointments, and, beyond all this, insisted on paying for everything herself. When she became ill, she paid for her nurses and doctors; and, according to her wishes, the cost of her funeral was borne out of her own funds. Only the burial plot was a gift; it was Katherine Baldwin's last kindness to her dear friend.

In an age when an escort or companion was deemed necessary for a lady, Martha moved through the world as a woman alone. Despite the possible stigma—and danger—Martha went from the Occident to the Orient, across every continent, from modern to ancient cultures, with no one to cushion her way through strange streets and rooming houses, newspapers and drawing rooms.

Everywhere she went, from hospices to royal apartments, she made friends; and she constantly kept up her round of contacts with heads of state, the media, educators, humanitarians, librarians, as well as anyone she met who would listen. At the end of long days, tired, often sick, she would return to her tiny, modest quarters in some strange city and write long into the night. Often she would rise between five and six in the morning to finish the article, interview, or letters she had been writing. Her output was prodigious.

As Martha traversed the globe, her presence was humble, self-effacing, and seemed to radiate a palpable sense of love. She changed the lives of a multitude of disparate persons simply because she made the effort to come to them. Although many could not remember her face or form, they would never forget the intangible essence that was Martha. The former Princess Ileana wrote, over half a century after meeting her:

> I remember her quite well but . . . I couldn't really even tell you what she looked like.
> I retain rather a general impression of a very charming, small woman whose general coloring was grey, with a remarkable inner fire of her own deep faith which made her stand out in a crowd in spite of her extreme modesty. . . . one just had to like her.[9]

Toward the close of Martha's life, when her health was truly broken, she spent her last ounces of strength spreading Bahá'u'lláh's teachings in the Eastern Hemisphere, which represents more than half the world's population. Only Russia remained closed to her, which was a keen disappointment, especially as she frequently skirted its borders in her travels. In one of her notebooks was the plea: "God come back to Russia."[10]

Nevertheless, much of the rest of the world did hear Martha's voice. Her travels in the last two years were only an undiminished version of earlier years and the capstone to a monumental life's work. In the end the feats of physical endurance that emanated from such a fragile, afflicted frame continued to be Olympian. Although she succumbed, at last, to her long-delayed rest, her precious spirit, through the many who caught her fire, still reverberates around the globe.

The wonder that was Martha goes on.

Notes

Notes

Part 1 / Beginnings

Chapter 1 / Beginnings

1. Genealogical book of the Root family, personal papers of Ruth Root Canfield. The book was shown to Bahiyyih Winckler during a visit to Cambridge Springs.
2. Ibid.
3. Martha L. Root, "What People Drink At Cambridge Springs," *Index of Pittsburg Life*, 8 February 1902.
4. Ibid.
5. Hotel Rider later became the home of Alliance College, a school for Polish male students. It was destroyed by fire and rebuilt on a new site in Cambridge Springs.
6. Georgia King, interview with author, Cambridge Springs, Pa., October 1980.

Chapter 2 / Growing and Learning

1. Martha L. Root, "Her Father, The Prince Charming," *Cambridge Springs Enterprise-News*, 7 November 1922.
2. Ibid.
3. Ibid.
4. Bahiyyih Winckler to author (tape recording), n.d., author's personal papers.
5. Ibid.
6. Root, "Her Father, The Prince Charming."

Chapter 3 / Careers

1. A 1937 newspaper article referred to the Burt family as cousins of Martha, but no verification has been found.
2. Bahiyyih Winckler to author (tape recording), n.d., author's personal papers.

3. *Cambridge Springs Enterprise*, 13 February 1900. The original spelling of Pittsburgh was changed when, in 1894, the U.S. Geographic Board of Names dropped the "h." In 1911 it was restored, and *Pittsburgh* became the official spelling.

4. Martha L. Root, "Romance at Cambridge Springs," *Pittsburg Dispatch*, 6 May 1900.

5. *Cambridge Springs Enterprise*, 6 May 1900.

6. *Pittsburg Press*, 27 January 1901.

7. Martha L. Root, "A Man and a Woman," *Index of Pittsburg Life*, 3 August 1901.

8. Martha L. Root, "New York to Buffalo Endurance Test," *Index of Pittsburg Life*, 14 September 1901.

9. Martha L. Root, "Outward Bound on a Dutch Liner," *Index of Pittsburg Life*, 19 April 1902.

10. Ibid.

11. Martha L. Root, "Automobiles in Paris," *Index of Pittsburg Life*, 19 April 1902.

12. Ibid.

13. Martha L. Root, "A Ride to Versailles in the Berg Automobile," *Index of Pittsburg Life*, 17 May 1902.

14. Ibid.

15. [Martha L. Root], "An Automobile Trip to Cambridge Springs and Return," *Index of Pittsburg Life*, 6 September 1902.

16. Ibid.

17. Ibid.

18. Ibid.

19. Ibid. In 1906 there was a six-mile-per-hour speed limit in Cambridge Springs. It was eight miles per hour in Pittsburgh.

20. The S.S. *Cedric* was the ship on which 'Abdu'l-Bahá, the son of the Prophet-Founder of the Bahá'í Faith, would sail to America nine years later.

Chapter 4 / Incidents

1. "Civic Improvement," *Cambridge Springs Enterprise*, 18 March 1904.

Part 2 / Gathering the Threads

Chapter 5 / Changes

1. Wilhelm to Bahiyyih Winckler, 10 October 1946, personal papers of Bahiyyih Winckler. The letter was written in response to Bahiyyih Winckler's urging and was sent to her via Agnes Alexander, a well-known early Bahá'í.

2. Root to Munavvar <u>Kh</u>ánum ['Abdu'l-Bahá's youngest daughter], Dr. Susan I. Moody, Edith Landerman, Mírzá Maḥmúd, Mírzá Valí'u'lláh, Helen Goodall, Ella Goodall Cooper, Roy Wilhelm, Lua Getsinger, Mr. and Mrs. Howard Struven, Gertrude Buikema, Albert Hall, Mr. and Mrs. Harlan Ober, and George Latimer, 30 September 1912, Ella G. Cooper Papers, National Bahá'í Archives, Wilmette, Ill.

3. Arthur Agnew, untitled notes, Arthur S. Agnew Personal Recollections, 1901–1922, National Bahá'í Archives, Wilmette, Ill.

4. Martha L. Root, "The 'Bab' and the New Persian Religious Movement," *Pittsburgh Post*, 26 September 1909.

5. Ibid.

6. Bahá'u'lláh wrote that "All the Divine Books and Scriptures have predicted and announced unto men the advent of the Most Great Revelation. None can adequately recount the verses recorded in the Books of former ages which forecast this supreme Bounty, this most mighty Bestowal" (Shoghi Effendi, *God Passes By*, rev. ed. [Wilmette, Ill.: Bahá'í Publishing Trust, 1974], p. 100).

7. Root, " 'Bab' and the New Persian Religious Movement."

8. Edward G. Browne, an Orientalist at Cambridge University, England, was the only Westerner ever to have an audience with Bahá'u'lláh. He has left an account of this meeting in the introduction to his translation of ['Abdu'l-Bahá], *A Traveller's Narrative: Written to Illustrate the Episode of the Báb*, trans. Edward G. Browne (New York: Baha'i Publishing Company, 1930), pp. xxxix–xli.

9. Root to Goodall, 19 September 1909, Helen S. Goodall Papers, National Bahá'í Archives, Wilmette, Ill. In the early days of the Bahá'í Faith in this country the term *assembly* referred to the group of Bahá'ís in a locality. Today, it refers to an elected body of nine Bahá'ís.

10. Allan L. Ward, *239 Days: 'Abdu'l-Bahá's Journey in America* (Wilmette, Ill.: Bahá'í Publishing Trust, 1979), p. 16.

11. 'Abdu'l-Bahá', *The Promulgation of Universal Peace: Talks Delivered by 'Abdu'l-Bahá during His Visit to the United States and Canada in 1912*, comp. Howard MacNutt, 2d ed. (Wilmette, Ill.: Bahá'í Publishing Trust, 1982), pp. 172, xv.

12. *New York City Evening Mail*, 13 April 1912. For other accounts of 'Abdu'l-Bahá's trip to North America see H. M. Balyuzi, *'Abdu'l-Bahá: The Centre of the Covenant of Bahá'u'lláh* (London: George Ronald, 1971); and Ward, *239 Days*.

13. Martha L. Root, "White Roses of Persia," *Bahá'í Magazine*, 23 (Nov. 1932), 255–59. The entire article was published in four parts, beginning with the June issue of *Bahá'í Magazine*, and continuing in the September, October, and November issues.

14. 'Abdu'l-Bahá, *Promulgation of Universal Peace*, p. 469.
15. Martha L. Root and Roy C. Wilhelm, "Gasoline Gypsies Four," *Collier's* (10 Jan. 1914), 41–44.

Chapter 6 / Shifting Winds

1. Wilhelm to Root, 12 November 1912, Martha L. Root Papers, National Bahá'í Archives, Wilmette, Ill.
2. Martha L. Root, passport, 18 January 1915, Root Papers.
3. They were turned over to friends when she left for China in 1923.
4. Root to unnamed "Friends," 25 March 1915, personal papers of Bahiyyih Winckler.
5. Ibid.
6. "Woman Journalist Saw Jews Flee From Turks," *(Honolulu) Pacific Commercial Advertiser*, 14 August 1915.
7. Martha L. Root, "The Jewish Flight From Palestine to Egypt," *American Review of Reviews* (June 1915), 710–11.
8. 'Abdu'l-Bahá to Root, 20, 21 April 1915, Tablets of 'Abdu'l-Bahá, International Bahá'í Archives, Haifa, Israel. (Approved translations of these tablets do not yet exist; consequently, these translations cannot be considered authentic.—ED.)
9. Khosrove to author, February 1981, author's personal papers.
10. Root to Wilhelm, 29 May 1915, Ella G. Cooper Papers, National Bahá'í Archives, Wilmette, Ill.
11. Ibid.
12. "10 Days in a Mandalay Harem," *New York Evening Sun*, 2 August 1920.
13. Root to Wilhelm, 29 May 1915, Cooper Papers.
14. "10 Days," *New York Evening Sun*, 2 August 1920.
15. Root to Wilhelm, 29 May 1915, Cooper Papers.
16. Ibid.
17. Martha L. Root, "Japan and the Coronation: I—An Interview with Premier Okuma," *American Review of Reviews* (Nov. 1915), 594.

Chapter 7 / New Challenges at Home

1. Root to unnamed "Dearly Beloved Bahai Friends," 18 April 1916, Agnes S. Parsons Papers, National Bahá'í Archives, Wilmette, Ill.
2. *Pittsburgh Sunday Press*, date unknown, reprinted in "Magazine Woman Quits Her Work," *Cambridge Springs Enterprise*, 15 December 1916.

3. Georgia King, interview with author, Cambridge Springs, Pa., October 1980.

4. Bahiyyih Winckler to author (tape recording), n.d., author's personal papers.

5. Doris McKay to author, 5 August 1980, author's personal papers.

6. Winckler to author, n.d., author's personal papers.

7. Martha L. Root, "Pot-Pourri of Convention Fragrances," *Star of the West*, 8 (20 Aug. 1917), 106–11. The Tablets were written in 1916 but were not officially presented until the 1919 annual convention at the Hotel McAlpin, New York City. The five geographical areas that 'Abdu'l-Bahá mentioned were expanded upon and nine other Tablets read.

8. Replicas of these booklets were presented to the youth, "in the pioneering spirit of Martha Root," at the First National Bahá'í Conference of the Five Year Plan, St. Louis, 1974.

9. See Loulie Albee Mathews, *Not Every Sea Hath Pearls* (Milford, N.H.: The Cabinet Press, 1951), pp. 7–8. Bahiyyih Randall Winckler later moved to the Transvaal, South Africa, where she is a Bahá'í teacher.

10. Winckler to author, n.d., author's personal papers.

11. After Harry Randall's death Ruth Randall and Bishop Brown married.

12. Root to Parsons, 29 October 1917, Parsons Papers. Most of the Bahá'ís had met 'Abdu'l-Bahá during His visit to America.

13. Hall to Root, 15 July 1916, Martha L. Root Papers, National Bahá'í Archives, Wilmette, Ill.

14. Annie Ellsworth Smith was the daughter of Henry L. Ellsworth (son of Chief Justice Oliver Ellsworth), the first commissioner of patents and a college friend of Samuel F. B. Morse, inventor of the telegraph. Since 1838 they had been seeking a grant of thirty thousand dollars from Congress to finance the trial line between Washington and Baltimore, but the bill was not passed until the last five minutes of the 1843–44 session. It was seventeen-year-old Annie Ellsworth who carried the news to Professor Morse the next morning, and he promised that she would send the first message. Her mother suggested the words from the Psalm, "What hath God wrought?" She died in New York on 21 January 1900. Symbolically, it was a woman who opened the new age of communication.

15. Root to Munavvar Khánum, Dr. Susan I. Moody, Edith Landerman, Mírzá Mahmúd, Mírzá Valí'u'lláh, Helen Goodall, Ella Goodall Cooper, Roy Wilhelm, Lua Getsinger, Mr. and Mrs. Howard Struven, Gertrude Buikema, Albert Hall, Mr. and Mrs. Harlan Ober, and George Latimer, 30 September 1912, Ella G. Cooper Papers, National Bahá'í Archives, Wilmette, Ill.

16. Winckler to author, n.d., author's personal papers.

17. Bahá'u'lláh, *Surat 'ul Hykl: Sura of the Temple* (Chicago: Behais Supply and Publishing Board, 1900).

18. Root to Parsons, 10 April 1918, Parsons Papers.

Chapter 8 / South America

1. 'Abdu'l-Bahá to Root, 10 January 1919, personal papers of Emanuel Reimer. (At the time of Martha Root's decision to travel to South America, an approved translation of this tablet did not yet exist; consequently, this translation cannot be considered authentic.—ED.)

2. Martha L. Root, "Eighth Annual Feast of Commemoration," *Star of the West*, 10 (13 July 1919), 134-35.

3. Martha L. Root, "A Bahai Pilgrimage to South America," TS, personal papers of Emanuel Reimer. Portions of this account were published in Martha L. Root, "A Bahai Pilgrimage to South America," *Star of the West*, 11 (13 July 1920), 107-11, 113-18.

4. Ibid.

5. 'Abdu'l-Bahá, *Paris Talks: Addresses Given by 'Abdu'l-Bahá in Paris in 1911*, 11th ed. (London: Bahá'í Publishing Trust, 1969), p. 15.

6. Root, "Bahai Pilgrimage."

7. Ibid.

8. Ibid.

9. Ibid.

10. 'Abdu'l-Bahá to Root, 10 January 1919, personal papers of Emanuel Reimer.

11. For the text of the letter see p. 167.

12. 'Abdu'l-Bahá, "Unveiling of the Divine Plan for the Western World," *Star of the West*, 10 (12 Dec. 1919), 282.

13. Root, "Bahai Pilgrimage."

14. Ibid.

15. Ibid.

16. Ibid.

17. Ibid. Lua Getsinger was one of the early American Bahá'ís, who on occasion was a special emissary for 'Abdu'l-Bahá. She taught the Bahá'í Faith in India and Egypt and died in Alexandria in 1916.

18. Root, "Bahai Pilgrimage."

19. Ibid.

20. Ibid.

21. Ibid.

22. Ibid.

23. Ibid.
24. Another street was named "President Wilson," and there was a town in Brazil named "Elihu Root."
25. Root, "Bahai Pilgrimage."
26. Ibid.
27. Ibid. It was of this, perhaps the richest short railroad in the world, that an American railroad president said he knew of nothing to improve it unless its rails be set with diamonds.
28. Root, "Bahai Pilgrimage."
29. Ibid.
30. Ibid.

Chapter 9 / The Other Side of the Mountain

1. Martha L. Root, "A Bahai Pilgrimage to South America," TS, personal papers of Emanuel Reimer.
2. Ibid.
3. Ibid.
4. "Miss Martha Root Will Enunciate Bahai Cause this Morning," *Austin (Texas) Statesman*, 6 November 1921.
5. Root, "Bahai Pilgrimage."
6. Ibid.
7. Ibid.
8. Ibid.
9. Ibid.
10. Ibid. See also the footnote on p. 87.
11. Root, "Bahai Pilgrimage."
12. Ibid.
13. 'Abdu'l-Bahá to Root, 27 January 1920, Tablets of 'Abdu'l-Bahá, International Bahá'í Archives, Haifa, Israel. (An approved translation of this tablet does not yet exist; consequently, this translation cannot be considered authentic.—ED.)
Martha Root's letters to 'Abdu'l-Bahá were dated 14 July; 21 August; 11, 12, 14, 30 September; 20 October; and 3 November 1919.

Chapter 10 / Home Again

1. "First Woman to Talk at Chamber of Commerce," *Cambridge Springs Enterprise*, 12 December 1919.
2. Ibid.

Chapter 11 / Excursions

1. Martha L. Root, "Disciples of the New Deal," *National Teaching Committee Bulletin* (28 Aug. 1920), 2, Alfred E. Lunt Papers, National Bahá'í Archives, Wilmette, Ill.
2. Ibid.
3. Ibid., p. 1.
4. Ibid., p. 3.
5. Ibid.
6. Bahiyyih Winckler to author (tape recording), n.d., author's personal papers.

Chapter 12 / Confusion and Confirmation

1. 'Abdu'l-Bahá, quoted in Mariam Haney, "Mrs. Agnes Parsons," in *The Bahá'í World: A Biennial International Record, Volume V, 1932-1934,* comp. National Spiritual Assembly of the Bahá'ís of the United States and Canada (New York: Bahá'í Publishing Committee, 1936), p. 413.
2. "Bahá'u'lláh . . . taught that prejudices—whether religious, racial, patriotic or political—are destructive to the foundations of human development . . . [and] are the destroyers of human happiness and welfare. Until they are dispelled, the advancement of the world of humanity is not possible. . . ." ('Abdu'l-Bahá, *The Promulgation of Universal Peace: Talks Delivered by 'Abdu'l-Bahá during His Visit to the United States and Canada in 1912,* comp. Howard MacNutt, 2d ed. [Wilmette, Ill.: Bahá'í Publishing Trust, 1982], p. 181.)
3. Root to Parsons, 1 October 1920, Agnes S. Parsons Papers, National Bahá'í Archives, Wilmette, Ill.
4. Ibid.
5. Root to Parsons (cablegram), 11 October 1920, Parsons Papers.
6. Root to Parsons, n.d., Parsons Papers; Root to Parsons, n.d., Parsons Papers.
7. Maxwell to Root (copy to Harry Randall), n.d., Parsons Papers.
8. Root to Parsons, n.d., Parsons Papers.
9. May Maxwell, untitled article, *National Teaching Committee Bulletin* (15 Nov. 1920), 3, Alfred E. Lunt Papers, National Bahá'í Archives, Wilmette, Ill.
10. Ibid., p. 5.
11. Root to Parsons, 30 November 1920, Parsons Papers.
12. Root to unnamed "Beloved Brothers and Sisters," 6 December 1920, Lunt Papers. The reference to "the city" that "had no need of the sun" is from Rev. 21:23.

13. Root to unnamed "Members of the Ideas Committee," 7 December 1920, Lunt Papers.

14. Root to Parsons, 13 January 1921, Parsons Papers.

15. Root to unnamed "dearest Friends," 25 February 1921, Lunt Papers.

16. Root to Parsons, 13 January 1921, Parsons Papers. Leonora Holsapple (Armstrong) left on 15 January 1921 and lived in South America until her death in 1980, working for the Bahá'í Faith.

17. Root to Parsons, n.d., Parsons Papers.

18. Eugene Debs had been jailed on a charge of espionage. President Harding pardoned him late in 1921. He died in 1926 at the age of seventy-one. Theodore Debs wrote Martha every two or three weeks; he said she was the only one able to get press clippings through to his brother.

19. Root to Parsons, 5 April 1921, Parsons Papers.

20. Ibid.

21. Lucy Wilson, untitled notes, written by Elizabeth Hopper, 5 September 1945, National Bahá'í Archives, Honolulu, Hawaii.

22. Root to Parsons, 1 May 1921, Parsons Papers.

23. Root to Agnes Parsons and Harry Randall, 5 May 1921, Parsons Papers.

24. An account of the amity convention, with reproductions of the program, can be found in Louis G. Gregory, "Convention for Amity Between the Colored and White Races," *Star of the West*, 12 (24 June 1921), 115–24. See also Gayle Morrison, *To Move the World: Louis G. Gregory and the Advancement of Racial Unity in America* (Wilmette, Ill.: Bahá'í Publishing Trust, 1982), pp. 138–43.

25. Zia M. Bagdadi, "Now is the time for the Americans to unite both the white and colored races," *Star of the West*, 12 (24 June 1921), 120. The comments recorded by Mr. Bagdadi are pilgrim's notes, unauthenticated remarks of 'Abdu'l-Bahá. However, Shoghi Effendi, in *Citadel of Faith: Messages to America, 1947–1957* (Wilmette, Ill.: Bahá'í Publishing Trust, 1965), p. 126, refers to similar comments by 'Abdu'l-Bahá.

26. Root to Parsons, 25 May 1921, Parsons Papers.

Chapter 13 / Creating Opportunities

1. Although there were further indications that Martha Root was working on a book about the Bahá'í Faith, no record was found of its ever having been published.

2. Root to unnamed recipients (copy), 21 August 1921, Ella G. Cooper Papers, National Bahá'í Archives, Wilmette, Ill.; Root to unnamed "Beloved Friends," 19 August 1921, Martha L. Root Papers, National Bahá'í Archives, Wilmette, Ill.

3. Cowles to Root, 7 September 1921, Root Papers.
4. Root to Agnes Parsons, Lethia C. Fleming, and W. H. Randall, 19 September 1921, Agnes S. Parsons Papers, National Bahá'í Archives, Wilmette, Ill.
5. Root to Parsons, 4 October 1921, Parsons Papers.
6. Ibid.
7. Ibid.

Chapter 14 / Mexico and Guatemala

1. 'Abdu'l-Bahá, *Tablets of the Divine Plan: Revealed by 'Abdu'l-Bahá to the North American Bahá'ís*, rev. ed. (Wilmette, Ill.: Bahá'í Publishing Trust, 1977), p. 32.
2. Martha L. Root, "A Teaching Tour Through Texas and Mexico," 7 November 1921, personal papers of Bahiyyih Winckler. Martha always wrote first to the prison warden about her plans to visit and would send copies of the clippings to be given to Mr. Debs. Her diplomacy succeeded where others failed.
3. Root, "Teaching Tour."
4. Ibid.
5. Ibid.
6. Ibid.
7. Root to National Teaching Committee, "Notes of a Month's Pilgrimage Through Mexico and Guatemala," n.d., personal papers of Bahiyyih Winckler.
8. Ibid.
9. Ibid.
10. Ibid.
11. Ibid.
12. Ibid.
13. "Martha Root Returns Home After Another Perilous Trip South," *Cambridge Springs Enterprise-News*, 23 December 1921.
14. Root to National Teaching Committee, "Notes of a Month's Pilgrimage."
15. Ibid.

Chapter 15 / Tests and Vital Changes

1. Mountfort Mills, quoted in Louis G. Gregory, "The Bahai Congress for Teaching and the Fourteenth Annual Convention," *Star of the West,* 13 (17 May 1922), 68.
2. Bahá'u'lláh, quoted in Louis G. Gregory, "The Bahai Congress for Teaching and the Fourteenth Annual Convention," *Star of the West*, 13 (17

May 1922), 74. (An approved translation of this tablet does not yet exist; consequently, this translation cannot be considered authentic.—ED.)

3. Root to Randall, 29 April 1922, personal papers of Bahiyyih Winckler.

4. Ibid.

5. Martha Root, "Happiness from the Bahai Viewpoint," *Roycroft Magazine* (June 1922). Reprinted in *Star of the West*, 13 (Aug. 1922), 101.

6. Root to unnamed "Members Bahai Temple Unity," 30 May 1922, Ella G. Cooper Papers, National Bahá'í Archives, Wilmette, Ill.

7. Ibid.

8. Ibid. See Bahá'u'lláh, *The Hidden Words of Bahá'u'lláh*, trans. Shoghi Effendi (Wilmette, Ill.: Bahá'í Publishing Trust, 1939).

9. Root to unnamed "Members Bahai Temple Unity," 30 May 1922, Cooper Papers.

10. Root to Cooper, 30 May 1922, Cooper Papers. Helen Goodall died on 19 February 1922.

11. *Cambridge Springs Enterprise-News*, 25 July 1922.

12. Root to Lunt, 14 October 1922, Alfred E. Lunt Papers, National Bahá'í Archives, Wilmette, Ill.

13. Lucy Wilson, untitled notes, written by Elizabeth Hopper, 5 September 1945, National Bahá'í Archives, Honolulu, Hawaii.

14. Ibid.

15. Martha Root, "Her Father, The Prince Charming," *Cambridge Springs Enterprise-News*, 7 November 1922.

16. Root to Lunt, 14 October 1922, Lunt Papers.

17. Root to Harry Randall, Alfred Lunt, Roy Wilhelm, Mountfort Mills, and Ella Cooper, 21 November 1922, Cooper Papers.

18. Root to Harry Randall, Alfred Lunt, Roy Wilhelm, Mountfort Mills, and Ella Cooper, 18 November 1922, Cooper Papers.

19. Ibid. Andrew, one of the twelve disciples of Christ, traveled extensively to promote Christ's teachings.

20. Root to Randall et al., 21 November 1922, Cooper Papers.

21. Bahiyyih Winckler to author (tape recording), n.d., author's personal papers.

22. Ibid.

Part 3 / Weaving the Tapestry

Chapter 16 / The Journey Begins

1. 'Abdu'l-Bahá, *Tablets of the Divine Plan: Revealed by 'Abdu'l-Bahá to the North American Bahá'ís*, rev. ed. (Wilmette, Ill.: Bahá'í Publishing Trust, 1977), p. 39.

2. Root to Ella Cooper and Dr. Frederick D'Evelyn, 2 January 1923, Ella G. Cooper Papers, National Bahá'í Archives, Wilmette, Ill. Seven letters from 'Abdu'l-Bahá to Martha Root are known to exist and are dated 14 November 1914, 20 April 1915, 21 April 1915, 10 January 1919, 20 July 1919, 27 January 1920, and 28 March 1920.

3. Root to Cooper and D'Evelyn, 2 January 1923, Cooper Papers.

4. Ibid.

5. "The Voice of the West," National Teaching Committee Bulletin (9 April 1923), Alfred E. Lunt Papers, National Bahá'í Archives, Wilmette, Ill.

6. Ibid.

7. Root to unnamed relatives and friends, "What It Is Like On the Kaga Maru," 29 March, 3 April, 9 April 1923, Cooper Papers.

8. Ibid.

9. Ibid.

10. Ibid.

11. Ibid.

Chapter 17 / Back in Japan

1. Martha L. Root, "Bahai Sky-Larking in Japan," 10–25 April 1923, personal papers of Bahiyyih Winckler.

2. Ibid.

3. Ibid.; Agnes Baldwin Alexander, History of the Baha'i Faith in Japan 1914–1938 (Tokyo: Baha'i Publishing Trust Japan, 1977), p. 46.

4. "Pittsburgh Girl Trailed by Tokio Police as 'Red,'" Pittsburgh Post, 21 April 1923.

5. Root, "Bahai Sky-Larking."

Chapter 18 / China

1. 'Abdu'l-Bahá, "China is the Country of the Future" (from Diary of Mirza Ahmad Sohrab, entry for 3 April 1917), reprinted in Star of the West, 8 (28 Apr. 1917), 37. (Since neither documentation nor an approved translation exists for this passage, it cannot be considered authentic and must be regarded as "pilgrim's notes."—ED.)

2. "Earning A Living In China," Adelaide (Australia) Mail, 25 February 1939.

3. Root to Agnes Parsons, Roy Wilhelm, and Harry Randall, 20 May 1923, Agnes S. Parsons Papers, National Bahá'í Archives, Wilmette, Ill.

4. "Earning A Living In China," Adelaide (Australia) Mail, 25 February 1939.

5. Root to Parsons et al., 20 May 1923, Parsons Papers.
6. Root to unnamed "Precious Friends," 16 June 1923, personal papers of Bahiyyih Winckler.
7. Ibid.
8. Ibid.
9. Ibid.
10. Ibid.
11. Ibid.
12. "Earning A Living In China," *Adelaide (Australia) Mail*, 25 February 1939.
13. Ibid.
14. Martha Root, "Can You Hear China Calling?," *Magazine of The Children of the Kingdom*, 4 (Sept. 1923), 95-96; Martha Root, "The Art of Reading God's Word Aloud," *Magazine of The Children of the Kingdom*, 5 (Mar. 1924), 29.
15. Ida A. Finch, "The Tokyo Earthquake," *Star of the West*, 14 (Nov. 1923), 244-45. The Greatest Name, "Alláh-u-Abhá," means "God is All-Glorious." It is often said during times of stress, as one would say a prayer for assistance.
16. "Baha'i World News: Miss Alexander in Japan and Korea," *Star of the West*, 14 (Jan. 1924), 311.
17. Agnes Baldwin Alexander, *History of the Baha'i Faith in Japan 1914-1938* (Tokyo: Baha'i Publishing Trust Japan, 1977), p. 59.
18. Ibid.
19. Ibid., p. 60.
20. Root to Roy Wilhelm and Mrs. J. O. Wilhelm, and Mrs. Grant, 11 January 1924, personal papers of Donald Kinney.
21. Ibid.
22. Root to unnamed recipients, March 1924, personal papers of Bahiyyih Winckler; Martha L. Root, "Bahai Sky-Larking in Japan," 10-25 April 1923, personal papers of Bahiyyih Winckler.
23. Root to unnamed recipients, March 1924, personal papers of Bahiyyih Winckler.
24. Ibid.

Chapter 19 / Hong Kong

1. Editorial, *Hongkong Telegraph*, 19 April 1924, reprinted in "Miss Root lectures at Hong Kong and is Reported by Chinese Press," *Cambridge Springs Enterprise-News*, 8 July 1924.
2. *South China Morning Post*, English ed., 25 April 1924, reprinted in

"Miss Root lectures at Hong Kong and is Reported by Chinese Press," *Cambridge Springs Enterprise-News*, 8 July 1924.

3. F. L. Falk to Root, 11 April 1924, personal papers of Bahiyyih Winckler.

4. "Ways of the World: A Travelling Journalist's Observations," *Adelaide (Australia) Register*, 11 November 1924.

5. Martha L. Root, "A Trip to Indo-China on a Cargo Boat," *Bahá'í Magazine: Star of the West*, 15 (May 1924), 40.

6. Ibid., p. 43.

7. Ibid.

Chapter 20 / Australia, New Zealand, and Tasmania

1. Martha L. Root, "A Trip to Indo-China on a Cargo Boat," *Bahá'í Magazine: Star of the West*, 15 (May 1924), 42.

2. Root to unnamed "Precious Loved Ones," n.d., personal papers of Bahiyyih Winckler.

3. Martha Root, "How the Baha'i Message Came to Australia and New Zealand," *Bahá'í Magazine: Star of the West*, 15 (Feb. 1925), 334.

4. Root to unnamed "Precious Loved Ones," 19 July 1924, personal papers of Bahiyyih Winckler.

5. Root to unnamed "Precious Loved Ones," 8 September 1924, personal papers of Bahiyyih Winckler.

6. Martha L. Root, "Notes from Martha Root, Now Travelling in Australia," 9 September 1924, TS, Ella G. Cooper Papers, National Bahá'í Archives, Wilmette, Ill.

7. "Miss Martha Root on the Wireless," *Adelaide (Australia) Saturday Journal*, 8 November 1924.

8. Root to unnamed "Precious Loved Ones," 8 September 1924, personal papers of Bahiyyih Winckler.

9. Ibid.

10. Root to unnamed "Precious Loved Ones," 14 October 1924, Martha L. Root Papers, National Bahá'í Archives, Wilmette, Ill.

11. Root, "Notes from Martha Root."

12. Root to unnamed "Precious Loved Ones," 14 October 1924, Root Papers.

13. Root to unnamed "Precious Loved Ones," 8 September 1924, personal papers of Bahiyyih Winckler.

14. Root to unnamed "Precious Loved Ones," 14 October 1924, Root Papers. Mariam Haney reported that "five thousand Socialists" were present at the talk (M[ariam] H[aney], "Martha Root in Australia and Other Countries," *Bahá'í Magazine: Star of the West*, 15 [Mar. 1925], 375).

Chapter 21 / South Africa

1. Root to unnamed "Precious Relatives and Friends," 20 November 1924, personal papers of Bahiyyih Winckler.
2. Root to unnamed "Precious Loved Ones," 7 December 1924, Ella G. Cooper Papers, National Bahá'í Archives, Wilmette, Ill.
3. One of Fanny Knobloch's sisters, Pauline, married Joseph Hannen of Washington, D.C. The other sister, Alma, went to Germany to teach the Bahá'í Faith.
4. Fanny Knobloch to Pauline Hannen and Alma Knobloch, 19 December 1924, personal papers of Bahiyyih Winckler.
5. Root to unnamed "Dearest Loved Ones," 3 February 1925, personal papers of Bahiyyih Winckler.
6. Fanny Knobloch to Pauline Hannen and Alma Knobloch, 19 December 1924, personal papers of Bahiyyih Winckler.
7. Root to unnamed "Precious Relatives and Friends," 2 February 1925, personal papers of Bahiyyih Winckler.
8. Ibid.; Root to Roy Wilhelm and unnamed "Dearest Friends," 14 January 1925, personal papers of Bahiyyih Winckler.
9. Root to unnamed "Precious Relatives and Friends," 2 February 1925, personal papers of Bahiyyih Winckler.
10. Ibid.

Chapter 22 / The Approach to Palestine

1. Root to unnamed "Precious Loved Ones," 8 March 1925, personal papers of Bahiyyih Winckler. For a description of Ḥájí Mírzá Ḥaydar-'Alí's imprisonment see *Stories from The Delight of Hearts: The Memoirs of Ḥájí Mírzá Ḥaydar-'Alí*, trans. and abridged by A. Q. Faizi (Los Angeles: Kalimát, 1980).
2. Root to unnamed "Dearest Loved Ones," 6 March 1925, personal papers of Bahiyyih Winckler.
3. Ibid.
4. 'Abdu'l-Bahá, *Will and Testament of 'Abdu'l-Bahá* (Wilmette, Ill.: Bahá'í Publishing Trust, 1944), pp. 3, 11.
5. Shoghi Effendi to Root, 13 February 1924, Martha L. Root Papers, National Bahá'í Archives, Wilmette, Ill.
6. Shoghi Effendi (through his secy.) to Root, 1 January 1925, Root Papers.
7. The Western Pilgrim House would later serve as the center of activities for The Universal House of Justice, the international administrative institution for the worldwide Bahá'í community.

Chapter 23 / Haifa: The Spiritual Center

1. Shoghi Effendi, *God Passes By*, rev. ed. (Wilmette, Ill.: Bahá'í Publishing Trust, 1974), p. 194; Isa. 2:2-3.

2. Martha L. Root, "Days in Haifa, Palestine," entry for 14 March 1925, MS, Martha L. Root Papers, National Bahá'í Archives, Wilmette, Ill.

3. Ibid.

4. Ibid.

5. Root to unnamed "Precious Friends," 7 April 1925, Agnes S. Parsons Papers, National Bahá'í Archives, Wilmette, Ill.

6. Ibid.

7. Martha L. Root, untitled notes about meeting the Greatest Holy Leaf, 1925, MS, Root Papers.

8. Ibid.

9. Ibid.

10. Ibid.

11. Martha L. Root, untitled notes about visit with Rúḥá Khánum, 1925, MS, Root Papers.

12. Esslemont to Root, 21 October 1925, Root Papers.

13. J. E. Esslemont, *Bahá'u'lláh and the New Era* (London: George Allen & Unwin, 1923). In October 1924 Brentano's brought out the first American edition (J. E. Esslemont, *Bahá'u'lláh and the New Era* [New York: Brentano's, 1924]). Since then the book has been reprinted numerous times in English and has been published in fifty-eight languages. For a recent edition see J. E. Esslemont, *Bahá'u'lláh and the New Era: An Introduction to the Bahá'í Faith*, 4th rev. ed. (Wilmette, Ill.: Bahá'í Publishing Trust, 1980).

14. Martha Root, "An Appreciation," *Bahá'í Magazine: Star of the West*, 16 (Feb. 1926), 718.

15. Esslemont to Root, 21 October 1925, Root Papers.

16. Root, untitled notes about meeting the Greatest Holy Leaf.

17. Shoghi Effendi to Root, 27 April 1925, Root Papers.

18. Root to Roy Wilhelm and Mrs. J. O. Wilhelm, 5 May 1925, personal papers of Bahiyyih Winckler.

19. Root to Wilson, 7 May 1925, personal papers of Bahiyyih Winckler.

Chapter 24 / Modes and Mores

1. Root to unnamed "Precious Relatives and Friends," 16 May 1925, personal papers of Bahiyyih Winckler.

2. Winckler to author (tape recording), n.d., author's personal papers.

3. Root to Parsons, 5 April 1921, Agnes S. Parsons Papers, National Bahá'í Archives, Wilmette, Ill.

4. Lucy Wilson, untitled notes, written by Elizabeth Hopper, 5 September 1945, National Bahá'í Archives, Honolulu, Hawaii.
5. Root to Wilson, 4 April 1923, personal papers of Bahiyyih Winckler.
6. Winckler to author (tape recording), n.d., author's personal papers.
7. Root to Ella Cooper, 31 October 1927, Ella G. Cooper Papers, National Bahá'í Archives, Wilmette, Ill.
8. Root to unnamed "Precious Loved Ones," 19 July 1924, personal papers of Bahiyyih Winckler.
9. Winckler to author (tape recording), n.d., author's personal papers.
10. Root to unnamed "Dearest Loved Ones," 3 February 1925, personal papers of Bahiyyih Winckler.
11. Meherangiz Munsiff, "Miss Martha Root: Reminiscences of Mrs. Meherangiz Munsiff," n.d., TS (copy), p. 5, author's personal papers.
12. Root to Roy Wilhelm and Mrs. J. O. Wilhelm, 5 May 1925, personal papers of Bahiyyih Winckler.
13. Root to Cooper, 21 October 1925, Cooper Papers.
14. Root to Mrs. J. O. Wilhelm, 24 December 1925, personal papers of Bahiyyih Winckler.
15. Root to Roy Wilhelm, 5 May 1925, personal papers of Bahiyyih Winckler. The Wilhelms donated funds to light the Bahá'í shrines and to purchase land in order to protect the area of the shrines.

Chapter 25 / Switzerland and Its Neighbors

1. Root to unnamed "Precious Relatives and Friends," 16 May 1925, personal papers of Bahiyyih Winckler.
2. Ibid.
3. Ibid.
4. Root to Lucy Wilson, 7 May 1925, personal papers of Bahiyyih Winckler.
5. Root to unnamed "Precious Relatives and Friends," 16 May 1925, personal papers of Bahiyyih Winckler.
6. Root to Roy Wilhelm, [early June 1925], personal papers of Bahiyyih Winckler.
7. Root to unnamed "Precious Relatives and Friends," 16 May 1925, personal papers of Bahiyyih Winckler.
8. Root to Roy Wilhelm and Mrs. J. O. Wilhelm, 27 June 1925, personal papers of Bahiyyih Winckler.
9. Martha L. Root, untitled report of Esperanto congress enclosed with letter to unnamed "Dearest Friends," 27 August 1925, TS, p. 4, National Bahá'í Archives, Honolulu, Hawaii.

10. Ibid.

11. Root to Cooper, 29 December 1925, Ella G. Cooper Papers, National Bahá'í Archives, Wilmette, Ill.

12. Root to Cooper, 21 October 1925, Cooper Papers.

13. Ibid.

14. Root to Julia Culver, 2 November 1935, Julia Culver Correspondence, National Bahá'í Archives, Wilmette, Ill.

15. Ibid.

16. Ibid.

17. Stanwood Cobb, "The World-Wide Influence of Qurratu'l-'Ayn," in *The Bahá'í World (Formerly: Bahá'í Year Book): A Biennial International Record, Volume II, 1926-1928*, comp. National Spiritual Assembly of the Bahá'ís of the United States and Canada (New York: Bahá'í Publishing Committee, 1928), pp. 257-62.

18. Martha Root, "The Servant Apostle," *Bahá'í Magazine: Star of the West*, 16 (Mar. 1926), 749.

19. Root to Mrs. J. O. Wilhelm, 24 December 1925, personal papers of Bahiyyih Winckler.

20. Root to Cooper, 29 December 1925, Cooper Papers.

21. Root to Mrs. J. O. Wilhelm, 24 December 1925, personal papers of Bahiyyih Winckler.

22. Ibid.

23. Root to Cooper, 19 February 1926, Cooper Papers.

24. Ibid.

Chapter 26 / Royalty

1. When Bahá'u'lláh sent a letter to Queen Victoria announcing His station and mission, she, of all the monarchs, left room for the possibility that His words were true. " 'If this is of God,' " she said, " 'it will endure; if not, it can do no harm' " (Shoghi Effendi, *The Promised Day Is Come*, 3d ed. [Wilmette, Ill.: Bahá'í Publishing Trust, 1980], p. 65). Czar Alexander's minister in Iran demanded that the sháh release Bahá'u'lláh from the Síyáh-Chál and later offered his guards to protect Bahá'u'lláh and His family along the exile route.

2. Root to Shoghi Effendi and Roy Wilhelm, 26 January 1926, Ella G. Cooper Papers, National Bahá'í Archives, Wilmette, Ill.

3. Root to Ella Cooper, 19 February 1926, Cooper Papers. The Seven Valleys is one of Bahá'u'lláh's mystical writings, composed in response to the questions of a Muslim Ṣúfí. See Bahá'u'lláh, *The Seven Valleys and the Four*

Valleys, trans. Ali-Kuli Khan and Marzieh Gail, 3d ed. (Wilmette, Ill.: Bahá'í Publishing Trust, 1978).

4. Martha L. Root, "Her Majesty, Queen Marie of Rumania," *Bahá'í Magazine: Star of the West*, 17 (June 1926), 85.

5. Martha L. Root, "Queen Marie of Rumania," in *The Bahá'í World: A Biennial International Record, Volume VI, 1934-1936*, comp. National Spiritual Assembly of the Bahá'ís of the United States and Canada (New York: Bahá'í Publishing Committee, 1937), p. 580.

6. Root to Cooper, 19 February 1926, Cooper Papers.

7. "Homespun: Small Town Comment on Big Town Stuff," *Cambridge Springs Enterprise-News*, 6 July 1926. The article was also printed in Martha L. Root, "Her Majesty, Queen Marie of Rumania," *Bahá'í Magazine: Star of the West*, 17 (June 1926), 84-87.

8. *Toronto Daily Star*, 4 May 1926, reprinted in Marie, Queen of Rumania, "Open Letters of Queen Marie of Rumania," in *The Bahá'í World (Formerly: Bahá'í Year Book): A Biennial International Record, Volume II, 1926-1928*, comp. National Spiritual Assembly of the Bahá'ís of the United States and Canada (New York: Bahá'í Publishing Committee, 1928), p. 174.

9. Marie, Queen of Rumania, to Root (copy), 8 June 1926, Martha L. Root Papers, National Bahá'í Archives, Wilmette, Ill.

Chapter 27 / Staying on Course

1. Root to Ella Cooper, 19 February 1926, Ella G. Cooper Papers, National Bahá'í Archives, Wilmette, Ill.

2. Root to Shoghi Effendi and Roy Wilhelm, 26 January 1926, Cooper Papers.

3. Root to Cooper, 19 February 1926, Cooper Papers.

4. Ibid.

5. Root to Shoghi Effendi and Roy Wilhelm, 26 January 1926, Cooper Papers.

6. Root to Cooper, 29 December 1925, Cooper Papers.

7. Root to unnamed "Precious Loved Ones," 12 April 1926, Cooper Papers.

8. Martha L. Root, "Count Leo Tolstoy and the Bahá'í Movement," in *The Bahá'í World: A Biennial International Record, Volume V, 1932-1934*, comp. National Spiritual Assembly of the Bahá'ís of the United States and Canada (New York: Bahá'í Publishing Committee, 1936), p. 644.

9. Root to unnamed "Dearest Loved Ones" (copy), 15 June 1926, personal papers of Bahiyyih Winckler.

10. Ibid.

Chapter 28 / The British Isles

1. Coles to Culver, 13 June 1926, Julia Culver Correspondence, National Bahá'í Archives, Wilmette, Ill.
2. Martha L. Root, "The Universal Esperanto Congress at Edinburgh," *Bahá'í Magazine: Star of the West*, 17 (Sept. 1926), 183.
3. Root to Ella Cooper, 3 September 1926, Ella G. Cooper Papers, National Bahá'í Archives, Wilmette, Ill.
4. Root, "Universal Esperanto Congress," p. 184.
5. John Craven was the uncle of Lucy Hall, whose father was one of the first Bahá'ís in England.
6. Lucy Hall, "Personal Memories of Miss Martha Root's Visit to Manchester in 1926," n.d., TS, personal papers of Martha Garman.
7. Root to Cooper, 3 September 1926, Cooper Papers; Root to unnamed "Dearest Loved Ones," 16 June 1926, Cooper Papers.
8. Root to unnamed "Dearest Loved Ones," 16 June 1926, Cooper Papers.

Chapter 29 / Iberia and Stuttgart

1. Rúḥíyyih Rabbaní, *The Priceless Pearl* (London: Bahá'í Publishing Trust, 1969), p. 102.
2. Root to Ella Cooper and Lena [Lee?], January 1927, Ella G. Cooper Papers, National Bahá'í Archives, Wilmette, Ill. See ['Abdu'l-Bahá], *The Mysterious Forces of Civilization*, trans. Johanna Dawud (Chicago: Bahai Publishing Society, 1918); for a more recent edition see 'Abdu'l-Bahá, *The Secret of Divine Civilization*, trans. Marzieh Gail and Ali-Kuli Khan, 2d ed. (Wilmette, Ill.: Bahá'í Publishing Trust, 1970).
3. Root to unnamed "Precious Loved Ones," 25 December 1926, Cooper Papers.
4. Ibid.
5. Ibid.
6. Root to Shoghi Effendi and Roy Wilhelm, 26 January 1926, Cooper Papers.

Chapter 30 / Germany and the North Countries

1. Root to unnamed "Dearest loved ones," January 1927, Ella G. Cooper Papers, National Bahá'í Archives, Wilmette, Ill.
2. Ibid.
3. Root to unnamed "Dearest loved Ones," 22 January 1927, Cooper Papers.

4. Root to "Dearest Holy Leaf" [Bahíyyih Khánum], Rouhanieh Latimer, Harry Randall, and Roy Wilhelm (copy), 22 August 1924, personal papers of Bahiyyih Winckler.

5. Root to Ella Cooper and Lena [Lee?], 23 January 1927, Cooper Papers.

6. Root to unnamed "Dearest loved ones," January 1927, Cooper Papers.

7. Annie and Harry Romer to unnamed "Dearest Friends at home," 28 November 1926, personal papers of Bahiyyih Winckler.

8. Root to Ella Cooper and Lena [Lee?], 23 January 1927, Cooper Papers.

9. Root to Annie Romer (copy), March 1927, Cooper Papers.

10. Ibid.

11. Ibid.

12. Root to unnamed "Beloved Ones," 13 May 1927, personal papers of Bahiyyih Winckler.

13. Ibid.

14. Root to Spiritual Assembly of Meshed [Mashhad], Persia, George P. Simpson, and Mr. Asgarzadeh, 22 February 1927, personal papers of Bahiyyih Winckler. Transliterations of Persian names often vary: Meshed, Mashhad, and Mashaad are all the same place.

15. Ibid., handwritten note penned on carbon copy to Harry Randall.

16. Ibid.

17. Root to unnamed "Beloved Ones," 13 May 1927, personal papers of Bahiyyih Winckler.

Chapter 31 / Northward

1. Root to unnamed "Beloved Ones," 13 May 1927, personal papers of Bahiyyih Winckler.

2. Ibid.

3. Ibid.

4. Ibid.

5. Root to unnamed "beloved Friends," 24 August 1927, Ella G. Cooper Papers, National Bahá'í Archives, Wilmette, Ill.

6. See Bahá'u'lláh, *The Kitáb-i-Íqán: The Book of Certitude*, trans. Shoghi Effendi, 2d ed. (Wilmette, Ill.: Bahá'í Publishing Trust, 1950); and J. E. Esslemont, *Bahá'u'lláh and the New Era: An Introduction to the Bahá'í Faith*, 4th rev. ed. (Wilmette, Ill.: Bahá'í Publishing Trust, 1980).

7. Root to unnamed "beloved Friends," 24 August 1927, Cooper Papers.

8. Ibid.
9. Ibid.
10. Ibid.
11. Ibid. See 'Abdu'l-Bahá, *The Promulgation of Universal Peace: Talks Delivered by 'Abdu'l-Bahá during His Visit to the United States and Canada in 1912*, comp. Howard MacNutt, 2d ed. (Wilmette, Ill.: Bahá'í Publishing Trust, 1982).

Chapter 32 / The Summer of 1927

1. Root to unnamed "beloved Friends," 24 August 1927, Ella G. Cooper Papers, National Bahá'í Archives, Wilmette, Ill.
2. Root to Julia Culver, n.d., Julia Culver Correspondence, National Bahá'í Archives, Wilmette, Ill.
3. Root to Culver, 14 July 1927, Culver Correspondence.
4. Shoghi Effendi, "Letter from Shoghi Effendi," *Baha'i News Letter,* no. 31 (Apr. 1929), p. 4.

Chapter 33 / Return to the Balkans

1. Martha L. Root, "Her Majesty Queen Marie of Rumania; Her Royal Highness Princess Ileana," *Bahá'í Magazine: Star of the West*, 18 (Mar. 1928), 366.
2. Root to Ella Cooper, 31 October 1927, Ella G. Cooper Papers, National Bahá'í Archives, Wilmette, Ill.
3. Root, "Her Majesty Queen Marie," p. 367.
4. Ibid.
5. Ibid.
6. Ibid., p. 368.
7. Ibid.
8. Ibid., p. 369.
9. Ibid., p. 370.
10. Ibid.
11. Root to Cooper, 31 October 1927, Cooper Papers.
12. Ibid. Later there was another story of Princess Ileana's running away. It was all blown out of proportion, and Ileana wrote Martha that the rumors were false and horrid. Years later Princess Ileana told the author: "Actually this escapade was innocent enough. My cousin and myself decided to sleep in another wing of the palace where the guest rooms were unused at that time and we thought it very enterprising of ourselves to sneak out of a legitimate bedroom to the wing which was off bounds and my poor old nurse

had a fit when she found our beds empty. But as you see, this was really an innocent adventure and not really dangerous. It was the planning of it that was such fun" (Mother Alexandra [the former Princess Ileana] to author, 25 March 1981, author's personal papers).

13. Root to Cooper, 31 October 1927, Cooper Papers.

14. Ibid.

15. Shoghi Effendi to Root (copy), 11 September 1927, Martha L. Root Papers, National Bahá'í Archives, Wilmette, Ill.

Chapter 34 / Bulgaria and Constantinople

1. Root to unnamed "Beloved members of my family and beloved friends" (copy), 24 November 1927, Ella G. Cooper Papers, National Bahá'í Archives, Wilmette, Ill.

2. Root to Cooper, 31 October 1927, Cooper Papers. The paper to which Martha Root referred was the Tolstoi Journal, December 1927.

3. Root to unnamed "Beloved members of my family and beloved friends" (copy), 24 November 1927, Cooper Papers.

4. Root to Agnes Parsons, 30 October 1927, Agnes S. Parsons Papers, National Bahá'í Archives, Wilmette, Ill.

5. Ibid.

6. Ibid.

7. Root to unnamed "Beloved members of my family and beloved friends" (copy), 24 November 1927, Cooper Papers.

8. Ibid.

Chapter 35 / Greece, Yugoslavia, and Czechoslovakia

1. Horace Holley, "Survey of Current Bahá'í Activities 1928–1930," in The Bahá'í World (Formerly: Bahá'í Year Book): A Biennial International Record, Volume III, 1928–1930, comp. National Spiritual Assembly of the Bahá'ís of the United States and Canada (New York: Bahá'í Publishing Committee, 1930), p. 44.

2. Martha L. Root, "Tea with a Queen and a Princess," Bahá'í Magazine: Star of the West, 19 (Sept. 1928), 172.

3. Root to Roy Wilhelm and Mrs. J. O. Wilhelm, 6 July 1928, personal papers of Donald Kinney.

4. Ibid.

5. Martha L. Root, "Prague and the International Congress: 'What the Schools Can Do for Peace,'" Bahá'í Magazine: Star of the West, 18 (June 1927), 75–76.

6. Martha L. Root, "President Thomas Masaryk," *Bahá'í Magazine: Star of the West*, 19 (Oct. 1928), 200.

7. Root to Shoghi Effendi and Roy Wilhelm, 5 April 1928, personal papers of Donald Kinney.

8. Ibid.

9. Ibid.

10. Ibid.

11. Ibid.

12. Ibid.

13. Root to Roy Wilhelm and unnamed "Friends," 13 April 1928, personal papers of Donald Kinney.

Chapter 36 / The Summer of 1928

1. Root to Marshall (copy), 29 April 1928, Ella G. Cooper Papers, National Bahá'í Archives, Wilmette, Ill.

2. Ibid.

3. Ibid.

4. Root to Roy Wilhelm and Mrs. J. O. Wilhelm, 6 July 1928, personal papers of Donald Kinney.

5. Ibid.

6. Root to unnamed "beloved Friends," 5 January 1929, personal papers of Donald Kinney.

7. Root to Roy Wilhelm, 9 September 1928, personal papers of Donald Kinney.

8. Ibid.

Chapter 37 / The Universities of Germany

1. Root to unnamed "beloved Friends," 30 November 1928, personal papers of Donald Kinney.

2. Ibid.

3. Root to unnamed "dear Friends," 22 January 1929, personal papers of Donald Kinney.

4. Ibid. Professor Babinger's description of the Bahá'í Faith appeared in his revision of Ignas Goldsiher's *Verlesungen Über den Islam*, which he prepared after Mr. Goldsiher's death.

5. Root to unnamed "dear Friends," 22 January 1929, personal papers of Donald Kinney.

6. Ibid.

7. Ibid.

8. Root to Culver, 16 March 1929, Julia Culver Correspondence, National Bahá'í Archives, Wilmette, Ill.

9. Ibid.

10. Root to the Randall family, 19 April 1929, personal papers of Bahiyyih Winckler.

11. Root to Culver, 16 March 1929, Culver Correspondence.

12. Root to unnamed "Beloved Friends in El-Abha!," 15 April 1929, Martha L. Root Papers, National Bahá'í Archives, Wilmette, Ill.

13. Root to Culver, 26 April 1929, Culver Correspondence.

14. Ibid.

15. Root to Culver, 28 March 1929, Culver Correspondence. The Tablet of Aḥmad (Arabic), written by Bahá'u'lláh around 1865 for Aḥmad, a native of Yezd, Iran, "is endowed with a special potency; and for this reason . . . [Bahá'ís] often recite it at times of difficulty or trouble" (Adib Taherzadeh, *The Revelation of Bahá'u'lláh: Adrianople 1863-68* [Oxford: George Ronald, 1977], p. 116). For the text of the Tablet of Aḥmad see Bahá'u'lláh, the Báb, and 'Abdu'l-Bahá, *Bahá'í Prayers: A Selection of Prayers Revealed by Bahá'u'lláh, the Báb, and 'Abdu'l-Bahá*, new ed. (Wilmette, Ill.: Bahá'í Publishing Trust, 1982), pp. 209-13.

16. Root to Culver, 16 April 1929, Culver Correspondence.

Chapter 38 / An Unfamiliar Face of the Balkans

1. Root to unnamed "Beloved Friends," 15 August 1929, personal papers of Donald Kinney.

2. Ibid.

3. Root to Culver, 16 March 1929, Julia Culver Correspondence, National Bahá'í Archives, Wilmette, Ill.; Root to Culver, 19 April 1929, Culver Correspondence.

4. Root to Culver, 16 April 1929, Culver Correspondence.

5. Root to unnamed "Beloved Friends," 6 September 1929, personal papers of Bahiyyih Winckler.

6. Ibid.

7. Ibid.

8. Ibid.

9. Ibid.

10. Ibid; Root to Roy Wilhelm, 14 September 1929, personal papers of Donald Kinney.

Chapter 39 / Turkey and Balcic, Rumania

1. H. M. Balyuzi, *'Abdu'l-Bahá: The Centre of the Covenant of Bahá'u'lláh* (London: George Ronald, 1971), p. 16.

2. Root to Roy Wilhelm and Mrs. J. O. Wilhelm, 14 September 1929, personal papers of Donald Kinney.

3. Root to unnamed "Dearest Loved Ones," 16 October 1929, personal papers of Donald Kinney.

4. Martha L. Root, "A Visit To Queen Marie of Rumania," *Bahá'í Magazine: Star of the West*, 20 (Feb. 1930), 333.

5. Ibid., p. 331.

6. Ibid., p. 335.

7. Root to Roy Wilhelm and Mrs. J. O. Wilhelm, 14 September 1929, personal papers of Donald Kinney.

8. Root to Roy Wilhelm (cablegrams), 8, 15 October, 7 November 1929, personal papers of Donald Kinney.

9. Root to unnamed "Dearest Loved Ones," 16 October 1929, personal papers of Donald Kinney.

10. Ibid.

11. Root to Sidney Hart and Roy Wilhelm, 21 November 1929, personal papers of Donald Kinney.

12. Root to Roy Wilhelm, 21 November 1929, personal papers of Donald Kinney.

13. Ibid.

14. Ibid.

15. Martha L. Root, "A Great Prince Speaks of 'Abdu'l-Baha," *Bahá'í Magazine: Star of the West*, 20 (Jan. 1930), 301.

16. Gulick to author (tape recording), November 1980, author's personal papers.

17. 'Azíz Yazdí to author, 29 December 1980, author's personal papers.

Chapter 40 / Haifa Revisited—Damascus Discovered

1. Root to Roy Wilhelm and Mrs. J. O. Wilhelm, 3 December 1929, personal papers of Donald Kinney.

2. Ibid.

3. Ibid.

4. Ibid.

5. Ibid.

6. Ibid. The lighting of the Bahá'í shrines was made possible by Roy Wilhelm. He chose Curtis Kelsey, a Bahá'í from Utah, to engineer the project. For an account of Mr. Kelsey's work at the Bahá'í shrines see Nathan Rutstein, *He Loved and Served: The Story of Curtis Kelsey* (Oxford: George Ronald, 1982).

7. Root to Roy Wilhelm and Mrs. J. O. Wilhelm, 3 December 1929, personal papers of Donald Kinney.

8. Ibid.

9. Martha L. Root, untitled address at the home of Cinita Knowles, Portland, Oreg., from notes written by Fay Swain Mathews, probably January 1931, Portland Bahá'í Archives, Portland, Oreg.

10. Root to Roy Wilhelm and Mrs. J. O. Wilhelm, 3 December 1929, personal papers of Donald Kinney.

11. Rafaat to author, 2 December 1980, author's personal papers.

12. Root, untitled address, Portland, Oreg., probably January 1931.

Chapter 41 / Iraq and Iran

1. Martha L. Root, "An Audience with King Faisal," *Bahá'í Magazine: Star of the West*, 20 (Mar. 1930), 365.

2. Y. A. Rafaat to author, 2 December 1980, author's personal papers; Martha L. Root, untitled address at the home of Cinita Knowles, Portland, Oreg., from notes written by Fay Swain Mathews, probably January 1931, Portland Bahá'í Archives, Portland, Oreg.

3. Bahá'u'lláh, *Gleanings from the Writings of Bahá'u'lláh*, trans. Shoghi Effendi, 2d ed. (Wilmette, Ill.: Bahá'í Publishing Trust, 1976), p. 114.

4. Ibid., p. 115.

5. H. M. Balyuzi, *Bahá'u'lláh: The King of Glory* (Oxford: George Ronald, 1980), pp. 154, 159. For translations of these works see Bahá'u'lláh, *The Hidden Words of Bahá'u'lláh*, trans. Shoghi Effendi (Wilmette, Ill.: Bahá'í Publishing Trust, 1939); Bahá'u'lláh, the Báb, and 'Abdu'l-Bahá, *Bahá'í Prayers: A Selection of Prayers Revealed by Bahá'u'lláh, the Báb, and 'Abdu'l-Bahá*, new ed. (Wilmette, Ill.: Bahá'í Publishing Trust, 1982), pp. 221–29; and Bahá'u'lláh, *The Kitáb-i-Íqán: The Book of Certitude*, trans. Shoghi Effendi, 2d ed. (Wilmette, Ill.: Bahá'í Publishing Trust, 1950).

6. Dhikru'lláh Khádem, telephone conversation with author, 4 July 1980.

7. Root, untitled address, Portland, Oreg., probably January 1931.

8. Ibid.

9. Ibid.

10. Martha L. Root, "A Pilgrimage Through Persia: 1.—Baghdád and Kirmansháh," *Bahá'í Magazine: Star of the West*, 21 (July 1930), 104.

11. Shoghi Effendi to Root, December 1929, Martha L. Root Papers, National Bahá'í Archives, Wilmette, Ill. (An approved translation of this letter does not yet exist; consequently, this translation cannot be considered authentic.—ED.)

12. Ibid.

13. Rafaat to author, 1 November 1980, author's personal papers.

14. Martha L. Root, "A Pilgrimage Through Persia: 2.—Hamadan," *Bahá'í Magazine: Star of the West*, 21 (Aug. 1930), 139.
15. Martha L. Root, *Táhirih the Pure: Irán's Greatest Woman* (n.p., 1938), p. ii; for a recent edition see Martha L. Root, *Ṭáhirih the Pure*, rev. ed. (Los Angeles: Kalimát, 1981).
16. Root, untitled address, Portland, Oreg., probably January 1931.
17. Ibid. See Root, *Táhirih the Pure*.
18. Root, untitled address, Portland, Oreg., probably January 1931.

Chapter 42 / The Heart of Persia

1. Martha L. Root, untitled address at the home of Cinita Knowles, Portland, Oreg., from notes written by Fay Swain Mathews, probably January 1931, Portland Bahá'í Archives, Portland, Oreg.
2. Ibid.
3. Ibid.
4. Root to Teymúrtásh, 11 April 1930, personal papers of Donald Kinney.
5. Root to Roy Wilhelm and Mrs. J. O. Wilhelm, 22 February 1930, personal papers of Donald Kinney.
6. Bahiyyih Imani, interview with author, Eliot, Maine, August 1980.
7. Shoghi Effendi, *God Passes By*, rev. ed. (Wilmette, Ill.: Bahá'í Publishing Trust, 1974), p. 52.
8. Ibid.
9. Ibid., p. 53.
10. Root, untitled address, Portland, Oreg., probably January 1931.
11. Robert Gulick to Bahiyyih Winckler, 16 April 1952, personal papers of Bahiyyih Winckler.
12. Root to Roy Wilhelm and Mrs. J. O. Wilhelm, 20 May 1930, personal papers of Donald Kinney.
13. Ibid.
14. Ibid.
15. Ibid.
16. Ibid.
17. Rafaat to author, 2 December 1980, author's personal papers.
18. Horace Holley, "Survey of Current Bahá'í Activities 1928-1930: An International Bahá'í Teacher," in *The Bahá'í World (Formerly: Bahá'í Year Book): A Biennial International Record, Volume III, 1928-1930*, comp. National Spiritual Assembly of the Bahá'ís of the United States and Canada (New York: Bahá'í Publishing Committee, 1930), p. 46.

Chapter 43 / India and Burma, 1930

1. Root to unnamed "Beloved Friends," 25 June 1930, personal papers of Donald Kinney.
2. Root to unnamed "Beloved Ones in El-Abha!," 2 July 1930, personal papers of Donald Kinney.
3. Root to unnamed "Beloved Friends in El-Abha!," 21 July 1930, Martha L. Root Papers, National Bahá'í Archives, Wilmette, Ill.
4. Root to Roy Wilhelm and Mrs. J. O. Wilhelm, 9 July 1930, personal papers of Donald Kinney.

Chapter 44 / Return to the Far East and Hawaii

1. Root to unnamed "Beloved Friends in El-Abhá!," 18 October 1930, author's personal papers.
2. Ibid.
3. Ibid.
4. Root to unnamed "Beloved Friends," 6 July 1937, Martha L. Root Papers, National Bahá'í Archives, Wilmette, Ill.
5. Agnes Baldwin Alexander, *History of the Baha'i Faith in Japan 1914–1938* (Tokyo: Baha'i Publishing Trust Japan, 1977), p. 79.
6. Martha L. Root, untitled notes, 1930, Root Papers.
7. Ibid.
8. Alexander, *History of the Baha'i Faith in Japan,* p. 79.

Chapter 45 / On Native Soil

1. Root to National Spiritual Assembly of the Bahá'ís of the United States and Canada, and to the National Bahá'í Teaching Committee, 20 January 1931, National Spiritual Assembly of the Bahá'ís of the United States and Canada Records, National Bahá'í Archives, Wilmette, Ill.
2. Allen to Martha Garman, 10 July 1980, author's personal papers, by kind permission of Martha Garman.
3. "Martha Root Visibly Affected by the Welcome of Childhood Associates," *Cambridge Springs Enterprise-News,* 2 April 1931.
4. Root to Parsons, 14 April 1931, Agnes S. Parsons Papers, National Bahá'í Archives, Wilmette, Ill.
5. Ibid.
6. Louis G. Gregory, "The Annual Convention," *Baha'i News,* no. 52 (May 1931), p. 3.

7. Morton to H. G. Pauli, 29 June 1931, personal papers of Miriam Wiener.

8. Parsons to Root, 30 April 1931, Parsons Papers.

9. Martha L. Root, untitled report, *National Teaching Committee Bulletin* (1 Aug. 1922), 2, Alfred E. Lunt Papers, National Bahá'í Archives, Wilmette, Ill.

10. McKay to author, 5 August 1980, author's personal papers.

11. Root to Parsons, n.d., Parsons Papers.

12. Ibid.

13. Shoghi Effendi to Root (cablegram, copy in Martha Root's handwriting), 14 November 1931, Martha L. Root Papers, National Bahá'í Archives, Wilmette, Ill.

14. A letter from Martha Root to Agnes Parsons that was written on 10 November 1932 stated: "I think how hard we tried to give them our greatest gifts. I pray God to be with them and now when he is not President, he and she may still remember about the Cause and perhaps they did and do read the books" (Root to Parsons, 10 November 1932, Parsons Papers).

15. See Gayle Morrison, *To Move the World: Louis G. Gregory and the Advancement of Racial Unity in America* (Wilmette, Ill.: Bahá'í Publishing Trust, 1982), pp. 191–92.

16. McKay to Lorna Tasker, 5, 16 December 1931, personal papers of Lorna Tasker, quoted in McKay to author, 17 September 1980, author's personal papers.

17. Diary of Lorna Tasker, entry for January 1932, personal papers of Lorna Tasker, quoted in McKay to author, 17 September 1980, author's personal papers.

18. Winckler to author (tape recording), n.d., author's personal papers.

19. Roy Wilhelm to Root, n.d., Root Papers.

Chapter 46 / A Change of Pace

1. Shoghi Effendi, *The Goal of a New World Order* (n.p.: National Spiritual Assembly of the Bahá'ís of the United States and Canada, n.d.). For a new edition see Shoghi Effendi, *The Goal of a New World Order,* 2d ed. (Wilmette, Ill.: Bahá'í Publishing Trust, 1971). The work is also included in Shoghi Effendi, *The World Order of Bahá'u'lláh: Selected Letters,* rev. ed. (Wilmette, Ill.: Bahá'í Publishing Trust, 1974).

2. Root to Shoghi Effendi and the National Spiritual Assembly of the Bahá'ís of the United States and Canada, 9 June 1932, Martha L. Root Papers, National Bahá'í Archives, Wilmette, Ill.

3. Ibid.

4. Ibid.

5. Shoghi Effendi to Root, 15 September 1932, Root Papers.
6. Root to Cooper, 21 August 1932, Ella G. Cooper Papers, National Bahá'í Archives, Wilmette, Ill.
7. Root to unnamed "Dearest Loved Ones," 25 September 1932, Agnes S. Parsons Papers, National Bahá'í Archives, Wilmette, Ill.
8. Root to Parsons, 10 November 1932, Parsons Papers.
9. Shoghi Effendi (through his secy.) to Root, 1 November 1932, Letters of Shoghi Effendi, National Bahá'í Archives, Wilmette, Ill.
10. Root to unnamed "Beloved friends," 22 June 1933, Parsons Papers.
11. Root to Lucy Wilson, 5 March 1934, personal papers of Bahiyyih Winckler. The picture appeared in Martha L. Root, "Appreciations from Yugoslavia," *Bahá'í Magazine*, 24 (Oct. 1933), 209.

Chapter 47 / Adrianople—Land of Mystery

1. Shoghi Effendi, *The Promised Day Is Come,* 3d ed. (Wilmette, Ill.: Bahá'í Publishing Trust, 1980), p. 61.
2. Martha L. Root, "A Visit to Adrianople," in *The Bahá'í World: A Biennial International Record, Volume V, 1932–1934,* comp. National Spiritual Assembly of the Bahá'ís of the United States and Canada (New York: Bahá'í Publishing Committee, 1936), p. 590.
3. Ibid., p. 584.
4. Ibid.
5. Winckler to author (tape recording), n.d., author's personal papers.
6. Root, "Visit to Adrianople," p. 593.
7. Ibid., p. 581.

Chapter 48 / New Struggles and Victories in Europe

1. Root to Parsons, 7 December 1933, Agnes S. Parsons Papers, National Bahá'í Archives, Wilmette, Ill.
2. Ibid.
3. Root to Wilson, 5 March 1934, personal papers of Bahiyyih Winckler.
4. Shoghi Effendi, *God Passes By,* rev. ed. (Wilmette, Ill.: Bahá'í Publishing Trust, 1974), p. 394.
5. Root to Wilson, 5 March 1934, personal papers of Bahiyyih Winckler.
6. Root to Wilson, 29 July 1934, personal papers of Bahiyyih Winckler.
7. Shoghi Effendi (through his secy.,with a postscript in Shoghi Effendi's handwriting) to Root, 9 September 1934, Letters of Shoghi Effendi, National Bahá'í Archives, Wilmette, Ill.

8. Shoghi Effendi to Root (cablegram), 22 January 1935, Martha L. Root Papers, National Bahá'í Archives, Wilmette, Ill.

9. Root to Cooper, 1 February 1935, Ella G. Cooper Papers, National Bahá'í Archives, Wilmette, Ill.

10. St. Barbe Baker to author, 18 February 1981, author's personal papers.

11. Ibid.

12. Ibid.

13. Ibid.

14. St. Barbe Baker to Root, 7 February 1935, Root Papers.

15. Root to Cooper, 1 February 1935, Cooper Papers.

16. Root to Mrs. Clarence Root (copy of cablegram in Martha Root's handwriting), n.d., Root Papers.

Chapter 49 / The Rhythm Quickens

1. Root to unnamed "Beloved Bahá'í brothers and sisters in El-Abhá!," 24 November 1935, Ella G. Cooper Papers, National Bahá'í Archives, Wilmette, Ill.

2. Root to Shoghi Effendi and Roy Wilhelm, 19 September 1935, Martha L. Root Papers, National Bahá'í Archives, Wilmette, Ill.

3. Ibid.

4. Root to unnamed "Beloved Bahá'i brothers and sisters in El-Abhá!," 24 November 1935, Cooper Papers.

5. *The Bahá'í World* is a multivolume work that chronicles the world-wide development of the Bahá'í Faith from 1925 to the present. For a recent edition of *Gleanings from the Writings of Bahá'u'lláh* see Bahá'u'lláh, *Gleanings from the Writings of Bahá'u'lláh,* trans. Shoghi Effendi, 2d ed. (Wilmette, Ill.: Bahá'í Publishing Trust, 1976).

6. Root to Ella Cooper, 23 February 1936, Cooper Papers. See Bahá'u'lláh, *Gleanings from the Writings of Bahá'u'lláh.*

7. Shoghi Effendi to Root (cablegram), 29 February 1936, Root Papers.

8. Martha L. Root, "President Eduard Beneš," in *The Bahá'í World: A Biennial International Record, Volume VI, 1934–1936,* comp. National Spiritual Assembly of the Bahá'ís of the United States and Canada (New York: Bahá'í Publishing Committee, 1937), p. 591.

9. Bolles to Root, 14 February, 9 May 1937, Root Papers.

Chapter 50 / The Skylark at Home

1. National Spiritual Assembly of the Bahá'ís of the United States and Canada, minutes, 1–2 August 1936, p. 3, National Spiritual Assembly of the

Bahá'ís of the United States and Canada Records, National Bahá'í Archives, Wilmette, Ill.

2. McKay to author, 5 August 1980, author's personal papers.

3. Winckler to author (tape recording), n.d., author's personal papers.

4. Martha L. Root, date book, 1936, Martha L. Root Papers, National Bahá'í Archives, Wilmette, Ill.

5. Edith Carpenter to Martha Garman (copy), 31 August 1980, author's personal papers.

6. Loulie Albee Mathews, *Not Every Sea Hath Pearls* (n.p., 1963), pp. 71–72.

7. Martha Root, "The Individual's Responsibility," address given to Bahá'ís in New York, 12 December 1936, personal papers of Donald Kinney.

8. McKay to author, 5 August 1980, author's personal papers.

9. McKay to author, 17 September 1980, author's personal papers.

10. Root to Wilson, 28 January 1937, personal papers of Bahiyyih Winckler.

11. Root to Wilson, 10 February 1937, personal papers of Bahiyyih Winckler.

12. Root to Setz, 28 January 1937, personal papers of Virginia Gregg.

13. McKay to author, 5 August 1980, author's personal papers.

14. McKay to author, 17 September 1980, author's personal papers.

15. Baker to Root, 9 March 1937, Mountfort Mills Papers, National Bahá'í Archives, Wilmette, Ill.

16. Root to Roy Wilhelm, Horace Holley, and Mountfort Mills, 10 March 1937, Mills Papers.

17. Root to Roy Wilhelm, Horace Holley, and Mountfort Mills, 17 March 1937, Mills Papers.

18. Ibid.

19. Amelia Collins (1873–1962) was a dedicated worker for the Bahá'í Faith and was named a Hand of the Cause of God. Among other gifts she provided the money for the wrought-iron gate leading to the Shrine of Bahá'u'lláh at Bahjí. Today the gate is known as the Collins Gate.

20. Root to Wilhelm et al., 17 March 1937, Mills Papers.

21. Wilhelm to Root, 3 May 1937, Root Papers.

22. Root to Ella Cooper, Lucy Marshall, Lena Lee, and Leroy Ioas, 6 April 1937, Ella G. Cooper Papers, National Bahá'í Archives, Wilmette, Ill.

23. Virginia Orbison to Martha Garman (copy), n.d., author's personal papers.

24. Root to Cooper et al., 6 April 1937, Cooper Papers.

25. Ibid.

26. Dahl to author, 28 June 1980, author's personal papers.

27. Hofman to author, 17 February 1981, author's personal papers.

28. Ibid.
29. Lucy Marshall, "Martha Root Again Fares Forth," 20 May 1937, TS, personal papers of Bahiyyih Winckler.
30. Ibid.
31. Dahl to author, 28 June 1980, author's personal papers.
32. Anita Ioas Chapman to author, 3 July 1980, author's personal papers.

Part 4 / The Warp and the Weft

Chapter 51 / Cataclysmic Moods of Man and Nature

1. Root to unnamed "Beloved friends in El-Abhá," 6 July 1937, Martha L. Root Papers, National Bahá'í Archives, Wilmette, Ill. A portion of this letter is printed in Horace Holley, "Survey of Current Bahá'í Activities in the East and West: International," in *The Bahá'í World: A Biennial International Record, Volume VII, 1936-1938,* comp. National Spiritual Assembly of the Bahá'ís of the United States and Canada (New York: Bahá'í Publishing Committee, 1939), pp. 89-93.
2. Martha L. Root, "War in Shanghai," 20 August 1937, TS, p. 1, personal papers of Bahiyyih Winckler.
3. Ibid.
4. Ibid., p. 2.
5. Ibid.
6. Ibid., p. 3.
7. Ibid.
8. Ibid.
9. Ibid.
10. Ibid.
11. Ibid.
12. Ibid., pp. 3-4.
13. Ibid., p. 4.
14. Ibid.
15. Ibid., pp. 4-5.
16. Martha L. Root, "The Aftermath: The Earthquake," n.d., TS, personal papers of Bahiyyih Winckler.
17. Ibid.
18. Shoghi Effendi, quoted in Root to National Spiritual Assembly of the Bahá'ís of the United States and Canada (copy), 25, 27, 28 August 1937, Carl Scheffler Papers, National Bahá'í Archives, Wilmette, Ill.
19. Root to National Spiritual Assembly of the Bahá'ís of the United

States and Canada (copy), 25, 27, 28 August 1937, Carl Scheffler Papers, National Bahá'í Archives, Wilmette, Ill.

20. Ibid.

21. Ibid.

Chapter 52 / India—Beyond the Possible

1. Horace Holley, "Survey of Current Bahá'í Activities in the East and West: International: The International Activities of Martha L. Root," in *The Bahá'í World: A Biennial International Record, Volume VII, 1936–1938,* comp. National Spiritual Assembly of the Bahá'ís of the United States and Canada (New York: Bahá'í Publishing Committee, 1939), p. 94.

2. Ibid., p. 98.

3. Martha L. Root, "A continuation of our report about the Burma Work: A short report from Miss Martha Root," n.d., TS, Martha L. Root Papers, National Bahá'í Archives, Wilmette, Ill. Siyyid Muṣṭafá Rúmí was martyred in Burma during the Second World War and was posthumously accorded the rank of Hand of the Cause of God.

4. Martha L. Root, "A Few High Lights on the Baha'i Teaching Tour Through Southern India," n.d., TS, p. 1, Root Papers.

5. Ibid., p. 5.

6. Ibid., p. 6.

7. Monira Sohaili, interview with author, Wilmette, Ill., 24 January 1981.

8. Ibid.

9. Ibid.

10. It was not only the Bahá'ís who were impressed by Martha and who remembered her years after her visit. On 8 July 1974 Dr. Raymond Johnson, the Bahá'í headmaster of the New Era High School in Panchgani, called on the headmaster of a college in Poona, where he had been invited to speak. In one hallway he was amazed to find a picture of Martha Root hanging on the wall. He learned that she is remembered in the school assembly every year on her birthday. The Bahá'í books that she had left there with the well-known guru who had started the college had been thoroughly read and studied. The present headmaster said, to Dr. Johnson's astonishment, "How interesting that we should meet on the eve of the martyrdom of the Báb." A statue of the founding guru stands near the college in a busy traffic circle. Carved into the stone are inspiring and visionary phrases—the words of Bahá'u'lláh. Martha's work had firmly taken root. (Jane Grover, interview with author, Eliot, Maine, 30 May 1980.)

11. Root, "Few High Lights," p. 3.

12. Ibid.

13. Aronson to author, 28 October 1981, author's personal papers.

14. Sohaili, interview, 24 January 1981.

15. Meherangiz Munsiff, "Miss Martha Root: Reminiscences of Mrs. Meherangiz Munsiff," n.d., TS (copy), pp. 1–2, author's personal papers.

16. Ibid., p. 2.

17. Ibid., p. 6.

18. Martha L. Root, " 'Letter-Report Home,' sent by Martha L. Root, from Karachi, India, August 1, 1938," p. 1, Root Papers.

19. Ibid., p. 2.

20. Ibid.

21. Martha L. Root, *Táhirih the Pure, Irán's Greatest Woman* (n.p., 1938), p. 5.

22. Ibid., pp. 21, 3.

23. Root, "Letter-Report Home," 1 August 1938, p. 3.

24. Ibid.

25. Ibid., p. 4.

26. Martha L. Root, "Another 'Letter-Report Home', sent by Martha L. Root, from Lahore, India, October 2, 1938," p. 1, Root Papers.

27. Ibid., p. 3.

28. Ibid., p. 4.

29. Root to Wilson, 2 December 1938, personal papers of Bahiyyih Winckler. An outline of Martha's tour through northern India can be found in Martha L. Root, "Bahá'í Message to the Universities of Northern India," in *The Bahá'í World: A Biennial International Record, Volume VIII, 1938–1940,* comp. National Spiritual Assembly of the Bahá'ís of the United States and Canada (Wilmette, Ill.: Bahá'í Publishing Committee, 1942), pp. 809–18.

30. National Spiritual Assembly of the Bahá'ís of India and Burma, quoted in Horace Holley, "Survey of Current Bahá'í Activities in the East and West: Martha Root's Travels in India, Burma and Australia—Her Death in Honolulu," in *Bahá'í World, Vol. VIII,* p. 61.

31. Shoghi Effendi to Root, 25 January 1939, Letters of Shoghi Effendi, National Bahá'í Archives, Wilmette, Ill.

32. Martha L. Root, untitled address, Bombay, India, 27 December 1938, Root Papers.

Chapter 53 / Australasia—Finishing the Work

1. Root to unnamed "Beloved Friends," 1 August 1938, personal papers of Bahiyyih Winckler.

2. Root to unnamed "Precious loved ones," 26 January 1939, personal papers of Bahiyyih Winckler.

3. Ibid.

4. Root to unnamed "Beloved Friends," 3 February 1939, author's personal papers.

5. Root to unnamed "Beloved friends," 10 February 1939, National Bahá'í Archives, Honolulu, Hawaii.

6. Ibid.

7. Root to unnamed "Beloved friends," 10 February 1939, personal papers of Bahiyyih Winckler.

8. Root to Ella Cooper, Lucy Marshall, Leroy Ioas, and unnamed "loved friends," 25, 27 April 1939, Ella G. Cooper Papers, National Bahá'í Archives, Wilmette, Ill.

9. Ethel Blundell to Otto Swezey, 12 November 1939, National Bahá'í Archives, Honolulu, Hawaii.

10. Ibid.

11. Horace Holley, "Survey of Current Bahá'í Activities in the East and West: Martha Root's Travels in India, Burma and Australia—Her Death in Honolulu," in *The Bahá'í World: A Biennial International Record, Volume VIII, 1938-1940,* comp. National Spiritual Assembly of the Bahá'ís of the United States and Canada (Wilmette, Ill.: Bahá'í Publishing Committee, 1942), p. 71.

12. Blundell to Swezey, 12 November 1939.

13. Root to unnamed "Beloved Ones of my heart, all you Auckland 'Angels,' " 1 June 1939, National Bahá'í Archives, Honolulu, Hawaii.

Chapter 54 / The Skylark Soareth

1. From to Sidney Hart, Frank Root, Claude Root, and Lucy Marshall, n.d., National Bahá'í Archives, Honolulu, Hawaii.

2. Ibid.

3. Ibid.

4. Ibid.; Root to Roy Wilhelm, the National Spiritual Assembly of the Bahá'ís of the United States and Canada, and unnamed "loved Friends," 9 June 1939, Ella G. Cooper Papers, National Bahá'í Archives, Wilmette, Ill.

5. From to Hart et al., n.d.

6. Larsen to Baldwin, 27 July 1939, National Bahá'í Archives, Honolulu, Hawaii.

7. From to Hart et al., n.d.

8. Ibid.

9. Baldwin to Roy Wilhelm, 30 July 1939, National Bahá'í Archives, Honolulu, Hawaii.

10. Bahá'u'lláh, *Prayers and Meditations,* trans. Shoghi Effendi (Wilmette, Ill.: Bahá'í Publishing Trust, 1938), p. 258.

11. Root to Sidney Hart, Mr. and Mrs. Claude Root, Mr. and Mrs. Frank Root, Mr. and Mrs. Roy Canfield, other unnamed relatives, Roy Wilhelm, and the National Spiritual Assembly of the Bahá'ís of the United States and Canada, 7, 9 September 1939, National Bahá'í Archives, Honolulu, Hawaii.

Chapter 55 / Epilogue

1. Root to unnamed "Beloved friends in El-Abhá," 6 July 1937, Martha L. Root Papers, National Bahá'í Archives, Wilmette, Ill.

2. Shoghi Effendi to the Iranian Bahá'í community (translation of cablegram), 10 October 1939, National Bahá'í Archives, Honolulu, Hawaii. (An approved translation of this cablegram does not yet exist; consequently, this translation cannot be considered authentic.—ED.)

3. Shoghi Effendi (through his secy.) to Wilhelm, 20 October 1939, Letters of Shoghi Effendi, National Bahá'í Archives, Wilmette, Ill.

4. Shoghi Effendi to National Spiritual Assembly of the Bahá'ís of the United States and Canada (copy of cablegram), 3 October 1939, National Spiritual Assembly of the Bahá'ís of the United States and Canada Records, National Bahá'í Archives, Wilmette, Ill.

5. Marjory McCormick, untitled notes taken during a pilgrimage to the Holy Land, 3–16 November 1937, personal papers of Virginia Gregg. (Since documentation does not exist for this statement, it cannot be considered authentic and must be regarded as "pilgrim's notes."—ED.)

6. Mariam Haney to Baldwin, 24 August 1939, National Bahá'í Archives, Honolulu, Hawaii.

7. Roy Wilhelm, quoted in Bahiyyih Winckler to author (tape recording), n.d., author's personal papers.

8. 'Abdu'l-Bahá, *Tablets of the Divine Plan: Revealed by 'Abdu'l-Bahá to the North American Bahá'ís,* rev. ed. (Wilmette, Ill.: Bahá'í Publishing Trust, 1977), p. 39.

9. Mother Alexandra (the former Princess Ileana) to author, 19 May 1981, author's personal papers.

10. Root, untitled notebook, n.d., Root Papers.

Index

Index to Places

Other Countries

General Index

two Belgrade professors are friends of, 298
Fozdar, K. M., 454–55, **454**
Fozdar, Shirin, 454–55, **454**, 456, 460, 462
From, Henriette, 480–81, 482, 485, 486
Frost, C. P., 140
Fukuta, Mr., 69, **69**

Gail, Marzieh. *See* Carpenter, Howard and Marzieh
Gandhi, Mahatma, 353, 451
  Bahá'í book sent to, by Root, 354
  Rabindranath Tagore influences, 457
Garrels, Arthur, 59, 440
George II (king of Greece), 413
Getsinger, Lua, 59, 95, 504 n.17
Goodall, Ella. *See* Cooper, Ella Goodall
Goodall, Helen, 47–48, 71
  Root dreams about, 148–49
Gourlie, Mr., 448
Gray, D. H., 9
Green Acre Bahá'í School, Root enjoys visiting, 149, 150, 376, **417**, 418
Gregory, Louis, 138, 160, 372, **375**, 380
  helps plan race amity convention, 128
Gregory, Louise, 251, 257, **300**
  invited to visit Czech parliament, 299
Guardian. *See* Shoghi Effendi
Gulick, Mrs. Robert (Bahia Faraj'u'lláh), 328
Gustav Adolph, Crown Prince (of Sweden), 276

Haakon, King (of Norway), 409
Hainisch, Marianne, 236
Hall, Albert, 80–81
Hamaker, Edward, 30

Hands of the Cause of God, **425**, **490**, 493–94, 531 n.19, 533 n.3
Haney, Mariam, 128
Hanko, D. J., 125
Hanna, Ethel, 48
Hannen, Joseph, 79
Hart, Nancy. *See* Root, Nancy Hart
Hart, Sidney, 14–15, 153, 226, 450, 484
Ḥaydar-'Alí, Mírzá, 145
Hazel, Judge John, 24
Henderson, George, 138
Herrera, Carlos, 141–42
Herrigel, Mr. and Mrs., 265
Hinduism, 357
  N. R. Vakil is first adherent of, to become a Bahá'í, 458
Hitler, Adolph, 265
Ho, Chien Yung. *See* Chien Yung Ho
Hoagg, Emogene, 260–61
Hofman, Marion Holley, 432–33
Holley, Horace, 125, **375**, 417
Holley, Marion. *See* Hofman, Marion Holley
Holsapple, Leonore. *See* Armstrong, Leonore Holsapple
Hoover, Pres. Herbert, 379, 528 n.14
Hubbard, Elbert, 32
Hume, Robert, 373, 420
Hummel, Arthur, 373
Ḥusayn, Mullá, 348
Ḥusayn, Siyyid, 347

Ileana, Princess (of Rumania and, later, archduchess of Austria), 246, 288, **289**, 296, 297, 323–24, 386, 414, 520 n.12
  Root described by, 496
Ilich, Draga, 390, **391**, 401, 413
Ioas, Monroe, 427, 429
Isaiah, 207

Root, Martha *(continued)*
  money from Roy Wilhelm reimbursed, 226, 326
  money from Siegfried Schopflocher, 217
  National Spiritual Assembly of India and Burma subsidizes teaching expenses, 451–52
  Shoghi Effendi gives proceeds from sale of translated books to Root, 404
  translator paid with fur coat, 413
  Harry Randall and. *See* Randall, Harry
  health of
    'Abdu'l-Bahá gives advice about, 53
    'Abdu'l-Bahá's hopes for, 371
    Agnes Parsons asks 'Abdu'l-Bahá to pray for, 135
    altitude of Johannesburg affects, 199
    chiropractic treatments, 422, 474–75
    comments on handling physical distress, 403, 424
    diet during travels, 307, 322–23
    dislike of doctors, 34, 418–19, 474
    Dr. Esslemont expresses concern for, 215
    Ella Cooper worries about, 233–34, 261–62
    fasting, 202
    improvement of, in Switzerland in 1928, 307
    Julia Culver monitors, 307
    little regard shown for own health, 459
    malaria, 201
    medical consultation in Germany, 261

  pain, illness, and fatigue, 90, 107, 135, 172, 178, 180–81, 191, 233–34, 248, 252, 280, 301, 325, 371, 373, 387, 401, 406–09, 410, 412, 423, 468
  rest rarely taken, except when ill, 152, 160–61, 180, 261–62
  rests taken in 1936, 416–18
  seasickness, 25, 100, 186, 197, 218, 383
  Shoghi Effendi asks committee to monitor, 417, 418, 419, 424–25, 426–27, 431, 439
  Shoghi Effendi is concerned about, 330
  surgery renders Root unable to have children, 34
  warm weather preferred, 128, 358
  health of, during final year, 480–86
    bedridden during first day in New Zealand, 476
    constant pain, 472, 478–79
    Dr. and Mrs. Bolton accompany Root to Hawaii, 477–79
    Dr. Bolton treats Root in Australia, 474–75
    Dr. Molyneux confirms existence of cancer, 482
    hope that Shoghi Effendi does not learn of her illness, 482
    insistence on paying own medical expenses, 484
    morphine prescribed to ease pain, 483
    plans for Honolulu rearranged because of illness, 480–81
    seemed half in spirit world during final days, 484
    slight heart attack in Sydney, 476

difficulty of physical arrangements for, 495
document printed with letters of thanks and commendation to use as introduction, 376
first thoughts of traveling and teaching discouraged, 57–58
general techniques used during, 109, 159, 236, 376
in later travels, began arriving unannounced to get some work done first, 193
scope of, 205
Shoghi Effendi cables greetings to give her a reason to meet various persons, 379
Shoghi Effendi urges Bahá'ís to help her during, 283–84
soil touched in each country of Bahá'u'lláh's exile, 398
undertaken in response to Tablets of the Divine Plan, 88, 110, 157–58, 494–95
wish to travel until death, 412
(trips below listed in chronological order)
South America in 1919, 88–110, **105**
'Abdu'l-Bahá's response to achievements of Root in, 111–12
activities during first day in South America, 93
activities during three hours in Lima, 108
Andes, winter crossing of, 103–06
Arab met who knows 'Abdu'l-Bahá, 95–96
Bahia visited in spite of difficulties, 94–98
Havana, 109–10

lecture about, at 1921 Bahá'í convention, 130
lecture about, in Cambridge Springs, 113–14
lectures on board ship, 91, 108, 109
Lillyan Vegas assists Root in, 95–96
meeting with Esperantists, 98
meeting with Theosophists, 99, 101
neighbors take care of father during, 89
observations made about South Americans, 96–97
palm reading makes friends, 91–92
Panama, 108–09
pattern of teaching, 109
press response to, 93, 95, 96, 97, 98, 101
results of, 110–12
strikers who delay start of trip to, told about Bahá'í teachings, 90, 92
trip motivated by 'Abdu'l-Bahá, 88, 89
visit to leper colony prevented by weather, 109
written account of, mailed worldwide, 114–15
United States and Canada, as advance person for Jináb-i-Fádil in 1920, 116–19, 121–25
New York (state) tour, 116–19
press response, 125
success of Canadian trip, 123–25
talk at Chautauqua arranged, 116, 118
Southern U.S., Mexico, and Central America in 1921, 137–43

Root, Martha *(continued)*
Root passes two Esperanto
exams, 277
Swedish National Esperanto
Congress, 277
The Netherlands, Belgium, Poland, Germany, and Switz-
erland in 1927, 280–84
Congres Mondial Des Associations in Belgium, 279, 280
first-class room given to Root
during voyage to Rotter-
dam, 279
19th Universal Esperanto
Congress, 280, **281**
soil from Haifa and New Jersey used at Jubilee Tree
planting ceremony in Dan-
zig, 282
Balkans and Constantinople in
1927, 285–95
Armenian translation of
Bahá'í book arranged, 295
Esperanto lecture in Vratza
very well attended, 292
Queen Marie receives Root
again, 285–89
visit warmly received in Bulgaria, 291–92
Greece, Yugoslavia, and Czechoslovakia in 1928, 296–303
blue booklets translated into
Serbian and Croatian,
297–98
meeting with Pres. Masaryk
of Czechoslovakia, 300–01
meeting with Prof. Popovitch,
297
meeting with Prof. Straitch, 298
pass granted to visit many cities in Czechoslovakia,
300–01
Queen Marie receives Root in
Yugoslavia, 296–97
two articles by Root well received in Athens, 296

Belgium, Switzerland, Germany, and Poland in
1928–29, 304–15
extremely cold in Germany,
314
extremely cold in Poland,
311–12
financial strain during trip to,
315
friendship made with Prof.
Babinger, 310–11
lecture at Berlin University,
312–14
misunderstanding between
Esperantists and Bahá'ís,
305–06
outline of work in Germany,
308–09, 314–15
Thanksgiving celebrated in
Munich, 309
various conferences concentrated on during summer,
304–05, **305**, 306–07
work with Lydia Zamenhof
on Esperanto translation of
*Bahá'u'lláh and the New
Era*, 312
Balkans in 1929, 316–21
meeting with king of Albania
and his family, 319–20
press response, 319
talk given to Hungarian Press
Club in Budapest, 316
Turkey, Rumania, Egypt, and
Palestine in 1929, 322–29
arrival in Cairo in third-class
train seats, 329
meeting with governor and
grand muftí of Jerusalem,
329
meeting with minister of foreign affairs in Turkey, 323
meeting with nephew of king
of Egypt, 328
pleasant voyage to Constanti
nople, 322